The HOWELL Book of
SADDLERY
AND TACK

A QUARTO BOOK

The HOWELL Book of
SADDLERY
AND TACK

Consultant Editor   Elwyn Hartley Edwards

1988

HOWELL BOOK HOUSE Inc.
230 Park Avenue
New York, N.Y. 10169

Country life book of saddlery and equipment.
The Howell book of saddlery and tack.

Reprint. Originally published: The Country life book of saddlery and equipment. New Burlington Books, 1981.
Includes index.
1. Saddlery. 2. Horsemanship—Equipment and supplies. 3. Horses—Equipment and supplies.
4. Saddlery—History. 5. Horsmanship—Equipment and supplies—History. 6. Horses—Equipment and supplies—History. I. Edwards, Elwyn Hartley.
SF309.9.C68 1988   636.1'0837   88-6869
ISBN 0-87605-873-X

Published in North America 1988 by
Howell Book House Inc.
230 Park Avenue
New York, N.Y. 10169

Copyright © 1988 Quarto Publishing plc

Consultant Editor: Elwyn Hartley Edwards
Contributing Editors: Jenny Baker, Geoff Clothier, Elwyn Hartley Edwards, Janet Macdonald, Judy Payne, Diana Tuke, Sallie Walrond

Art Editor: Moira Clinch
Art Assistant: Helen Kirby
Editor: Patricia Mackinnon
Picture Researcher: Marion Eason
Photography: Ian Howes
Art Director: Bob Morley
Editorial Director: Jeremy Harwood

Special thanks to Michale Gidden of W & H Gidden Ltd., Len Courtice of Western Saddles of America Ltd., Sutton, Mandy Chapman of Westerham Riding School, Jabez Cliff & Co. Ltd., Evelyn Slack of York Harness Raceway, Warcop Working Farm Museum, Matthew Harvey and Company, Anthony Parker of George Parkers and Sons Ltd., Major Phelps of The Royal Mews, London

All rights reserved. No part of this publication may be reproduced, stored in a retrieval system, or transmitted, in any form or by any means, electronic, mechanical, photocopying, recording or otherwise, except in the case of brief excerpts quoted in reviews, without the prior written permission of the publisher and copyright holder

Typeset in Great Britain by Tradespools Ltd., Frome, and Flowery Typesetters, London
Origination by Hong Kong Graphic Arts, Rodney Howe Ltd, London, Speedlith Photolitho Ltd., Manchester

Printed in Hong Kong by
Leefung-Asco Printers Limited

Contents

Christine Stückelberger on her horse, Granat, at Goodwood, England in 1980. A turnout as perfect as this is probably beyond the aspirations of all but the most determined, but it sets a splendid example of how, even at a more humble level, equipment should be well-kept, well-fitting and appropriate for the event in which horse and rider are competing.

INTRODUCTION · PAGE 6

CHAPTER ONE · PAGE 8
History and Development

CHAPTER TWO · PAGE 42
Making the Modern Saddle

CHAPTER THREE · PAGE 54
The Twentieth-Century Saddle

CHAPTER FOUR · PAGE 90
Specialist Saddles

CHAPTER FIVE · PAGE 114
Bits, Bridles and Additional Aids

CHAPTER SIX · PAGE 146
Driving and Farm Harness

CHAPTER SEVEN · PAGE 186
Training Aids

CHAPTER EIGHT · PAGE 196
The Well-Equipped Stable

CHAPTER NINE · PAGE 222
Ceremonial Trappings

CHAPTER TEN · PAGE 238
Riding Dress

Introduction

PERHAPS THE MOST SURPRISING fact to emerge from a study of horse equipment is the realisation that so little significant change has occurred over the centuries during which the horse has been closely associated with man. It is interesting, for instance, to see how the bits employed to control and direct the horse have been named and re-named over the years after a particular horseman or notable personality – each generation claiming to have made an original contribution to the equestrian science. In fact, there is really nothing, in this area at least, which cannot be shown to have originated hundreds, and in some cases thousands, of years ago.

Throughout the history of horse equipment it is possible to follow a clearly discernible development which is marked by only a very few innovations of any consequence. Of these the stirrup, an almost accidental discovery, is the most important. In general, original thought is not particularly noticeable in the equestrian progression, but there are the occasional exceptions which stand out like beacons in the darkness, and whose contributions are either unknown to the modern rider or not appreciated. The great masters of classical riding such as Pluvinal and de la Guerinière are, without doubt, accorded their place in history and regarded with the respect they deserve.

Caprilli, the prophet of forward riding, is less appreciated, despite the continuing influence of his system, while Ilias Toptani has certainly not attained the stature which is his due. Yet these two alone accelerated the development of modern riding to a most remarkable degree. It could indeed be that they were the first original thinkers in something like 2,000 years and certainly Toptani's breakthrough in saddle design and construction marks a real watershed in the development not only of equipment but of competitive precision riding.

Similarly, Western riding and in particular, perhaps, the hackamore reining system, is greatly under-rated outside the USA. It belongs to a far older school of horsemanship than that currently practised in Europe and involves skills of the highest order.

This book seeks to show how the evolution of equipment is entwined inextricably with the overall equestrian development, and to place men like Caprilli, Toptani and even perhaps those like Rarey and Galvayne firmly into the perspective of history. In doing so, it acts as a reference volume and gives detailed coverage of the range of equipment available today. If it can also pay tribute to the craftsmen who, over centuries of endeavour, made possible the conquest of the horse and all that it was to mean in the extension of our civilisations then no better purpose could have been realised.

E.H.E.
DEDHAM

CHAPTER ONE

History and Development

The search for control, from domestication of the horse to present day

A gentleman's saddle of about 1640, with a doeskin seat and the flaps stitched with silver thread. This saddle is part of the Barnsby collection at Walsall, England.

CHAPTER ONE · HISTORY AND DEVELOPMENT

History and Development

The development of harness—the equipment of the driving horse—and saddlery—the equipment of the ridden horse—begins at the point when man began the domestication of the animals which were to help him conquer his environment and to be the cornerstones for future civilizations. The horse, however, was not the first animal to be domesticated for the former purpose. Probably the first domestic animal was the dog, whose association with man began in the Palaeolithic age, around 6750 BC. But, although dogs have been used in draught for centuries—and are still used in Arctic regions and until recently also in western Europe, where they were employed to pull small carts—their influence on equine equipment is scarcely an important factor.

This is not, however, the case as far as cattle, reindeer, donkeys and onagers—the first of these in particular—are concerned. All of these were domesticated and used in draught long before the horse. Additionally, reindeer, donkeys and onagers were used as riding animals well before the horse was employed for that purpose. Archaeological evidence suggests that reindeer, for instance, were pulling sledges in northern Europe as long ago as 5000 BC, whilst cattle, domesticated by Neolithic man prior to 4000 BC, were used in Mesopotamia to draw land sledges before 3500 BC. At about the same time, pack asses are depicted in Egyptian art.

The domestication of the horse took place sometime during the 3rd millennium BC (3000–2000 BC)—probably, as nearly as a date can be fixed, in around 2700 BC. It was effected by a nomadic Aryan people, speaking an Indo-European language, who inhabited the steppes bordering the Black and Caspian Seas. These tough, highly adaptable people kept no records but we know of them through the clay tablets kept by their neighbours to the south, on which mention is made of them.

Initially these people would have used horses in much the same way as cattle, keeping them in herds and relying upon them as a source of food. Mares would have been milked, hides used for making tents and clothing and the dung for supplying fuel for fires. The same lifestyle still exists in these steppe lands today.

The first equipment
Naturally, when the horse began to be used for domestic purposes, the equipment employed was for the most part nearly identical to that which had proved successful with oxen, onagers and so on as far as draught harness was concerned. Saddlery—the equipment of the riding horse—evolved far later and much more slowly. One item of equine equipment—the bit—was a notable exception, however. Oxen, although occasionally guided by a rope fastened to the horns, were, and still are, controlled by either a nose rope threaded through the nasal septum, or by a cord attached to a ring through the nose. The onager, too, was controlled on the same principle. Sumerian art of the 3rd millennium BC shows yokes of four onagers abreast pulling two- and four-wheeled vehicles, being guided by reins attached to rings passed through the nose or upper lip and kept firmly in place by a strap under the jaw. But, though there is evidence to suggest that horses were controlled in this fashion in North Africa—the Greek geographer Strabo mentions the use of such a method—the introduction of a bit seems to have taken place at a fairly early stage in the association between man and the animal.

The very earliest form of control was probably no more than a woven grass halter wound around the nose, from which, it is thought, the idea of a thong tied round the lower jaw developed. This device was used centuries later by the American Indians. North African horsemen, on the other hand, particularly the Numidians, in the century either side of the Christian era, contrived to ride horses without benefit of any form of bridle, 'plying a light switch between their horses' ears', according to Silius Italicus, and evidently obtaining satisfactory results. Today, people in that part of the world ride donkeys in a similar fashion.

Bridles and bits initially made of horn or bone, seem to have been introduced in Mesopotamia in about 2300 BC, when the horse replaced the less amenable onager.

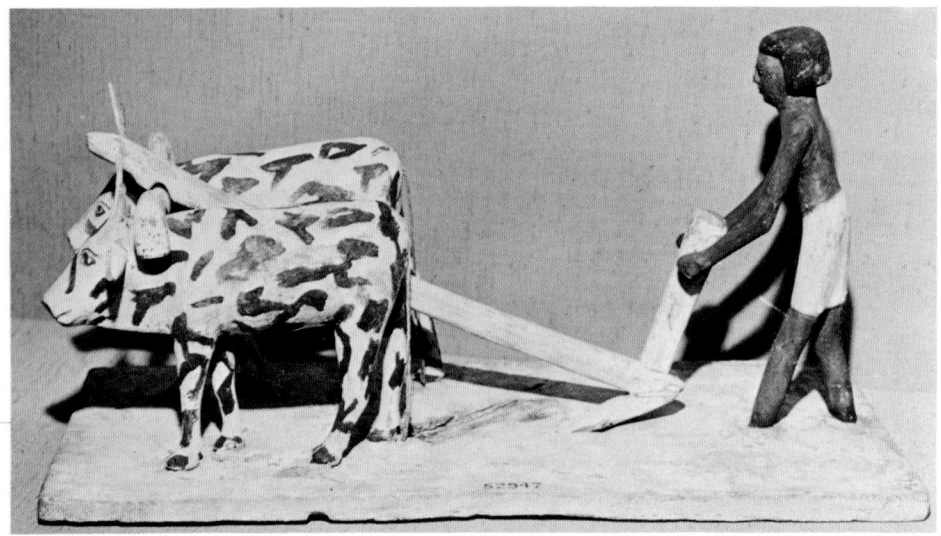

Left: A very early cave painting at Castillo, Puerto Viesgo, in the Altamira region of Spain, dated at 15000 BC. **Below:** An Egyptian tomb model of 2000 BC depicting a plough drawn by yoked oxen. The yoke survived until the time when horses were first used to pull vehicles, although it did not suit the equine conformation. **Right:** Mesopotamian mosaic of about 3000 BC showing a slightly adapted yoke. The horses (very small) are pulling by the strap at the base of the neck, a method of traction almost general until the invention of the collar.

CHAPTER ONE · HISTORY AND DEVELOPMENT

By 1400 BC a jointed metal snaffle bit was in general use throughout the Near East. Although there were numerous variations in the design of the bit rings and in the plain bar and jointed mouthpieces—some of which are remarkably modern in appearance—no important alteration in the shape or action of the bit occurred until possibly the 4th century BC, when the Greek general and writer Xenophon (430–355 BC) mentions a curb bit. Since then, nothing revolutionary in the way of bits has been produced, despite variations on the basic themes of snaffle and curb.

Yokes and harness
It is likely that horses were ridden bareback before they were generally used in harness, but much of the surviving evidence about early usage relates only to draught animals drawing chariots. Possibly the development of wheeled vehicles —largely for the purposes of war but also for travel and transport—took place before riding became widespread. The small size of the horse as it then existed would have prohibited the carrying of an armed man for any distance, while in flat country a wheeled vehicle is a better proposition than a pack animal for transporting goods.

The wheel, an invention which marked a watershed in human progress almost commensurate in importance with the discovery of fire, dates from before 3000 BC. Solid wheels dating from about 3500 BC have been found in Sumerian graves excavated in the Tigris–Euphrates valley. Spoked wheels made their appearance about 1000 years later, when they were used in chariots in Syria and Egypt. Wheeled vehicles drawn by animals were in use in the Indus Valley by 2500 BC, in Continental Europe by 2000 BC, in Egypt by 1600 BC, China by 1300 BC and in Britain by 500 BC.

Whatever the argument, it is an undisputed fact that the horse eventually superseded the onager in the war chariot. When this happened, the harness of the latter, with the exception of the nose rope, was transferred virtually in the same form to the horse, just as the yoke of the oxen had been put to use previously on the onager-drawn vehicle. Basically, a yoke is a baulk of timber attached to a pair of oxen, with a vehicle or a plough then being fastened to this. Anatomically, this simple arrangement is ideally suited to the ox, since the yoke can be placed firmly against the animal's high shoulders. It is not, however, nearly as well suited to the conformation of the horse but, nevertheless, it was adapted satisfactorily enough for chariots to operate effectively over level ground for a period of many centuries.

The ox yoke, lightened and bowed, was secured to a centre pole and fitted with a pad, which rested on the horses' withers just in front of where the pommel of a riding saddle would fit. It was kept in place by a girth and a broad neck strap, so that in fact the horses were pulling their load from their necks. This completely contradicted the accepted principle of equine traction, which is centred on the shoulder.

The yoke system had another disadvantage. The neck strap could rise up in motion and press severely upon the windpipe and jugular vein of the horses. The greater the effort made by the animals, which would result in an extension of the neck, the greater was the pressure exerted on the windpipe by the neck strap. It is the use of this strap which must presumably account for the powerful muscle development on the underside of the neck and the general ewe-necked attitude depicted in the art of the period.

To counteract the throttling action of the neckstrap, an additional strap, the equivalent of the modern harness martingale, was attached to the centre of the neck collar and passed between the forelegs to fasten on the girth. The system was still mechanically inefficient, but the vehicle was light, while the addition of two more horses largely obviated the inefficiency of the pulling power which could be applied. The extra horses were placed on the outside of the two yoke horses, these outriggers being fastened to the chariot by a single trace fitted to a simple neck strap. This was the principle involved in the Roman *quadriga*, in which the basic crew of three manning this forerunner of the modern armoured car (the charioteer, a

CHAPTER ONE · HISTORY AND DEVELOPMENT

Right: The 'Desert Hunt' from the casket of Tutankhamun. The detail is remarkable and the relief is a good example of the early use of a central pole to which the two horses were fastened. The fixed rein to the pad appears to involve the use of some form of restraining noseband. The yoke principle is, of course, still evident. **Bottom:** The cylinder seal, probably from Thebes (c. 500 BC) showing King Darius of Persia hunting lions. The very small stature of the chariot ponies is surprising.

bowman and a general help) was sometimes augmented by a fourth soldier riding postillion on the right hand outrigger.

The Roman improvements

Yoke harness which is very similar to the ancient models, still survives today in parts of India—the Bombay 'chariot rig' being a notable example. The Romans, however, adapted the yoke still further to achieve a better fit by curving the ends and adding curved side pieces, which fitted down the neck rather like a modern collar. The Romans, too, must be given credit for the equipment which led ultimately to the modern breast collar. This derives from the arrangement perfected by the Romans to take the place of the early neck collar and trace fitted to the two outriggers in a team of four. The outside horses were given a pad kept in place by a girth to which a breast band was attached. Traces were then fitted to either side of the band and hooked either directly to the vehicle

or on to a length of wood at the front of the chassis, which would today be recognized as a swingle tree. In essence the modern breast harness used for every other type of driving activity, is the same as the Roman pattern.

The padded collar resting on the shoulders and made rigid by supporting metal hames was similarly developed from the adaptations made by the Romans to the basic yoke. It is claimed to provide the most efficient method of traction, since it does not impair the horses' breathing or circulation and allows the full weight of the animals to be thrown into the pull. As an instance of this, it has been proved that a team of horses in modern harness is able to pull a load four to five times the weight of the one that could be shifted by an equivalent team in ancient yoke harness.

Asiatic influence

In common with most of the innovations in riding horse equipment, however, modern harness appears to have developed to its fullest extent in Asia. For instance, although the collar existed in its rudimentary shape in the Roman Empire, it reached its most sophisticated form in China during the same period. It was in China, too, that the single horse vehicle drawn from lateral shafts emerged. The frescoes of Kansu, dating from AD 500, show detailed depictions of modern harness, but it was not until the end of the 9th century that such harness was used generally in Europe. Tandem harness also seems to have been perfected in China.

Simultaneous with the invention of shafts came the provision of a padded cart saddle to take the weight off the horse's back and to minimize the risk of chafing. Additionally a simple breeching was introduced to help in braking the load.

Blinkers and bearing reins

Blinkers on harness bridles, however, appear to be a far more modern addition to driving equipment. They also are used for reasons which obviously could not have been matters of concern to the horsemen of ancient times. Though it is worthy of note that North African horsemen ride their Barbs in blinkered bridles, the origin of the practice, as far as driving is concerned, is more probably European and dates from the latter part of the 18th century.

The object of blinkers, leather patches fastened to the bridle cheeks thus preventing lateral vision, is to ensure that the horse can see only to his front. It is held that this will help him to concentrate on the job in hand and ensure that he will not be frightened by objects coming up behind him and will not shy away from objects or happenings on either side. It has never been proved that this is the case, however, and it is more likely that blinkers give the driver a greater (if unjustified) sense of security than they do the horse. Another reason put forward for their use is that the blinkers prevent the driver's whip from hitting the horse's eye.

Blinkers of a different pattern, but operating on the same principle, are used in modern racing where their employment can be fairly successful—at least initially—on horses which might otherwise run in a half-hearted fashion. In the racing context blinkers are often referred to as the 'rogues' badge' and horses wearing them have the reputation for being un-generous. The circumstances in which blinkers are used on the racetrack are not, however, the same as those applicable to their use with the harness horse.

Bearing, or check reins, on the other hand, are of very early origin; ancient sculptures show bearing reins attached to harness yokes. Their purpose was essentially practical, since their prevention of the extension of the horses' heads and necks not only gave greater control to the driver but prevented the neck strap from riding up on the windpipe, where it could affect the horse's breathing. Judiciously adjusted they could be used additionally as a regulator to keep the performance of the individual members of a team at a common level. The reins, however, had the potential for abuse. Centuries later, men of far more highly developed civilizations misused these reins to impose a high arched-neck head carriage which was as artificial as it was inhumane.

The growth of saddlery

Although the racing of chariots survived in the Roman circus, while horses were used increasingly in transport and agriculture, the accent in the centuries approaching the Christian period shifts decisively towards the mounted warrior. In the centuries which followed the death of Christ, this emphasis becomes ever more evident. From soon after 2300 BC, when recognizable bits and bridles were introduced, the Sumerians were in possession of written manuals on horse-management and kept records of pedigrees, presumably for breeding purposes. It is clear, therefore, that there was an awareness of the need to produce bigger, stronger and faster horses, together with the ability to do so through improved methods of land and animal husbandry. These would have involved the feeding of grain and possibly a degree of selective breeding. From this point in history, the development of saddlery for the riding horse runs parallel with the

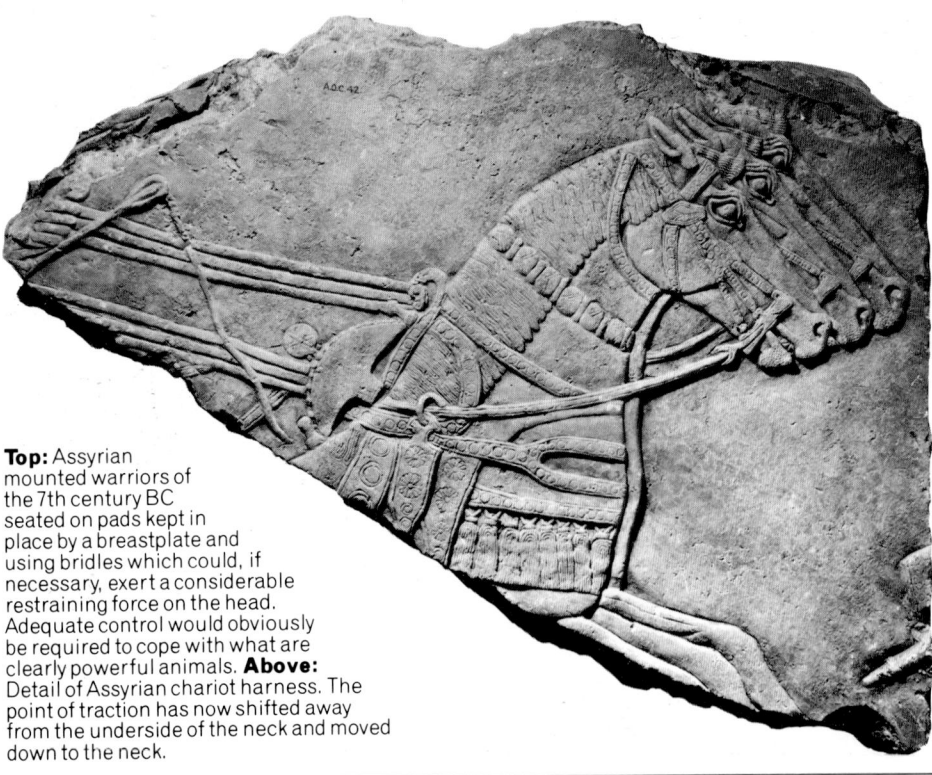

Top: Assyrian mounted warriors of the 7th century BC seated on pads kept in place by a breastplate and using bridles which could, if necessary, exert a considerable restraining force on the head. Adequate control would obviously be required to cope with what are clearly powerful animals. **Above:** Detail of Assyrian chariot harness. The point of traction has now shifted away from the underside of the neck and moved down to the neck.

CHAPTER ONE · HISTORY AND DEVELOPMENT

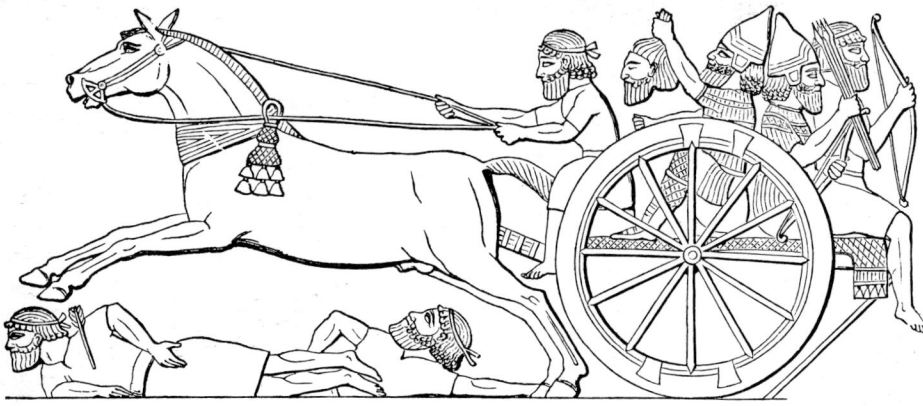

Left: Elements from the highly-ornamented Assyrian bridles can still be seen in the East and in the cavalry formations of Europe. **Bottom:** This is an Elamite cart captured by the Assyrians. The bridle is simple by comparison with those shown above and the horse pulls from the neck. It is, however, reasonable to suppose that a transport cart would not have the same requirements as a war chariot.

development of the equine species itself and the purposes to which men put horses in their constant struggle to maintain, consolidate and expand their control over their environment.

The Sumerians were not a horse-riding people on the whole and the few plaques surviving from the period which show mounted men are more likely to depict onagers, which as we know were domesticated before the horse. The first pictures of men riding what are beyond doubt spirited horses and controlling them by means of a recognizable bridle are to be found on the tomb of the 14th century BC Egyptian Pharaoh, Horenhab. Thereafter, it is the Assyrians who provide us, for a period, with the bulk of evidence about the ridden horse and its equipment.

The early Assyrians are depicted sitting well back, as men did on the onager and as men do in the east today when riding donkeys. Since, as archers, they needed to be free to handle their weapons, these early equestrians were led by grooms. A century later, however, the cavalry of Tiglath-Pileser III (747–727 BC) presented a very different picture. These were bold horsemen, sitting much further forward on cloths which are secured by a breastplate and girth, whilst they controlled their horses by means of a sophisticated bridle comprising headpiece, throatlatch and browband. The bit is a snaffle, probably jointed, while the cheekpieces of the bridle are divided like an inverted Y to fasten onto the oblong cheek of the bit. The latter is a general feature of the snaffle used in the Ancient World. The horses are stallions, almost certainly corn-fed, and probably requiring some effective means of control if their riders were to use them effectively in either the fields of battle or sport.

Control without the aid of a saddle is a matter of considerable importance. From this point in history, as horses became bigger and were fed increasingly on grain, the trend was constantly towards bits of increased severity, imposing a strong, mechanical control. The idea of the horse being pushed by the legs into accepting

CHAPTER ONE · HISTORY AND DEVELOPMENT

Above: An Assyrian relief showing the horseman wearing an armoured suit of sophisticated design. **Opposite left:** Greek warriors of the Leontis tribe (400 BC). No bridles are visible, but the position of the horses' heads, and in particular the muscle development of the underside of the neck, is indicative of an outline obtained by the use of a snaffle bit by a rider sitting bareback.

the hand is something that did not enter the horseman's philosophy for almost another two millenniums.

Developments in Persia

Up to the time of the Assyrians, horses are depicted, for the most part, with head and neck extended. The first time that horses are shown overbent is in the sculptures of Persian horses of the 6th century BC. During this period, the Persian Empire was the most important and powerful military force in the world and supported large numbers of cavalry mounted on heavier animals than seems previously to have been the case. Certainly, too, the Persian horses were far more common specimens than most of those of the preceding horse peoples.

It is possible that these horses came about as a result of the Persian connection with the neighbouring Mongolian territories to the east into which they had extended their influence. There, it would seem more than likely that Persian horses could have been crossed with the primitive Przewalskii (Mongolian wild horse), which would account for the coarse appearance and the heavy, Roman-nosed head of the Persian troop horses. Ridden without saddles and corn-fed, such horses, often thick-necked stallions, of this conformation would be difficult to control, quite apart from becoming overbent, unless some form of strong restraint, such as a curb bit, was used. But the curb bit had yet to be invented, so how did the animals become overbent in the way demonstrated by surviving ancient artefacts?

One authority, the British writer Charles Chenevix Trench, suggests that the noseband, which is obviously present in the reliefs of Persian horses, might, in fact, have had a spiked nosepiece, like the present-day Spanish *careta*. This would certainly account for the overbent position of the head and it seems reasonable to suppose that this first appearance of a noseband has a significance beyond mere decoration.

Persian bridles are also of particular interest, because they established a design convention which can be seen repeated continually in the equipment of the horse peoples of following centuries. The points of attachment are made with toggles—the buckle had yet to be invented—in much the same form as the present-day bridles used in South America and parts of Mexico. The cheek of the bridle is divided to fasten to the phallus-shaped cheek of the bit, which is ornamented with a horse's hoof at the lower end. Both are possibly symbolic of the stallion's fertility

CHAPTER ONE · HISTORY AND DEVELOPMENT

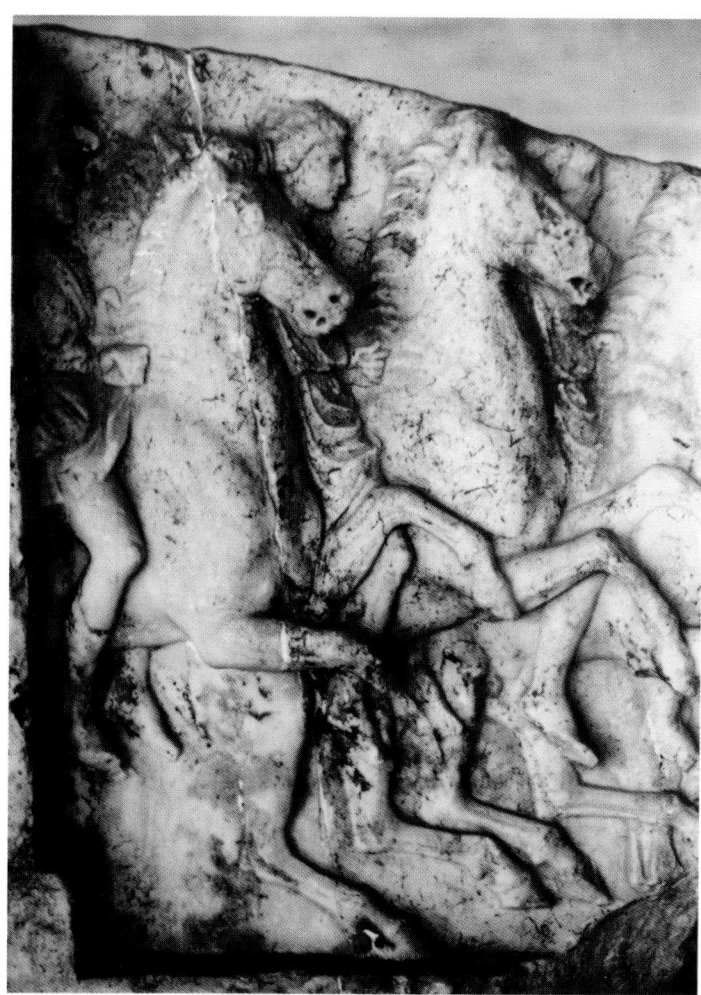

Top: An interesting variation on the usual pattern of Assyrian bit. An animal motif was often a feature of early bitting arrangements. **Above:** A bit of a slightly later period from Western Asia, which employs a very 'modern' central link. **Right:** An ornamental terret, also from Western Asia, which employs another animal motif, in this case a horse model which is again remarkably 'modern' in execution.

and the design, suitably modified, persists up to the present day, a very common showing bit for stallions having 'horseshoe' cheeks. There is no way of knowing the exact form of the mouthpiece, but it seems very possible that the shape of the bit cheeks, in combination with the divided cheekpieces of the bridle and the connection to the noseband, would bring the latter into play when the rein was used. Furthermore a degree of pressure would also have been exerted on the poll, via the cheekpieces and the bridle head. This in itself contributes to a lowering of the head and is one of the actions produced by a curb bit.

The use of a noseband by the Persians was not the first time that a device of this sort had been employed. The Egyptian charioteers of nearly a millennium before had used a 'drop' noseband which was brought into action by the use of the rein. The principle of the drop noseband then, as now, was to cause the horse to drop his nose and thus come more easily to the hand. In the Egyptian version, the fitting was so low that a strong pull on the rein would cause a severe restriction of the animal's breathing, imposing an unmistakable check on the most headstrong

The search for greater control

From the very earliest times, horsemen were concerned with the need to devise methods of restraint that would give them greater control over their mounts, which were for the most part stallions. As horses increased in size and strength and the practice of grain feeding became more widely established, the necessity for more effective braking and steering systems became commensurately more urgent.

The first modification to the plain bar bit of the early horsemen was the introduction of the jointed mouthpiece. This produced a squeezing effect across the lower jaw or on either side of the face, depending upon the position of the head at the moment the action was applied by the reins. The severity of the action was fairly quickly increased by modifications to the bit rings or cheeks. The most usual of these was the addition of spikes to the inside of the rings, an innovation which not only increased the stopping power of the bit but also simplified the business of turning to one side or the other.

From the 6th century BC onwards, attention was focussed on the mouthpiece, to which was fitted spiked rollers, sharp discs or spines like those of a hedgehog. These were the bits termed 'rough' by Xenophon, though the Greeks also employed 'smooth' bits once the horse was sufficiently schooled. Xenophon, the first recorder of equestrian theory in a number of technical treatises, also mentions mouthpieces fitted with rollers or short lengths of chain, encouraging the horse to 'mouth' his bit, thus relaxing the lower jaw. Xenophon talks about the horse 'pursuing the bit' with his tongue, which is

CHAPTER ONE · HISTORY AND DEVELOPMENT

exactly what modern horsemen are trying to achieve when they put a mouthing bit, fitted with 'keys' in the centre of its mouthpiece, on a young horse.

The curb bit

The Greeks did not use a curb bit, although Xenophon knew of this important innovation, which was invented by the Celts of Gaul in the 4th century BC. The curb bit, indeed, constitutes something of a landmark in the development of horse equipment, since it was to dominate equestrian thinking in nearly every area up to the present day. It is only in the past three or four decades that the emphasis in riding has been on the snaffle bridle, with or without a drop noseband. Up to the Second World War (and even after) hunting men would have been familiar with the maxim that 'there are three kinds of fool: the fool, the damn fool and the fool that hunts in a snaffle', and in some areas it would have been considered 'incorrect' (the most heinous of hunting crimes) to ride with so rudimentary a bridle as a simple snaffle.

The curb bit achieves control by a simple system of levers, with the curb chain, or its early equivalent, acting as the fulcrum. It causes the mouthpiece to act against the bars of the mouth, encouraging flexion at the poll and in the lower jaw. The severity of the bit and the degree of leverage obtainable depends upon the length of the cheek below the mouthpiece, whilst the length of the cheek above the mouthpiece, to which is attached the cheekpiece of the bridle, governs the degree of pressure which can be applied to the horse at the poll.

From skins to saddles

The development of the saddle in the pre-Christian era is less notable and no specific improvement or discovery comparable to those connected with bitting seems to have occurred. Cloths and skins had been in use since early times. The saddle cloths of the Assyrians, kept in place by a girth and breast strap—sometimes by a 'breeching' passing around the quarters as well—were improved by the addition of cloth rolls in front and behind the rider. On the whole, however, nothing emerged which contributed materially to the security of the rider; indeed, many of the ancients scorned the use of coverings as effete and unmanly, although most, like Xenophon, appreciated the desirability of riding 'round-backed' horses rather than those of an opposite inclination.

Whilst mounted troops were used extensively in the pre-Christian period—it was, after all, the demands of war which made the greatest contribution to both the development of saddlery and harness and to the art of riding itself—their use was limited. Without saddles the distances which could be covered, as well as the speed with which a march could be made, depended, largely, upon the endurance of the riders. Furthermore, no horseshoes were then available—they were not invented until the 1st century AD. Although the Greek military genius Alexander the Great (c. 300 BC) is reported to have used 'boots' or 'sandals' on his horses' feet in rough country, these would have given no more than rudimentary protection and were certainly not in general use.

Nor was it possible for mounted men riding bareback to close with infantry. Their seats were far too insecure for this and therefore they had to confine their

CHAPTER ONE HISTORY AND DEVELOPMENT

action to the throwing of javelins or attacking from a safe distance with bow and arrow. Nonetheless, these early cavalry soldiers must have been considerable horsemen, although it seems reasonable to suppose that many of them would have fought dismounted once they had reached the field of battle.

At the start of the Christian era therefore, horsemen were riding virtually bareback and for the most part controlling

Opposite: Horsemen from the Parthenon frieze. Once more the position of the head and the development of the lower neck is an example of the collection achieved by the use of the snaffle. **Above:** Decoration on a Greek vase of about 500 BC. This is a racing chariot so the vehicle and its harness are as light as possible. The breastplate is prevented from rising up the neck by a martingale or strap passing between the forelegs. **Left:** Early Greco/Roman horse sandal made of iron. The horseshoe, in one form or another, began to come into general use during the first century AD.

CHAPTER ONE · HISTORY AND DEVELOPMENT

Above: A Roman prick-spur discovered during an excavation in the City of London in 1935. **Left:** Celtic horseman of the first or 2nd century BC, from a relief in the Gunderstrup Cauldron found in Denmark. These warriors sit on pads secured firmly both by breastplate and crupper and they wear spurs.

their horses in a variety of snaffles, with and without the addition of nosebands. The Celtic barbarians and their close neighbours, for the moment, were alone amongst the horse peoples in their use of the curb. The security of the rider under these circumstances depended upon the strength of his legs and it must be assumed, in some degree, to how tightly he could hold the reins.

Two styles of riding in this period are also evident. People like the Greeks and Persians of the civilized world sat upright on horses which, because of the rocky terrain, were 'collected' in so far as the quarters were engaged well beneath the body. In nearly all instances with the exception of the Persians, the heads are held high, however, with the nose poked out rather than 'tucked in', as in the Parthenon frieze. This attitude is what would be expected of riders sitting bareback on spirited stallions and using a snaffle, the action of which is predominantly an upward one against the corners of the horse's lips.

An opposite style is evident amongst people, such as the Scythians, living in flatter country with open plain or steppe lands. These horsemen, too, rode in snaffles, but they rode fast with a loose rein, for they were horse-archers, needing two hands to use their weapons. Their horses, with no bit contact to govern the position of their heads, are extended from nose to tail. The riders themselves adopted a more crouched seat in accordance with the outline of their galloping horses and also in accordance with their own conformation, for many are short, squat men, with less length of leg than the more elegant Greek horseman.

Revolutionary improvements

It is from this point, in the first 500 years of the Christian era, that the most significant developments in horse equipment took place. The effect of these was remarkable. The improvements made to the saddle in particular influenced not only the advance of equitational skills but also altered the practice and even the concept of warfare. The horseshoe, invented and brought into general use during the first century of Christianity, played its part as well, since it made it possible for a horse to remain fit for service over extended periods of time and without regard for the nature of the terrain covered.

Initial improvements are most evident in the saddlery of the Scythians, one of the greatest horse peoples of all time. The Scythians were hardly cast in the academic mould and there is therefore no direct information obtainable about these fierce nomadic horsemen. Their delight was in war and feasting rather than in letters. Nonetheless, there are sufficient accounts from people associated with them to appreciate that their saddlery, derived from practical necessity, was in advance of that of their contemporaries. We know of their predilection for the taking of scalps, their grisly trophies being used to adorn their bridle reins or being hung from their saddle bows, and it is these same saddles which mark an important stage in the long story of the development of horse equipment.

Scythian and Sarmatian

Unlike the Greeks, Romans and Persians, who used a simple pad laid on the back secured by girth, breastplate and perhaps a crupper or breeching, the Scythians employed a felt saddlecloth or 'numnah', which, as demonstrated by the examples found intact in the frozen tombs of Pazyryk in the High Altai, was often gorgeously embroidered. Such saddlecloths, however, were by no means for decorative purposes alone. They were given hard usage and doubled as a blanket for the rider at night. On the march they would have been folded under the Scythian saddle and would have constituted an effective protection

The saddle, made of leather and felt, comprised two cushions well-stuffed with deer hair, joined by straps or by a connecting piece of leather from end to end. The cushions, put on over the saddlecloth, lay on either side of the spine, thus ensuring that the rider's weight was carried on the dorsal muscles and ribs. Such an arrangement conforms to the current principle of saddle-fitting, which requires the saddle to clear the backbone both along its length and width. When this principle is observed, the spine itself is not subjected to weight. It is, therefore, unlikely that sores will occur in this sensitive area and, just as importantly, there will be no restriction of the horse's free movement, such as occurs when weight is carried directly on the spine. Horses thus equipped, like those of the Scythians, were therefore less likely to develop sore backs which would limit their effective serviceability, while, because their saddles allowed freedom to the spinal process, they would be physically better able to undertake long marches. That is the measure of importance of the Scythian saddle; it, together with the easy snaffle bridle employed, endowed its inventors with a mobility superior to that of other mounted peoples of the period.

It is interesting to note that the Argentine *gaucho*, perhaps the last in the line of 'horse peoples', uses a saddle today that in its essentials differs little from that of his Scythian predecessor. In the pampas where high grasses obstruct his view, the *gaucho* stands on his saddle, placing a foot on either cushion, so as to be able to see further. The Scythians employed the same tactic, while Mongolian horsemen, themselves the most probable descendants of the Scythians, act in just the same fashion to this day.

Another link with the Scythian saddle, which is not easily explained, concerns the Plains Indians of North America. Since no horses existed on the continent until their re-introduction by the Spanish *conquistadores* in the 16th century, these Indians were pedestrian by necessity until possibly the mid-17th century, when they had acquired horses in sufficient quantity to become riders. Their saddles were almost an exact counterpart of those of the Scythians and, like that war-like people, there were Indian tribes who decorated their saddles and bridles with the scalps of their enemies.

To the east of the Scythians there lived another horse people, the Sarmatians. Unlike the Scythians, the Sarmatians fought as heavy cavalry, using a long, heavy lance which the Greeks called a 'barge-pole', and wearing armour. The Sarmatians, using this heavy lance, were probably the first troops to charge bodies of infantry in the accepted cavalry fashion—previously spears and javelins carried by mounted warriors were hurled at the enemy from a distance. The Sarmatians, too, must be given the credit for the first saddle built on a wooden frame or 'tree'. Such a saddle, built high at the cantle, was essential if horsemen, riding without benefit of stirrups, were to retain their seats at the moment of impact as they

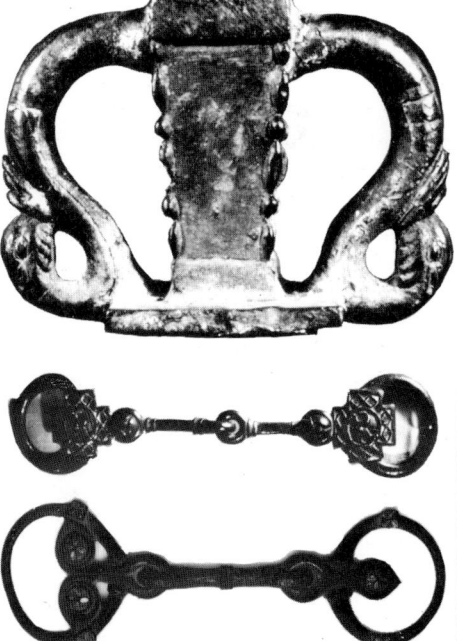

Left: A Gallo-Roman passenger vehicle, forerunner of the stage-coach. The horses are equipped with a recognisable pad and collar and traces are being used. **Above, top:** Greco-Roman rein terret in bronze. **Centre:** A Roman bit found in London. **Bottom:** A chariot bit, found in Yorkshire, with a double-bossed bit ring for fitting to the outside once the horses were in position.

CHAPTER ONE · HISTORY AND DEVELOPMENT

charged into a body of infantry. Without the high cantle, against which the horseman could brace himself, it would have been impossible for him not to have made a rapid exit over his horse's tail.

Thereafter, numerous horse peoples used the shock tactic made possible by the Sarmatian saddle. Having pushed westward from their original homelands between the Black and Caspian Seas, the Sarmatians eventually absorbed the Scythians, who in turn became part of the Goths. All used the couched lance in one form or another but there is no evidence to show that any of them used a stirrup. This was also true of a Negroid race of obscure African origin employed by the Romans as cavalry *foederati*. They are known as the X Group and exactly from where they came is a matter of conjecture.

The X Group used highly sophisticated saddles, which were extravagantly decorated and built high at front and rear, so that the rider was encased between pommel and cantle. Arab saddles of the present day are almost identical to the

Above: Saddle-cloth from the Pazyryk tombs (5th century BC) decorated in felt **appliqué** with an eagle, griffon and ibex. **Left, top:** Carved wooden facing of a saddle arch from the same source. **Bottom:** Elaborate gold belt buckle of Sarmatian origin (first century BC – first century AD). The noseband fitted below the bit is an early form of drop noseband, used to give the rider greater control. The saddle pad is equipped with thongs to which the rider would have attached his belongings. **Opposite:** This gaily attired horseman appears on a decorated felt wall-hanging found in Barrow 5 at Pazyryk. All the items illustrated on these two pages are in the collection at the Hermitage Museum, Leningrad, which houses the large number of items removed from Pazyryk. Without doubt this collection is one of the most comprehensive and valuable in the world.

CHAPTER ONE · HISTORY AND DEVELOPMENT

CHAPTER ONE HISTORY AND DEVELOPMENT

Left: A Sasanian silver-gilt dish from the collection at Leningrad's Hermitage Museum. The illustration is of King Ardnashir III (628-630 AD) hunting with a bow. The saddle he uses has a clearly defined forearch and is probably kept in place by a girth as well as by the breastplate and breeching. The discs hanging from these items may well be charms to ward off evil, rather like the horse brasses used on heavy harness horses. The tail decoration is unusual and of particular interest. There is no evidence of a stirrup, but this does not seem to inhibit King Ardnashir in his firing of a 'Parthian shot'.

saddles of this mysterious people, whom the Romans called Nobades.

In Africa the lance was customarily used overhand in a stabbing action, but the Nobades couched their weapons like the Sarmatians. Additionally they employed the notorious ring bit, which is often referred to as the Mameluke. This is because the Mamelukes used a similar device much later in time. It would seem reasonable to assume that the ring-type curb bits of the Renaissance masters derived from this source and, indeed, a very similar bit can be found in North Africa today.

Invention of the stirrup

But the greatest advance was yet to come. This was the invention of the stirrup. It seems fairly certain that this came from Mongolia with Attila the Hun, known to the world as 'the scourge of God'. It is impossible to date this momentous happening exactly, but there is written evidence of the stirrup's existence around the middle of the 5th century AD.

The Russian scientist W W Arendt put forward the suggestion that the stirrup could have been incorporated into the girth of Scythian saddles, but it is difficult to substantiate the claim, which was based largely on an illustration on the Chertomlyk vase (4th century BC) and on material discovered in tombs at Novo-Alexandrovska in 1865. If such an item did exist, it seems very unlikely that it took some 700 to 800 years to come into general use. On the other hand, some evidence suggests that Indian horsemen rode with a toe stirrup, a leather loop into which was placed the big toe, perhaps as much as 200 years before Attila. If this were so, it is not unreasonable to suppose that the nomads of Central Asia would, in time, have become acquainted with the practice, adapting the toe thong so as to accommodate the thick felt boots which protected their feet against the cold. In parts of southern India today and in Malaya and Singapore the natives still use a toe stirrup—even when racing.

The advantages bestowed by the stirrup were numerous and far reaching in their effect. Cavalry was able to increase its mobility and range, since the comfort given to the rider by the presence of a pair of stirrups reduced fatigue and allowed longer marches to be made at high speeds. Naturally, it also increased the rider's security a hundred-fold. Heavy cavalry were able to close with bodies of infantry with far less risk of being un-horsed at the moment of impact and, as a result, assumed a far greater importance on the battlefield. However, the clear division between heavy horsemen and the light cavalry of the barbarians like Attila's Huns persisted. The two distinct styles of riding continued to exist alongside each other and continued to do so right through the centuries. Both heavy and light cavalry adopted the stirrup, but the style of riding

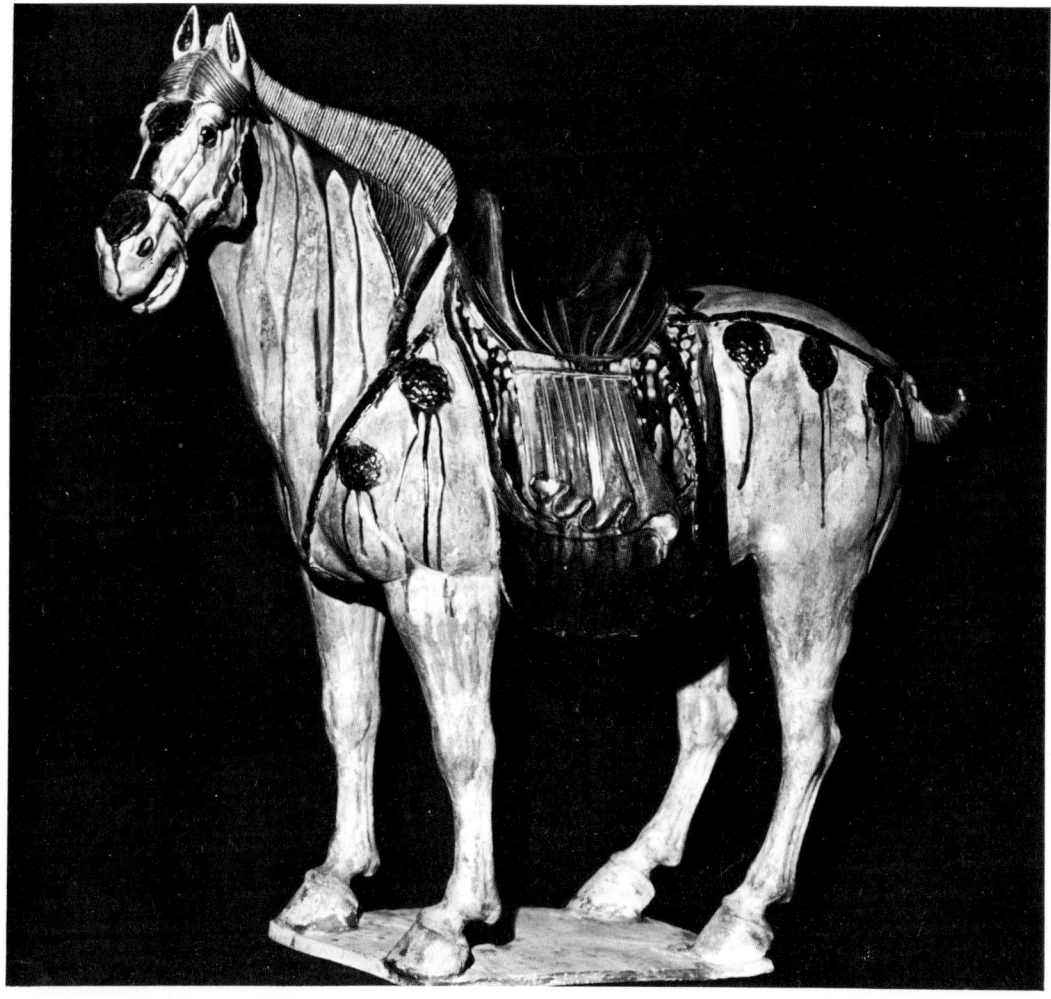

Left: Chinese glazed, earthenware figure from a tomb of the Tang Dynasty (7th-10th century AD). The practice of burying equine representations and equipment, and even the horses themselves, with chieftains and noblemen was widespread throughout Asia. This is a particularly fine example of a tomb figure and the characteristic features of the saddle are clearly defined. The dipped seat persisted until well after the Renaissance period and survives, in a less extreme form, in modern saddles.

and the use made of it was determined by the weapons employed and by the type of horses being ridden.

Heavy cavalry, weighted with armour, had the lance as a principal weapon and used the charge against infantry, or other cavalry, as their tactic. Their horses needed to be strong, robust sorts, but did not need to be excessively swift. This type of mounted soldier used a pretty fierce curb bit to control his horse, achieving a form of mechanical collection by its action, and preserved his equilibrium in the charge by pushing hard on his stirrups and bracing himself against the high cantle of his saddle. He rode, therefore, with seat firmly in the saddle using a fairly long leather and pushing his feet to the front, a position which was enforced by the stirrup attachment being placed well to the front of the saddle.

For the most part the light horsemen originated in the east. They rode smaller horses and relied far more upon speed. They were horse-archers, riding short so as to be able to stand in their stirrups and adopting a remarkably modern-looking seat, with the lower leg drawn back behind the vertical. They rode in snaffles, making no attempt to collect their horses, since their bows required the use of both hands. Their tactic was to gallop across the enemy's front usually from left to right to facilitate the drawing of the bow, then to loose three or four shafts before peeling off and despatching, over the horse's rump, a 'Parthian shot'.

A shift in emphasis

This style of riding persisted long after the bow, fired from horse-back, had given way to other weapons. It was the opposite cavalry school, however, which for centuries dominated the battlefields of the world and was the most significant factor in the development of equitation and of horse equipment.

What was happening was a shift in emphasis from the east to the west. The old horse cultures of Asian origin—the originators of man's association with the horse—were to be overtaken by the practices of Europe. It was the latter which were to exert the greater influence on the future, but not, as will be seen later, exclusively, everywhere or for ever. Hundreds of years later, the two streams of equitation were to merge to produce the modern system of riding.

The first steps in this progress are less well documented than later ones. Man's knowledge of the Dark Ages is sparse in comparison with later periods, from which fairly detailed records survive. Obviously, equipment was adapted and improved in accordance with immediate local needs, but no notable advance in equitational method and theory occurred which was reflected in corresponding improvements in the equipment used.

From about 1066 onwards, however, documentation in words and in pictures

CHAPTER ONE · HISTORY AND DEVELOPMENT

Far right: Paolo Ucello's painting of the battle of San Romano gives a very complete picture of the equipment of the mounted knight and illustrates clearly the need for a saddle which afforded maximum security to the rider and for a bit strong enough to control an excited (and probably heavy) horse with one hand in 'press of battle'. The wide leather reins embossed with heavy brass discs were not entirely decorative – such a rein would have presented a considerable difficulty to a foot soldier attempting to cut it. **Right:** An illustration from the medieval Luttrell Psalter, showing a black St. George killing the dragon using the overhand thrust employed by Eastern horsemen. **Below:** Norman knights preparing to embark for Hastings in 1066, from the Bayeux tapestry. The forward attachment of the stirrup leather, causing the leg to be pushed to the front, is seen clearly on the saddle of the rider leading the group.

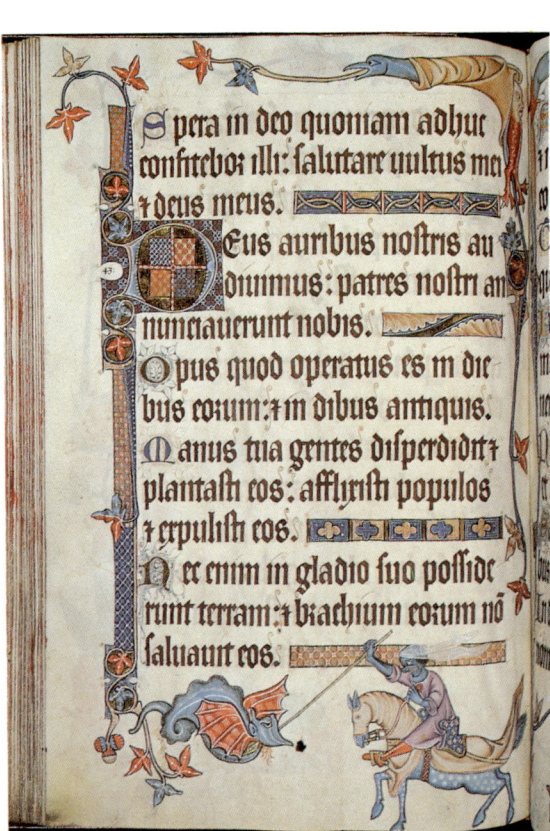

becomes increasingly detailed and, as far as equitation and equipment is concerned, a development is easily discernible. These two facets—the practice of riding and the equipment used by the horseman in improving techniques and advancing his mastery of the horse—of necessity must be considered in parallel, for they are largely interdependent. Sometimes, it is true, the horseman appears to be in advance of his equipment, his physical strength and skills overcoming, if only in part, his lack of the constructions of wood, metal and leather which could have endowed him with greater comfort, security and control in his partnership with the horse. There are also periods, however, when the equipment available seems almost to be a step or two ahead of the rider; there have certainly been occasions when the horseman has been so overwhelmed by a surfeit of saddlery and forceful devices that the art and the empathy he should possess have been reduced to a matter of applied mechanics.

Knights and the Great Horse

In the equestrian context, the tendency is for the Middle Ages to be associated with the Great Horse and the armoured knight. Both became a notable feature on the battlefields and tourney grounds of the time. At the beginning of this period, however, horses were light in build, as can be seen from the Bayeux tapestry, while their riders wore relatively light chain-mail shirts. With all weapons included, plus saddles, the average warrior did not probably weigh more than 16 stone. This was the average burden of a single cavalry troop horse in the First World War.

From the numerous illustrations which have survived, it seems that a snaffle of one sort or another was in more general use than the curb bit. The mouthpieces of these snaffles, however, may very well have been made more severe by the addition of spikes, sharpened edges and so on,

CHAPTER ONE · HISTORY AND DEVELOPMENT

while many are obviously connected to a low-fitting noseband. The action of this could also have been strengthened by the addition of a rough metal plate on the inner surface, or by a row of small spikes.

Nonetheless, whilst it is possible that such additional restraints could have been present, the horses are neither overbent nor highly collected, like those of the earlier Persians or those of some 200 to 300 years later. In the former instance, it has to be remembered that, unlike the Norman horsemen depicted on the Bayeux tapestry, the Persians had no stirrups and precious little saddle to give them security of tenure. It is not unreasonable to suppose, therefore, that they would have had some recourse to the reins not only to control their apparently strong horses but also to ensure a safe seat.

As the shattering effect of a co-ordinated charge of cavalry became increasingly appreciated, bigger, heavier horses were bred and employed. They would have required stronger forms of restraint than those afforded by the snaffle; since it was also essential 'in press of knights' that the horses should be responsive and schooled, the more immediate bitting arrangement represented by the curb became a necessity.

Even so the heavier horses used in the 12th and 13th centuries did not approach the Great Horses produced in the following 200 years. The Great Horse evolved as a result of the usual tit-for-tat escalation of the arms' race, which was as much in evidence in the Middle Ages as in today's nuclear era. To counter the effect of charging cavalry, the weapons carried by the foot soldier had to be improved. The most effective of all these weapons was the long-bow, a Welsh product, used with the most devastating effect to cut swathes in the concourse of French chivalry at the decisive moment at Crécy in 1346.

For as long as horses were integral to the battlefield, the developing practices of war

CHAPTER ONE · HISTORY AND DEVELOPMENT

Opposite: Knight of the late 15th century in full armour, with his horse armoured and caparisoned with rich cloths. The latter, at least in a form as exaggerated as this, would not have been used other than for full-dress parade occasions. **Left:** Late 15th-century German armour, the horse being equipped with plate and chain mail. The length of the bridle cheeks would allow for tremendous leverage against the jaw: they measure more than 20 inches.

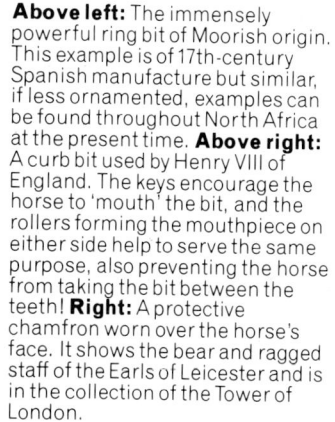

Above left: The immensely powerful ring bit of Moorish origin. This example is of 17th-century Spanish manufacture but similar, if less ornamented, examples can be found throughout North Africa at the present time. **Above right:** A curb bit used by Henry VIII of England. The keys encourage the horse to 'mouth' the bit, and the rollers forming the mouthpiece on either side help to serve the same purpose, also preventing the horse from taking the bit between the teeth! **Right:** A protective chamfron worn over the horse's face. It shows the bear and ragged staff of the Earls of Leicester and is in the collection of the Tower of London.

would have their influence upon equitational methods and the complementing equipment used in support of the latter. It was so in this situation.

The cavalry's answer to the long-bow was to equip the knight with body armour. This became increasingly complex and weighty, as the bowmen became more and more skilled with their murderous tool. At Crécy, for instance, the Welsh archers could fire enough arrows to produce a dense, lethal and continuing barrage on the advancing cavalry. To carry the rider's increased weight, a stronger, heavier horse was needed; when it became necessary to provide the horse with protective armour as well, an even more massive—and slower—horse was required for the purpose.

The seat of the knight remained much the same. He positioned himself deep in his dip-seated saddle, its high pommel affording him a little extra protection as well as contributing to his security, whilst bracing himself, with leg straight and thrust forward in the stirrup, against the equally high cantle. As has been seen, this position, encouraged by the forward placement of the stirrup leather attachment, suited the knight's purpose admirably, allowing him to withstand the shock of the charge without becoming unseated. He wore extremely long and very sharp spurs in order to be able to reach his horse and to ensure that so heavy an animal would react to the indications implicit in their use. Without doubt, the ability to control the horse with the legs was now appreciated and understood. The remaining element of control, the bit, was used with one hand only—the left. This held the reins and also the knight's shield and therefore had to be carried high—certainly as high as the chest. The right hand held the sword, lance or mace.

The bit employed was a curb bit of fearsome dimensions. The mouthpiece might be jointed in its centre and made 'sharp' by serrations, spikes or something similar; alternatively it might be fitted with a very high port. This not only allowed the bit to bear directly upon the

CHAPTER ONE · HISTORY AND DEVELOPMENT

Right: A Luttrell Psalter lady hands her caparisoned knight his helm whilst the other lady (a rival out of favour perhaps) is left holding his shield. The saddle encasing the rider is of a type used for jousting before this pastime became so professional that knights, preferring to exit by the back door, had the cantles cut away.

CHAPTER ONE · HISTORY AND DEVELOPMENT

Right: A 15th-century French tournament scene. Although the saddle fixed the rider firmly in position the high cantle was a dangerous feature and could cause serious injury. It was later removed and replaced by a less restrictive support. The fashion of a flower growing out of the top of the head is surely an entirely Gallic conceit!

bars of the mouth by accommodating the tongue, which would otherwise lie over the bars and thus mitigate the pressure imposed by the mouthpiece of the bit, but also bore painfully on the roof of the mouth to provide a horrific degree of leverage. The extent of this can easily be imagined, when it is appreciated that the length of the cheeks could be as much as 15in. The other type of curb bit employed was the fierce, jaw-breaking ring bit of North Africa, similar to that used by the X Group nearly a millennium previously.

Most dressage riders of the present day, more particularly those influenced by German teaching, would break a horse's jaw in five minutes with such a bit if they rode in their customary manner, always supposing that the horse did not rear over backwards first. There is no reason to suppose that the mounted knights would have fared better had they employed our modern 'contact' system, despite the lack of quality in their elephantine mounts.

Instead they rode with one hand on a looped rein, which implies that their horses were schooled to the neck rein for changes of direction and to the raised hand as an indication to decrease the pace or to stop. This is the way the Californian cowboy schools his horse, arriving at the final potentially severe 'spade' (port) bit by a progression of nosebands. In fact, the system of the hackamore (*jaquima*, in Arabic *hakma*) on which the cowboy's method of bitting is based, derives from the practices of the 16th-century Spanish *conquistadores*, who, in turn, had learnt them from the Moors during the latters' 700-year presence on the Iberian peninsula.

The knights of Europe were therefore probably borrowing parts of a system widely used in the Middle East, which had been learnt from contacts made during the long period of the Crusades and from Portuguese and Spanish acquaintances.

As a training ground for war, the knights of the Middle Ages employed the tournament and joust. These sports were directly related to the demands of the battlefield, as, indeed, are many other horse sports. Particularly as the role of the mounted knight became less tenable as a result of the devastating long-bows, tournaments became increasingly artificial and professional—tournament knights 'doing the circuit' much like the modern show jumper. The sport, too, produced specialist equipment. This was often exaggerated in the extreme, particularly as far as the jousting saddle was concerned, but it also advanced the standards of equitation. The horses, heavy or not, had to be schooled to a very high degree if they were to stand any chance in this first of the equestrian 'spectator-sports'.

The saddles for the sport were often built so that the rider was completely encased from the waist to the hips. Eventually the pommel became a vast iron shield, like the windscreen of a motorcycle, while great leg guards were also incorporated. Finally, since fake action with blunted lances had taken the place of conflict to the death, the contenders decided on the sensible option of ejecting via the back door rather than risk being maimed or killed by being imprisoned in the cockpit of the saddle. For this reason,

CHAPTER ONE · HISTORY AND DEVELOPMENT

CHAPTER ONE · HISTORY AND DEVELOPMENT

Opposite: 18th-century prints depicting the High School movements. They are by the Austrian artist Ridinger, who made the subject his speciality. In all the illustrations, except the top right, the upper rein is attached to the cavesson. In the two bottom pictures a draw rein passing through the cavesson ring is in use. **Right:** This elegant rider also employs a rein to the cavesson and displays commendable restraint in the use of the curb. The tail casing has a practical purpose during execution of the 'airs' or leaps above the ground. It is still used at the Spanish School and by the Cadre Noir. The saddle in these pictures is the **Selle Royale**, a streamlined version of the saddle of the medieval knight.

the cantle was removed. This naturally could not have been the case in actual battle.

The riding masters

The tournament had become the medieval equivalent of the jumping arena and the conventional role of the knight in battle had declined by the time that the phenomenon of the Renaissance (literally 'rebirth') of the 16th century, opened a new gateway to rediscovering and developng the old learning in the arts and sciences within the civilized world. Men enthusiastically discovered the classical glories again, amongst them the works of the great Greek general, Xenophon, the first master of equitation. Young gentlemen began to take an interest in equitation as an art form, regarding it as on a level with an appreciation of music and poetry, an understanding of mathematics and the other varied attributes which now made up the intellectual equipment and social graces of those of gentle birth.

In Italy, at first, and then over Europe baroque riding halls arose and the foundations of 'classical' riding were established. Spain and France were also important centres. In fact, like the tournament this new riding was initially mirrored on war, but without the latter's danger. In the extravagant carousels, the riders performed the same movements which the mounted knight would have executed in battle. The *volte, levade, pirouette* and *capriole* ensured the handiness of the horse and displayed his ability to overawe opponents and discourage the attentions of ill-disposed enemy infantry. Then, too, there were the glories of the *passage* and *piaffe*, the elevated trots which showed off the victorious general and his noble horse to best advantage.

Dominating the horse

In the 16th century the horses used in the *manège* (school) were those which would have carried knights into battle; they were coarse, heavy animals and in order to put them back on their haunches so as to perform the highly collected movements required, it was deemed necessary to use strong curb bits and sometimes the *careta*, the studded noseband from which is derived the ringed lunge cavesson and of which the plain cavesson, which does no more than set off a bridle, is a relic, which survives in riding up to the present day.

The accent, indeed, in the early days of classical riding was on 'breaking' the horse. The only reward he received was when the punishment stopped. Grisone, the first of the great riding masters, who wrote his book *Gli Ordine di Cavalcare* in 1550, used some appalling devices, as did his pupil and successor Pignatelli. But in an age when the rack, the thumbscrew and the stake were commonplace, the cruelties practised on animals were no more than relative, while, in spite of their use of some barbarous items of equipment, both Grisone and Pignatelli were swift to condemn any practice that would harden the mouth itself.

The bits were curbs, with or without ports. Some of them had the forerunner of the bradoon—a thin bit which was called a 'flying trench'—attached. The curb was used with a noseband—a cavesson—to which, following loosely the Moorish fashion, the 'false rein' was secured. The cavesson could be studded, like the *careta*, or it might occasionally be of plain leather. Later, the 'false rein' would be fitted to the 'flying trench', or to the top ring of the curb, in the fashion of what has

CHAPTER ONE · HISTORY AND DEVELOPMENT

become known as a Pelham. Finally the curb rein was added to supplement the top rein. What this meant was that the curb, however severe, was never brought into full use. It was, as it were, only the threat of its severe action which was employed to obtain the desired result. The Western horseman of today uses the same system through the *bosal*, a noseband weighted at the rear, and the hackamore, the bosal fitted with heavy *mecate* ropes which are attached to the knot lying behind the curb groove and act as reins. This art, however, is virtually lost to the modern European horseman, who frequently inflicts far more pain upon the mouths of his horses while criticizing the 'barbarity' of the Western bit, or those used by the horsemen of the Iberian peninsular.

Both Grisone and Pignatelli, in common with other riding masters of their era, would attach metal 'keys' to the bit so that the horse should play with the bit and retain a wet mouth. Such 'keys' are frequently seen on modern-day breaking bits.

The saddle, initially, was to all intents the war saddle of the Middle Ages. However, it was gradually adapted to appear more elegant and provide additional comfort and security. It became a padded affair, straight cut in its flap, of course, but as with the saddle of the knight high in front and with a pronounced cantle. For additional security, pads were often fitted into which the riders' thighs could be

Top: A 16th-century Italian saddle presented to Charles V. This is essentially the **Selle Royale** of classical equitation. A very similar saddle is used today in the Spanish Riding School in Vienna and is still made in some numbers in Portugal and Spain where it is in general use.
Right: A horseman of Andalucia riding in a saddle of the same design, but with the heavy Iberian 'slipper' stirrups of that country. He rides with one hand on a cavesson rein and a looping curb rein. Note again the tail casing which differs only slightly from those found in the Pazyryk tombs.

CHAPTER ONE · HISTORY AND DEVELOPMENT

Left: The English master, William Cavendish, Duke of Newcastle (1592-1676), inventor of the running rein but here seen riding with a single curb rein. The heavy horses used for school riding compelled riders to make use of very strong curb bits to obtain the required control.

on that used in the *manège*. Military saddles were often no more than utility versions of the school saddles, but they were practical, as they retained the dip seat, although for the most part the stirrup bar was still placed so far to the front as to prevent the leg from being held other than somewhat in advance of the girth.

The British tradition

In Britain, 'scientific' equitation never really became established. However, riding and the equipment that went with it was to undergo a change following the Stuart Restoration of 1660. Hunting had always been the great sport of the British, but, until that time, it had been confined to the hunting of the stag and hare. Then, as a result of the serious depletion of the deer population in the Civil War, foxes, previously considered as vermin, became the chief quarry. To pursue this swift, straight-running animal, hounds had to be bred lighter and faster. Horses, too, had to be able to gallop and, increasingly, those who rode them had to be prepared to jump if they wished to be in at the kill. In the first place, there was no time to go round obstacles and remain in touch with hounds, while, in the second, the new enclosures of hitherto open pasture and common land were not only changing the face of the countryside but also providing ever more jumping for foxhunters.

By the 18th century foxhunting was a popular sport and the British, either disdainful or unaware of academic riding as carried on outside their island, rode their good horses, largely by the light of nature, over and through whatever came in their way in their devotion to the pursuit of the fox.

The British foxhunter was not an 'educated' horseman in the Continental sense, but followers of the sport were brave, adaptable and willing to let their horses do their full share of the work involved. In a sense they were more in the mould of the ancient horsemen from Asia, although, of course, they rode much longer. Frequently, however, they used a light snaffle bridle, without even the adornment of a

wedged. It survives in only slightly altered form in the *selle royale* of the classical schools of Vienna (the Spanish Riding School) and of Saumur in France, while examples can still be bought throughout Spain and Portugal.

Refinements over the centuries

As far as the classical form of indoor riding was concerned, equipment altered little over the next 200 years, though it perhaps became more streamlined. The 'flying trench' became a bradoon proper and the curb bit became more refined and often also more ingenious in its construction. England's Duke of Newcastle, a notable, though conceited, master of the equestrian art, invented the running or draw rein and placed great reliance on its efficacy. The side-rein attached to a body roller or to a saddle was in general use and was, in fact, the forerunner of Newcastle's running rein. Long-reining, following the use of the lunge rein in the exercise of 'treading the ring', was practised in the early 16th century as, too, was the ploy of fitting weights to a horse's feet to encourage the elevated action in collected paces. The weights were often wooden balls attached to a strap which encircled the fetlock, the ball lying above the heel. A modern version of this instrument can be seen in any stable where American Saddlebreds or Tennessee Walkers are kept.

Nonetheless the accent by the 18th century had shifted decisively from the forceful methods of Grisone to a form of scientific equitation in which the horse was trained with understanding and kindness. This change in emphasis was profoundly influenced by the teachings of François Robichon de la Guérinière (1688–1751). Academic equitation dominated European thinking throughout the century and beyond it—except perhaps in England—and most equipment was based

CHAPTER ONE · HISTORY AND DEVELOPMENT

noseband, which in its drop version—that is, fitted low and below the bit—was virtually a compulsory schooling device on the Continent. Sometimes they might employ a martingale, but all in all their main aim was to encourage their horses to go on freely rather than discourage them from this. Later, however, the snaffle bridle went out of fashion, and in many hunting 'countries' it became 'incorrect' to hunt in anything other than a double bridle—the term used to describe the combination of bit and bradoon.

The necessity of jumping fences meant that foxhunters wisely eschewed the high pommel of the medieval saddle and, to meet their needs, a saddle which by comparison had a flat seat was developed. It was neat, unobtrusive, not exaggerated and extremely durable. Such saddlery was, indeed, to become the envy of every other nation and would in time be avidly sought after by riders everywhere.

The hunting saddle

Although the saddle was fairly straight in its flap, in accordance with the length of stirrup leather in general use, it was wide in the seat and waist, thus distributing the weight of the rider over as large an area as possible. The panel of this saddle (the cushion between the tree and the horse's back) was correspondingly large and followed the shape of the flaps. In later years it was called a 'full panel'. For the most part the panels of these saddles were covered in serge cloth, which might sometimes be overlaid with a covering of linen so as to prevent the serge being dirtied and the panel from absorbing too great a quantity of sweat. The stuffing material used was short, springy wool of various qualities, which could be 'regulated' by the saddler so that the saddle fitted correctly to the horse's back.

This type of saddle, built on a handmade beechwood tree, persisted with no more than minor variations throughout the 19th century and well into the 20th century. In time, saddles of this general outline came to be known by the common title of the 'English hunting saddle'.

In fact, the saddle naturally underwent changes over the course of years as particular makers produced their own specialities, but the pattern remained, nonetheless, the example for saddle manufacturers to follow in many parts of the world. As a saddle it had disadvantages, but it was not entirely ill-suited to its purpose.

In the days before motorized transport, a hunting man spent many hours in the saddle during a day and covered distances which many modern riders would consider unthinkable. Tired riders naturally shift in their saddles to ease their fatigue, but this is hardly the best thing for a horse's back, since the friction which a fidgeting rider produces between panel and back can cause soreness. The shape of these saddles, with their broad bearing surfaces distributing the weight over a wide area of the back, certainly helped to mitigate the possible detrimental effects of long days in the saddle, but whether their durability was an advantage or not is uncertain. It is probable that, because they lasted so long—saddles 50 years old and more were by no means uncommon—they helped to delay the acceptance of the purpose-designed saddles which were so much needed when sport, in terms of show jumping and eventing, became the greatest influence in saddlery design.

Variants and developments

One of the first outside influences was polo, a game played in Persia and in areas of Assam in pre-Christian times and introduced to England in 1869 by army officers who had learnt the game in India. It influenced the construction of saddles in a number of ways. Polo players needed to sit close to their ponies, which the full panels of the traditional hunting saddles did not always allow. To overcome this problem, the bottom part of the panel, which would have come under the lower leg, was removed, the remaining 'half' panel being called, in time, a 'Rugby' panel. Rugby was an early British polo centre. In addition, polo, more than any other equestrian sport, was responsible for the narrowing of the waist or 'twist' of the saddle. The waist is the tapered area between the pommel or head of the saddle and the seat proper. A narrow twist does not spread the rider's thighs and allows him greater contact down the length of the leg. Short-legged riders will appreciate the discomfort which could be caused by a wide-waisted saddle, since the thighs are spread so much that the effective use of the leg becomes difficult.

Increasingly, too, saddle panels began to be lined with leather. This, although it made the job of regulating the panels more

difficult, resisted the absorption of sweat more efficiently and was easier to keep clean. A further innovation was the use of felt pads to replace the traditional wool stuffing and felt panelled saddles, their Rugby-type panels lined with leather, became extremely popular. Right up to the time when the modern spring-tree saddles became available, they were made in fairly large quantities, although they never superseded their stuffed wool predecessors.

Other late 19th-century innovations included the use of numerous patented 'safety bars', designed to release the stirrup leather in the event of a fall. They reflected a period when horsemen seemed more than usually concerned with 'devices' of one sort or another, not so much

CHAPTER ONE · HISTORY AND DEVELOPMENT

Left: The picture of Eclipse by George Stubbs. Eclipse, unbeaten in all his races, was arguably the world's greatest racehorse and Stubbs the world's greatest painter of horses. Eclipse is wearing a light racing saddle, which is in fact no more than a cut-down hunting saddle of the period, and a racing bridle, without a noseband and fitted with a simple cheek snaffle. The surcingle is an extra precaution against the saddle slipping.

perhaps so far as their saddles were concerned, but more particularly as far as bits and bitting were concerned.

At the same time, the shape of the saddle tree began to vary. This was a more useful development than the one described above. The head of the tree was shaped back to accommodate high withers. A head might be either half or full cutback, while, in the case of saddles made for American-gaited horses, the head was cut back so far as to earn the name 'cowmouth'.

In the area of bitting, which was dominated again to a considerable degree by Britain, the centre of the bit and the horse furniture industry being the Midlands town of Walsall, the 19th century, in particular, saw bits produced in enormous quantity and in quite astonishing variety. But, for all the ingenuity expended, nothing really new emerged; the designs were no more than variations—sometimes quite complex ones—on the basic forms of bit which had existed for almost 2,000 years.

The principal influence at this time on equestrian developments was the equipment demanded for the carriage horse, an important aspect of the social scene. All manner of bits were devised to impose the high head carriage demanded by the high society of the time. The gag, taken over with enthusiasm by polo players, had its origin in the variety of checks and bearing reins used in the carriage trade, although once more, the device had been known hundreds of years previously. Other riding bits in every shape and size also abounded, most of them designed to produce a high carriage of head and neck.

American saddlery followed the pattern of the British product on the eastern side of the continent and was for the most part imported from Britain. In general terms, this applies today, though imports increasingly came from West Germany, and other Continental countries. But the Americans also had a further requirement in respect of the breeds which they had developed for their own particular purposes. The American gaited horses—the American Saddlebred, the Missouri Foxtrotter and the Tennessee Walker—used paces which are now lost to Europe and required specialist saddlery as a consequence. They needed in particular the flat-

CHAPTER ONE · HISTORY AND DEVELOPMENT

seated, wide-flapped saddle and the various training equipment used to encourage the extravagant gaits. The curb bits used resemble the Western 'spade' bit, but the saddle itself is unique. The native industry naturally produces high quality Western saddles and related equipment in vast quantity, but surprisingly the USA does not have an industry producing European-type saddlery.

The Caprilli watershed
At the start of the present century, however, one of the great watersheds in the evolution of horse tack occurred. This, perhaps the most significant development in the context of modern equitation, came about as a result of the theories expounded by a little known Italian cavalry captain, Federico Caprilli, whose short life spanned the years between 1868 and 1907. In the context of his time, and having regard for the very narrow and conservative field in which he operated, Caprilli's brief and necessarily incomplete *Principi di Equitazione di Campagna*, published in 1901, had much the same impact on the equestrian world as did Darwin's *Origin of the Species* on the more general one.

At the turn of the century, and for many years before, Continental riding was dominated by the cavalry schools, particularly those of Germany. Unlike their British counterparts, the cavalry officers these schools produced did not hunt on horseback and civilians had virtually no influence. The German cavalry schools employed a near-'classical' method of instruction, demanding considerable collection but devoting little time to jumping and cross-country riding. Basically, instruction of recruits was within the confines of the school and the purpose of cavalry was still enshrined in the philosophy of the charge—even though much of their instruction would hardly have fitted the recipients with the necessary skills involved, unless the nature of the terrain had been that of a billiard table.

Caprilli appreciated, somewhat in advance of the generals, that the traditional role of cavalry was no longer valid. A charge against machine-guns was simply not viable—the modern role of cavalry would be increasingly concerned with reconnaissance, which, indeed, had been its original role in the distant past. What

CHAPTER ONE · HISTORY AND DEVELOPMENT

was needed was a cavalry arm that would be able to move swiftly over all types of country, returning, in fact, to the early light horsemen of Asia.

Caprilli saw clearly, however, that existing cavalry instruction would not produce a mounted arm of the sort he thought necessary and it was for that reason that he evolved a new system of training which is now termed the Italian or 'Forward Seat'.

Caprilli abolished the work in the indoor schools. Instead, he trained riders and horses over the kind of terrain in which they might expect to operate. He sought to teach natural balance by natural training. He demanded that the head and neck of the horse be given full freedom, and that his riders do nothing to disturb the horse's balance. By establishing

Top: Lady riders in the 1920s often competed in point-to-point races riding side-saddle. As the sport became more professional and came closer to steeplechasing, equipment and dress changed accordingly. **Above:** Portrait of a park hack by the English artist Herring (c. 1880). The saddle is typical of the period, the seat probably quilted for comfort, with the panel swelling in front of the knee. **Left:** Henry Alken's view of the Belvoir field, all riding with a long leather in plain hunting saddles which were renowned throughout the world for their style and superlative craftsmanship. All the riders use double bridles but there is not a noseband to be seen. **Far left:** To obtain maximum control the polo player has to resort to martingales, side reins and fairly heavy bridles, but he rides in what is virtually an improved version of the conventional hunting saddle.

CHAPTER ONE · HISTORY AND DEVELOPMENT

Far right, top: Long-distance riding in Britain. The saddles are conventional general purpose ones but the rider in the centre is using a hackamore bridle.
Bottom: The classical forward position is not always possible or desirable on the cross-country course and for this reason a general purpose rather than a pure jumping saddle is preferred.
Centre: Trail riding in America. The riders are by no means proficient but they manage well enough with the help of the big Western saddle. **Right:** Christine Stückelburger, the former world dressage champion, riding her horse Granat. She uses a very typical dressage saddle which allows for the long leg position.
Below: An American rider in the classic jumping position of which Federico Caprilli would have approved.

this definite policy of non-intervention, Caprilli was not so much overturning the classical precept as re-affirming it. In essence he was saying that, if it was correct for the rider to sit in balance with his horse at the slower paces, then it was correct for him to do so at the faster ones as well. Therefore, he encouraged his riders to shorten their leathers and to 'perch' in their saddles, the seat at the gallop being raised out of the plate, the hands following the head through the rein and the lower legs being drawn back behind the vertical with the knees pointed. The body weight at the faster paces was then positioned well over the horse's centre of balance and was the least possible burden to the horse, particularly over fences.

Caprilli's theories were expanded after his death by his pupil, Piero Santini. Though they were never accepted in their entirety, they nevertheless form a very large part of modern equestrian thought and practice. Current teaching is possibly a system of half-intervention practised in conjunction with a mixture of Caprilli's forward riding and classical schooling on the flat.

Although Italian teams won show jumping contests in the first decade of the century employing the Caprilli seat, the effect of Caprilli's teaching on saddle design was not immediately apparent. Flaps were cut further forward to accommodate the shorter length of leather used, but the seat of the saddle and in particular the bars remained much the same as ever. In other words, a forward flap was grafted on to what was basically an English hunting saddle. In consequence, whilst riders aimed at sitting or perhaps leaning forward over fences, their actual weight was carried too far back; the result was that they were behind the horse's movement.

The Italian firm of Pariani produced a 'forward seat' saddle between the two world wars, the first in fact with a flexible seat (spring tree), and in Britain Santini produced a similar saddle on what was termed a 'parchment' tree. Both were an

CHAPTER ONE · HISTORY AND DEVELOPMENT

improvement on the old hunting saddle, but in neither was it appreciated that the positioning of the bars was critical.

The jumping saddle

It was not until nearly 50 years after Caprilli's death that a correctly designed jumping saddle (which would act as a base for a less exaggerated all-purpose riding saddle) gained acceptance. It came about, surprisingly, in the one country where its acceptance would have been thought most unlikely—Britain. There, hunting folk until well into the 1950s poured scorn on the 'monkey-up-a-stick' style of riding and clung tenaciously to the saddles left to them by their fathers and grandfathers. Even more surprising is not only the fact that the new saddle was produced in Britain but that it was promoted vigorously by a Spanish nobleman, Count Ilias Toptani. To him, together with his collaborators Colonel F E Gibson and Messrs George Parker of London, should go the credit for the development of saddles which were designed specifically for the precision riding demanded by the equestrian sports of the latter half of the 20th century. Without such saddles, the standards would not be as high today.

Not only was Toptani the first to appreciate the significance of the stirrup bar position, but was also the first to design a saddle in which riders could sit in balance at speed and over fences without undue physical effort. In fact, the Toptani saddle helped the rider to ride and to ride more effectively. It, together with other modern saddles, is discussed in the following chapters. Interestingly enough, these new saddles, the precision instruments of riding, resemble, at least as far as their dipped seats are concerned, the very earliest saddles.

As for the methods of bitting, these have followed the advances in equestrian thinking and have become far more simple. The snaffle and drop noseband has become the accepted bridle, with the double bridle (the bit and bradoon) being used with the horse in a more advanced stage of training.

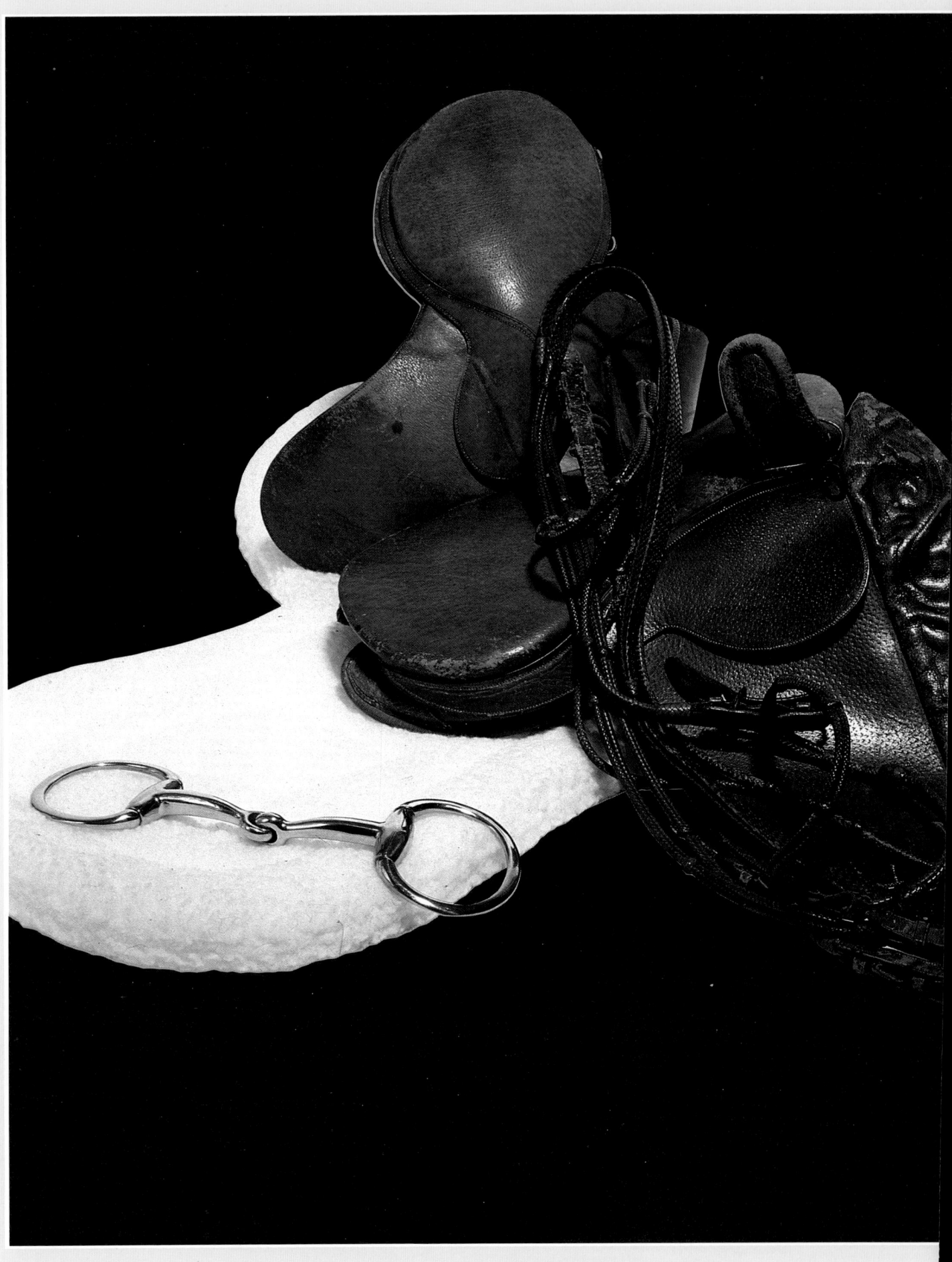

CHAPTER TWO

Making the Modern Saddle

Tanning and currying, the leather-making skills

Saddle construction

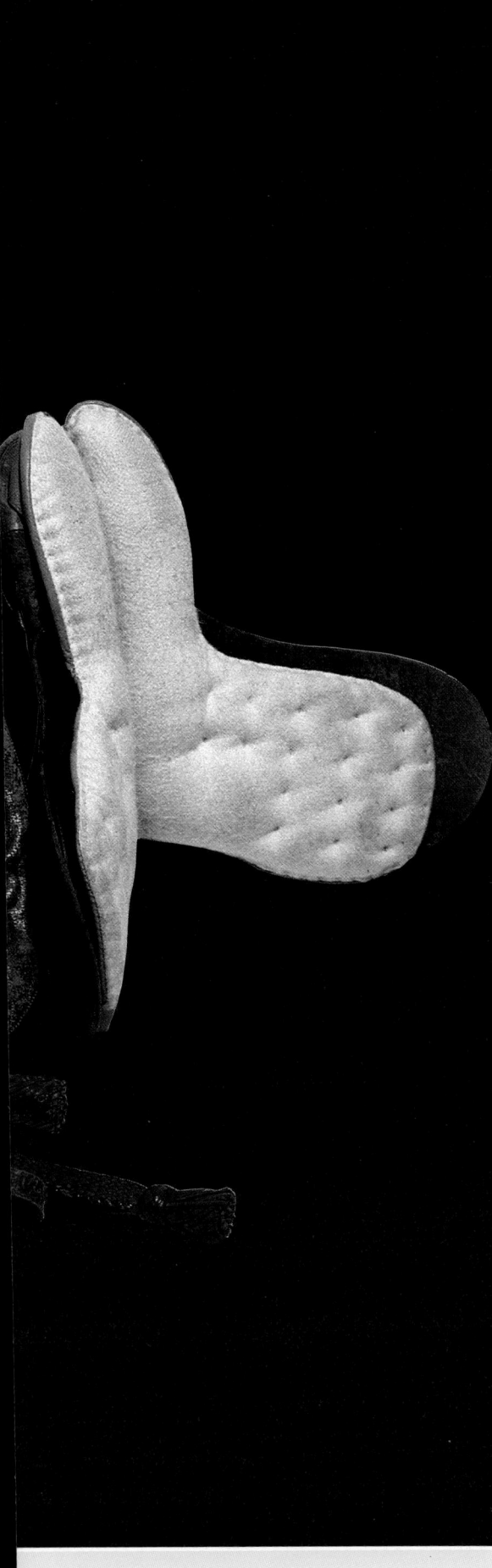

A group of 19th-century English 'apprentice' saddles made in miniature as an exercise and used as samples by commercial travellers. The snaffle bit gives an idea of their size.

Making the Modern Saddle

CHAPTER TWO · MAKING THE MODERN SADDLE

Traditionally, leather has been the principal material used in the manufacture of saddlery. During the last decade or so, however, other materials have been introduced in order to reduce the heavy costs involved. Nevertheless, leather still remains the first choice for saddles and bridles of the best quality. New saddlery should always be examined carefully. The presence of a greyish overtinge is a good sign, since it indicates the presence of grease in the leather, which should be supple as a consequence.

The quality of leather varies greatly. Good leather will last for years and retain its strength, if cared for correctly. Poor leather, on the other hand, may break as soon as it comes under stress. The latter is naturally less expensive than the former, but, if used for either saddles or bridles, it can be dangerous; a broken stirrup leather, girth strap, bridle rein or headpiece can cause serious accidents, even to the extent of endangering the lives of both horse and rider. This point should govern the selection of all leather for horse equipment, whether it is for straps on rugs or the ends of a leading or lungeing rein. A horse is a very strong animal, capable of exerting tremendous pressure and stress on the straps which are used to control him.

The quality of leather

The finest leather has a distinct 'feel' to it. It is firm but supple, slightly greasy and of good substance—that is, thickness. It is this quality which is commensurate with the material's strength. Dry leather will be brittle and thus likely to break. Leather that is 'pappy' or spongy to handle should never be used, as it is totally unsatisfactory in all respects. The natural reaction of good leather is to wrinkle when bent by hand on both the flesh—the inside—and the grain—the treated outside. On no account, however, should it 'bubble'; when released and straightened out it should return to its normal state.

Leather is made from animal skins. Some 90 per cent of the leather used in the saddlery trade comes from cow hides—the best of this coming from slow-maturing cattle, such as the Aberdeen Angus. The slower the growth, the more the leather's substance has a chance to develop and the greater will be the eventual strength of the hide. The remaining 10 per cent is accounted for by pigskins, which are used primarily for saddle seats and, at one time, for covering saddle flaps; by doeskins, used for seats, covering flaps and knee grips; and sheepskin, known in the saddlery context as basil. The skin has the wool removed; it is used, reversed, for backing saddle panels and lining cheaper saddles.

Possible defects

Imported and home-produced hides are used equally in the major saddle producing countries of the world today. Usually, imported hides have one distinct advantage as far as the temperate countries are concerned. They are less likely to be damaged by warble holes—holes made by the small grubs of the warble fly. These small breathing holes enlarge as the grub ripens. Once the grub has emerged, the hole closes over, but an extremely weak spot is left in the hide as a result.

Wire scars, caused by the extensive use of barbed wire fencing, also cause problems in the selection of sound leather. Such scars, sometimes evident on the panels of less expensive saddles, weaken the leather. They should not be seen on the tops of expensive saddles, nor on bridle leather. Wire marks can not only be a serious weakness; they can cause the

Right: After the raw skins have been cleansed they are placed in lime pits for some ten days. The lime has the effect of loosening the covering hair which is removed during the next tanning process.

CHAPTER TWO · MAKING THE MODERN SADDLE

Modern tanneries are as highly mechanised as is consistent with an industry which still has to depend upon a degree of hand working. **Left:** Rotating drums are used in the cleansing and liming of the hides. **Above:** A machine is also employed for scudding – the removal of surplus matter such as hair roots and fat.

leather to split when it is under stress.

Some wire marks on saddle flaps are erased when the pigskin finish is embossed on ordinary hide to make it match the characteristic grain of pigskin. Only very light racing saddles have real pigskin flaps. Brushed pigskin—the flesh side is brushed and used outwards—gives a suede-like finish—while doeskin is also used when extra gripping properties are required. In this instance, the skin is taken from fallow deer.

Show saddles are often entirely covered in doeskin, whereas it is more usual for show jumping and eventing saddles to have just padded knee-grips of doeskin let in, or sewn, to the flaps.

The making of leather
Hides cannot be used in their raw state; like all animal matter, they soon begin to rot. The manufacture of leather involves the twin processes of tanning and currying so as to render them imperishable. Tanning is an extremely ancient process, dating back to the days of early man. Then, tree bark—this contains tannin or tannic acid—was used to convert raw skins into leather. Mixed with water, the bark produces a liquid in which the hides are soaked. Oak bark was considered the most suitable and is still in use today.

On arrival at the tannery, the raw skins are washed thoroughly to remove dirt, salt and other unwanted contents. They are then placed in pits containing lime. After about ten days, the lime will have loosened the covering hair—the chief object of the process—while the liquid will have swelled the skins' fibres and caused them to separate into their constituent fibrils. This process increases fullness and pliability.

After removal from the lime pits, the hides are thrown back into cold water ready for scudding and rounding. As a result of this the hides take on a recognizable form, the grain side, from which the hair is now removed, becoming relatively smooth. Both operations were once done by hand, but scudding—the removal of loose protein, hair roots, gland tissue, pigment, loose fat and so on—is now done largely by machine. Rounding—the trimming of the hides—is still a hand process. Firstly, the hides are sorted, with the best being set aside for the use of the saddlery trade and other industries requiring top-quality leather. The substance of the hide is one of the chief determining factors in selection. The decision on whether to round them or not depends on whether they are to be tanned whole. In the former case, the hides are rounded—trimmed—by a rounding frame; in the latter, this process takes place before the hides are curried, the stage after tanning.

After the lime has been removed, tanning can begin. Either vegetable tanning, using bark, can be employed; alternatively, mineral tanning, using alum salts or, more recently, chrome salts, can be used. The latter are very resistant to water. Chrome leather (characterized by a blue-grey finish) is extremely strong and is used for girths, the leg straps on New Zealand rugs and sometimes in the making of headcollars. The hides are put into suspenders (deep pits), where they are stacked in the liquor one on top of the other. After several weeks, they are removed so that the tanning liquid can be replaced and are then put back into the pits, this time for a longer period of several months.

CHAPTER TWO · MAKING THE MODERN SADDLE

The last stage in the tanning process is termed finishing, an operation which takes time and has to be done very carefully. The hides are oiled, rolled and then dried, the last process being critical, since it is essential that no variations in temperature occur. If a drying hide is exposed to even a slight draught, it will crinkle at the edges and become stained as a result.

Currying and completion
Once tanned, the leather is curried or dressed, but first the uncut hides are rounded. Hides can be cut either as a half-hide or side (split from shoulder to tail down the backbone), or as a back (in the same way as a half-hide, but with the thinner belly portion being removed). If the purchaser requires, the whole hide can be purchased without it being cut; alternatively, it can be cut to separate the belly and the shoulder from the best part of the leather. This area, known as the butts, is on each side of the spine and is used to make the best quality bridles and saddles. The shoulders, which are strong but coarse in texture, are used for headcollars and for the flaps of less expensive saddles.

After rounding, the hides are placed in vats of cold water overnight to swell the leather and remove the scum, which floats to the top of the vats. The swollen hides are then passed through a splitting machine to ensure that the leather is of uniform thickness—no hide is consistent in this respect—and then through the shaving machine to provide the correct substance. This machine is capable of very fine adjustment. After a further few days in the vats, the hides are placed in large revolving drums, fitted with slats on the inside. These drums are first filled with acid, which, in the beating process, both removes bacteria and other foreign matter and cleanses the leather thoroughly. When the acid has done its work, clean water is substituted to wash out the acid.

The next step is the drying process, known as slicking out, which removes the water from the hides. Then most of the natural growth marks are removed by machine. The leather is then at what is termed the russet stage and is hung up to dry on frames, being secured by toggles, a form of clip like a giant clothes peg. When dry, the best leather is put briefly through a buffing machine, before being dyed to the appropriate colour.

In the saddlery trade, dye is applied by

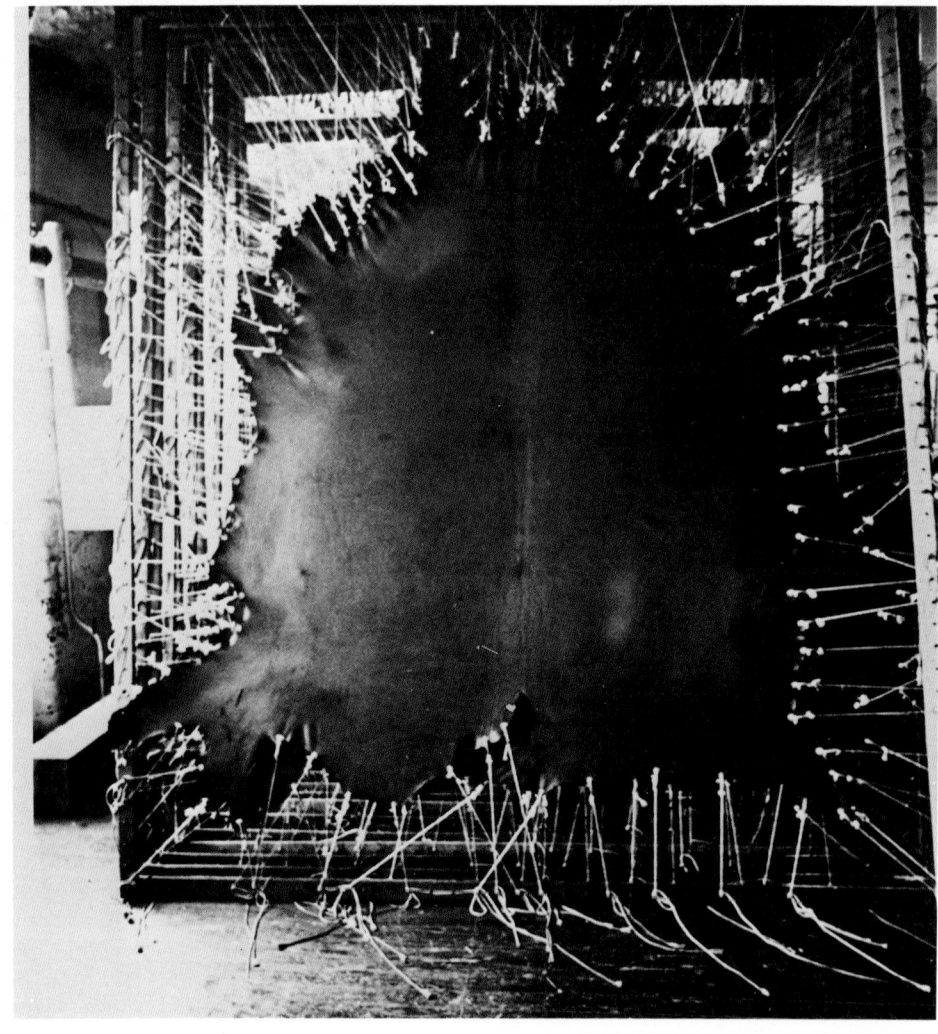

CHAPTER TWO · MAKING THE MODERN SADDLE

Opposite, top: Hides are passed through a splitting machine so as to obtain a consistent thickness. **Bottom:** This hide is pegged out for drying. It is important that the temperature remains constant during this process and that the hide is not subjected to draughts. **Top:** Pegging out the hide on the mesh drying frame. **Right:** Detail of the toggles used. **Left, above:** Although economics dictate the maximum use of machinery, there is no substitute for the skilled hand-polishing of leather. **Below:** Spraying the leather to the required colour.

Left: A store-room of top quality leather, which is always kept on racks and laid flat. Leather, like wine and cheese, improves with age, acquiring a greater firmness as it matures. Unfortunately, modern economic conditions do not always allow for long periods of storage.

pad staining (other leather is dyed in vats) or sometimes by spraying. The usual shades are London, a light colour; Havana, a richer brown; and Warwick, which is darker still. Black is also favoured, especially in the USA (this colour is, by convention, required on heavier harness leathers). The plating machine then flattens the leather again, while any embossing—of flap leather, for instance—is also applied. Finally the leather passes through the greasing department to be treated liberally with tallow and cod oil. The more the natural substance of the leather, the greater will be its capacity to absorb the two preservatives.

Saddlery manufacture
For the most part, the saddlery business relies upon individual craftsmen, rather than mass production. Much of the work is still done by hand, although machine stitching is now almost universal practice, except for countries where labour is cheap and plentiful, as in the east. The larger manufacturers employ production-line methods, but, for the most part, the construction of a top-quality saddle is still the work of individual craftsmen. However, the leather specialist's finished product depends on the work of his wood and metal counterparts, since they determine the shape and type of the tree, the foundation upon which the saddle is built. The larger saddle manufacturing companies sometimes have separate departments to produce trees, but most rely on specialist tree-making companies.

The types of tree
The three principal types of tree are the rigid tree, the spring tree and, to a lesser degree, that made of fibreglass. Use of fibreglass means that a somewhat different technique must be applied to the building of the saddle. Rigid trees, so-called to distinguish them from the sprung variety, used to be carved by hand from beechwood. Today they are made from strips of the same wood heat-bonded, or laminated, in a mould with *urea formaldehyde* resin. This technique makes the end product both stronger and considerably lighter than the older type. Spring trees are made in the same way, but achieve the resilience implied by the name by means of two pieces of sprung steel laid from head to cantle of the saddle.

From the foundation upwards
The basic framework is covered in muslin. A waterproof coating is then applied to make the framework and its covering stronger and more resistant to the moisture created by the heat from both horse and rider when the saddle is in hard use. The tree is reinforced with steel or Duralumin plates, the latter being lighter than the former. A gullet plate is fitted on the underside of the pommel, while a head plate is placed on top, the two being riveted together through the tree to form a very strong rigid arch that will be positioned, eventually, over the horse's back behind the withers and straddling the spine. The cantle is also reinforced with steel plates—those in a rigid tree being shorter than those in a spring tree—so as to hold the back of the saddle tree together. With spring trees, the springs—long strips of sprung steel—are riveted in place where the reinforcing plates are fixed underneath at each end to follow the line of the horse's back on either side of the spine. The stirrup bars are also riveted to the tree, usually with two rivets, but sometimes, in inexpensive saddles, with only one. Stirrup bars are either forged, which is the safest method, or cast. They are stamped accordingly.

The bars can be fitted on the outside of the tree, so that, in the finished saddle, they stand a little proud, or they can be shaped so that they are recessed into the flap. In the latter case, they will not cause an uncomfortable bulge under the rider's

CHAPTER TWO · MAKING THE MODERN SADDLE

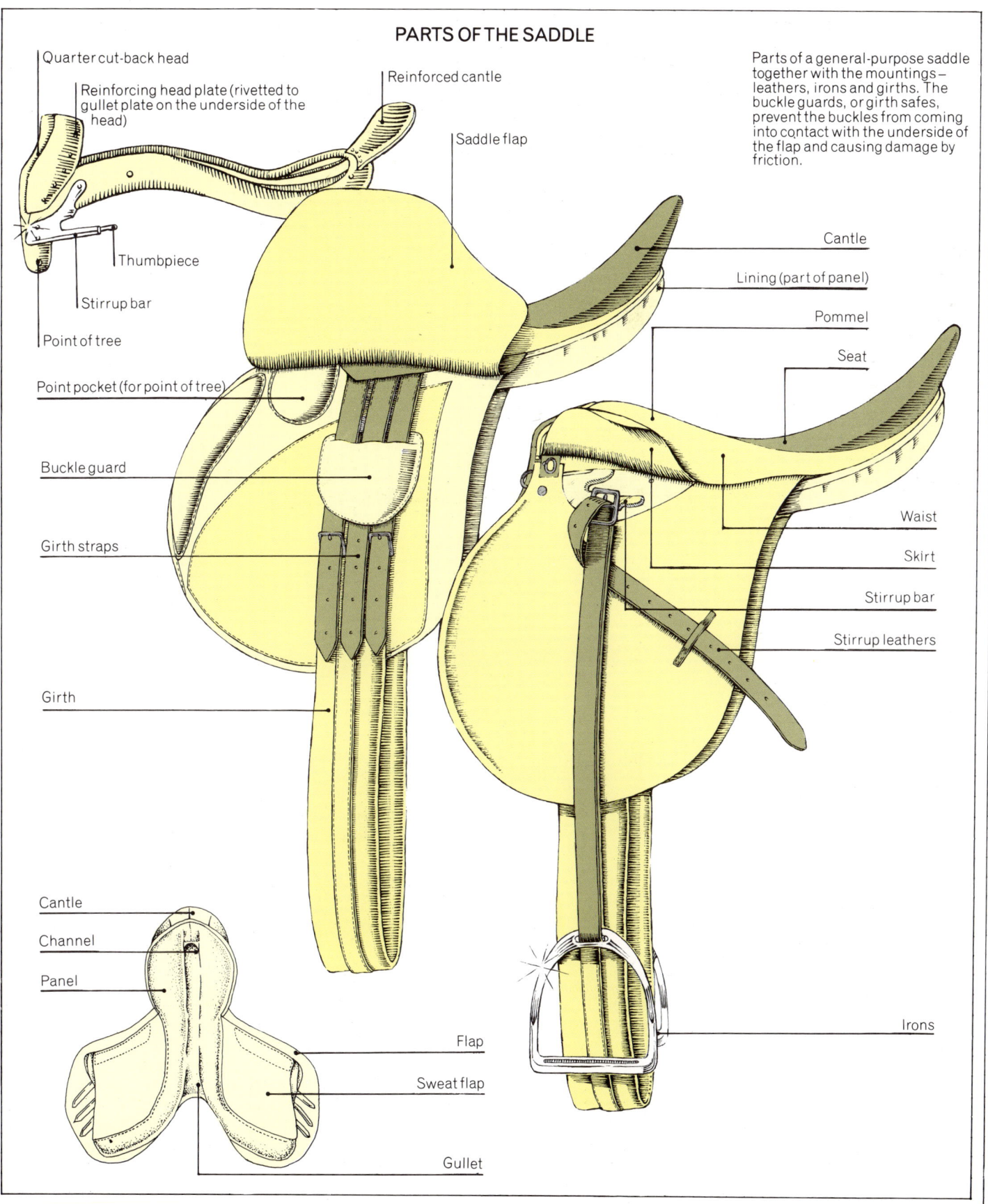

PARTS OF THE SADDLE

Parts of a general-purpose saddle together with the mountings — leathers, irons and girths. The buckle guards, or girth safes, prevent the buckles from coming into contact with the underside of the flap and causing damage by friction.

Trees of modern saddles are made in sections from strips of beech wood, heat-bonded in a mould. The sections are assembled **(right)** and trimmed with a fret **(below left)**. **Below right, top:** A cut-back spring tree. **Bottom:** A rigid tree without the metal springs set from front to rear.

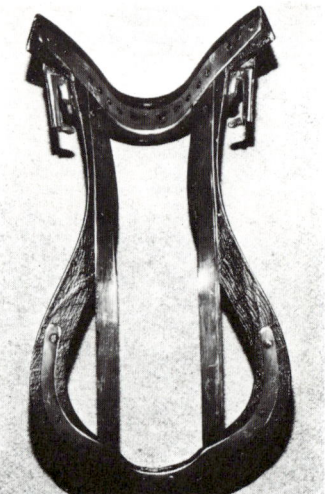
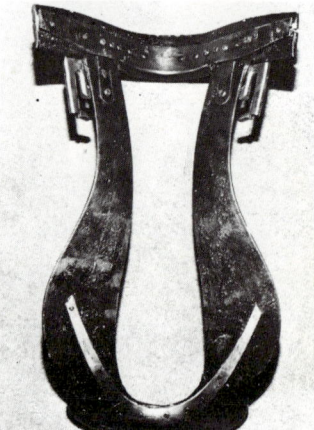

thigh. The ends of the saddle head, situated behind the shoulder, are called the points and largely determine how well the saddle will fit on the horse. In older saddles, the points were long and therefore the variety of horses the saddle would fit was limited as a result. In modern saddles, the points are cut off short and finished with leather to make what are known as flexible points. These have the advantage of allowing a greater range of fittings, while, as far as the rider is concerned, there is no chance of them projecting to form a lump under the thigh.

Trees are made in a number of sizes—ranging from 12in long up to 18in and sometimes bigger. Each size comes in a wide, medium or narrow fitting to suit the great majority of horses' backs, all of which differ in shape. Variations also occur in the type of head (the front arch of the tree). This depends, in part, on the purposes for which the saddle is intended. Dressage and show saddles, for instance, will employ either a vertical head or one that is cut back, so as to allow a greater range of fitting over the withers. Jumping and cross-country saddles usually have a sloped head, but they, too, may employ the cut-back variety. The technical object of the latter is to allow for high withers, but the present-day trend seems to be to use this type of head whether this is the case or not.

A relatively recent innovation is the fibreglass tree, which, after much initial experiment, seemed to be proving itself satisfactory. However, disadvantages became evident as saddles made with fibreglass trees were subjected to long use. The shape of the tree was liable to change, it was inclined to break and, despite the holes in the seat area—made to allow moisture to flow through—the heat and sweat naturally generated by a horse in work was insufficiently dispersed. In the field of racing, however, where the work load is concentrated, fibreglass trees are used extensively and with great success.

Setting the seat
The first stage in setting the saddle seat on the tree is the laying of pre-stretched

CHAPTER TWO · MAKING THE MODERN SADDLE

Left: Finishing the tree by rasping. **Above:** Fitting the metal reinforcement. **Bottom:** A cut-back, almost 'cow-mouth' tree, with laminations clearly visible.

canvas webs from head to cantle. The webs are secured by tingles, tiny, small-headed nails, which are tacked through a small strip of leather laid over the webs and so into the tree itself. The leather strip acts as a washer to prevent the webs from coming away from the tacks. The girth strap webs are then placed across the waist, or twist, of the tree, traversing the longer tree webs and again being tacked to the tree. The rear two girth straps are fastened to these webs, while the third—the forward one—is either stitched to a web going right over the tree, or to one fastened around the tree on either side. Behind the strap webs are placed the back webs and the back straining canvas, a piece of material shaped to cover the whole of the seat behind the waist. This is stretched tightly and then tacked down in position. The combination of tightly-drawn crossing webs—the ones that traverse the long webs force the latter downwards—gives a firm, springy base to the seat. Small crescent-shaped pieces of leather called bellies are nailed to the seat's edges. These save the rider from being forced to sit uncomfortably on the hard edges of the tree.

Covering and padding
The next stage in the preparation of the seat is covering and padding. In older

CHAPTER TWO · MAKING THE MODERN SADDLE

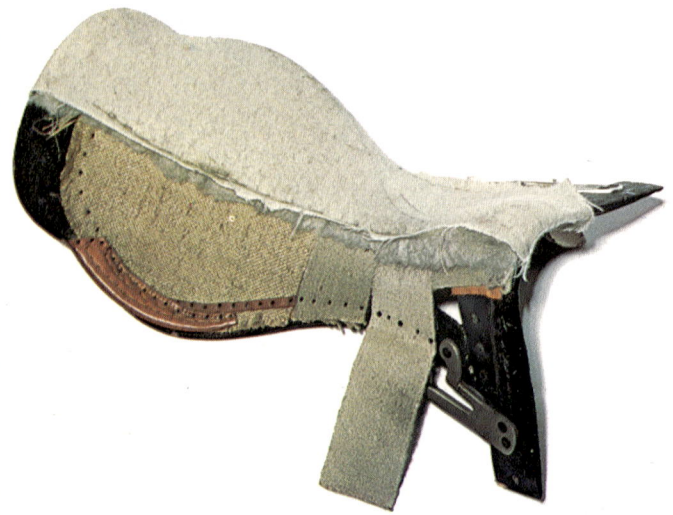

saddles—and in some modern ones, too—wool is the material used for the latter. Present practice, however, is to use rubber or plastic foam rather than wool to provide a resilient seat; this method also entails less labour.

Where wool is used, the seat is covered first with tightly-drawn serge. A small slit is made in this for the wool to be inserted with a seat steel, a thin rod especially designed for this purpose. The wool is spread evenly under the covering by means of an awl, which can be poked through the serge.

When spring trees are used, the two metal strips are covered either in thin leather or linen tape. The covering lessens the risk of the sharp edges of the springs cutting into a panel, if one becomes displaced; it also prevents moisture from rusting the springs.

Traditionally, the final covering of the seat is made of pigskin. As well as being hard-wearing, this has the advantage of being easy to stretch when it is wetted, preparatory to the seat being blocked on the tree. However, many modern saddles—particularly ones of German manufacture—employ calfskin for the seat. Though these are satisfactory, they are more inclined to split and, in general, do not wear as well as the pigskin ones.

The skirts are sewn to the seat, usually by hand but sometimes today by machine, using a hide welt. This is followed by the fitting of the girth straps to the doubled-up ends of the strap webs and then the fitting of the flaps. These can either be plain, blocked (shaped over the knee-roll of the panel), or inset with grips of doeskin or a similar material covering a foam plastic base.

Finally comes the fitting of the panel. Whatever its shape, the panel has the same function of providing a cushion between the tree and the horse's back. Today, it is almost invariably covered in a supple panel hide and is filled either with wool—the advantage of this is that its thickness can be regulated to suit the horse's back—or with pre-cut pieces of plastic foam. There are, however, saddles made with felt panels, like the English show saddles and the ones for the American Walking Horse. When completed, the panel is laced to the saddle top.

The only economy that can be made in the making of saddles is through the use of inferior materials. A seat, for instance, can be set with a covering of hessian, which will probably result in its collapse after a short period of use. The number of girth straps can be reduced to two, panels can be made entirely from the much cheaper, but far less satisfactory, basil, while seats are made from materials other than pig-

CHAPTER TWO · MAKING THE MODERN SADDLE

Opposite, top left: Section of a tree showing the initial web and canvas seat covered by the tightly-drawn, wool-stuffed serge. **Top right:** The pre-stretched webs being tacked across a tree to provide a foundation for the seat. **Below:** Cutting the component parts of the saddle is the work of a highly-skilled craftsman who cuts a hide with the minimum wastage. **Above left:** Using a razor-sharp saddler's knife the craftsman shapes the leather top on the tree. **Above right:** Fitting the girth straps to the tree webs. **Left:** A saddle panel ready for fitting. The slits in the body of the panel through which the stuffing wool is inserted are clearly visible, as are the leather point pockets into which the tree points are fitted.

skin and flaps from the roughest shoulder leather. In days gone by, saddle panels (stuffed with wool) were frequently covered with serge, a material which had some advantages in respect of comfort and ease of panel regulation, but was difficult to keep clean. For this reason, serge panels were frequently overlined with linen.

Bridlework
As with the manufacture of saddles, the pursuit of quality should be the keynote in the making of bridles and other accessories. The best bridles are cut from the butts, the finest leather, and the buckles must be of the same quality.

There are two ways of attaching the bit, or bits, to the bridle. They can be sewn to the bridle, which makes the changing of bits an expensive operation as well as weakening the area of attachment; alternatively, the bits are secured by neat hook studs, the billet passing round the bit ring and being fastened to the stud on the inside of the rein or cheekpiece. The width of a cheekpiece may vary from ½in—for a pony show bridle, for instance—to as much as ⅞in or more for a hunter's bridle.

The use of modern, man-made materials in place of the traditional ones is, of course, evident in the saddlery trade. Headcollars, girths and even bridles can be obtained in nylon, while plastic foam is used for a number of tasks. Nevertheless, **saddlery as a whole relies firmly on the basic natural materials that have been employed almost since the beginning of man's association with the horse.**

CHAPTER THREE

The Twentieth Century Saddle

Fitness for Purpose
Some Variations
Fittings
Mountings
Numnahs

The Toptani saddle, developed after the Second World War, has been a most important influence, making it easier for the rider to sit over the horse's centre of balance at all paces, particularly when jumping.

CHAPTER THREE · THE TWENTIETH-CENTURY SADDLE

The Saddle · Fitness for Purpose

The design of modern saddles has been governed by the requirements of the modern equestrian sports in the Olympic disciplines of show jumping, eventing and dressage. Naturally enough, there are variations from country to country, but the basic precept—certainly so far as jumping and cross-country saddles are concerned—is common to them all, with the over-riding influence being that of Count Ilias Toptani (see Chapter One). The saddle that evolved as a result of his work, plus that of others, has played, in its way, as important a part in the history of equipment as that of the Sarmatians or of the X Group people in pre-Christian times.

The first prototypes

As discussed in Chapter One, attempts were soon made to produce a saddle which would conform in its design to the teachings of Caprilli, or to modified versions of his method of riding. Pariani of Milan and Piero Santini, the pupil of Caprilli—his Santini saddles were made in Walsall, England—came nearer than most to producing such saddles, while, in England too, there was also the Distas Central Position saddle made by Colonel F E Gibson, just prior to the Second World War, in conjunction with the late Colonel Jack Hance. The latter was one of the greatest instructors of his day.

The story behind the invention of the Distas CP saddle is a curious one. In the days when Hance was teaching at his school in Malvern, he asked Gibson to make a saddle which would place his pupils correctly in its centre. The nearest thing he possessed to a saddle that would achieve this was an old one of foreign manufacture, which had a fairly pronounced dip to the seat. Because it was so comfortable, it was the most popular amongst his pupils. In fact, as Gibson was quick to see, the dip was unintentional, since it was caused by a broken tree. The result of the two men's work, however, was the Distas CP saddle. Though, at its first appearance at Olympia, the new saddle was greeted with derision by the more reactionary of the British hunting fraternity, the design might well have been developed much further had not the Second World War intervened.

The Toptani revolution

It was after the war that the work of Toptani came to the fore. In those years, he was concerned with the training of South American jumping teams and achieved great success with what were basically Caprillist methods. Not having the benefit of the big, scopy horses of Europe, it was necessary for him to utilize the powers of what were in many respects moderate animals to the full, training them meticulously and ensuring that the riders gave their horses every possible assistance.

Toptani's chief problem was with the saddles then in use, as they did not permit the rider to sit in balance with his horse over the fences. Discussions with first the saddler and then the tree-maker were not particularly fruitful; neither had ever sat on a horse, nor did they understand anything about the anatomy and movement of the animal for which they were making equipment. Still less did they know anything about the theory of riding over fences—in other words, jumping.

Toptani, however, made up some prototypes and then came to the London saddlery firm of George Parkers. There he met F E Gibson. Using the old Distas saddle and Toptani's prototypes, the first Toptani saddles were designed, starting

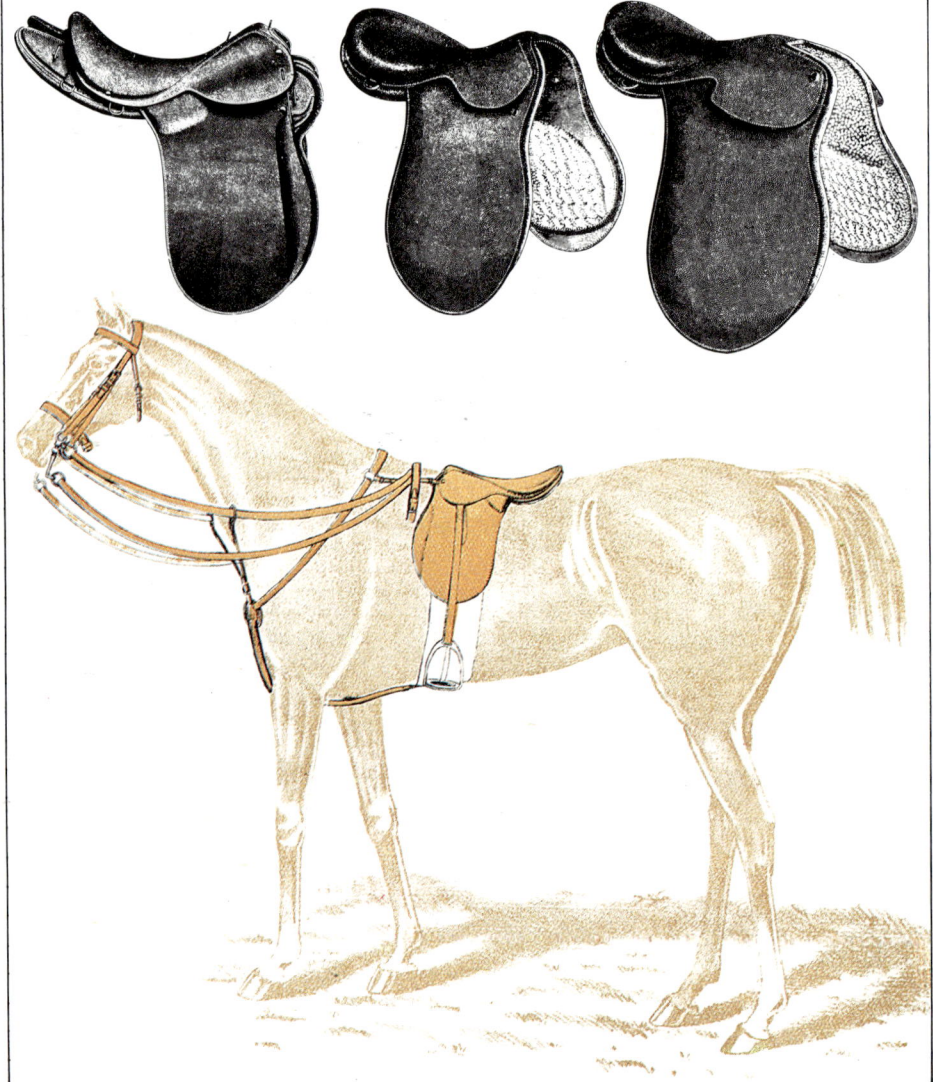

EARLY EXAMPLES

Below, left: An early 19th-century hunting saddle with a pronounced cut-back head which was popular in the American market. **Centre:** This saddle of the same period makes an attempt to provide a knee support in the panel. **Right:** An American saddle which was described as a 'Tourist' saddle and is an obvious adaptation of the Military Universal. All three were made in Walsall, England. **Bottom:** A conventional English pattern hunting saddle in common use at the turn of the century. In this example a knee swell is incorporated into the flap.

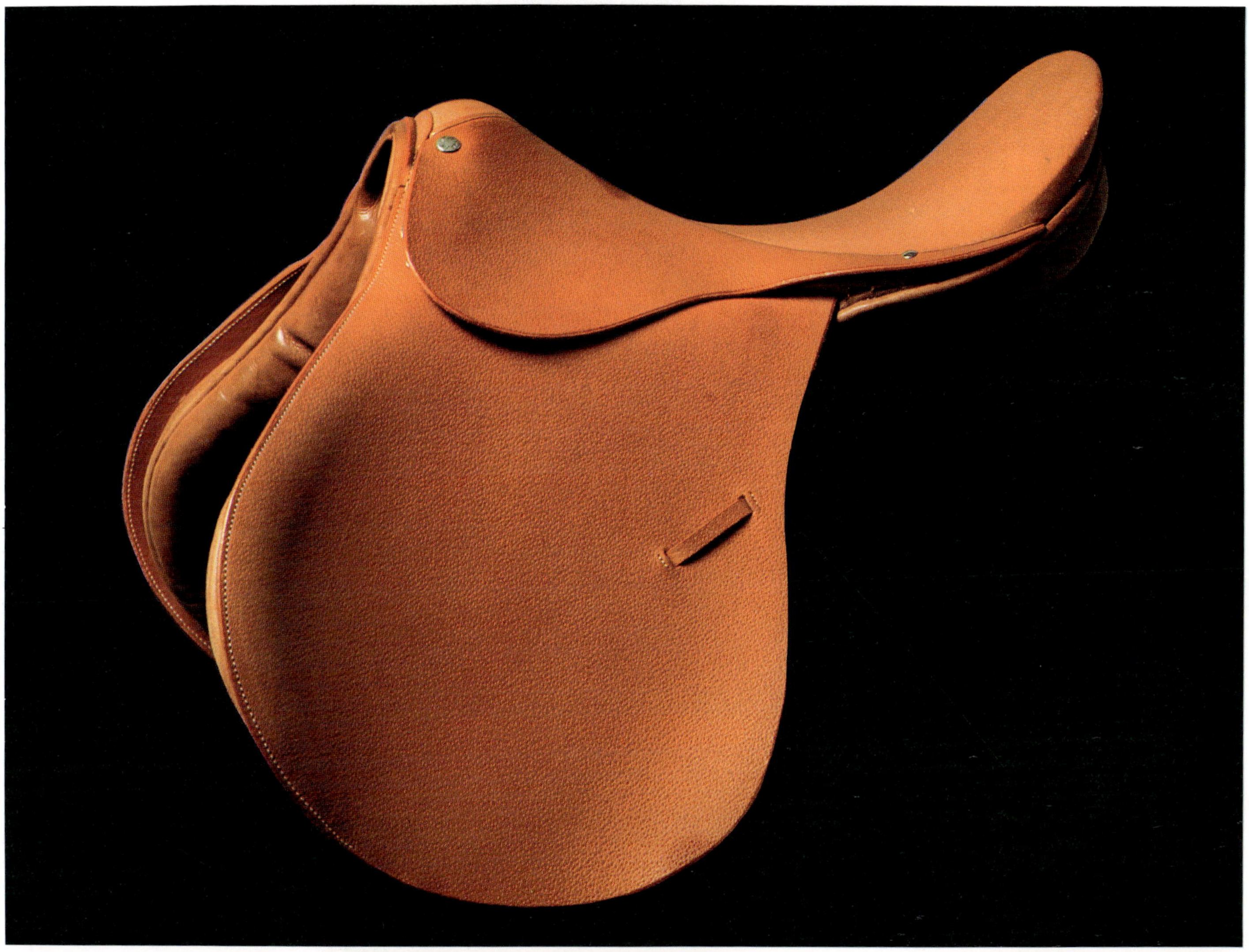

FITNESS FOR PURPOSE

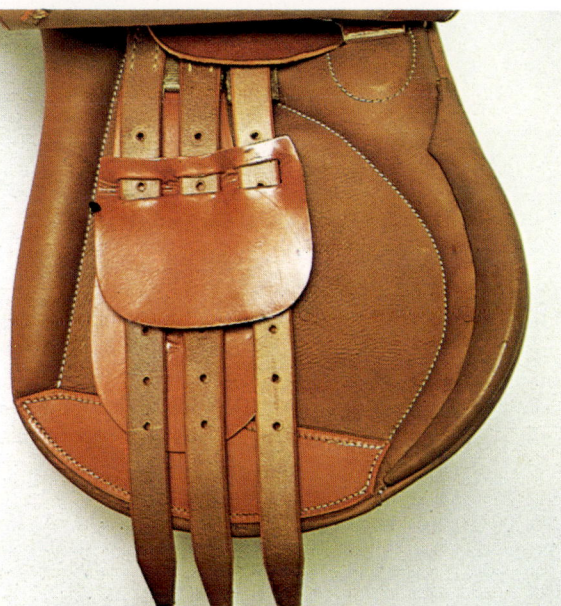

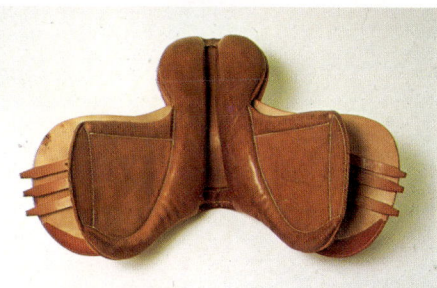

Above: A modern jumping saddle by the Italian firm of Pariani, Milan. Pariani was the first to produce saddles which attempted to conform to the Caprilli theory and was also responsible for the early 'spring' trees. The pleasing proportions are a notable feature of the Pariani marque. **Right:** Detail of the Pariani panel showing the knee and thigh rolls. The girth straps are placed so that the girth will lie in the sternum curve and so that the buckles, as long as the girth is of the correct length, will be clear of the rider's leg. The 'safe' over the girth straps prevents the buckles from damaging the flap.
Far right, top: The panel showing the narrow waist which places the rider close to his horse. **Bottom:** Inset stirrup bar, laid on the underside of the tree so that no bulk is formed under the thigh.

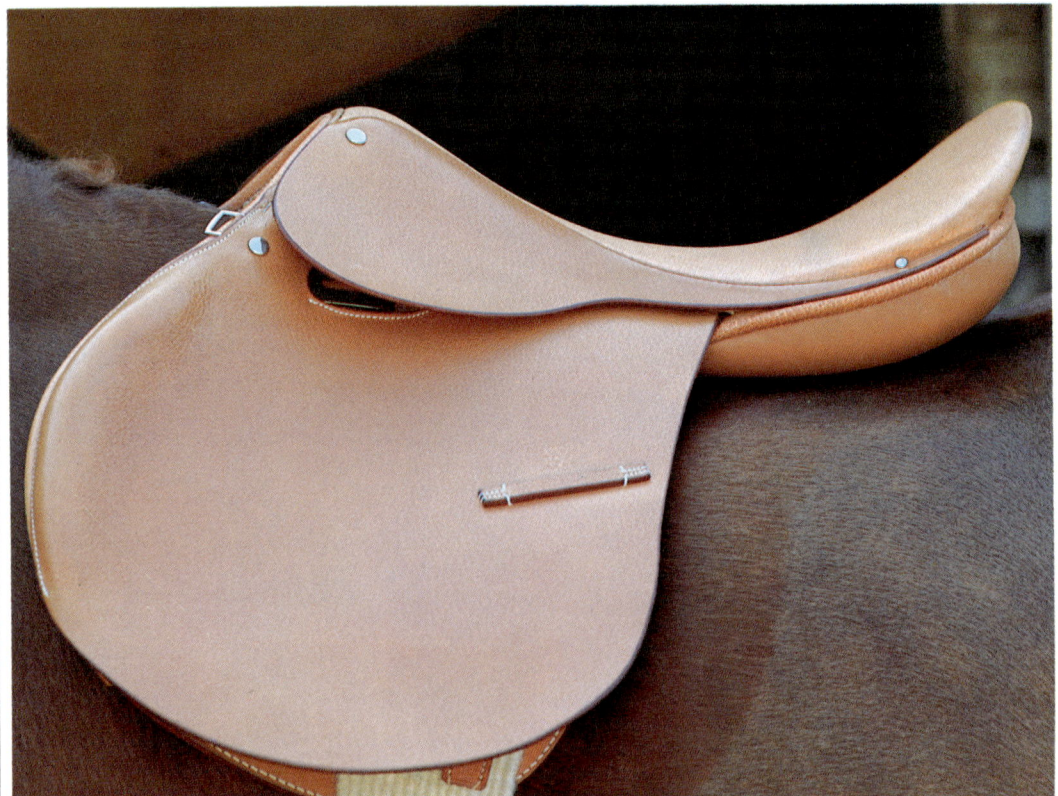

Left and Opposite The Toptani jumping saddle perfected by Count Ilias Toptani and marketed by George Parker and Sons of London. The accentuated slope of the head which positions the bars further to the front is a feature of a saddle which must be regarded as a turning point both in design and in equestrian practice. The left hand illustration shows the correct fitting and positioning on the horse's back. **Below, left:** The Toptani panel, showing the girth straps placed well to the rear out of the way of the rider's thigh. The squab on the rear roll keeps the girth straps in place. **Centre:** The characteristic waistline of the panel is an early design feature of the panel saddle and follows the line of the tree. **Right:** The inset bar which was first introduced by Toptani. The George Parker trademark, unchanged for nearly a century, appears on every Toptani saddle.

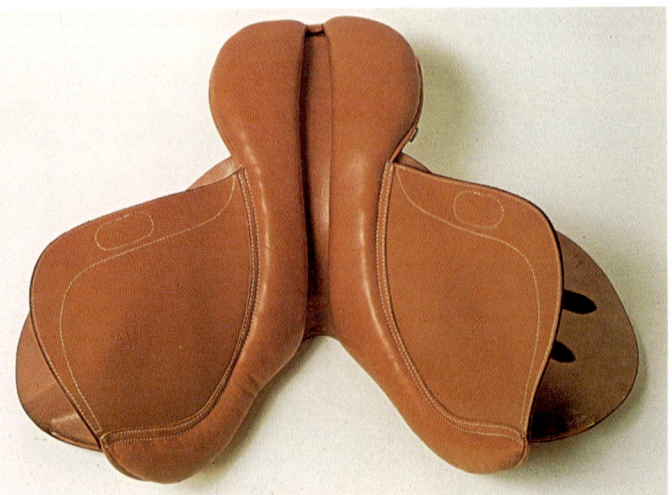

with the saddle's foundation—the tree. This, which was made in a mould with laminated wood so that each was identical, incorporated seven noteworthy design features. The tree was given a pronounced dip to the seat. It incorporated 'a spring seat'—two strips of light, tempered steel being laid along its length from the saddle's head to the cantle.

The waist, or 'twist', was shaped to lie parallel with the back on either side and was narrowed very considerably. The stirrup bar, which previously had been fastened always to the outside of the tree in two places—on the arm of the tree just to the rear of the head and on the point of the tree—was now set on the inside, so that the bar became recessed. The points, which, in previous designs, had extended for as much as 4in below the point of attachment of the bar, were now cut off short. The head of the saddle, instead of being vertical in relation to the body of the tree, was sloped *forward from the points,* so that the stirrup bar was positioned some inches *in front* of the conventional patterns. The metal reinforcements at the head and cantle were of alloy, which combined with the laminated construction to make the tree extremely light.

The completed saddle inevitably followed the lines of this tree. The flaps, in line with the points, were cut well forward; in addition, the leather used was thin in substance—especially when compared to that used in the conventional

hunting saddle—and very supple. The panel was of the so-called Continental type, which had been used in the early Pariani and Santini saddles. This one was narrow at the twist, to conform with the shape of the tree, and continued forward to provide the rider with a substantial knee roll. The so-called thigh roll, at the rear of the panel flap, was not to give support to the rider's thigh, but to prevent the girth straps from shifting backwards and off the panel at the rear, which happened occasionally with horses of a certain conformation.

Thus, the advantages of the Toptani saddle were substantial. It was extremely light in comparison with the older types. The dipped seat positioned the rider centrally and encouraged him to sit deep in the saddle. The narrow waist did not spread the rider's thighs. The recessed bars allowed the stirrup leather to lie flat under the rider's thigh, eliminating the very painful protrusion which was often a characteristic of the older saddles. The shortened points could not dig into the rider's thigh, while they also facilitated the correct fitting of the saddle to the horse's back. The forward position of the stirrup bars had the effect of placing the rider's weight further forward. It therefore made it easier for the rider to sit over the horse's centre of balance at all paces and when jumping. The spring tree gave resilience to the saddle seat, making the rider more comfortable. It also allowed the

CHAPTER THREE THE TWENTIETH-CENTURY SADDLE

influence of the rider's seat to be transmitted more directly to the horse. In a rigid tree saddle—that is, a saddle with no springs and therefore no resilience in the seat—much of the driving force of the seat bones, assuming they are used, is not immediately evident to the horse. Additionally, when the rider sat in the saddle, the spring in the tree 'gave' to the movement of the horse's back underneath it. The thin flap and panel, in conjunction with the narrow twist and deep seat, placed the rider as close as possible to the horse. This ensured that the aids of legs, seat and weight could be applied in the most effective manner. The forward roll of the panel combined with the other design features to assist materially the rider's security, helping him to maintain his leg position and virtually anchoring the lower half of the body in position.

In summary, like the theory of Caprilli,

Above: 'Danloux' pattern jumping saddle by the German firm, Stubben, based on the original design of Colonel Danloux. The panel, particularly the forward roll, is considerably heavier than in the majority of jumping saddles. The inclusion of padded suede inserts on the flap is thought to provide a better grip for the knee. **Left:** The saddle in position on a horse and sitting level from head to cantle with plenty of clearance at front and rear. **Right:** A lightweight adaptation of the basic Pariani jumping saddle with extended girth straps. The latter employ a special short girth and, of course, remove the buckle from under the rider's leg. The absence of the flap reduces the weight and the suede or doeskin covering gives a soft and firm grip. **Far right:** The saddle in position, the girth buckles being covered by a specially designed 'safe'.

FITNESS FOR PURPOSE

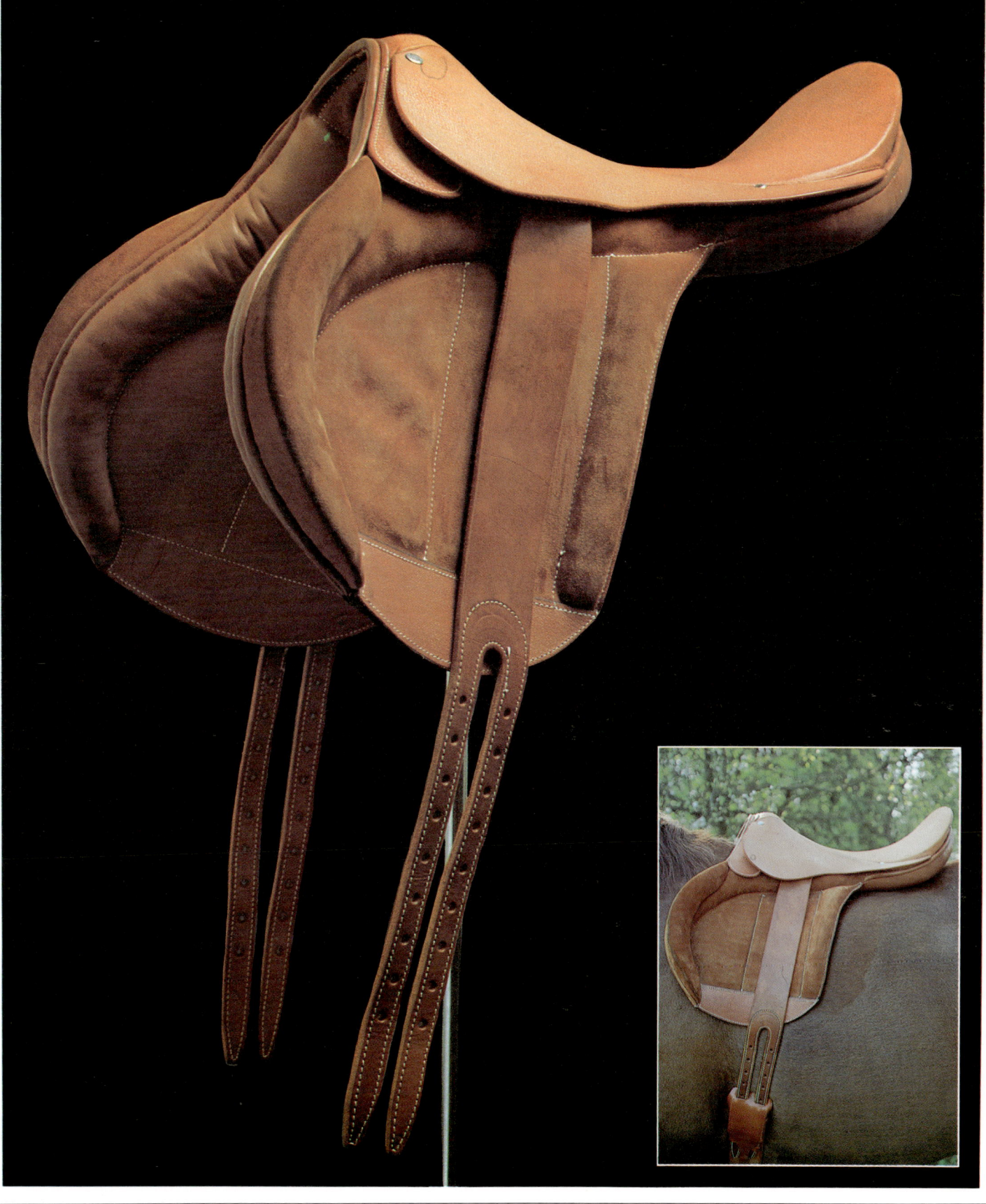

61

CHAPTER THREE · THE TWENTIETH-CENTURY SADDLE

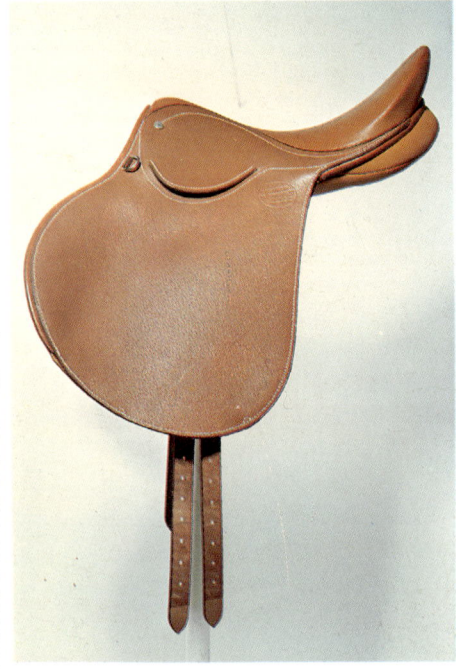

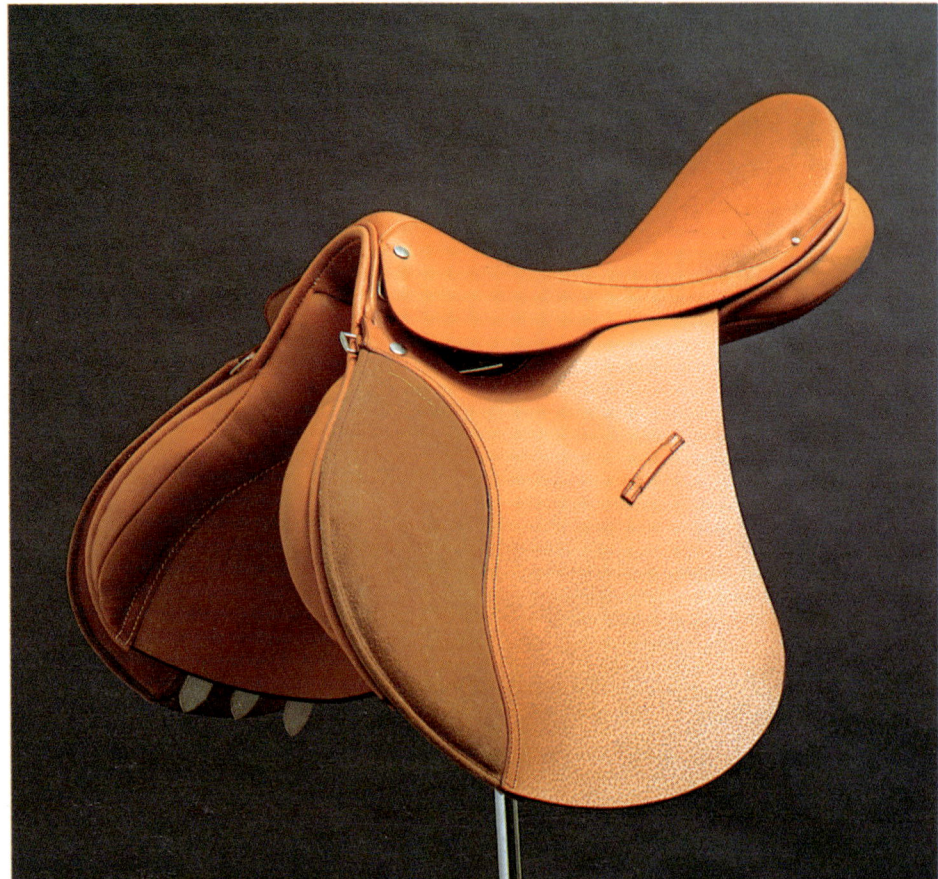

the Toptani saddle conformed to the basic principle of equitation. This is that the rider should be *in balance* with the horse by positioning his weight over the latter's centre of balance at all times.

The nature of balance
By experiment, the centre of balance of the horse both at the halt and when carrying the head and neck naturally has been shown to be in the centre of the body at the junction of two imaginary lines. One is drawn from a point some 8in behind the highest point of the withers vertically to the ground; the second is a horizontal line drawn parallel to the ground from the point of the shoulder to the rear. In effect, the point of balance is in the centre of the animal's body.

The point of balance alters as the horse moves and in relation to the gestures the animal makes with the head and neck, which are the balancing agents of the body mass. Thus, as the horse increases his pace, while at the same time stretching forward and lowering the head and neck, the point of balance advances. In order to position his body over that point, so as to be the least possible encumbrance to the horse, the rider must incline the trunk of his body forward. If the bars of the saddle, as in the case of the Toptani, are placed well forward in any case, it is easier for the rider (whose weight is carried over the bar) to position his body more in line with the horse's advancing centre of balance.

The most extreme instance of this is in jumping. Here, it is easy to understand how the point of balance is thrust forward very swiftly by the violence of the movement. Equally, it can be seen how easy it is for the rider to be left behind the movement, unless the position he takes when approaching the fence is such that he can, without great physical effort, follow the point of balance with the weight of the body. The Toptani saddle assisted the rider to do just this and, very importantly, without loss of security.

Another example shows not only how important this principle is, but also how simple it is to follow. Anyone who has ever given a child a piggyback will appreciate the importance of the weight being carried over the centre of balance. If the child sits still and upright there is no difficulty in carrying him, since his weight accords with the point of balance of the person carrying him. If, however, the child

Above left: A lightweight 'Barnsby' jumping saddle made by the English company of Jabez Cliff, Walsall. The flap is incorporated into the panel and extended girth straps are necessary. **Above:** Another example of a lightweight jumping saddle. In order to reduce weight it is necessary to use not only lightweight bonded trees but also correspondingly light leather. **Left:** The gusset, inset into the rear of the panel, assists in keeping the saddle level on the back.

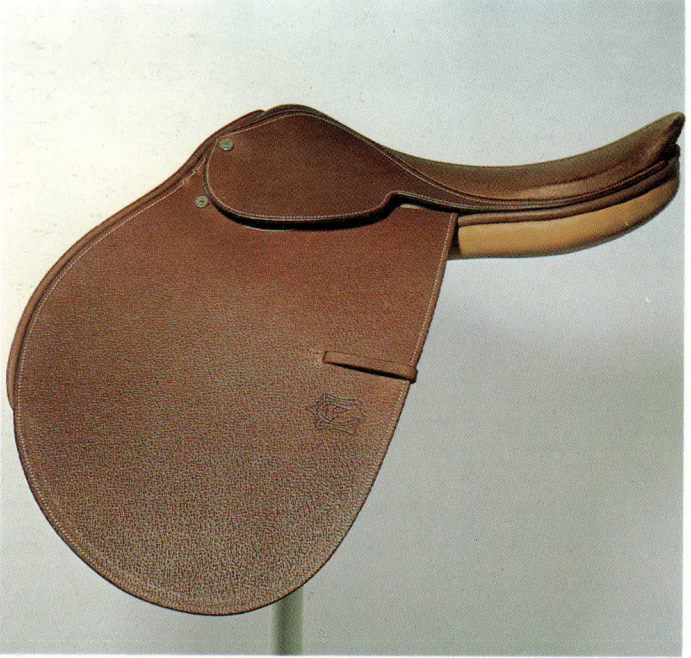

Two saddles reflecting another school of equestrian thought. **Left:** A saddle made by Gidden of London from a pattern produced by the leading French saddler Hermès. The seat is noticeably flatter, in the traditional Hermes line, and the shape of the flap is equally characteristic. Saddles of this type were popularised by the cavalry officers of Saumur. **Right:** A more exaggerated version of the Hermès pattern, produced specifically for the American market by Jabez Cliff, Walsall. The flat seat is a surprising feature; American riders employ a near classical Caprilli style.

leans backwards or throws himself too far forward, the difficulty of the task is increased immediately. Should he, instead of sitting still, shift his weight back and forth as the carrier attempts to run, it becomes almost impossible to carry him.

Conversely the position changes in the collected movements. There, the outline of the horse is shortened, the head and neck being held high and the croup slightly lowered as the hindlegs become engaged under the body. The point of balance moves slightly to the rear as a result, but this, naturally enough, does not concern the jumping rider, for whom the Toptani saddle was designed.

Advantages and disadvantages

In what ways did the conventional hunting saddle fail to assist the rider in these respects? It did have certain advantages—notably because it distributed weight over the largest possible area. But it was by no means ideally suited for the precision required in competitive riding.

The chief deficiencies of the conventional saddle in competition were as follows. The saddle was heavy. The seat was relatively flat and the head of the saddle, when it was in position on the horse's back, was often higher than the cantle. The twist was often so wide as to spread the thighs. The bars were placed on the outside of the tree, so forming, with the accompanying stirrup leather, a hard lump under the rider's leg. The points of the tree were long and similarly pressed uncomfortably into the leg. The head of the saddle was vertical in relation to the body of the tree. As a result, the bars were placed further to the rear and the flap, unless deliberately cut forward, was too straight for a rider riding with relatively short stirrup leathers. The tree was rigid in construction. There was no forward roll to the panel to give support to the thigh above the knee and to contribute to the rider's security. The flap leather was so thick and stiff that it might take years before it softened. The length of the panel could often prevent the rider from being in close contact with his horse.

It may well have been as a result of these deficiencies that the now notorious 'hunting seat'—leg thrust forward and seat to the rear of the saddle—developed. In all probability this was more the result of badly designed saddles, than of any conscious effort by the rider to emulate the armoured knights of the Middle Ages. The shape of the tree and the position of the bars, which were well behind the centre of balance, contributed to this behind-the-movement seat, whilst the uncomfortable lumps under the leg must have encouraged the rider to sit towards the rear in order to escape the discomfort. In fact, in many saddles it was difficult to sit other than at the cantle end.

The Toptani saddle, however, also has disadvantages. Though it was and is supreme for the purpose for which it was intended—show jumping and schooling for show jumping—it is not so satisfactory when used as a general purpose or cross-country saddle. Not surprisingly, it is of no use at all for competitive dressage. The Toptani's disadvantages in these fields are, firstly, that the waist is so narrow that the weight tends to be concentrated over a small area rather than spread over the

CHAPTER THREE · THE TWENTIETH-CENTURY SADDLE

FITNESS FOR PURPOSE

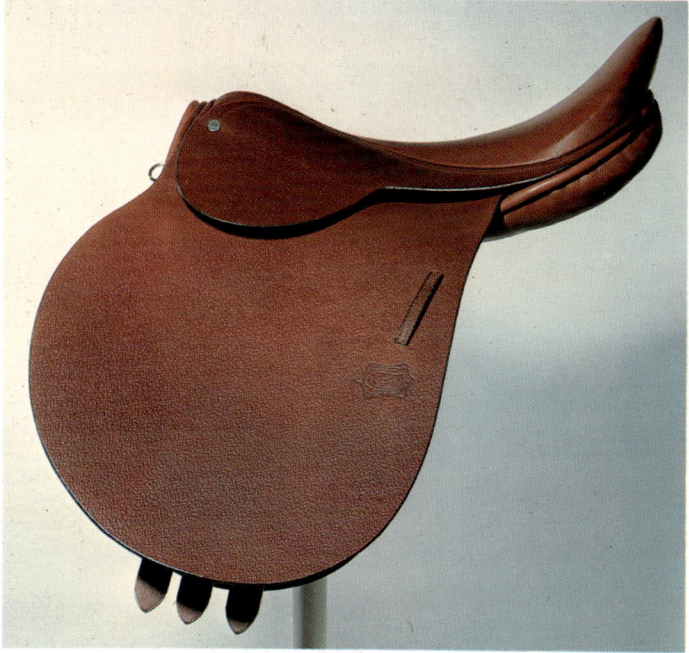

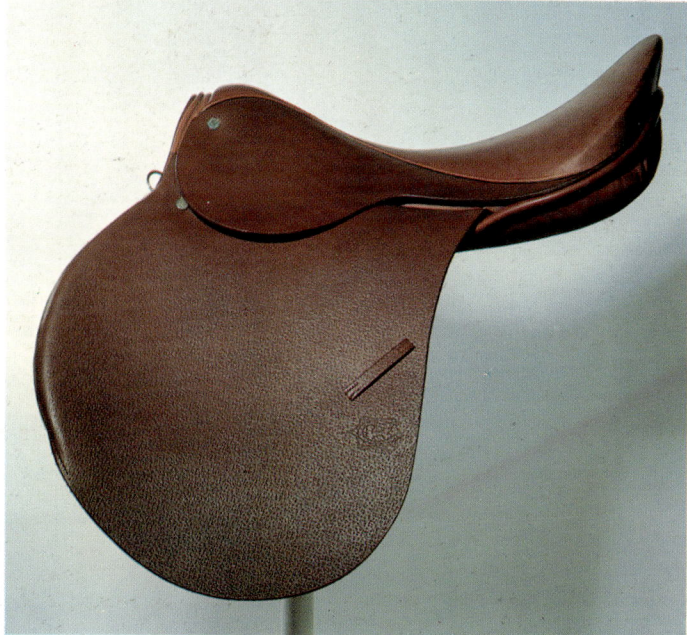

Left: A good example of a British-made general purpose saddle. The less extreme line, in comparison with the true jumping saddle, makes it suitable for hunting and general cross-country riding and it can also be used for dressage at lower levels of competition. **Inset:** A common fault in fitting is for the head to be higher than the cantle, so placing the rider's weight to the rear and behind the movement of the horse. The fault is caused either by too narrow a tree or by incorrect stuffing of the panel. **Top:** An example of a general purpose saddle, of which many types are currently marketed in Britain and America. The flap, as in the saddle on the left, is blocked round the forward roll. **Above:** A saddle for general use described as a 'working hunter's' saddle. 'Working hunter' is British terminology describing a show-ring class in which exhibitors are required to jump a course of rustic fences. Both saddles are strongly built to give long service.

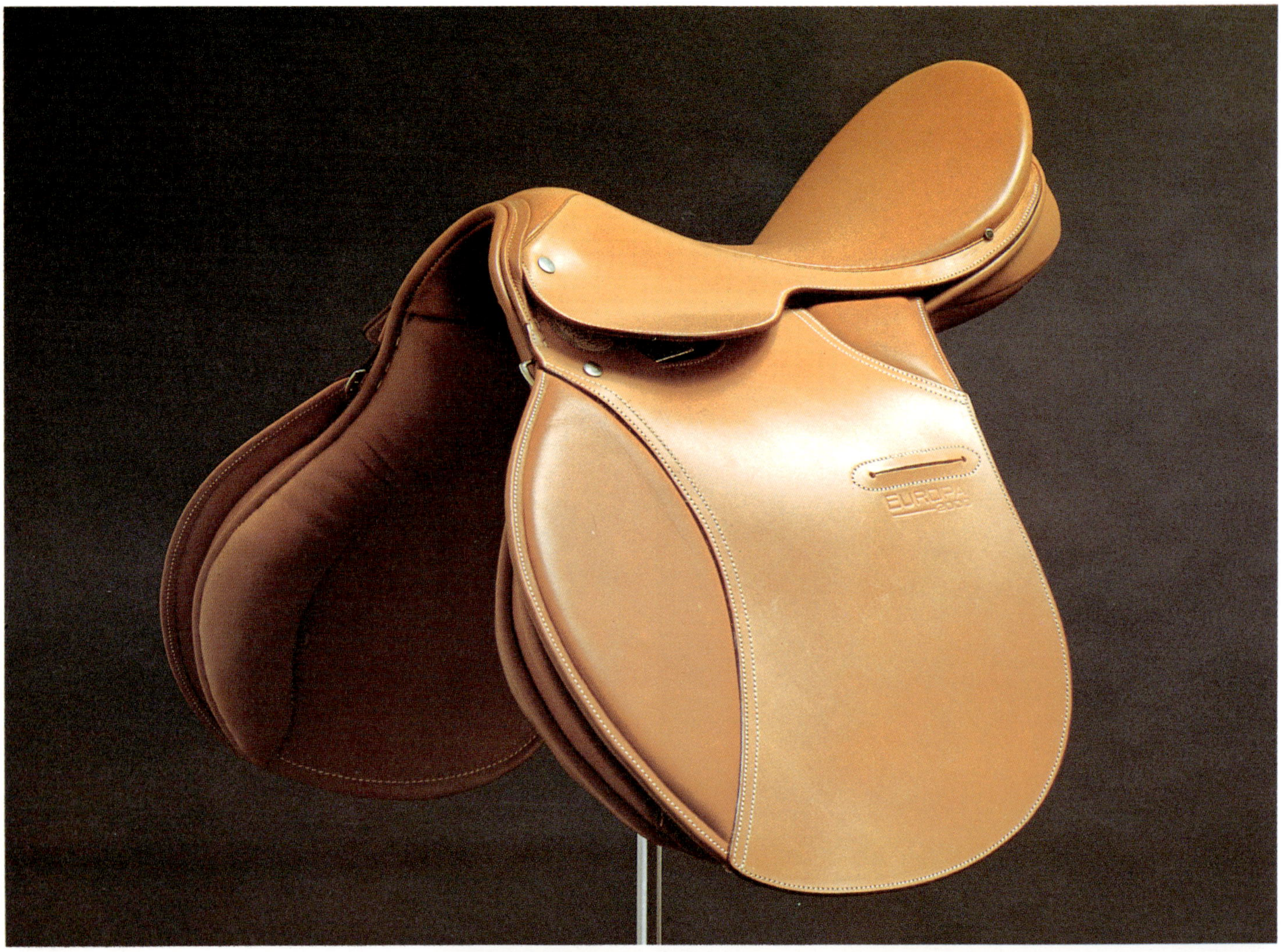

CHAPTER THREE · THE TWENTIETH-CENTURY SADDLE

bearing surface provided by the back. This does not matter if the rider is in the saddle only for short periods, as would be the case when jumping in competition. However, the continual concentrated pressure could cause the horse back troubles if the saddle was used for many hours at a stretch. Secondly, if the rider rides with relatively short leathers at jumping length and uses the saddle for any length of time, a 'rock' can develop in the saddle leading to its moving forward, with the resulting friction causing the horse soreness.

General Purpose and dressage

Largely because of these disadvantages, as far as general use was concerned, a general purpose saddle evolved. This was, in fact, a less exaggerated version of the jumping saddle. The slope of the head was reduced, so that the bars were not carried quite so far forward and so that a less forward-cut flap and panel could be fitted. This enabled a rider to use the somewhat longer leathers favoured for cross-country riding and hunting. The twist was made a little less narrow, so that the weight could be spread through the panel more evenly. These design changes considerably reduced the danger of sore backs.

The General Purpose saddle, however, failed to cope with one particular area. Though it is quite possible to use a general purpose saddle for dressage up to the level of event dressage, thereafter a properly designed dressage saddle is necessary.

The dressage saddle has nothing in common with the jumping or cross-country saddles, except that it seeks to position the rider in balance with the horse. In the case of dressage, where movements are slow and the outline of the horse is shortened, the balance remains central and the saddle is therefore designed to that end.

There is therefore no need for the head of the saddle to be slanted forward, since that would position the stirrup bars unnecessarily far to the front. As a result, the head is vertical, with the flap following that line so as to accommodate the longer leg position. Essentially, the stirrup bar should be an extended one, that is a bar longer than the normal fitting and 'extending' further to the rear. This ensures that the stirrup leather lies down the centre of the flap and

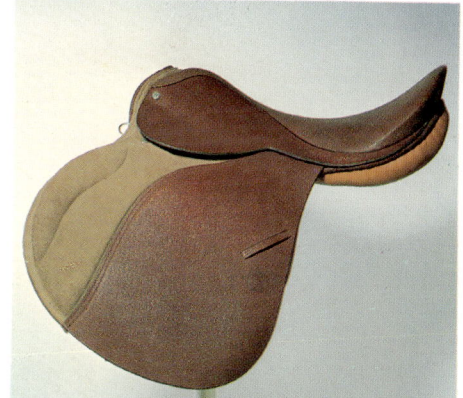
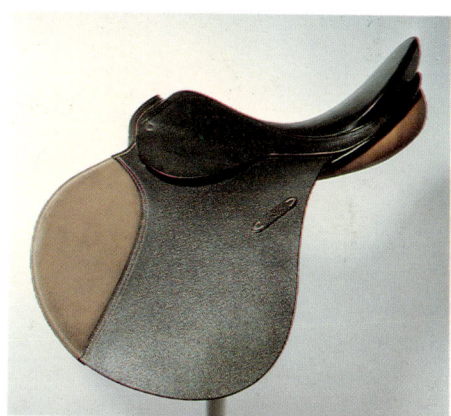

Opposite, top: A version of the General Purpose saddle made by Jabez Cliff, which shows a greater refinement of line and has a high quality finish. It is made on a cut-back tree, a fashion possibly made popular by the German saddle-makers and often employed quite needlessly. **Bottom:** The cut-back head does nothing to improve the fit on this particular horse. **Above:** Three versions of cut-back head General Purpose saddles incorporating different design features and varying in the extent to which the seat is dipped, the saddle on the right being the most extreme. **Right:** The Parzival saddle by the German makers, Stubben – a luxury saddle using top-quality materials and displaying a high standard of finish. The flaps and skirts of the saddle are lightly padded and constructed of specially soft leather to give maximum comfort.

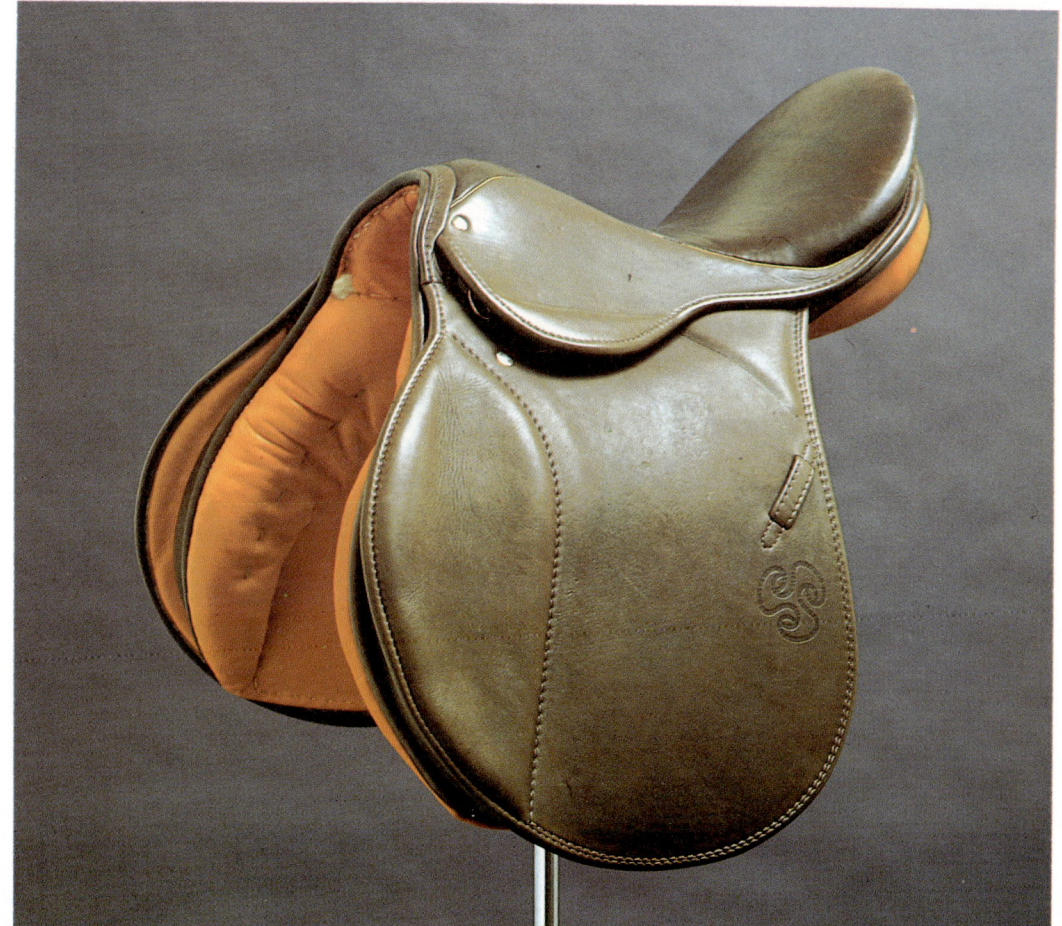

CHAPTER THREE · THE TWENTIETH-CENTURY SADDLE

thus positions the rider's weight directly above the point of attachment in accordance with the required balance. Such an arrangement will also allow sufficient flap in front of the rider's lower thigh and knee. This nicety, however, is not always appreciated or practised.

The seat of the saddle is certainly dipped, but not excessively. Nor must it be so short as not to allow movement of the rider's seat. Whether the tree is sprung or rigid is a matter of preference; there are arguments for both types. It is, however, absolutely essential that the saddle should sit dead level on the horse's back. To this end, the panels of the dressage saddles—these are of Continental type with knee supports—are often provided with a

Left: Modern dressage saddle built on a straight-headed tree and equipped with extended girth straps. The flap, following the tree, is straight and the panel gusset pronounced. **Below:** A deep-seated dressage tree. This example has a spring seat which would not be acceptable to every dressage rider. **Bottom:** An English-made dressage saddle in which the flap and panel are cut slightly forward of the classic vertical line which allows for the very long leather necessary for dressage riding.

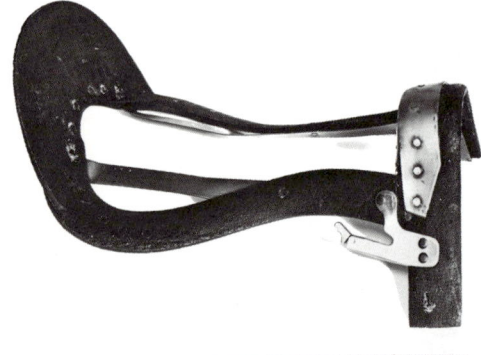

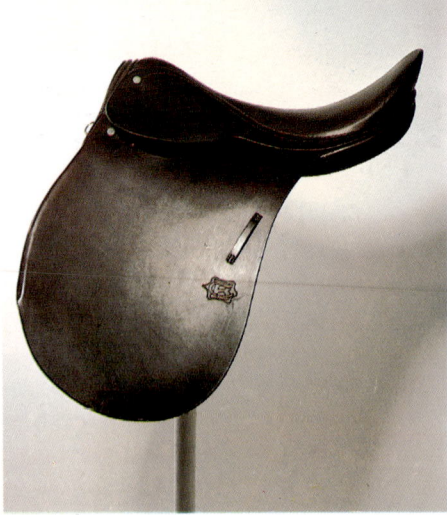

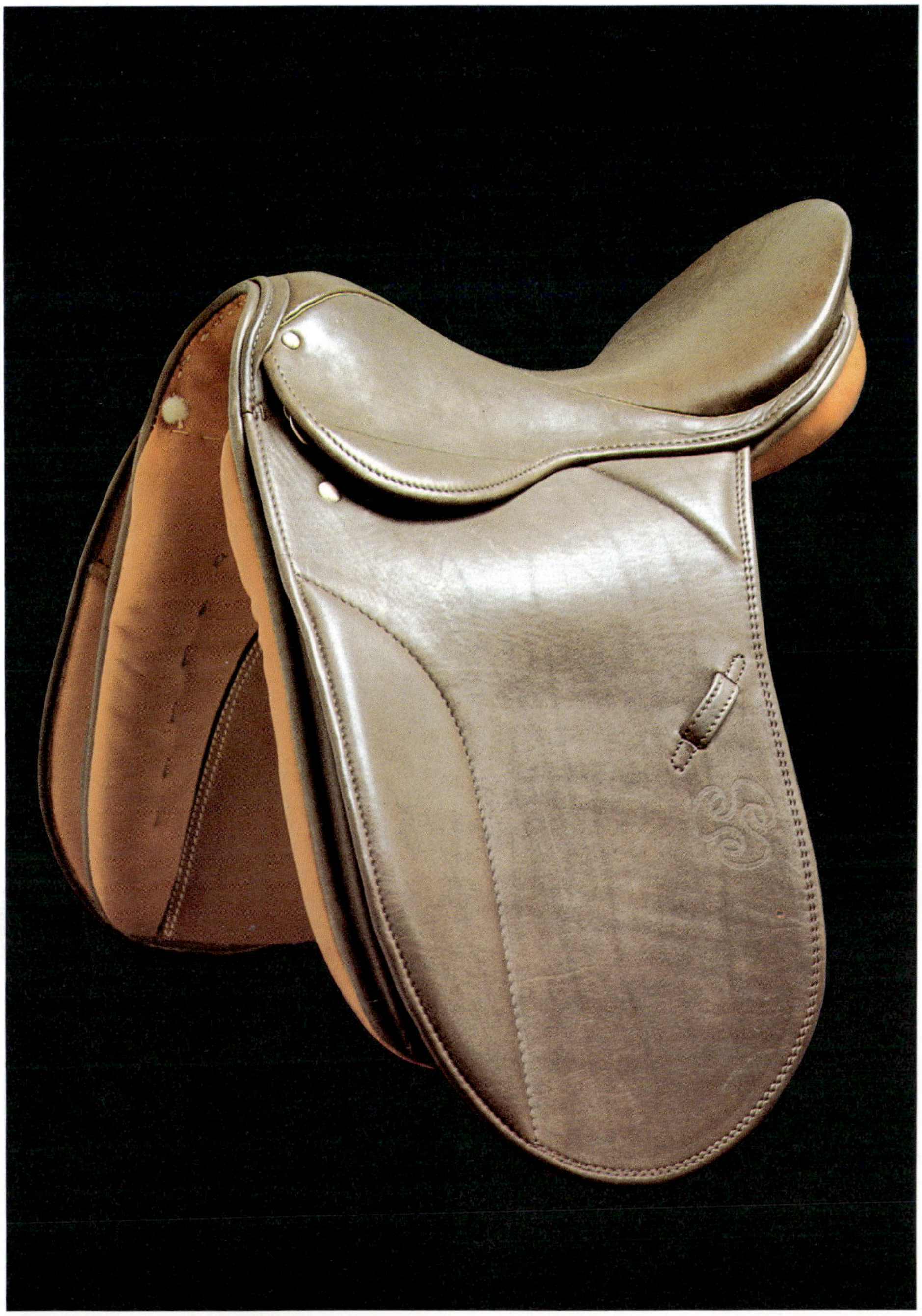

FITNESS FOR PURPOSE

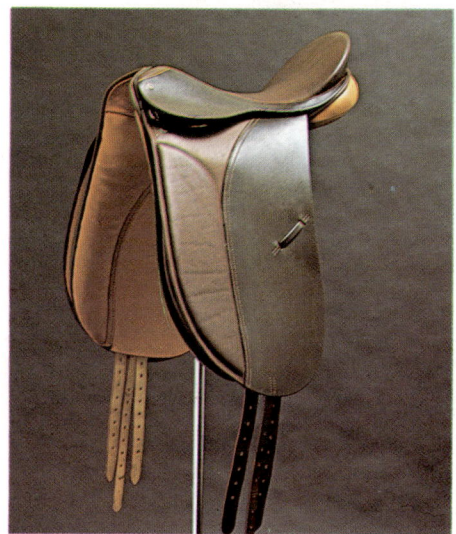

Left: A dressage saddle by Stubben, straighter in the flap than the English saddle at the bottom of page 68 and possibly, also, longer in this respect. **Bottom:** The Stubben saddle in position on the horse's back. **Top:** An English saddle, less dipped in the seat to allow the rider a little more freedom, and with the flap (which is blocked over the panel roll) swelled a little in advance of the vertical. **Above:** A German saddle with extended girth straps and long flap to accommodate long leg position of a tall rider.

gusset at the rear, which permits more stuffing to be inserted than would otherwise be the case.

The German influence

In recent years, Germany has had a wide influence on modern saddle design, as it has on riding practice, particularly in dressage.

Opinion is divided for the most part on the value of the influence. The majority of these saddles are made with cut-back heads, but there seems to be no obvious reason or advantage in this, particularly in the case of jumping saddles. The theoretical usefulness of a cut-back head is to accommodate very high withers, but, in fact, the modern sloped head is, in all but exceptional cases, perfectly able to accommodate this. In addition, a cut-back head weakens the structure of the tree and, by placing the bars further to the rear, makes it more difficult for the rider to sit in balance with his mount.

CHAPTER THREE · THE TWENTIETH-CENTURY SADDLE

The Saddle · **Some Variations**

A number of saddles have been designed with a specific purpose in view. They are either artificial or intensely practical.

The show saddle
This is a peculiarly English product. It is designed for use in the ring, to show off the horse's conformation to best advantage. In general use, it is not a practical item of equipment either for horse or rider, though it holds a firm place in the show ring. Many competitors, however, use a more conventionally shaped saddle.

Essentially the show saddle is a cutdown, streamlined version of the old hunting saddle and is fashioned in such a way as to enable horse and rider to present themselves to thier best ability. For instance, a particularly desirable feature in the show horse is the possession of a 'good front'—that is, a long, powerful and sloping shoulder in front of the saddle—combined (as such a shoulder must be) with a good 'length of rein'. (The 'length of rein' is the distance from the poll, down the crest of the neck to the withers.) The show rider seeks to display this second point by riding with as long a rein as he can while still maintaining perfect control, but even this aspect can be helped by the saddle. The 'front' of the horse, on the other hand, can definitely be emphasized and even exaggerated by the right saddle.

The classic show saddle is constructed on a plain, fairly flat-seated tree with either the usual vertical head or one of the cut-back variety. To be correct, as well as practical, the tree should be fitted with an extended stirrup bar. This fitting is particularly important, because the flap of the show saddle is cut absolutely straight, so as to display as much as possible of the horse's shoulder, and in some cases it is even cut to the rear of the vertical. The extended bar puts the stirrup leather further to the rear, so that it lies down the centre of the flap, and thus allows room for the rider's leg. With a normal bar, set further to the front, it would be impossible for the rider's knee not to be off the flap and lying in front of it. Such a knee position would reveal the saddle as being a stratagem to deceive the eye.

The panel of the true show saddle is made of relatively thin felt, covered with leather, and is nearly always a half panel.

Below: An Owen-type tree is ideal for use in building a show saddle. **Right:** An English show hunter at the Royal Windsor Horse Show wearing an original Owen saddle which although cut slightly forward in the flap, sits well behind the shoulder. **Opposite:** A modern straight-cut show saddle with a thin half-panel ('skeleton') made of felt covered with leather.

SOME VARIATIONS

This arrangement allows the saddle, with its relatively flat seat, to fit close to the horse's back and so not to interfere with the 'line'. Possibly the most important feature is the provision of a girth strap, which is laid under the point of the tree and is called a point strap for that reason. When this strap is used with the first of the two normally placed girth straps, the aim is to hold the saddle further to the rear than would otherwise be possible and so, once more, give emphasis to the 'front'. In other words, the saddle can be positioned inches further back than would be either usual or normally advisable.

The same thing can be achieved with the three girth straps on any saddle. These can be used to move the saddle either forward or back according to the conformation of the horse. A girth attached to the first two puts the saddle a little more to the rear, while the use of the centre and third strap will move it forward.

A particularly good saddle, which was extremely suitable for the show ring, was the pattern made by Hèrmes of Paris. Known as the 'English Saddle', this was a model of quiet restraint. The seat was just sufficiently dipped for comfort, the flap was not too straight and it was fitted with a light panel which included a flat, unobtrusive knee roll to give some support to the rider. A much older saddle, also extremely popular among show riders, was made by the old London firm of Owen. With its quarter cut-back head, rounded cantle—show saddles, as such, usually have a shaped, 'square' cantle—and flaps of exactly correct proportions it was a

CHAPTER THREE · THE TWENTIETH-CENTURY SADDLE

most elegant design and it showed off a horse very well.

The gaited horse saddle
In the USA, the American gaited horse saddle derives from the English show saddle, differing only in its extreme cut-back head ('cow-mouth') and the width of the flaps. In the American saddle, these extend to within two or three inches of the cantle and appear to be out of proportion as a result. There is, however, a practical purpose in so wide a flap. The attitude of the horse—very high in front and almost squatting over the hindlegs—together with the saddle's flat seat forces the rider to sit well back. In this position the rider's thigh would rest on the horse if a conventional saddle was used and, as a result, would be subjected to the inevitable sweat and dirt from the coat. The extra wide flap prevents this unpleasant happening.

The stockman's saddle
The show saddle and the gaited horse saddles are prime examples of artificiality in saddle design. That used by the Australian stockmen, on the other hand, must be considered, with the Western saddle, as one of the most practical and utilitarian saddles in the world.

Built to withstand the toughest treatment that can be imposed upon it, the Australian stock saddle is purpose planned to give comfort to both man and horse during droving trips that may last for as long as six months. It is made so that the stockman can make his own repairs with the minimum of tools and trouble and it is designed to keep the rider firmly in place.

Although the American cowboy and the stockman do similar work, their saddles

SOME VARIATIONS

Left: The ultra flat-seated, Walking Horse saddle made on a 'cow-mouth' Lane-Fox tree and fitted with an extra-wide flap to prevent the rider's leg coming into direct contact with the horse. **Below:** The tree together with a direct side-view of the saddle. Saddles for the American gaited horses (the American Saddlebred, the Tennessee Walker and the Missouri Foxtrotter) are supplied almost entirely by the Walsall-based British saddlery companies. In most instances these specialist saddles are fitted with a forward girth strap, as in the saddle on the left, which is laid under the point of the tree (point strap), enabling them to be fitted well behind the horse's shoulder.
Right: The attitude of the American Saddlebred in movement, 'very high in front and almost squatting over the hindlegs'.

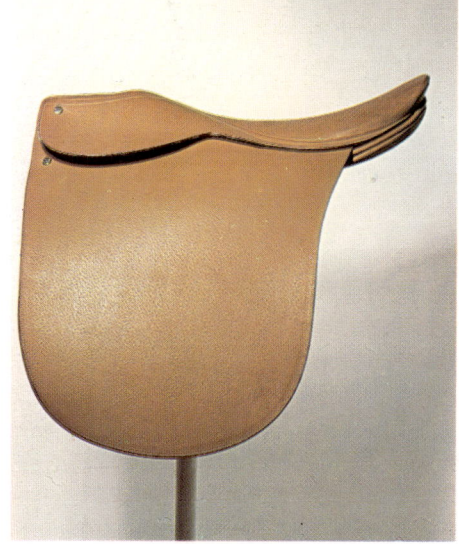

are entirely different. The American one owes its origins to the Spanish saddlery of the *conquistadores*, whilst the Australian saddle derives from the English hunting saddle, which was introduced to Australia by the early European settlers.

The saddle's characteristic shape is evident even in very early models; by 1911, the stock saddle had developed a narrow twist to the tree and a good dip to the seat. Obviously, security was a much appreciated commodity, so the Australian saddles of the turn of the century were fitted with very substantial knee rolls—some of wing-like proportions—set not as part of the panel but on the flaps themselves. Such rolls, though not as large, are to be found on some English saddles of the period and it is extremely likely that they inspired the Australian variety. Fairly quickly, too, an additional roll, smaller and placed high on the back edge of the flap, was also incorporated. The effect was to lock the thigh in position in an exactly identical manner to the medieval knight and his war saddle.

Later models, dating from about 1919, were made with shorter pads fitted high on the saddle to support the thigh but leaving the knee free. The back pad, however, remained to support the rear of the thigh and the design gave no less security to the rider. At least one maker put a horn on his saddles—the Humphreys Breaking-in Saddle is an example—similar, but smaller, to that found on American saddles. The purpose of the Australian horn was also different. It was intended as a 'grab' in emergencies; it was not used for roping, as in the American variety, since the Australian stockman does not use a lariat to the same extent or in the same fashion. From this time, too, the flap

CHAPTER THREE · THE TWENTIETH-CENTURY SADDLE

lengthened to give the rider's legs greater purchase—stockmen riding for the most part in cotton trousers.

The panels of the Australian saddle are admirable. They are very well stuffed, serge-covered panels fitted with gussets at the rear to ensure that the saddle lies level on the back.

As a practical, working saddle the Australian product is extremely hard to beat and it is interesting to note how the work involved produced a saddle that was ideally suited to its purpose. It is of equal interest to appreciate how close are the design features to those employed in the saddles of a thousand years ago—which goes to show, perhaps, how very practical were those features.

Trekking saddles
In view of the popularity of trekking as a holiday activity—particularly in Europe—it seems the more surprising that very few saddles suitable for this purpose have developed. The problem in this instance is the safeguarding of the horses' backs against inexperienced 'riders' of a very low standard. Many trekking operators very wisely rely on the military troopers' saddle, which is pretty well proof against the inexperience of the rider. It is, however, expensive to manufacture and in increasingly short supply as a sound secondhand article, but a utility saddle is being made following similar lines. In particular, it retains the traditional extended 'fans' bearing the panel, which ensure the horse's comfort.

This must certainly be the chief aim of any trekking saddle; the fact that the rider is carried high above the horse's back, generally a great disadvantage, and not in

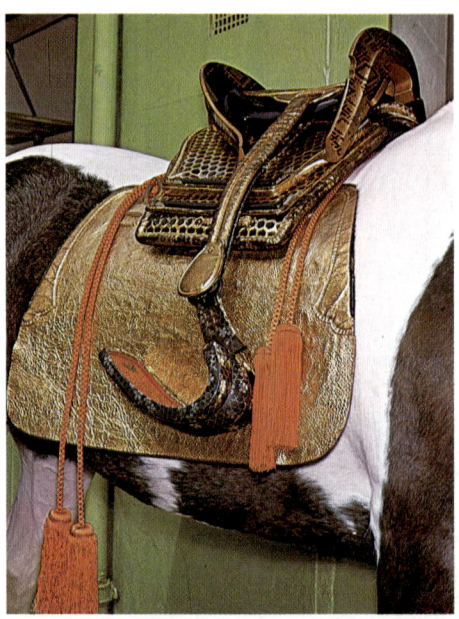

Top: An ornate and highly-decorated saddle of the Iberian Peninsula, richly quilted and infinitely redolent of its Moorish ancestry. Despite its extravagance it is none the less an essentially practical piece of equipment giving security to the horseman and comfort to his mount. **Right:** One of the most utilitarian saddles in the world is the Australian stock saddle. Built to stand up to the hardest use it still incorporates design features which give the rider a very high degree of comfort and security on what may on occasions be very rough horses. The seat is dipped and narrow in the 'twist', and the 'wings' set in front of the rider's upper thigh are a powerful support in times of emergency. The solid, well-stuffed panel of the Australian saddle, although adding to the weight, distributes the weight admirably over the whole bearing surface.

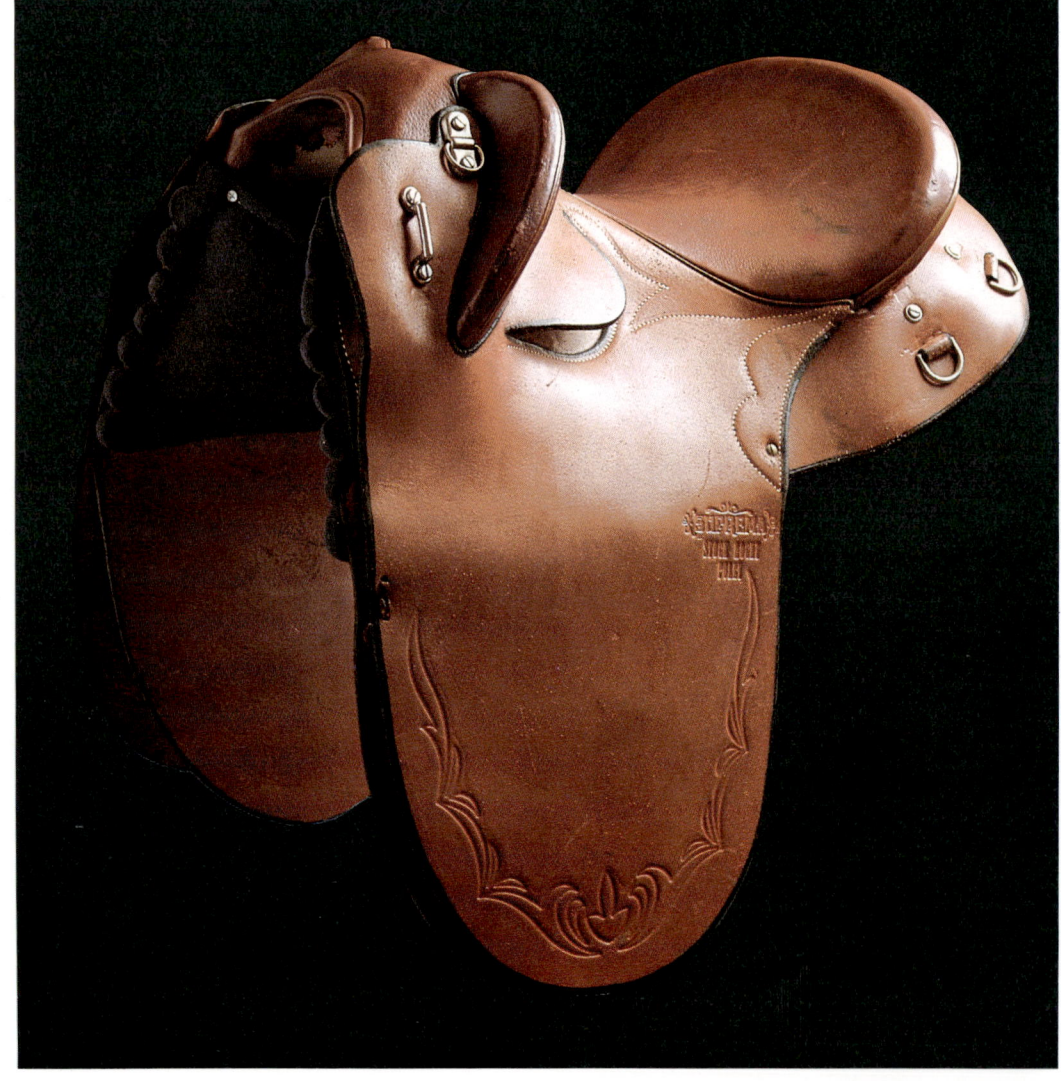

SOME VARIATIONS

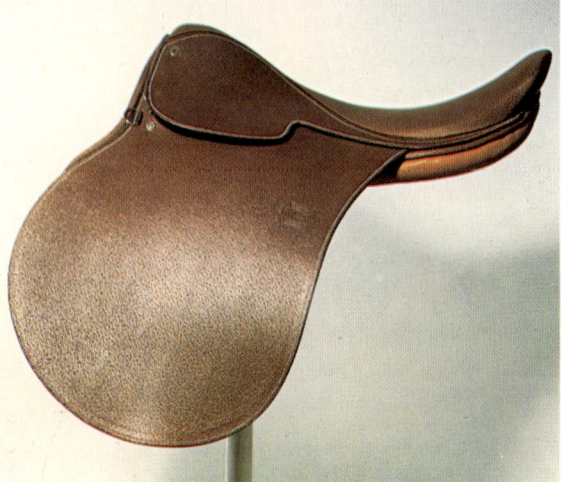

close contact with his mount is irrelevant in this instance.

Facsimile saddles
Harking back to the medieval saddle and, more particularly, to that of the Renaissance, it seems remarkable, at first thought, that modern facsimiles should still exist and, indeed, be widely used. This is so, however. The saddles of the Iberian Peninsula, particularly of Andalusia, do not differ at all from those which originated with the Moorish invaders and were in use four centuries ago. Built high in front and behind to encase the rider, and often quilted for comfort, they are used for all forms of general riding—for displays at the

CHAPTER THREE · THE TWENTIETH-CENTURY SADDLE

feria, for herding the black bulls, and as the saddle of the *rejeonadore*, when horse and man face a fighting bull in the ring.

The inflatable saddle

The one saddle which stands out on its own as being entirely original and 'modern' is an inflatable saddle, made of nylon fabric coated with neoprene synthetic rubber. The saddle was sold with a special pump adaptor and could be blown up to whatever degree of firmness was required with an ordinary bicycle pump.

When not in use, the saddle was deflated and could be rolled up rather like a plastic raincoat. No instructions were given as to what to do in the case of a sudden puncture, but obviously it was a wise precaution for users of the saddle to equip themselves with a repair kit. Surprisingly, for so modern a concept, the shape of the inflatable was distinctly medieval in appearance, as historical comparison shows.

Children's saddles

For the most part, children's saddles follow those of their elders in design, but there are saddles, produced specifically for small children, which have been in use in one form or another for a century or more.

The cheapest saddle of all is a pad of felt to which is attached a girth, a leather handle across the front for the small rider to hold, fittings for stirrup leathers and leather reinforcements to prevent stirrups

76

from wearing a hole through the felt. This is, in fact, a most satisfactory arrangement for the very young, whose diminutive ponies rarely have the conformation to carry a conventional saddle. There are no fitting problems to consider and it is far more comfortable for the riders' short little legs.

The felt pad, however, should not be confused, with the 'Cobbar' felt saddle. This, too, was a very practical saddle, which was comfortable for horse and rider and was neither too heavy nor too expensive. It was made of heavy quality felt, fitted to an attenuated tree. In fact, the tree was no more than the fore arch, with arms just sufficiently extended to allow the fitting of a stirrup bar. Unlike the simple felt pad, the 'Cobbar' had a panel, built conventionally with a channel between the two halves, and extended to provide a knee roll. Its principal use was as a race-exercise saddle, but there were occasions when it was used by point-to-point riders and by some show jumpers of perhaps two decades ago. In Australia, the country of its origin, it was certainly used in bush racing.

The other type of child's saddle was the 'basket' saddle, which resembled a miniature howdah. The basket was made with conveniently sited holes, through which the rider's legs protruded, or was sometimes fitted with a small seat. It was, of course, impossible for a child to fall out, but, naturally, the pony had to be led.

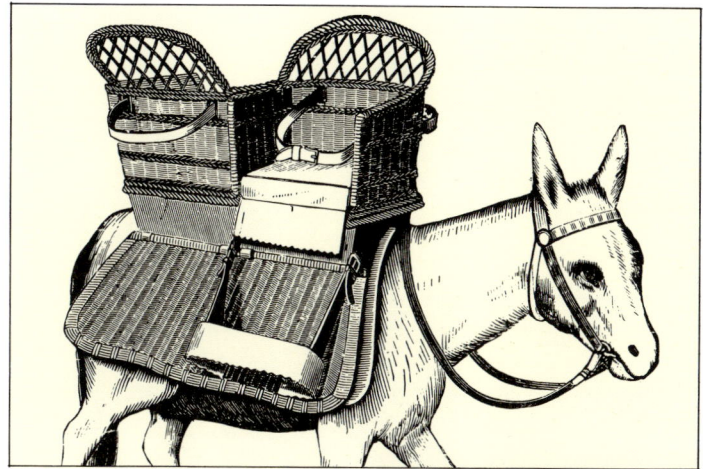

Opposite A child's basket saddle, resembling an elephant howdah, which was once in great demand. **Top left:** The ultimate – a 19th-century donkey two-seater for the larger Victorian family. **Top right:** The very practical modern felt pad with no fitting problems. **Above:** An elaborate quilted child's saddle of the 19th century. **Right:** A refinement on the felt saddle is the flexible leather pad made up on a half-tree, which is little more than a front arch and a pair of stirrup bars. It is, of course, a relatively cheap solution to the young rider's saddle requirement.

CHAPTER THREE · THE TWENTIETH-CENTURY SADDLE

The Saddle · **Mountings**

In the equestrian world, the accessories to the saddle are known by the collective name of 'mountings'. They consist of the girth, stirrup irons and leathers and also such items as breastplates.

The types of girth available can be divided in general terms into three basic categories—leather, webbing and, inevitably, nylon. There are the occasional exceptions made of cord and even of woven horse-hair, but they are hardly significant in comparison with the others.

The leather girth
There is no doubt that the best girth, in all circumstances and for every purpose outside racing, is one made of leather. There are three principal types—the Balding, the Atherstone and the Three-Fold. The first of these, named after the polo player who introduced it, is cut and then virtually 'plaited', so that it is shaped away from the elbow when in position, thus obviating any chance of the horse being galled in this area. The Atherstone girth is made and shaped with the same object in view—

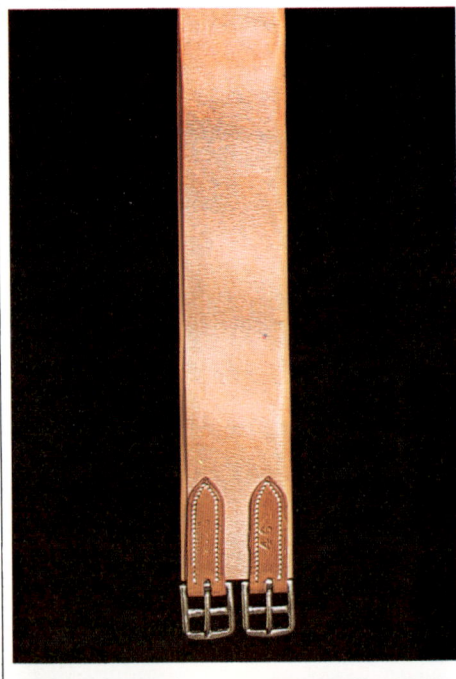
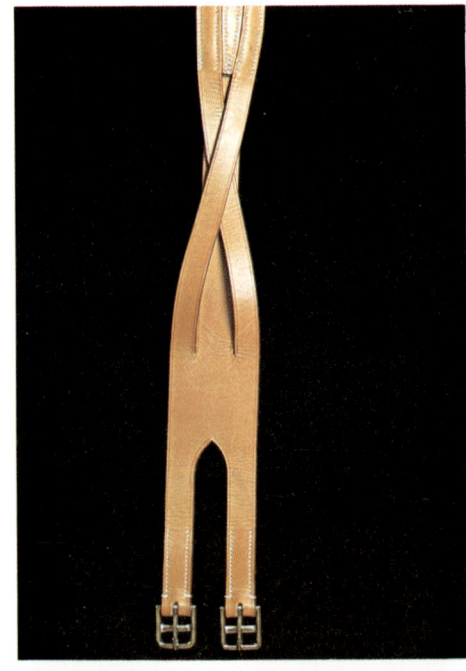

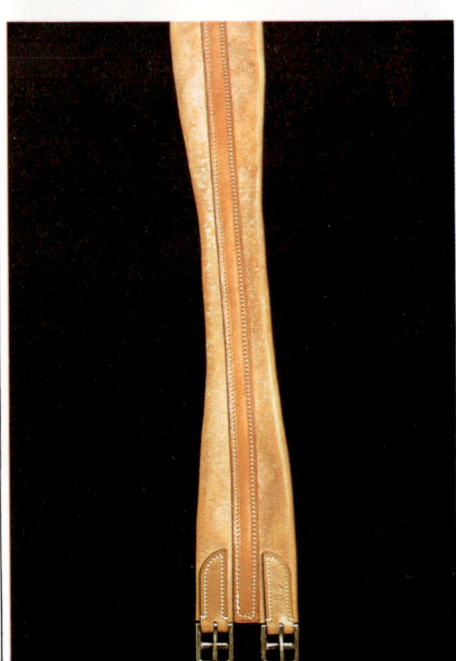
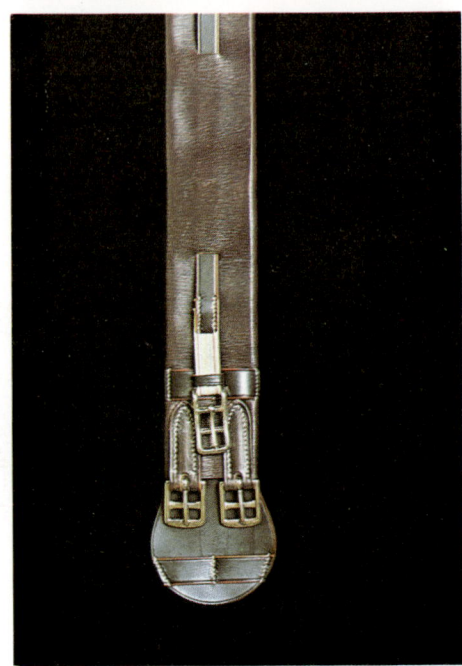
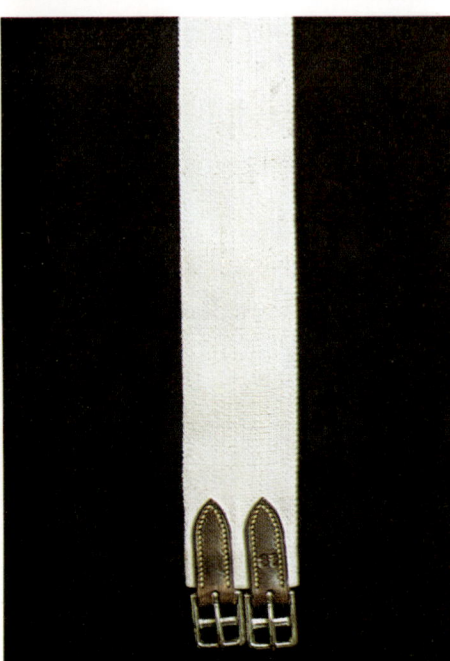

Top: The 3-fold baghide girth, usually made with an oiled flannel inlay. **Bottom:** The Atherstone pattern girth shaped to avoid galling at the elbow.

Top: Balding girth, originally designed for polo and again shaped to obviate chafing. **Bottom:** The short dressage girth, often termed Lonsdale, with the centre strap set on elastic.

Top: A wide woven horse-hair girth of a pattern more frequently seen in America. **Bottom:** The soft lampwick girth which is ideal for use on horses who are fat or susceptible to galling.

to prevent galling behind the elbow. It is usually made from a very soft baghide and, if properly treated, can become infinitely supple.

However, modern girths, both of this pattern and the Three-Fold variety are often unsatisfactory and should be examined carefully before purchase. Some varieties are made with a sharp crease at the fold, rather than a soft roll, which defeats their purpose, since the edge is sharp enough to chafe and even cut into the horse's skin.

The Three-Fold girth is no more than a piece of soft baghide folded in three, the leading edge naturally being the rounded one. Properly made, this excellent girth should be supplied with a piece of stout serge, or some similar wool cloth, laid inside the fold. If the serge is soaked in some kind of grease, the heat from the horse's body will ensure that the grease is absorbed by the leather to keep it in an exceptionally supple state. Ideally, the grease level in a Three-Fold girth should be checked and topped-up as frequently as the oil in a motor car. Leather girths in

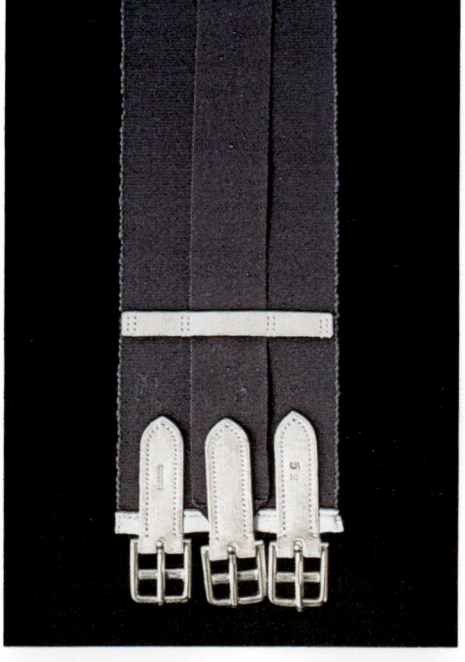
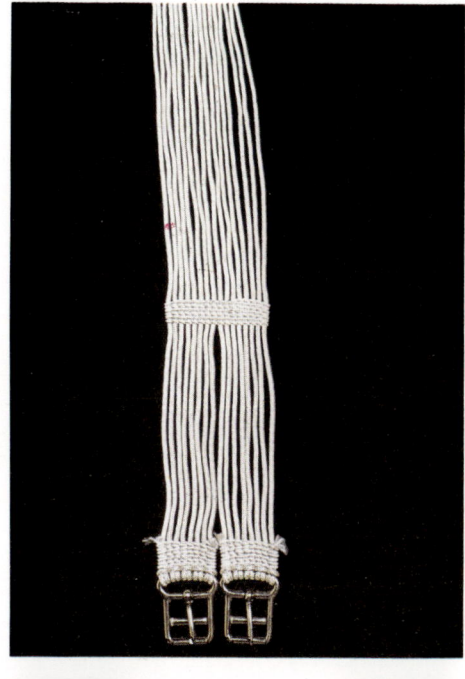

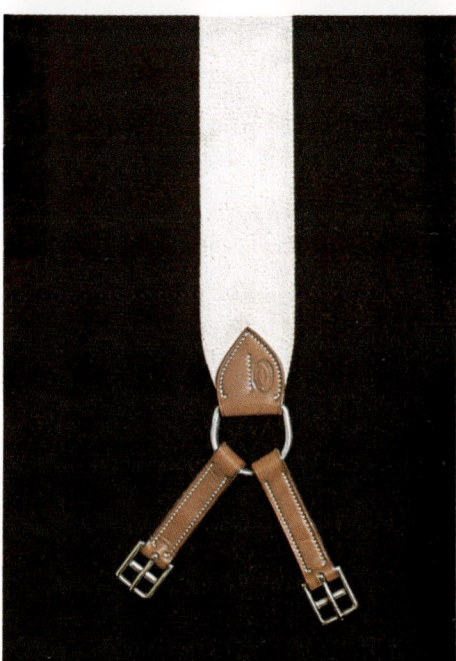
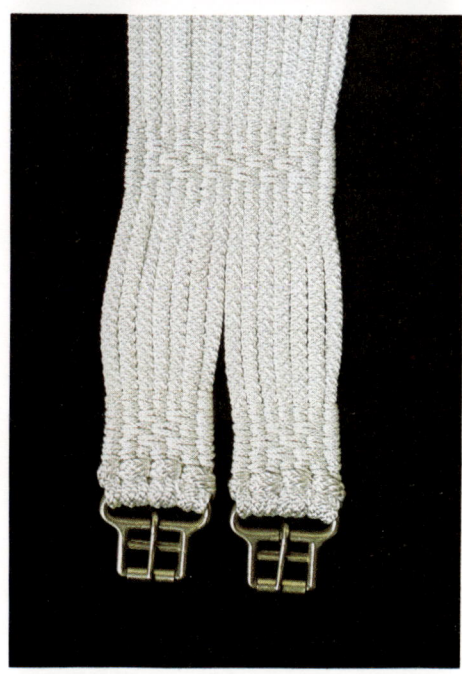
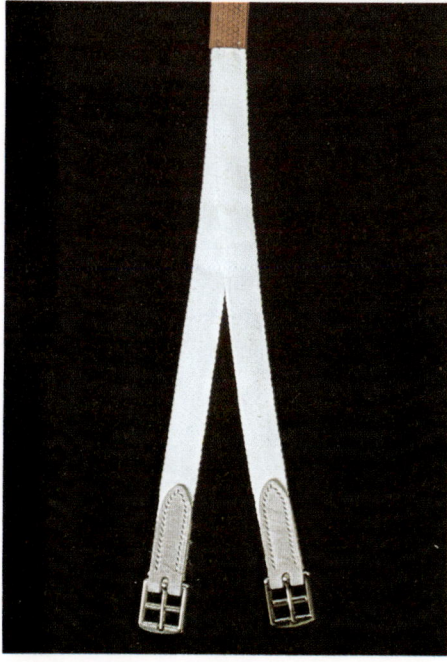

Top: A type of Fitzwilliam girth used on a side-saddle. **Bottom:** A variation on the 'Humane' pattern, designed to 'give' with the movement of the horse.

Top: The ubiquitous nylon girth, which has the advantage of being cheap but rarely has a satisfactory buckle. **Bottom:** The much superior cord girth, usually fitted with quality buckles.

Top: A pair of web girths which are in general use in European racing stables. **Bottom:** Tubular web, twin pony show girth fitted with rubber centre so as to prevent slipping.

CHAPTER THREE · THE TWENTIETH-CENTURY SADDLE

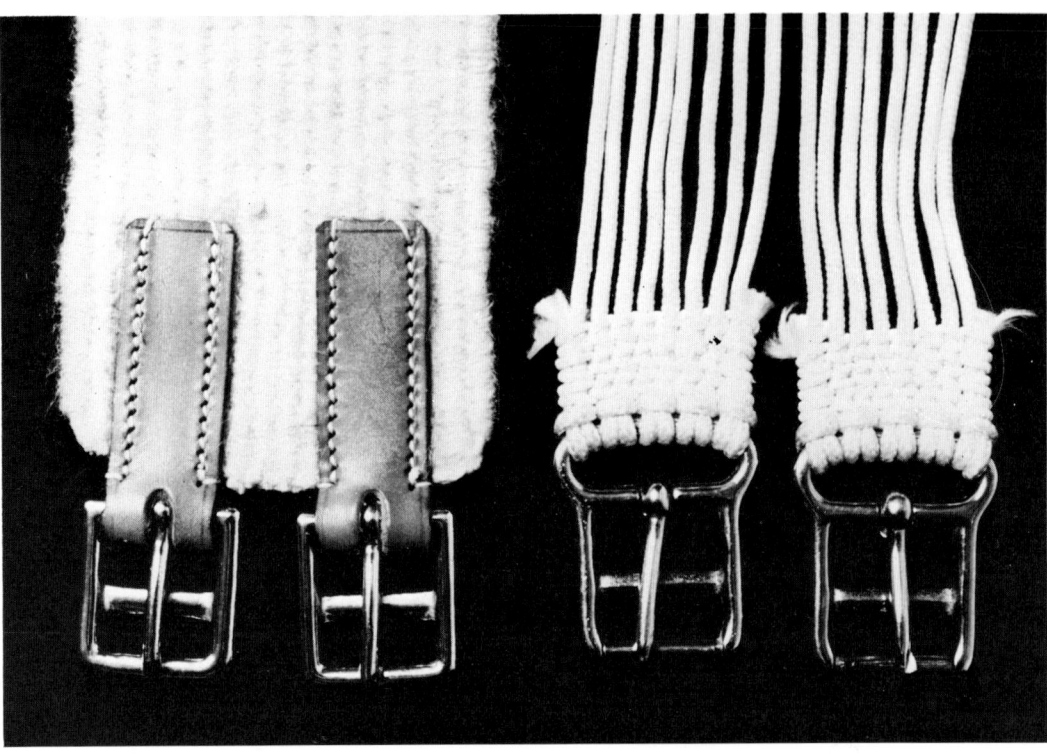

Right: Right and wrong. The buckles on the right are good, well-made ones with a groove for the tongue. Such buckles will not cut up the flap nor will the tongue slide out of its central position. On the left is a cheap, poor quality buckle which is nearly always unsatisfactory.

general must, indeed, be kept well-nourished, since the combination of body heat and sweat tends to reduce the essential fat content of the leather.

Webbing girths
Webbing girths, sold in pairs and each fitted with a single buckle, are not now so much in favour, except possibly in racing stables. If made of wool web, however, they are very satisfactory. Cotton web and even the mixtures of cotton and wool are not as adequate, since they will cut and chafe if not washed regularly and are anything but durable in use.

The lampwick
A girth which is now much neglected in favour of those made from easily washed man-made materials is that made of lampwick in a 3¼in width. Lampwick is a cotton and wool tubular web, used in days gone by, as the name suggests, as lamp wicks. Fitted with two buckles it will remain very soft if given reasonable care and it will not rub even the fattest and softest of horses.

A popular girth for showing, particularly where ponies are concerned, is the narrow, tubular web girth fitted with a centre of 'pimple' rubber (like that used on a table-tennis bat) which lies in the sternum curve. The girth is really two pieces of tubular web overlapping in the centre, the latter being covered with rubber for some 6in to 8in. Apart from being neat and unobtrusive this girth has considerable gripping properties and so helps to keep the saddle correctly positioned.

Racing girths
Racing girths are made in web, their width being as narrow as 2¼in, and are always worn with a surcingle of the same material. A surcingle passes over the top of the saddle and fastens under the belly to ensure that the saddle does not slip. They are also used for cross-country riding, show jumping and so on. A surcingle is not, however, a stable roller, though the latter is often incorrectly referred to by this name.

For racing and, indeed, for any form of active competitive riding girths of all types can be inset with a few inches of elastic below the buckles. The advantage of the elastic is that it will 'give' as the horse uses his lungs to their full capacity and, as a result, causes no restriction at moments of peak exertion. At one time, all-elastic girths were popular, but they are difficult to fit correctly and will rot when subjected to continual sweating.

Nylon girths
The ubiquitous nylon cord girth is both popular and relatively inexpensive but it is not as satisfactory as the majority of its users would like to think. It is held that the girth will prevent chafing by reason of its construction, but if it is allowed to become dirty this is not, in fact, the case. Nylon is, in any event, an abrasive material, and when hardened by the absorption of sweat is very likely to gall. Furthermore it is only too easy for a wrinkle of skin to become trapped between the cords, causing the horse discomfort and soreness.

Almost invariably, nylon girths are fitted with poor quality buckles, the top bar being fitted with a roller of thin metal which will almost certainly open to allow its sharp edges to cut into the areas of the saddle with which it comes into contact. The best buckles do not have rollers, the top bar in this case being grooved so as to accommodate the buckle tongue, which then lies flush and causes no unnecessary bulge. But, whatever the type of buckle used, the girth straps of the saddle should be fitted with leather pieces ('girth safes') which can be pulled down over the buckles and will prevent the latter from rubbing a hole in the saddle flaps.

On soft horses, brought into work after a summer at grass, a girth sleeve made from sheepskin, or, more cheaply, from an old rubber inner tube is a useful precaution

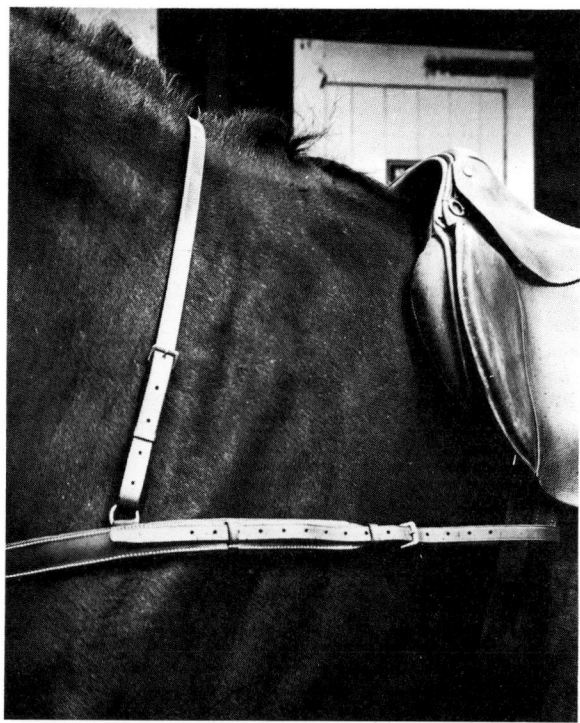
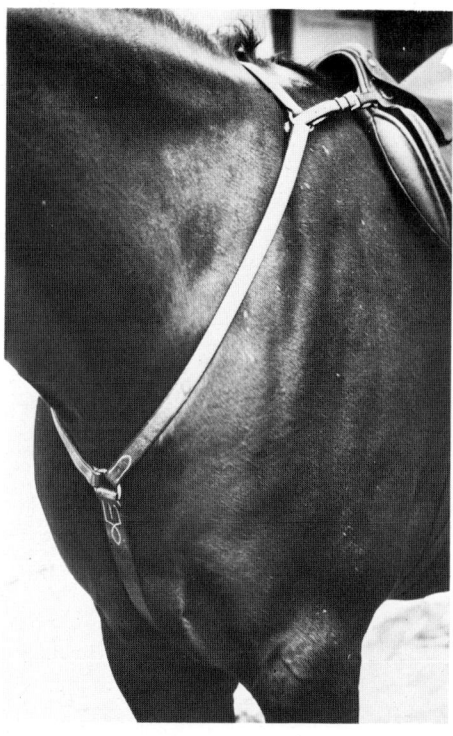

Far right: Leather hunting breastplate used to keep the saddle in place and prevent it sliding backwards. **Right and below:** Two types of 'Aintree' pattern racing breastplates, one made from leather and the other from webbing.

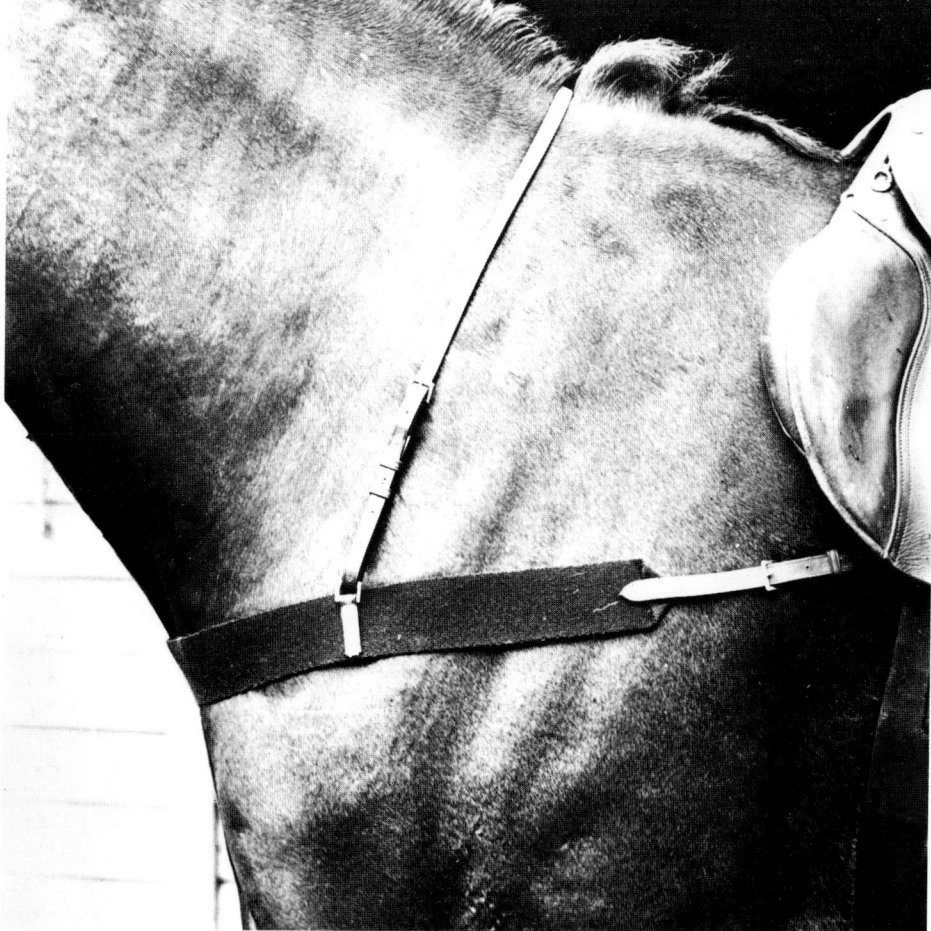

in guarding against galling.

Surprisingly very few riders pay sufficient attention to the length of the girth. It would always seem sensible to choose a length which places the buckles behind the bend of the knee and thus out of the way. Many dressage saddles, for instance, are fitted with extra long girth straps so that a short girth can be used and buckled below the bottom of the saddle flaps. This arrangement removes the bulk of the buckles from beneath the rider's thigh, allowing the leg to lie close to the saddle. Girths which are too long will naturally cause a bulge under the thigh. The girth straps of modern jumping and cross-country saddles are deliberately positioned so that the girth buckles can lie in the position described if the girth is of the correct length.

Use of a breastplate

There are two reasons for using a breastplate, a device which stops the saddle slipping backwards towards the horse's tail. The first is if conformation demands it; the second where riding in hilly country.

For hunting, the straightforward leather breastplate is the most suitable. This is fastened by adjustable straps to the front dees of the saddle and, after encircling the base of the neck, is secured to the girth between the forelegs. The same type—though much narrower in width and thus considerably lighter—can be used for racing, too. For the most part, however, racing breastplates are made of web, or sometimes elastic, and are of what is termed the Aintree pattern. These breastplates encircle the chest and need to be adjusted carefully, since it is possible for an ill-fitting one to ride upwards to the neck. A similar type, made more substantially in leather, is used for polo and has a loop on the inside of the chest strap through which a martingale can be passed. When martingales are used with a hunting breastplate they are shortened affairs, which are attached to the ring in the centre of the horse's chest.

Stirrup leathers

Stirrup leathers are made from either cowhide, rawhide or buffalo hide. In the case of the first two, the leathers are made up so that the flesh side faces outwards. The reason for this reversal of usual practice is so that the grain side, which is the harder wearing of the two, will receive the friction caused by contact with the 'eye' (slot) of the stirrup iron. When buffalo hide is used, this precaution is not necessary since the leather is virtually unbreakable. Buffalo hide which is characteristically red in colour has only one drawback, which is its propensity to stretch. All stirrup leathers stretch in use but the 'red leathers' stretch more than most. They are nonetheless extremely long lasting. A pair of leathers will not necessarily stretch equally, indeed they are most unlikely to prove so obliging. For this reason, plus the fact that all but the most skilled riders tend to put more weight upon one iron than on the other, it is advisable to change new leathers from side to side daily.

For convenience the holes punched in the leathers are usually numbered. It is best to insist on the holes being punched fairly close ('half holes'), so as to allow for a greater range of adjustment.

Racing leathers are necessarily very narrow, perhaps no greater than ½in in width. Often the material used is not leather at all, but lengths of tubular web, which are naturally very much lighter.

An annoying characteristic of the stirrup leather is the bulge it makes under the rider's thigh, a protrusion which, of course, will be more prominent if the

Above: Stirrup leathers in a variety of widths and leathers. It is preferable for the holes to be punched fairly close, to give greater adjustment, and for them to be numbered. Stirrup leathers are made from cowhide, rawhide or buffalo hide.
Below: The 'hook-up' or extending stirrup leather – a useful item for short-legged owners of tall horses.

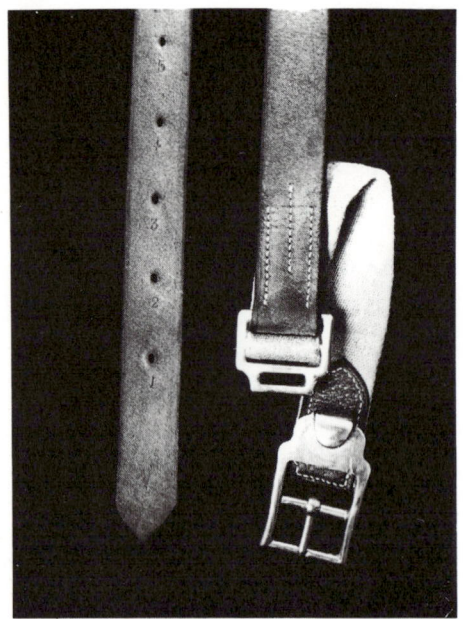

MOUNTINGS

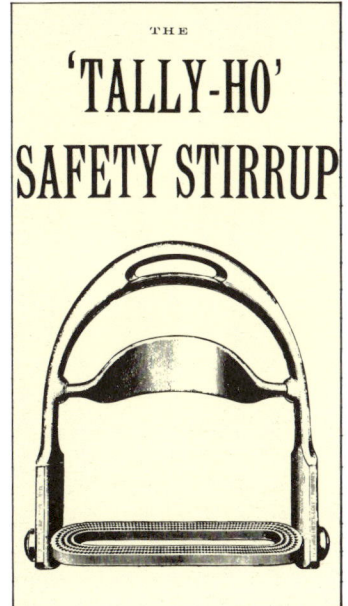

Top: A stockroom of stirrups at a Walsall foundry. **Far left:** The 'Tally-Ho', one of the many safety irons which proliferated in the 19th century. **Left:** Stirrup irons and, in the foreground, castings. **Above:** Example of finely-ornamented stirrups which were made by craftsmen in Europe well into the 17th and 18th centuries.

CHAPTER THREE · THE TWENTIETH-CENTURY SADDLE

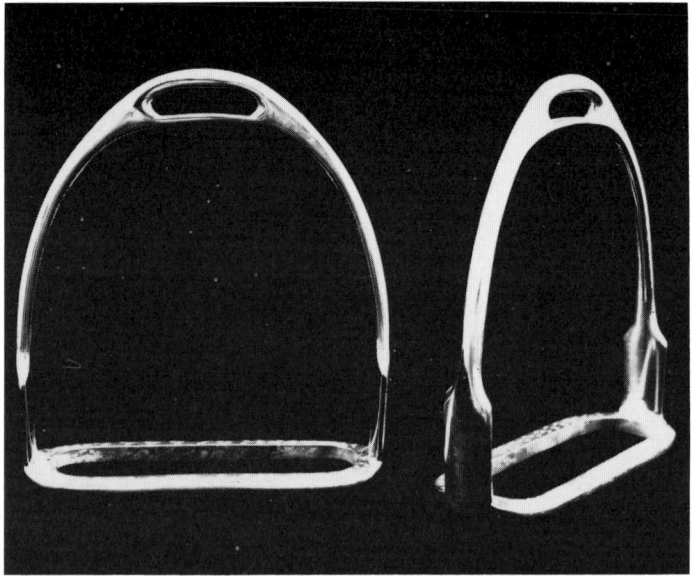

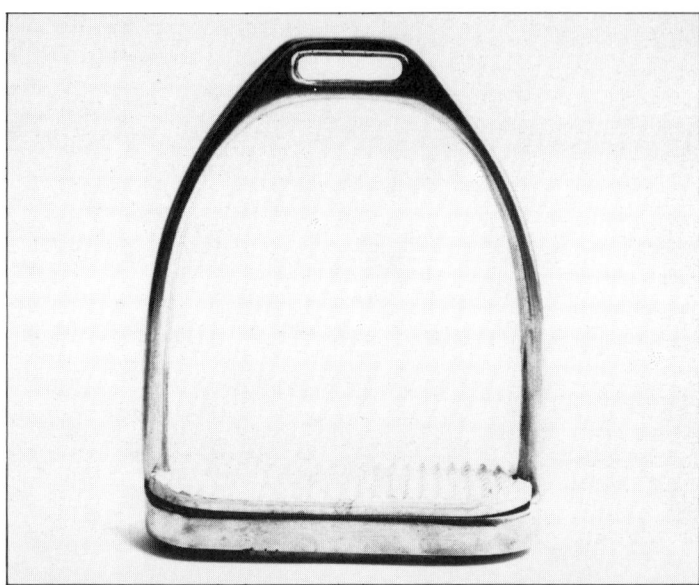

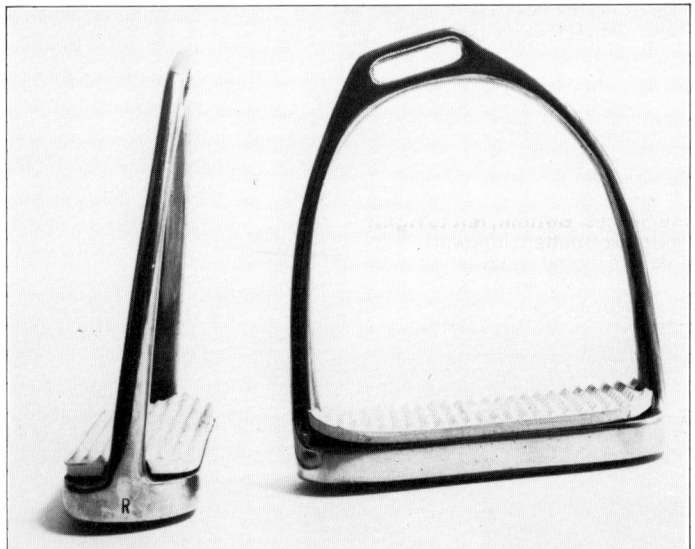

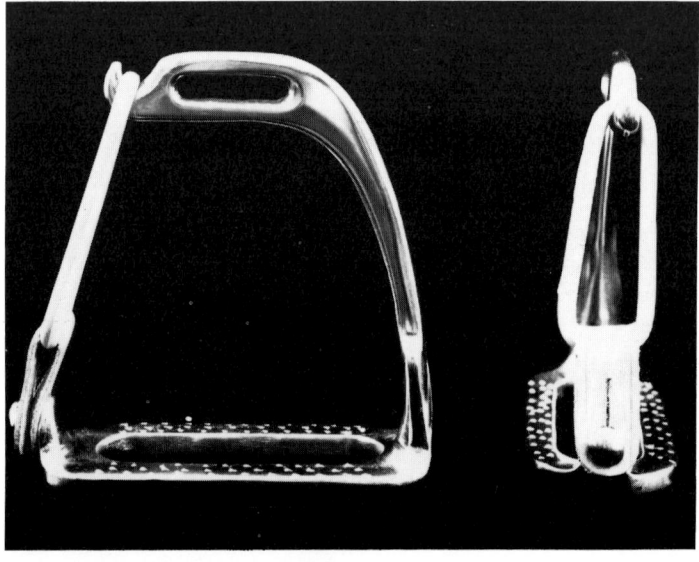

stirrup bars are not recessed in the manner described elsewhere. To overcome this problem, as well as to allow the rider's thigh to lie flat against the saddle, it is possible to obtain in some countries a stirrup leather, which is adjustable at a point some 8in above the stirrup iron, after the military fashion. This type of adjusting leather is found frequently on the Continent but rarely seen in Britain or the USA.

For those who experience difficulty in mounting, it is still possible to obtain a 'hook-up' or extending leather. This device consists of a hook and slot attachment connected by a length of approximately 8in of stout web. It allows the leather to be extended when mounting and it can then be easily hooked into place when the rider has gained the saddle. The disadvantage of the arrangement is its bulk when in position, but it is a help when short-legged persons are confronted with long-legged horses.

Stirrup irons

A notable feature in the saddlers' catalogues of the 19th century was the large number of safety stirrup irons—all designed so that in the event of a fall they would release the foot and thus prevent the rider from being dragged. There were many ingenious devices, some of which, however, acquired a reputation for anticipating a fall and thus leaving the rider in place but without benefit of stirrups.

With two exceptions—the Peacock safety iron, which is still used by children, and the Australian Simplex—modern irons are straightforward in design. Most, however, are used with a stirrup tread, a piece of equipment which seems to have become an essential part of the modern tack room. It assists the rider in keeping the foot position and it helps to keep the extremities warm by insulating them against the cold metal. Before the introduction of the stirrup tread (a relatively recent innovation), riders relied on the tread of the iron being roughed to give a better purchase to the sole of the boot.

The disadvantages of the Peacock iron are considerable and, in the light of these, it is probable that the provision of a fair-sized, heavy conventional iron, through

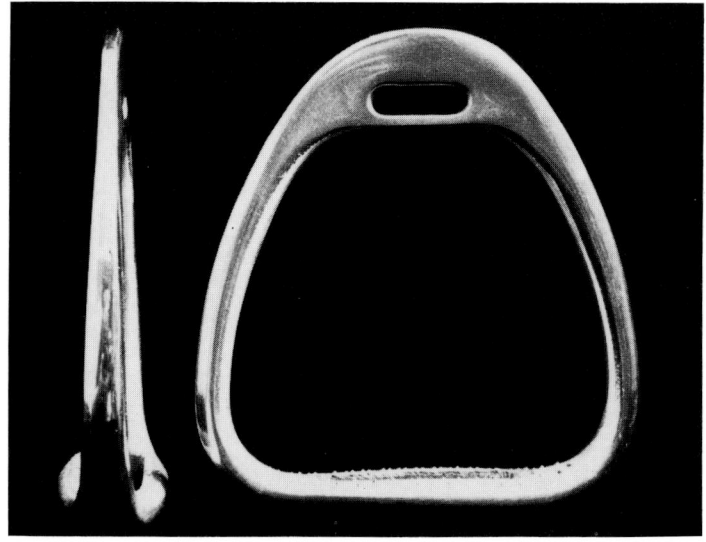
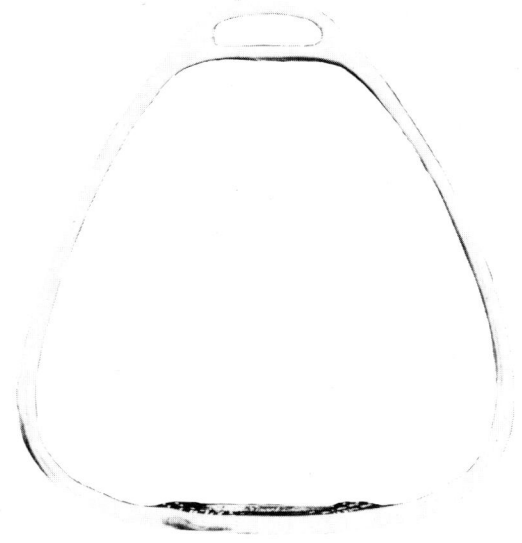
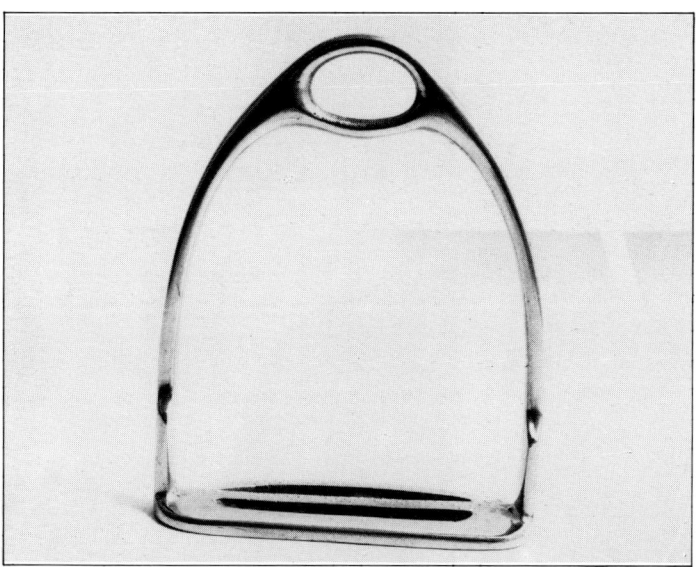

A selection of modern stirrup irons. **Top, left to right:** Plain, Prussian-side, open tread irons; knife-edge irons with heavy tread fitted in addition with anti-slip rubber treads which help the rider maintain the foot position; aluminium 'cradle' pattern race irons; cradle pattern stainless steel race irons, stronger for racing over fences. **Bottom, left to right:** Kournakoft pattern iron with shaped side and tread and cock-eye. The iron was developed for jumping and was designed to fix the rider's foot in what was thought to be the most secure position; the Peacock children's safety iron with quick-release rubbers; round eye side-saddle iron.

which a child's foot could not slip, as well as insistence upon the wearing of proper footwear would contribute just as effectively to the child's safety. Since, in effect, the Peacock has three sides instead of four, the outside of the iron being the rubber ring, its strength is correspondingly reduced. As a result, the tread can become bent by the action of mounting and will thus affect the child's foot and leg position. Furthermore, the rubber rings perish and are easily lost, frequently being replaced by binder twine or some similar substitute. Finally, it is quite surprising how many people fit the irons the wrong way round with the rubber ring on the inside.

Another pattern of stirrup iron with a built-in safety feature is the Australian Simplex, the forward bulge of the outside arm of the iron permitting the foot to slip out easily in emergencies.

A simple and very sensible variation to the basic pattern can be made by bending the top of the iron away from the instep. This will save the boot being worn in that area if the foot is placed fully home in the iron and is, of course, more comfortable for the rider.

A once popular jumping iron is that invented by a Russian cavalry officer and which takes his name—Kournakoff. This iron was designed to position the foot in accordance with Caprilli's system of forward riding. The eye is offset to the inside, the sides are sloped forward and the tread sloped upwards from the rear. In consequence, the rider's foot is held with toe up and heel down and with the outside of the sole higher than the inside. This position, in combination with that of the rest of the leg, is held to give very great security, since the knee and thigh are pulled inwards on to the saddle. The Kournakoff pattern is not suitable for dressage riding, however, while it is disastrous in the event that the left iron is fitted to the right hand side of the saddle by mistake and vice-versa.

Racing irons are usually made in a cradle pattern, which is more comfortable when wearing thin boots, and are as light as possible. Sometimes aluminium is used as an alternative material.

CHAPTER THREE · THE TWENTIETH-CENTURY SADDLE

The Saddle · **Numnahs**

Numnahs are items of equipment placed under the saddle to give greater comfort to the horse's back and to remove any risk of the animal becoming galled. In effect, anything of any substance placed between the saddle and the back may be regarded, in general terms, as a 'numnah', whatever the material from which it is made. A very basic form of 'numnah', for instance, is the folded blanket used under military saddles, which doubles as a rug for the horse or a cover for the rider at night or at other times when the horse is unsaddled.

Traditional numnahs
The traditional numnah is made of sheepskin, two skins being needed to make one numnah. The skins can be used in their natural state or the numnah can be covered with linen. Not surprisingly in recent times, sheepskin has been largely replaced by man-made material.

The advantage of the sheepskin is that the wool is resilient and is less likely to become flattened in use. On the other hand, it is difficult to wash and to keep clean, whereas the man-made fabrics can be put in a washing machine without coming to any harm. However, they become flat with use, while some types of fibre can prove to be abrasive. Foam plastic is another man-made product used in the making of numnahs and is usually covered in cotton or linen cloth. Whilst being soft and resilient it can, however, absorb sweat and is then something of a problem for horse and rider.

Another traditional type of numnah is made from thick felt. Consisting of two pieces, joined down the centre, it is shaped to the horse's back and is a very durable article, although again it will absorb sweat. A numnah of this type was often used in cases of sore backs, a 'chamber' being cut in the felt in the area of the sore place so that no pressure could be put on the wound.

Advantages and disadvantages
To what extent the use of numnahs is practical is a matter of doubt. It is certain that some horses appreciate the comfort they afford and resent the cold, leather

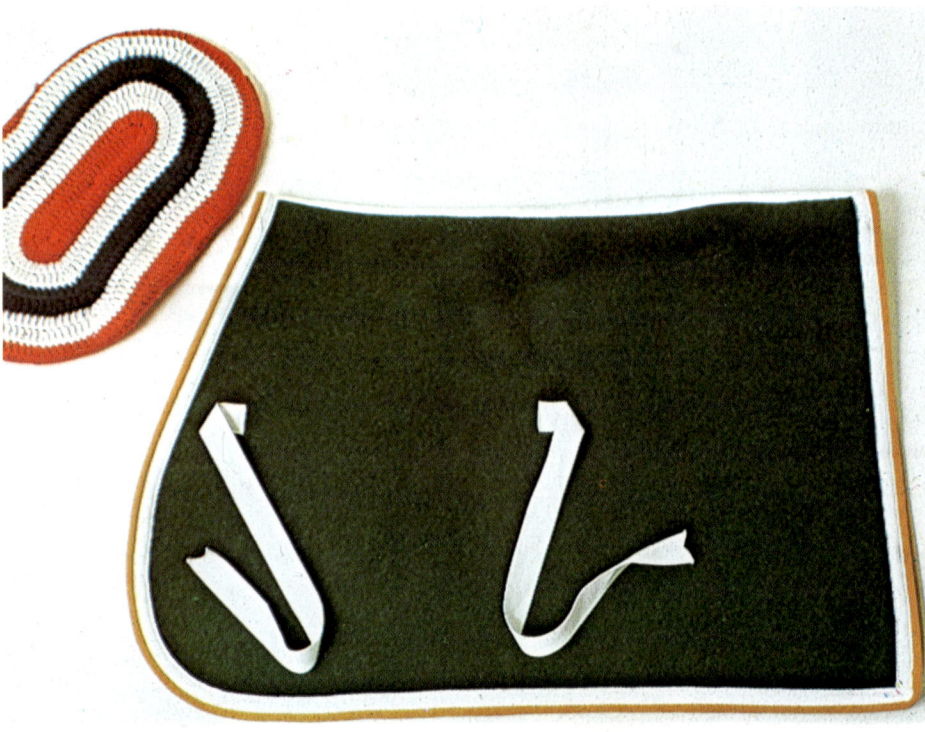

Above: A knitted wool wither pad always used under the head of a race saddle and sometimes under a riding saddle which is in need of stuffing and which bears too close to the wither. The saddle cloth is used to prevent the saddle becoming dirty from sweat, or for purely decorative purposes. **Right:** Brightly coloured Western blankets, always worn with a Western saddle.

panel of the saddle, while it is probably a wise precaution to put one on a young horse whose back has not hardened, or on one brought up from grass in soft condition.

In such instances the use of the numnah is entirely legitimate, but there are drawbacks. A numnah does not permit the free passage of air down the channel of the saddle; it can cause backs to become overheated and therefore more likely to be made sore, while, if it is used in dirty condition, it may gall the back of its own accord. From the viewpoint of the rider, the presence of a numnah places him that much further away from his horse, therefore preventing the close contact that is desirable. Its use therefore defeats one of the design objects of the modern saddle.

Finally, there is the temptation to employ a numnah to counter the effect of an ill-fitting saddle, when the real answer is to have the saddle regulated to the back.

There is, of course, another form of numnah which is designed purely for the benefit of the rider and contributes nothing to the comfort of the horse. It usually goes under the name of 'seat cover' and is made of sheepskin so as to fit over the top of the saddle. It is very comfortable for the tender-skinned but can become unpleasantly warm in hot weather.

Wither pads and saddlecloths

A wither pad can be used as a temporary measure, should a saddle have become too low in front, when there is a danger of the front arch bearing on the withers. It is therefore a useful tack room item. A wither pad may be made of foam plastic, an oval piece of sheepskin, or of a similar substitute. The best ones, however, are knitted from wool; these are far more satisfactory in use, being exceptionally soft and resilient.

Wither pads are nearly always used with the very light race saddles which would otherwise, because of their construction, bear down on the wither.

The purpose of a saddlecloth, other than for pure decoration, is to keep the panel of the saddle clean and free from the sweat deposits which would otherwise occur during use.

Left and inset: A selection of numnahs in various materials, from **left to right:** felt, cotton quilted, foam filled cotton, synthetic fur and real sheep wool. Numnahs, which are shaped to fit the saddle and are worn between the back and the saddle for greater comfort. **Top:** A sheepskin seat cover fitted over the saddle top provides comfort for riders with sensitive skins. **Above:** A waterproof saddle cover, a useful item for protecting the saddle against rain or damage.

CHAPTER THREE · THE TWENTIETH-CENTURY SADDLE

The Saddle · Fitting

The saddle lies on the horse's back behind the big muscle of the shoulder, the panel bearing on the blocks of muscle on either side of the spine. In order that the horse should be entirely comfortable and able to move and to jump without any restriction being imposed by the saddle, it is vital that the various key points concerning fitting are observed.

The importance of the saddle fitting correctly cannot be over-stressed. A badly fitting saddle, which pinches the horse or interferes with the movement of the back by pressing on the spine, detracts from the free movement of the limbs and can even cause the horse to move so unevenly as to appear lame. It will also prevent the horse from using himself fully over fences and, in extreme cases, may result in the animal refusing to jump at all. A saddle that distributes the weight of the rider unevenly, concentrating the pressure over one particular area, acts to unbalance the horse in movement. To compensate for this, the animal will become very stiff on one side of the body and the regularity and smoothness of the paces will be affected. In all cases the horse is likely to sustain injury to the back which will incapacitate him for normal working purposes.

The rules of fitting

The general rules of saddle fitting are as follows. In the first instance, the tree must fit the horse's back. It follows from this that, when the saddle is made up and as long as the panel is properly fitted, the completed article will be a correspondingly good fit. Too narrow a tree will cause the points to pinch the horse below and on either side of the withers. This cannot be changed by alteration, for it is rarely satisfactory to attempt widening the tree. Too broad a tree will mean that the fore arch will bear directly on the withers. To put more stuffing in the panel in an attempt to rectify this, puts the saddle out of balance and is more than likely to cause soreness.

The completed saddle must sit on the back so that when the rider is in position there is adequate clearance of the withers at the fore arch (it should be possible to insert three fingers); the saddle should at no point touch the backbone along the whole of its length; the channel dividing the panel must be wide enough to ensure that the weight is borne on either side of the spine and no pinching of the latter is

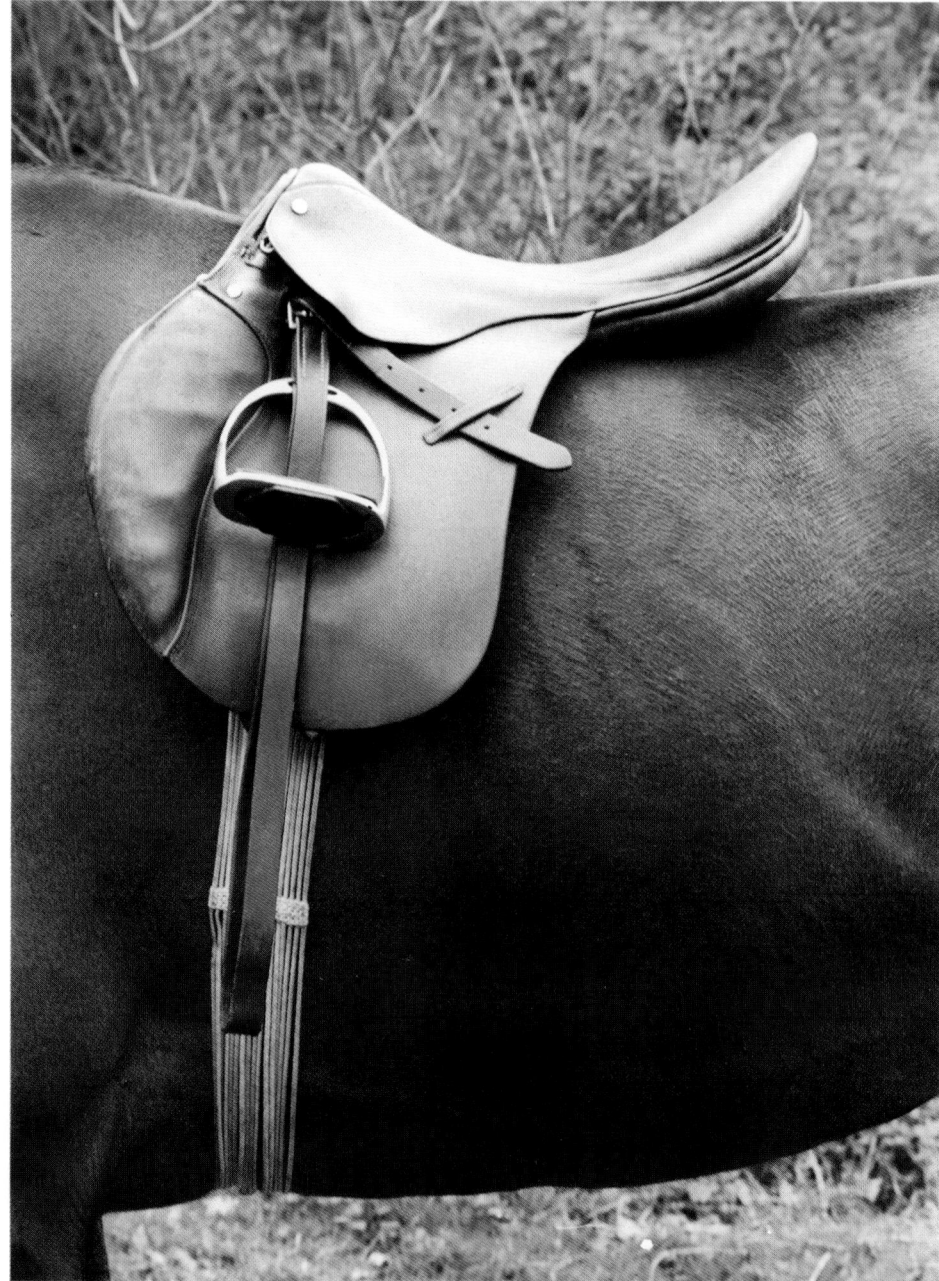

possible. If the channel is too narrow or becomes closed, pinching of the spinal vertebrae will occur. When viewed directly from behind with the rider in position, it should be possible to see daylight at the fore arch end of the channel.

The saddle must sit level on the back so that the weight of the rider is distributed evenly over the entire bearing surface of the panel. If the saddle is stuffed too high at the cantle, it will throw the rider forward, concentrating the pressure over the forepart of the saddle and thus creating the risk of a sore back developing. Similarly a saddle which is too high at the front throws the rider's weight to the rear. An unevenly stuffed panel will put the weight more upon one side than the other; this will also occur should the tree of the saddle be slightly twisted.

In all these instances, the concentration of weight over one part of the back is likely to cause soreness and all will affect the free movement of the horse. When viewed from behind it is very easy to see whether or not the saddle is sitting level and true.

The saddle must not be cut so far forward as to interfere with the action of the

Left: A modern saddle sitting level on the back but allowing clearance along the length of the backbone.

It is necessary for the saddle to lie level on the back so that the weight of the rider is distributed evenly over the whole bearing surface and points of pressure are avoided.

It is just as important for the cantle to be well clear of the back as it is for the head to have adequate clearance of the withers.

It should be possible to insert three fingers between the withers and the top of the front arch.

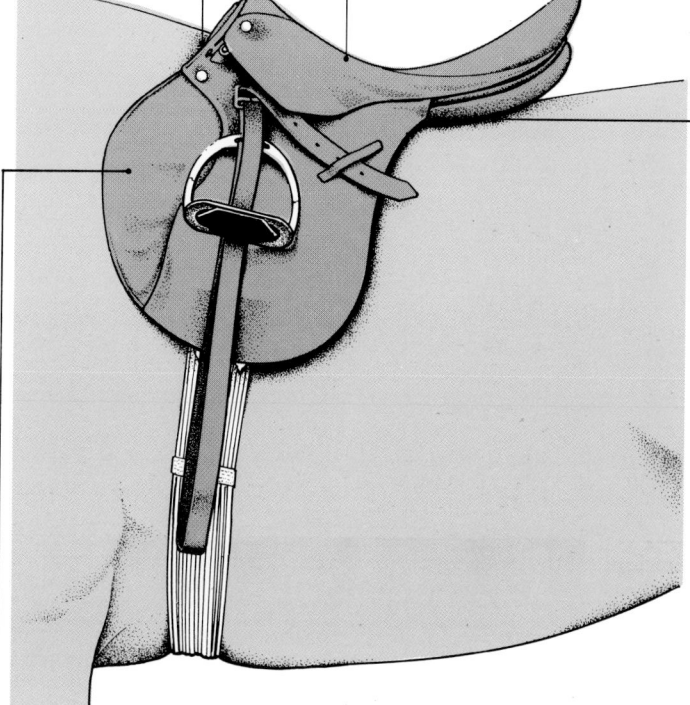

Panels must be level, clean and free from irregularities which might cause points of pressure and result in galling.

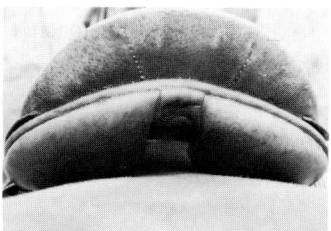

The forward inclination of the panel and the flap should not be such as to obscure the shoulder or interfere with its free movement. The saddle should at all times lie behind the shoulder, whatever the shape of the latter.

The channel has to be sufficiently wide to give clearance to the width of the backbone, and the panels must be stuffed sufficiently so that it is possible to look through the channel from back to front.

shoulder, while the panel must be clean, resilient and free of all irregularities. A lump on the panel creates a pressure point on the back which will cause soreness.

Whilst conforming to all these points the saddle should fit as closely as possible so that there is no chance of it rocking and causing soreness by friction. An overstuffed panel holding the saddle too high will cause this type of problem.

It is also important that the length of the saddle relates to the length of the back and the size of the rider. Short-backed horses and the back structures of many Arabians will prohibit the use of saddles that are, say, 17½in or 18in long. As far as the rider is concerned, it is a matter of the plate being big enough for the joint. Too small a saddle, coupled with an overlarge and overlapping posterior, will result in too great a concentration of weight over too small an area.

The problem of fatness

It is never advisable to fit a saddle to a fat horse, for what fits him when he is in gross condition will gall him when he is fit. Fat ponies will hold a saddle in place better if a point strap is fitted, as in a show saddle, plus a girth fitted with a centre of pimple rubber, which lies in the sternum curve (or where, in the case of ponies, the curve should be).

The problem can often be overcome by keeping the pony in a body roller. This, like a corset, is to encourage a better configuration.

Saddles with stuffed panels require, when new, to be regulated some three months after purchase if the use has been normal, and thereafter should be serviced once a year.

90

CHAPTER FOUR

Specialist Saddles

Western Saddles
Racing Equipment
Side-Saddles

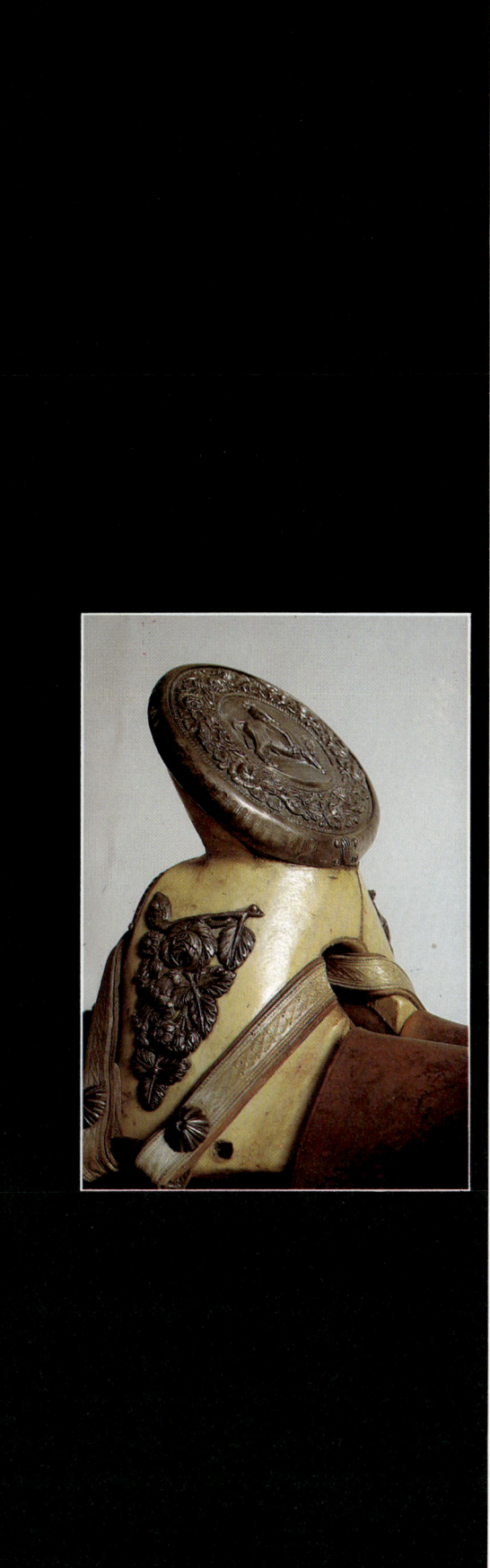

The Western saddle presented by Buffalo Bill Cody to King Edward VII when he was Prince of Wales. The horn is decorated with a silver relief of Buffalo Bill riding a bucking steer.

CHAPTER FOUR · SPECIALIST SADDLES

Specialist Saddles · **Western**

Just as the Spanish horses brought to the Americas by the 16th century *conquistadores* form the base of North American horse culture, so the Spaniards' saddle and bridle form the basis of Western riding equipment. The saddles used by the *conquistadores* were an amalgam of European and Moorish styles and had been evolved to suit the needs of the horseman in battle. Most important of those was the rider's security, both when wielding his own weapons and receiving blows from those of his adversaries. It was to provide maximum security that the saddle of that period was equipped with a very high pommel and cantle which, together with the metal armour which encased his legs, obliged the soldier to ride with a long stirrup and with his legs straight. The saddle sat high on the horse's back and the seat sloped steeply downwards from pommel to cantle so that the rider's weight was forced to the rear of the saddle.

This was the saddle inherited by the Mexicans, who became the west's first cattle ranchers in the southern states of North America. When cattle ranching became big business, it was natural enough that the saddlery already in use should form the basis of the cowboy's equipment. He needed a saddle which would fit any shape and size of horse—the cowpuncher worked on the *remuda* system, keeping a number of horses which he worked in rotation—and in this respect the high Mexican saddle served him well enough.

The cowboy saddle

The cattle ranching industry of the brief 'cattle kingdom' period that followed the US Civil War was of a different type from that practised by the Mexican *vaqueros*. Cattle were herded hundreds of miles from the southern plains where they were raised to the rail terminals which served the fast-growing towns of the northern states. Cowboys spent such long periods of time in the saddle that comfort also became a very important prerequisite and

This diagram shows the parts of the Western saddle

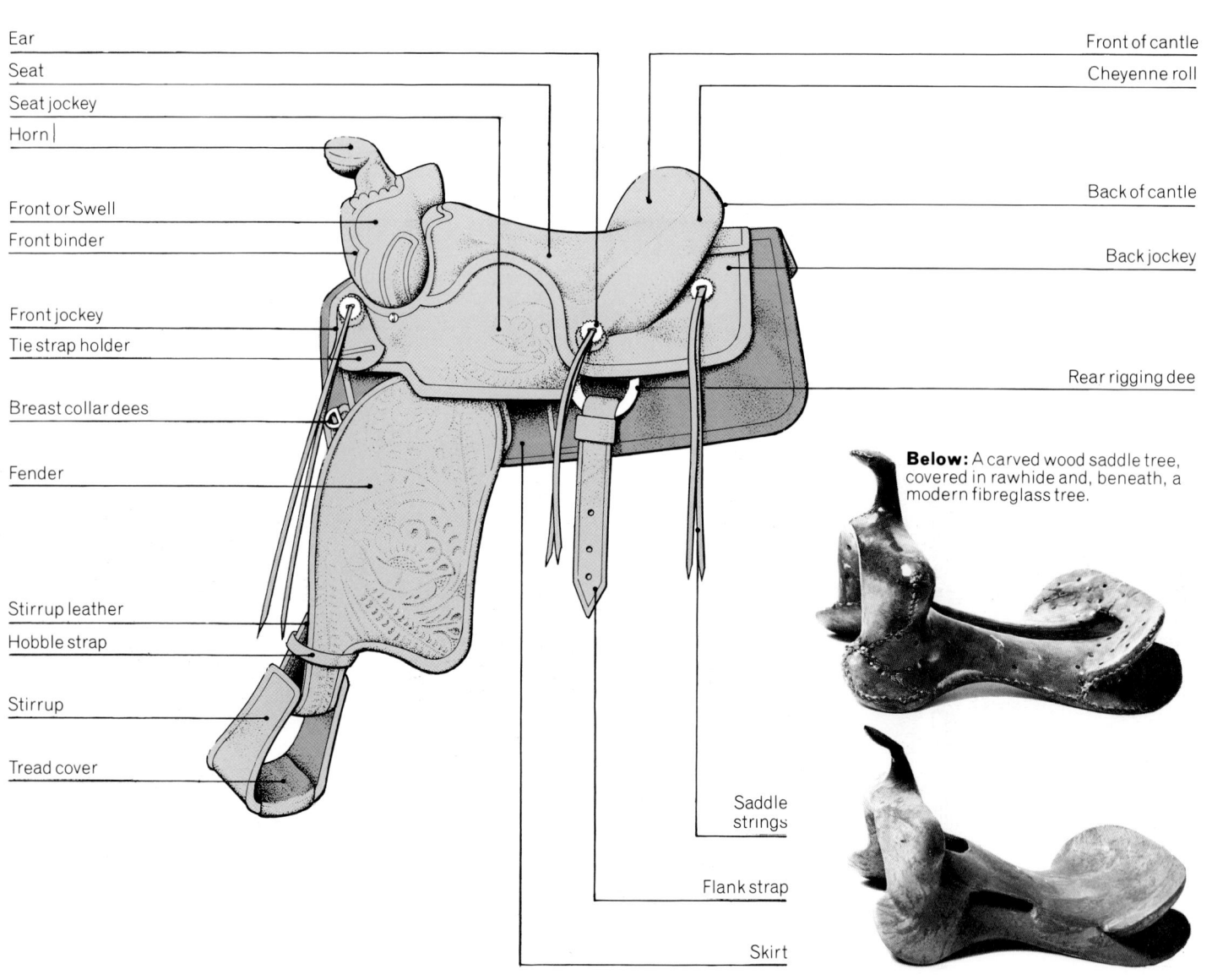

Below: A carved wood saddle tree, covered in rawhide and, beneath, a modern fibreglass tree.

WESTERN SADDLES

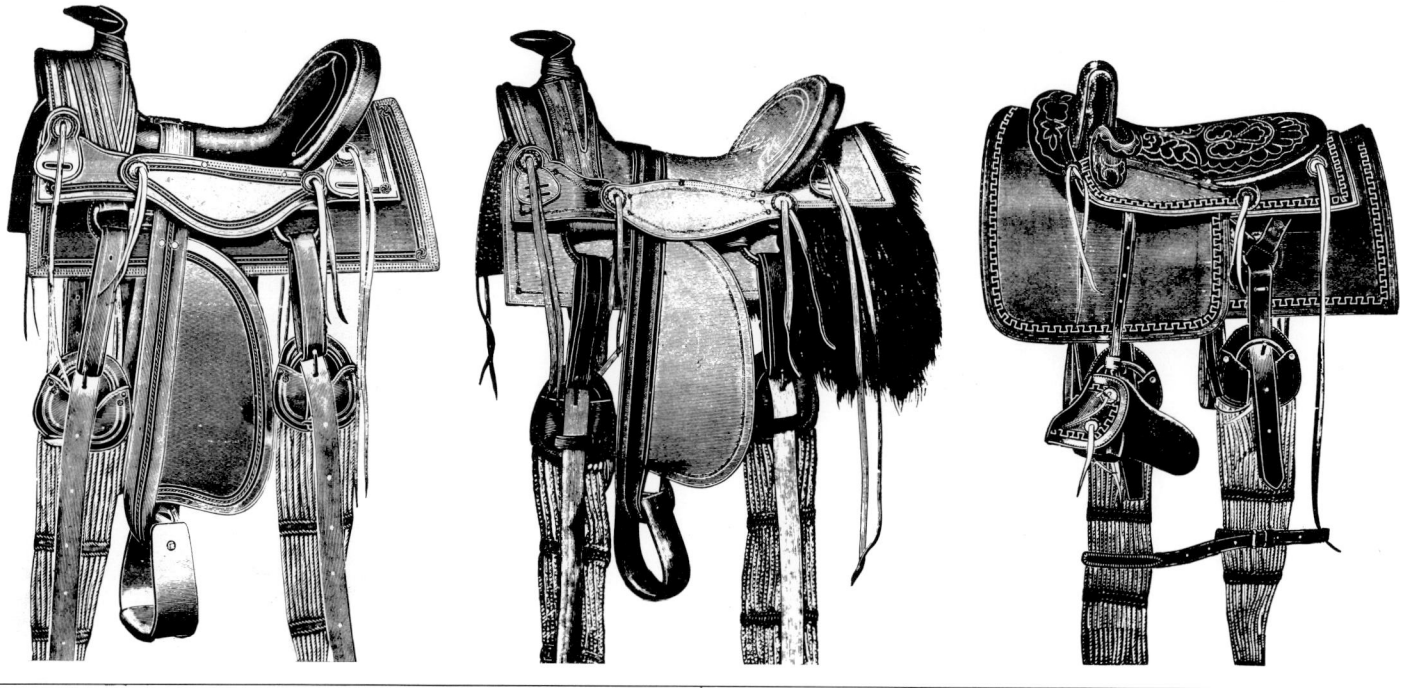

Left: A working cowboy of a century ago. His clothes are as practical as his saddlery: the broad-brimmed hat gives shade from the sun; the kerchief can be pulled up over the face in dusty conditions; the gloves protect his hands from rope burns; the chaps protect the legs from cactus cuts and keep out bad weather and the spurs, worn on strong, high-heeled boots, jangle as the horse moves and warn the cattle of the rider's approach. The saddle accommodates all his necessary possessions and affords a comfortable seat during long working hours. **Below, left:** A Great Plains saddle of the late 1800s. Saddle patterns varied from one territory to another and it was possible to tell a man's origin from his 'rig'. **Centre:** A similar saddle of the same period but with regional differences, for example the cinch fastening and connecting strap. **Right:** A skillfully-designed side-saddle, probably made in the early 1900s and certainly of Mexican origin.

CHAPTER FOUR · SPECIALIST SADDLES

various improvements were made to the Mexican-style saddle to prevent chafing and soreness of the seat and legs. The horse, too, had to be considered in this context, for he was the cowboy's lifeline. The saddle developed specifically for ranch work was a heavy item, weighing as much as 40 to 50lb. It was, however, so designed that this weight was spread over a large area of the horse's back, thus reducing the likelihood of saddle sores developing. To help achieve this, the skirts of the saddle were considerably enlarged. Further protection was afforded to the horse by the use of a thick blanket which was folded several times and placed under the saddle. This blanket had the added advantage of doubling as a bed roll for the cowboy, who often had to sleep rough in the open air and in all weathers for nights on end.

As well as enlarging the skirts, the pioneers of Western riding introduced fenders, which are, in effect, a much enlarged version of the narrow stirrup leathers used on the old Mexican saddles. The fender is a wide piece of stout leather which affords the rider's leg considerable protection, preventing sweat from the horse's sides from soaking into his clothes and also minimizing the risk of chafing. Stirrups were attached to the bottom of the fenders; the stiffness of the latter ensured that the stirrups themselves moved very little, a great advantage to the cowboy who often needed to mount in a hurry.

The cowboy's stirrups were made of wood, covered with rawhide. This was a much more satisfactory arrangement than metal, since the latter could be extremely cold on the feet in winter while becoming unbearably hot under the blazing summer sun. Stirrups were made with varying widths of sole supports and were heavy items of equipment. To protect his feet when riding in rough scrub country, the cowboy adopted the stirrup covers used by the Mexicans and known as *tapaderos*. These looked like boxes and were made of tough leather. The cowboy called them 'taps'. In cold weather they could be lined with fleece to give extra protection to the feet. Californian cowboys developed their own distinctive design.

The other major modifications which the Mexican saddle underwent were directly influenced by one particular aspect of the cowboy's work—roping. When he wanted to separate a steer from the herd, he did so by lassooing it. The cowboy secured his end of the lasso to the front of the saddle which had to take the strain when the roped animal struggled against the restricting rope. For this purpose the cowboy added a horn, shaped like an inverted Y, to the high pommelled Mexican saddle. The front arch of the saddle was strengthened with steel and widened to ensure complete clearance of the withers. The heavy shoulders, known as 'swells', thus created at the front of the saddle added to the rider's security by supporting the thighs.

The horn itself served the desired purpose satisfactorily. However, the enormous strain put on the saddle when the rope linking a calf to the horn was suddenly pulled taut caused the saddle to be

Left: A very rare example of an early Mexican-style saddle built before the advent of the dish horn. This saddle is a collector's piece and the inset shows the high quality embossed decoration. **Right:** A relatively lightweight saddle made on a carved wooden tree with laced-on seat covering.

CHAPTER FOUR · SPECIALIST SADDLES

Far left: Putting the Western saddle over a carefully folded blanket and attaching the cinch. **Left:** Detail of the way in which the cinch is buckled or, in this case, tied. **Above:** Having secured the cinch it is necessary to pull each leg forward in turn in order to ensure that there are no wrinkles of skin below the elbow.

dragged forward, often causing painful cuts to the horse's shoulders and elbows. Indeed, it was not uncommon for the rider to be unseated, or for the tree of a saddle actually to break, when subjected to such rough usage.

Strengthening the cinches
The solution to the problem lay in the positioning of the cinches, the Western term for girths. Mexican saddles were single-rigged—that is, they were secured by one girth placed around the horse's belly, not far behind the elbows. Since the roping process caused the cantle to be pulled upwards and then the whole saddle to shift forwards, the obvious solution was to employ a second cinch, fitted behind the rider's leg.

Under normal riding conditions, it was the front or forward cinch which continued to hold the saddle in position, the rear or flank cinch being fastened fairly slackly. The latter came into play when pressure was exerted on the horn, preventing the saddle being pulled upwards and forwards. It is a system which was soon in common use throughout most of the ranching country of the west and is known as double-rigging or full-double rigging.

The forward cinch of a cowboy's saddle was usually made of mohair, horsehair or cord, the ends of which were woven on to large rings. Leather straps were used to secure these rings to the rigging rings attached to the saddle itself. The nearside strap, called the latigo strap, was wrapped several times around the cinch ring and finished with a knot. The flank cinch was made of leather and had a buckle stitched to each end. These buckles were fastened to straps attached to another pair of rigging rings fitted on each side of the rear of the saddle.

The one disadvantage that arose from the provision of a loosely fastened flank cinch was its tendency to swing backwards and forwards. This could cause galling, while, in the case of geldings or stallions, the cinch could hit and damage the horse's sheath. To prevent this, a connecting strap was fitted, linking the two cinches under the horse's body.

These, then, were the major modifications made to the original Spanish-based Mexican saddle by the cowboy of the west. In addition he added sets of strings, which he fitted to the near and offside saddle skirts. To these strings, the cowboy, who was virtually a nomad, attached his personal possessions. There was usually another set of strings fitted to the front of the saddle at the base of the pommel and also a latigo carrier.

The Californian variant
Although the pattern of saddle described above spread throughout the main cattle ranching areas of Texas, Arizona and New Mexico, there was one regional variation, which was directly related to a difference in terrain. In the far western cattle rearing areas of California the countryside was much more open than elsewhere and this led to the development of a type of roping somewhat different in nature.

The Texan cowboy's method of roping was to wrap the end of the rope round the horn several times and to hold it firm when it was tautened by the weight of the steer, thus jerking the latter to a sudden, violent stop. In California, on the other hand, the cowboy had more room to manoeuvre and would play with the steer in much the same way as an angler plays with a fish. He, too, wound his lasso around the saddle horn, but, when the steer began to tauten the rope, the cowboy would pay out a few feet or so by allowing some of the coils to unwind from the horn. By repeating this process he brought the calf to a gradual halt. As a result the saddle did not have to withstand such a strain

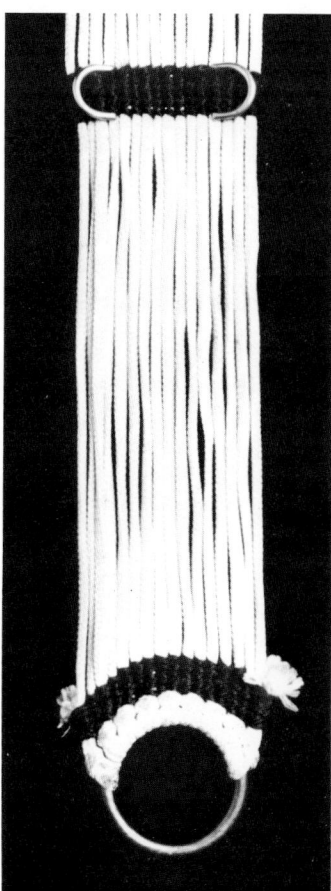
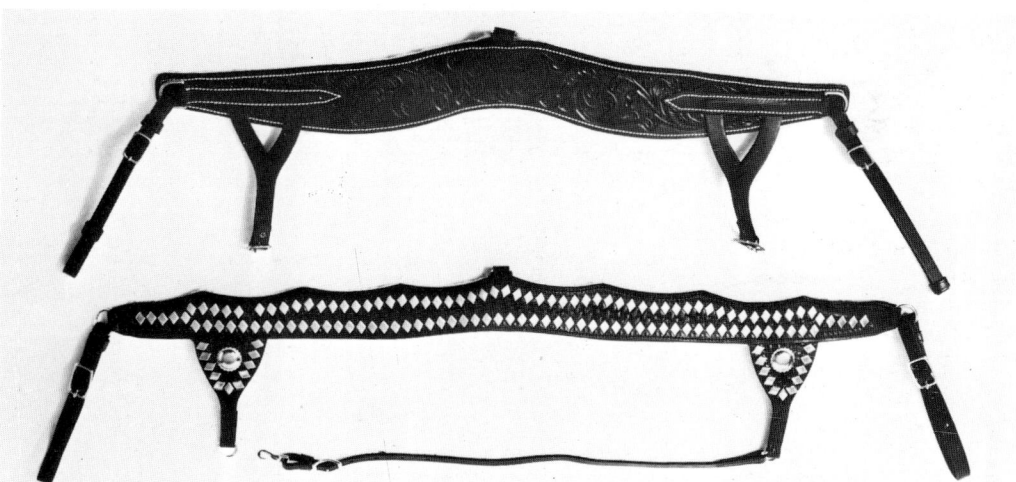
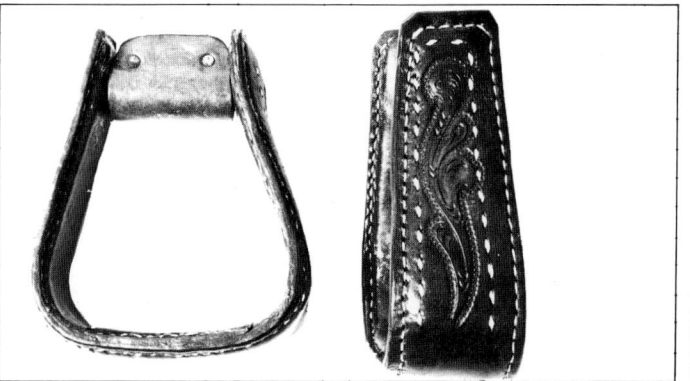

Left, top and bottom: Examples of woven hair and cord cinches, the former, in particular, giving a very firm, non-slip purchase. **Top:** A decorative Mexican saddle blanket which is as practical as it is colourful. **Above:** Two patterns of leather breastplate which again combine practicality with decorative effect. **Right:** The Western stirrup is made of willow wood shaped over wood and, in this instance, covered with leather.

CHAPTER FOUR · SPECIALIST SADDLES

and thus did not require the addition of a flank cinch. For many years, therefore, the Californian cowboy retained the single-rigging system of the Mexican saddle.

This type of roping became known as 'dallying', from the Spanish *de la vuelta* (to give a turn), and the cowboys who employed it were called dallymen. A disadvantage of their roping technique was its tendency to injure the hands—many dallymen apparently had the odd finger severed by means of a fast-moving rope.

One final item of equipment which was in general use, particularly in mountainous regions, was the breastplate, made of leather or cord and fastened to the rigging D rings situated at the front of the saddle. A strap, passed over the horse's withers, kept the breastplate in place; sometimes another strap was attached to the centre, passed between the forelegs and fastened to a D on the front of the forward cinch.

The McClellan saddle

While this modified version of the old Mexican saddle served the cowboy well for the duration of the ranching boom, another and quite different type of saddle was adopted by the US army. It hailed from Hungary and was taken to North America by an officer called McClellan, whose name it subsequently bore. Despite much criticism on account of its lack of comfort, it was used by the US cavalry until as late as 1940.

The earliest McClellan saddles did not have panels, so the rider's thighs were not protected from the risk of chafing against the horse's sweaty body. Soldiers are said

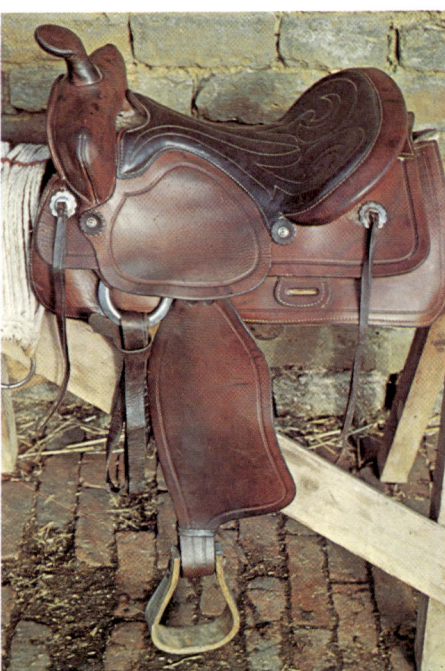

Above: Three-quarter size pleasure saddle with seven-eighth rigging and with the leather parts deeply engraved. It would be suitable for a teenager or a lightweight adult. **Top right:** Another teenager's saddle but with a cutting-type fork and plain wooden stirrups. **Right:** A lightweight pleasure saddle in position over a folded blanket.

Left: A lightweight barrel racing-type saddle with hand-tooled leatherwork and a padded seat. The wooden stirrups are sheathed in steel.

CHAPTER FOUR · SPECIALIST SADDLES

Left: An extravagantly-constructed Grand Parade saddle in black leather decorated with stainless steel studs. Elaborate saddles such as this are used in carnival and rodeo parades.
Above: Matching, similarly elaborate **tapaderos** or stirrup covers.

to have suffered a good deal from saddle sores before the advantage of panels was appreciated, although even then many saddles of the old type continued to be made. But, despite its drawbacks, the McClellan saddle had one advantage. It would fit any animal and did not, apparently, cause undue back troubles.

Modern changes
Some 20 years before the McClellan saddle finally sank into disuse, the cowboy's saddle began to undergo further modifications. As elsewhere in the world, the emphasis in riding had switched from work to pleasure. In the USA, trail riding, known in Europe as trekking, became popular, together with Western equitation show classes. While the existing saddle

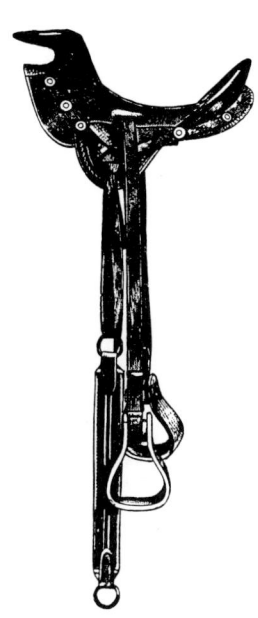

Below: A very well-constructed exercise or training saddle of the early 1900s. **Far right:** Its modern counterparts, pads made from fibreglass with the trees covered in fur fabric. **Right:** The strongest equipment is needed for the rough, tough sport of saddleback broncho riding.

was ideal in many respects for these sports—certainly its basic concept was what was required—it proved unnecessarily cumbersome for pleasure riding.

As a result the Western saddle as it exists today has a much smaller horn. In addition, this is sloped forwards, so as to eliminate any possibility of injury to the rider's midriff should he be pitched forward against it. Both cantle and pommel have been made lower and, while the excellent weight-distributing properties of the saddle have been retained, the saddle itself is now somewhat lighter. One of the reasons for this is that, unless the saddle is to be used for competitive calf roping, there is no necessity for it to be fitted with a heavily reinforced front arch. Such saddles, complete with a proper roping horn, are of course still made, but they are not necessary for the average pleasure rider.

Nor is the rear cinch absolutely essential and modern saddles have reverted to the old single-rigging system. This, however, has also undergone some modification, for a saddle secured solely with a cinch positioned so far forward that it is directly below the front arch (as was the Spanish system) lies on the horse's back in such a way as to force the rider to sit well back towards the cantle and to adopt a position not altogether suited to modern equitation. In addition, the conformation of some horses is such that the cinch can cause chafing to their elbows.

Consequently, saddles are made with a variety of cinch positions. The opposite extreme to the Spanish style of single-rigging is when the cinch is placed absolutely centrally between pommel and cantle. This is called centre-fire rigging (a term which derives from a gun cartridge in which the firing pin strikes the centre of the primer). Between Spanish and centre-fire rigging, there are alternative positions known as ⅞, ¾, or ⅝ rigging. Which system is favoured depends very much on the conformation of the individual horse and the purpose for which the saddle is to be used.

Unless they are to be used for roping contests, most modern double-rigged saddles are fitted with 'in-skirt' rigging for the back cinch. In other words, the rear rigging rings have been replaced by leather straps attached directly to the saddle. This arrangement, while not strong enough to withstand the strain of cattle roping, is adequate for other types of Western riding. It has the advantage of being less bulky and therefore more comfortable for the rider's leg, which also has closer contact with the horse's sides as a result. In some saddles the front rigging rings have also been eliminated to reduce the bulk still further.

The concept of the forward seat has also had a certain amount of influence on the Western saddle. Today the seat of the latter does not slope as steeply backwards as it did in the past, while the stirrup is placed further back, nearer to the centre of

CHAPTER FOUR · SPECIALIST SADDLES

Left: A typical Californian-type saddle of modern design. The deep seat, prominent horn and distinctive **tapaderos** are typical features.
Right: A deep-seat cutting saddle, silver-laced on the skirt and with Cheyenne roll and swell. The horn is covered with a laced raw-hide strip.

the saddle, than formerly. As a result the rider does not sit so far back. The leg is not as straight, nor is the foot pushed forward so exaggeratedly, as was the case with the old-time cowboys.

The lighter tree, lighter leathers and elimination of rigging rings for the back cinch mean that the modern Western saddle weighs around 30lb, a considerable improvement on its predecessor. Many modern saddles are elaborately tooled, stamped or engraved and decorated.

Broncho busting
A final variation on the Western saddle is the model developed for broncho busting, which derives from the cowboy's method of breaking in wild horses. Nowadays it is a popular sport, not a necessity, and the bucking horses are as professional as the competing riders with their eyes on the prize money. Saddles must conform to the rules laid down by the governing body of the sport, the Rodeo Cowboys' Association, and come in two types, the bronc saddle and the bareback rig.

The former is much like a normal Western saddle, but the exact dimensions such as the size of the tree and the height of the cantle, must be adhered to by all competitors. The bareback rig is little more than a piece of sturdy leather, with no seat or cantle, secured to the horse's back by means of centre-fire rigging. The rider is provided with stirrups and a leather handhold at the front, but otherwise the rig provides little security.

WESTERN SADDLES

CHAPTER FOUR · SPECIALIST SADDLES

Specialist Saddles · Racing Equipment

The making of racing equipment—in particular race saddles—is usually confined to specialist firms operating in the main racing areas. Apart from exercising tack for race purposes, it is not usually the province of wholesale saddlers.

Racing saddles for flat racing can be as light as 12oz when they are made and will weigh only a little over 1lb when mounted with girths, leathers and irons. Steeplechasing saddles are naturally bigger and heavier, but a 4lb or 5lb saddle is not unusual.

The lightest racing saddles are, indeed, little more than a convenient point of attachment for the stirrup leathers and irons. In common with conventional saddles, they can be made on a wooden tree or—a practice which is now increasingly

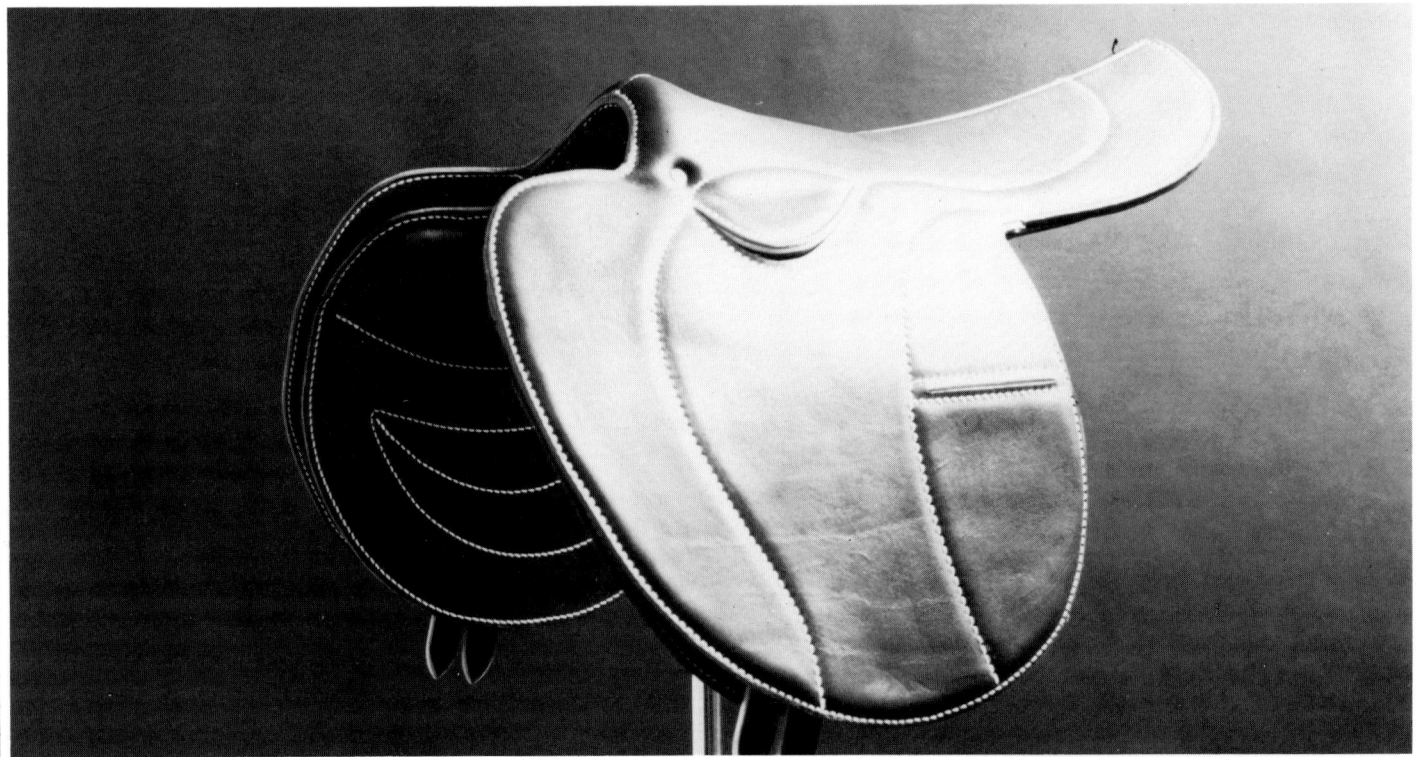

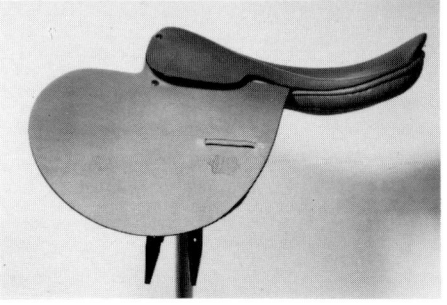

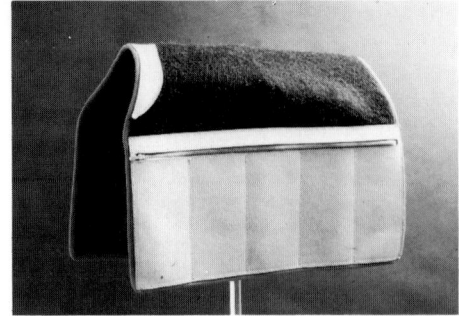

Top left: A race exercise saddle popular in America which could also be used for racing itself where weight requirements permitted. **Top right:** The half tree on which the race exercise pads are built and, underneath, a conventional racing tree without, of course, stirrup bars. **Above:** A flexible exercise pad, built on a half tree. **Right:** A heavier pattern race exercise saddle used extensively in Europe. **Far right:** A weight cloth, which might also be used for show jumping or eventing as well as for racing.

A contrast in styles. **Right:** A Vanity Fair cartoon of the American jockey Tod Sloan (1874-1933) who introduced the short-leather, crouching style into Europe in 1897. **Above:** The classic long-leg style favoured by jockeys before the adoption of the short leather. This picture is of Fred Archer, for many years English champion jockey, riding Iroquois, winner of the 1881 Derby.

frequent—on one made from fibreglass. Fibreglass has been used for riding saddles, as well as other forms of plastic, but it is only in the racing saddle that this material has been completely successful. Very light leathers, either pigskin or calfskin, are used, while the panels are no more than a thin layer of fine wool covered in silk. There are no stirrup bars; not only would these increase the weight but in view of the size of the tree, they would be impractical in any case. In fact, the stirrup leathers are passed round the tree on either side, a practice also frequently followed with the heavier saddles.

Design and fitting
Racing saddles are not made for sitting in and the seat is therefore almost flat. The flaps, however, are cut well forward to allow for the very short stirrup leather used, although in flat racing jockeys frequently ride so short that the knees are above the saddle and not in contact with it at all.

Steeplechasing saddles follow the same pattern, but are obviously more robust. It is important that they, too, are fairly flat in the seat. A conventional cantle is a very uncomfortable thing to land on should the jockey get even slightly 'left behind' at a fence. Probably the best 'chasing saddles were the Australian Boscas, made of kangaroo hide, and they still are much sought after.

The fitting of racing saddles, other than the heavier ones, differs completely from normal practice and principles. Most are used with a wither pad under the front arch and, since the weight is carried only for a very short time and then for the most part on the stirrup leathers, fitting in the conventional sense is of no consequence.

Saddles used in racing stables for exercising must naturally be much stronger in order to withstand the hard usage involved. These exercise saddles are made, therefore, on a stout, rigid tree, which has a little more of the conventional dip to the seat. The flaps are cut forward, so that the rider may ride with short leathers, and the panel is a 'full' one, following the shape of the flaps, and often, but not always, lined with serge. The American pattern race exercise saddle is a rather neater affair; it is nearly always leather lined.

Another form of race exercise saddle, sometimes used also for 'chasing, is that which is built on a 'half' tree. The tree is just the front arch, plus a sufficient length of arm on which the bars can be fitted. The seat and flaps are then made as one, as a sort of pad, with the leather panel built in beneath. This is a practical type of saddle, the absence of a tree being a definite advantage in a racing yard, where saddles are frequently treated with insufficient care and where, as a result, saddle trees are frequently broken.

Changing styles
Up to the early 1900s, racing saddles were made with very much straighter flaps. The reason for this was that jockeys up to that time rode with a long leg, much as they would have done in the hunting field, and sat in the saddle when riding a finish. The forward cut saddle, together with the practice of riding short, came about largely through the crouching style adopted by the American jockey Tod Sloan (1874–1933). He introduced the practice to England in 1897 and may have had some influence upon the theories expounded by Caprilli. The race saddle, as it exists today, conforms very closely to the Caprilli requirements in that it positions the jockey's body weight well forward and over the centre of balance of the horse.

For the most part the aim of all racing equipment is to achieve the maximum lightness possible, but there are exceptions to this general principle. These occur particularly in point-to-point racing where the stipulated weights the horses must carry may well be above the riding weight of the jockeys.

In order to make up the weight required a jockey can either use a heavy, and sometimes deliberately weighted, saddle, or the extra weight can be carried in the form of lead pieces inserted into the pockets of a weight cloth.

The guiding principle about carrying dead weight is to see that it is placed as far forward, and as near therefore to the centre of balance, as is possible. Weighted saddles are made by inserting lead into the tree itself. Every effort is made to keep the weight toward the front, although, in the case of a saddle weighing as much as 32lb, the lead would have to be introduced throughout the length of the tree and round the cantle as well.

CHAPTER FOUR · SPECIALIST SADDLES

Specialist Saddles · **Side-Saddles**

The origin of the side-saddle goes back 600 years, to the European courts of the 14th century. Anne of Bohemia, wife of Richard II, brought the fashion to England, for example, and soon ladies who had previously only ridden pillion behind a man—or, in some cases, astride in a split skirt—began to adopt the new fashion. The saddles at that time were little more than stuffed platforms, the rider sitting at a complete right angle to her horse's spine, with her feet resting on a platform called a *planchette*.

The rider would have had very little control over her horse in this position, and so the saddles soon acquired a pommel in front, over which the rider could hook one knee, which enabled her to face the way she was going. It is difficult to date the development of the pommel accurately, but it is known that Catherine de Medici invented a second pommel in about 1580. Both were still positioned on top of the saddle, the rider wedging her knee between them to gain a little more security.

Examples of these early saddles still survive in the Hermes collection in Paris. Another interesting feature is that the seats were level from back to front, with no sign of the dipped seat which was prevalent in the middle of the last century.

Improvements of the 1800s

A manual on riding for ladies published in 1826 shows a level-seated saddle, little changed from those used over 200 years previously, but by 1860 the dipped seat had been introduced. This may have been in an attempt to get the rider a little closer to her horse, for at that time the 'cut-back' head, which allows the horse's withers to rise through the front of the saddle had not been invented. If the seat was to be level, the whole saddle had to be much higher on the horse's back, and would, therefore, be more prone to slipping. A design of this sort was likely to give the horse a sore back, because of the friction arising from the lateral movement of the saddle and there was, additionally, a very real danger

Below: An elaborate and very beautifully worked saddle of the 19th century which has the characteristic deep seat of the period. **Bottom:** Detail of the tapestry used to cover the seat. **Right:** Up to the 14th century ladies either rode pillion behind a man or astride in a long split skirt in the manner of the equestrienne on the left of the pair.

CHAPTER FOUR · SPECIALIST SADDLES

of the rider being deposited on the ground. As a counter to the poor fit of the saddle grooms would often girth up so tightly that the horse had trouble breathing, or would even try to roll to get rid of its burden. Then some anonymous genius invented the balance strap. This first appears in drawings in the 1820s, when it was connected to the stirrup leather. In its modern form, however, it goes from the nearside front of the saddle to the offside rear, a balance being effected by pressures on opposite corners of the saddle. Some riders prefer a short balance strap sewn to the girth instead of buckling independently to the saddle—but this is a matter of taste since both types are effective.

The most important invention in the history of the side-saddle came in 1830, when a French riding master, Jules Pellier, invented the 'leaping head'—a pommel screwed into the saddle and curving over the rider's left thigh. It was this invention which gave the side-saddle its reputation for safety and security. Without a leaping head only the most intrepid rider would dare to jump, for if the horse chose to play up she had little chance of staying mounted. With it, any of the movements which might pitch the astride rider over the horse's shoulder, serve merely to strengthen the side-saddle rider's seat, as her thigh slides firmly into its support. It must have a left-handed thread to its screw, or it will loosen when the rider jams her leg against it when employing the emergency grip to retain her seat.

Changes dictated by fashion

By the 1860s, most saddles had three pommels—the two either side of the right knee, plus the leaping head—but the pommel on the extreme right was already becoming smaller. By the mid1870s it had almost disappeared and the side-saddle rider was equipped to enter the hunting field. Before then, while ladies might ride to the meet to see their menfolk off, it was not considered respectable actually to follow hounds. Then, in 1876, the Empress Elizabeth of Austria came to England to hunt and fashionable ladies followed her lead, taking to the hunting field with great enthusiasm. They soon began to give

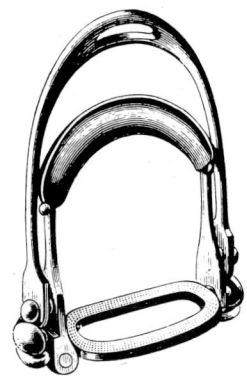
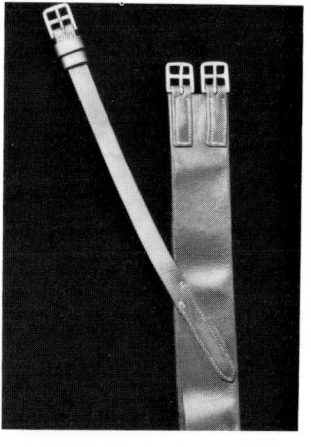
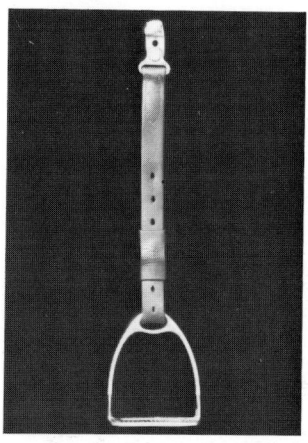
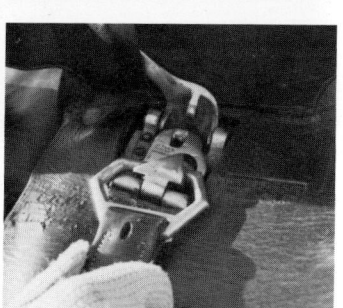

Opposite: J.F. Herring's picture of a pair of Queen Victoria's hacks. The saddles are fitted with two pommels but have no leaping heads. **Above left:** The balance strap, which obviates the danger of the saddle slipping round, was invented in the 1800s. **Left:** The ultimate safety device was the quick release which allowed both stirrup and leather to come away. **Top:** 'Safety' stirrups previously in general use. **Above, left:** The short balance strap sewn to the girth. **Right:** A modern leather with a hook for adjusting the length.

more thought to their saddles, for what was tolerably comfortable during a gentle ride was not necessarily suitable for a hard day in the hunting field.

The first casualty was the dipped seat. With this the rider had to sit facing over the horse's shoulder and had to twist at the waist in order to face forwards. A posture of this sort quickly becomes tiring, if not actually painful; at one time it was thought necessary to ride on different sides on alternate days in order to avoid a curvature of the spine. With the introduction of the cut-back head, however, saddles reverted to the level seat, so the rider was again able to ride on her right thigh, instead of her bottom, and face forward. She could then see where she was going, control her horse with both hands and jump safely.

The only problem remaining was what happened if the rider was to fall. Provided the skirt did not become entangled round the pommel (this problem was soon solved by the development of the apron skirt), the main worry was to ensure that the foot came free of the stirrup so that the rider was not dragged. A whole series of patent 'safety' stirrups were invented. These were mostly irons that broke open in various ways to release the foot, but they depended on the foot being placed in them the right way round, and they were not totally successful. The problem was finally solved by quick-release devices at the top of the stirrup leather, which allowed the stirrup *plus* the leather to come off the saddle.

The heyday of the side-saddle
The great heyday of side-saddle riding was between 1890 and 1930 and during this time the level seat became almost universal. Additionally, the doeskin seat, which gave greater purchase to the rider, became increasingly popular. The pommels were made wider and were better padded, while the leaping head altered its position and angle of rake as riders realized the advantages of a more forward seat for jumping.

The great side-saddle *marques*, like Owen, Mayhew, Whippy and Champion and Wilton became established and these are the makes still sought by connoisseurs.

CHAPTER FOUR · SPECIALIST SADDLES

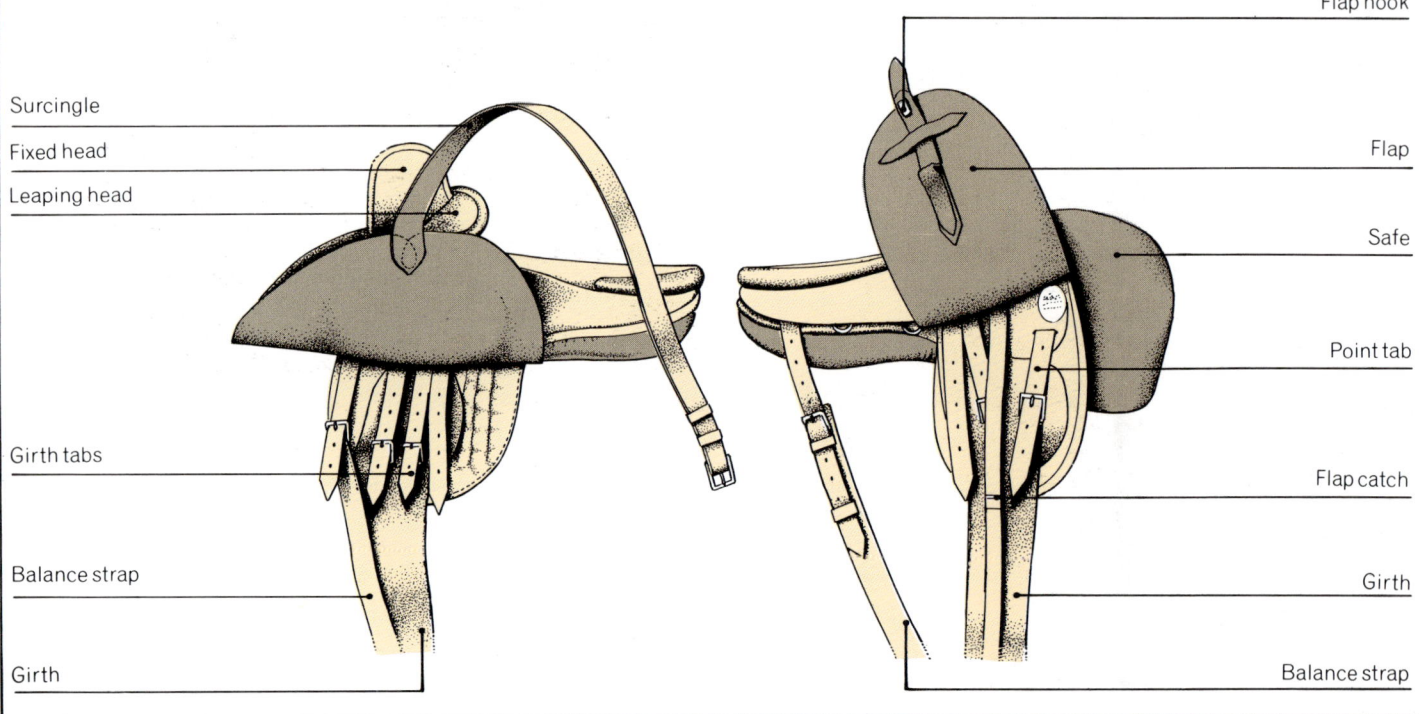

- Surcingle
- Fixed head
- Leaping head
- Girth tabs
- Balance strap
- Girth
- Flap hook
- Flap
- Safe
- Point tab
- Flap catch
- Girth
- Balance strap

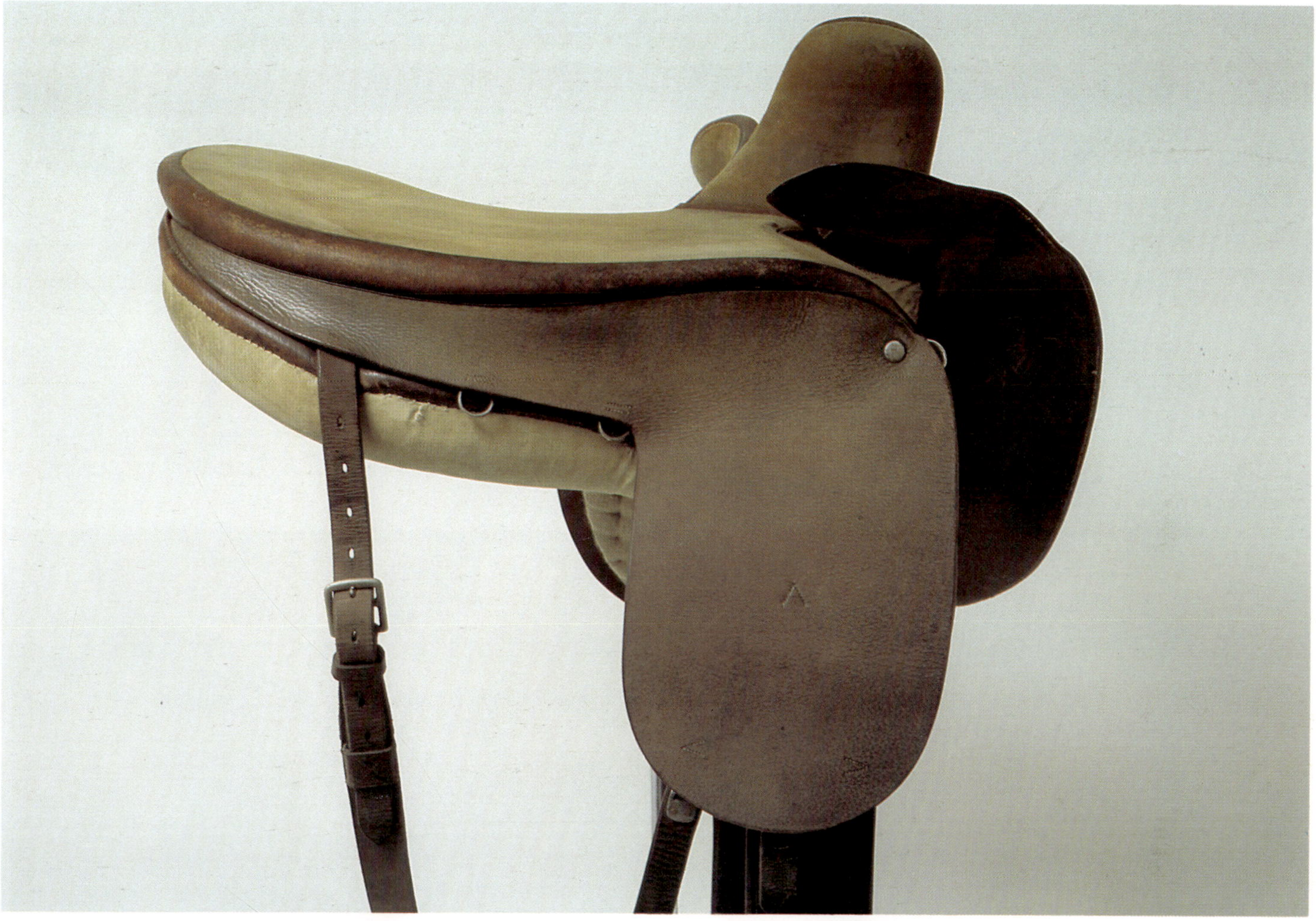

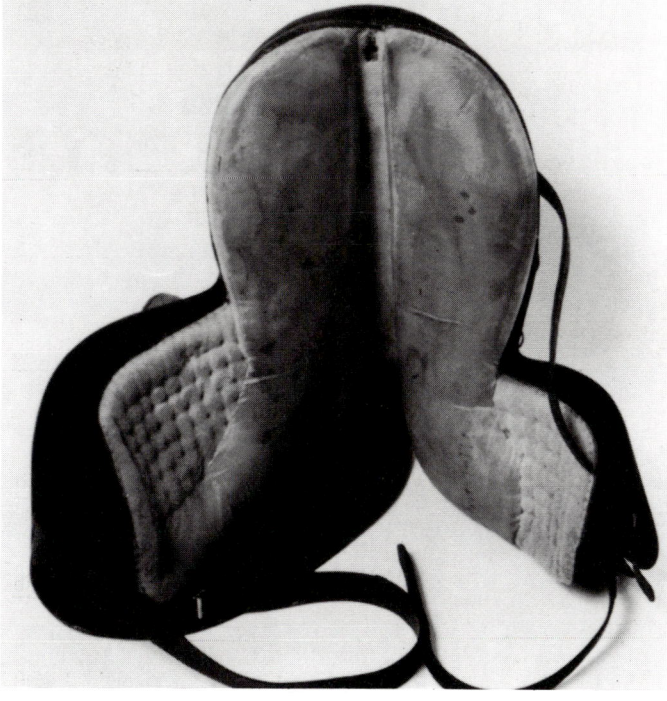

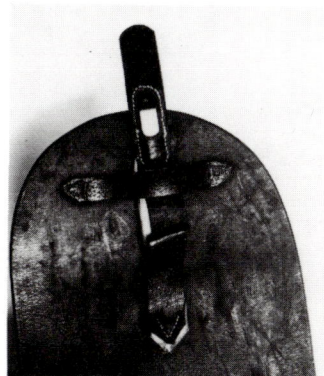

Opposite top and top: Near and offside views of a side-saddle. **Diagram opposite:** On the near side, the balance strap is on the front tab. Putting it on the back one is a common beginner's mistake and allows the girth to slip back. Note, on the offside, the girth buckled to the point tab, which helps to keep the point of the saddle down. **Left:** The lining, with linen overlining on the bearing surfaces and spot stitching on the points. **Above, left:** Detail of the doeskin and cut-back head. **Right:** Underside of flap, showing the hook for holding down the flap strap.

CHAPTER FOUR · SPECIALIST SADDLES

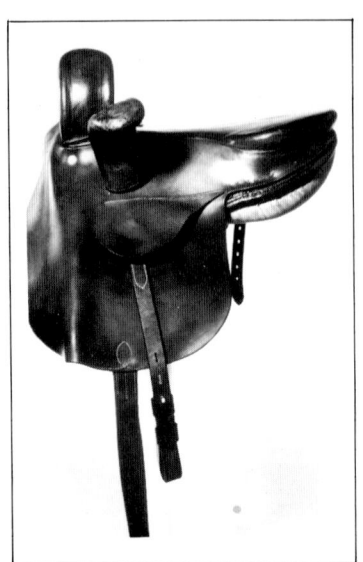

Left: A saddle made in about 1900. The large offside flap is characteristic of the period as are thin pommels and the notably dipped leather seat. It would not be suitable for a modern side-saddle rider. **Right:** A saddle made in Walsall between the wars. Although the quality was good, Walsall never really mastered the art of side-saddle manufacture, which remains the prerogative of the London houses. **Below left:** A saddle made by Owen of London in about 1920. The pommels are much narrower than in later models. **Below:** A very good model of a modern Owen, with the larger pommels shaped to accommodate the active rider and to position her securely and in balance.

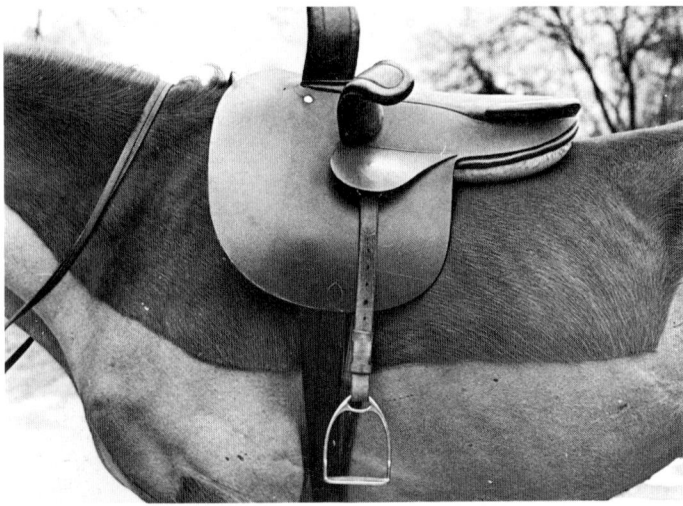
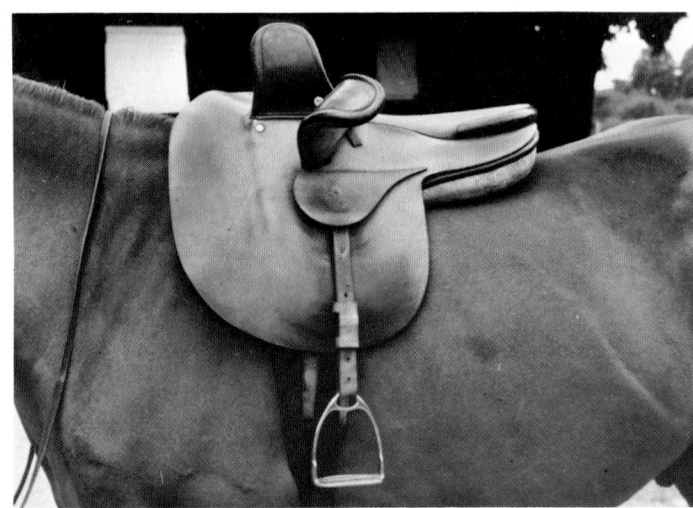

As well as excellent workmanship and good design in respect of the position and shaping of the pommel, they have the essential virtue of balance. It is noticeable that the seats of these saddles, if looked at from the rear, are deeper on the left side than the right. This is particularly evident in the case of the Owen saddles. The important point is that this extra depth is built into the top of the saddle, and is not achieved by putting extra stuffing in the panel. Added to this, the seat at the back is shaped to tilt the rider on her right seat bone, thus counteracting the effect of her having both legs on one side, and balancing her weight evenly on both sides of the horse's back.

Made to measure

It is, of course, essential that the saddle should fit the rider, or she will never be able to ride correctly. The main considerations here are length and pommel position. Side-saddles are measured from the extreme rear of the cut-back head straight across the seat to the centre of the cantle; the desired length corresponds to that of the rider's thigh from behind the knee to the back of the buttock as she sits. As a rough guide, a rider of 5ft 6in will probably need a 16in saddle. It is, however, always better to ride in a saddle that is too long than too short, as in the last instance the rider's weight will push the rear of the saddle down on the horse's spine.

Pommel position is even more important than length. When ladies had saddles made to measure, the saddler took the size of the thighs into account and positioned the pommels accordingly. Thus, a saddle made for a full-legged lady has the fixed head well to the left of centre to allow for the extra thickness on the inside of the thigh. A slimmer-legged rider would never be able to sit in the centre of a saddle made in this fashion with her right thigh parallel to the horse's spine; she would also find that the leaping head had too wide a curve to hold her left thigh in an emergency. Conversely, a saddle made for a slim lady will have too tight a curve for a larger thigh, while the fixed head will be positioned too far to the right and probably too low for safety also. Fixed heads cannot be altered without making radical changes to the saddle; for this reason beginners are advised against buying side-saddles without advice from an experienced instructor.

Having ensured that the saddle fits the rider, it is also necessary for it to fit the horse. Providing the saddle has a medium-fitting tree and the horse has a good back, withers and shoulders, this is comparatively easy. Problems arise if the horse's shoulders are asymmetrical, or square with a low wither development. This sometimes occurs with the Arabian type of horse and with the stuffy, cobby types. For this reason it may not be possible to fit a side-saddle to such an animal with any guarantee of its remaining in place.

A properly-made saddle should be fitted to the horse who is going to wear it, and this cannot be done entirely in a workshop. The correct method is for the saddler to put the saddle on the horse and do up the girth and balance strap; he must then study it from the rear and from both sides to assess what needs to be done in the way of regulation. Having decided, the saddle is removed and wool stuffing inserted into the front through slits in the top of the panel near the tree points should this be necessary. Stuffing is introduced to the rear of the panel by slitting a few of the stitches that hold the lining material to the leather backing and inserting as much wool as may be required. The position of the saddle can then be checked again on the horse and with the rider up, further adjustments being made if they are required.

To check the correctness of the fit, the saddle should be viewed from behind, without a rider. It should sit with its seat sloping markedly from left to right, with the gullet sitting to the right of the horse's spine. Once the rider is on the saddle, it should settle with the seat level and the gullet should fall exactly over the spine. Viewed from the side, the seat should be level from front to back. The weight should be borne by the inside two-thirds of the offside of the panel and the outside two-thirds of the nearside.

Only when all these criteria are satisfied can the rider be sure that the saddle will not throw her off balance, or slip and cause damage to the horse's back.

The usual lining material for side saddles is serge, with a linen overlining. Leather linings are rare and the old school of saddlers do not like them, as they consider them difficult to stuff correctly. Some older saddles have a panel of felt covered with red 'sorbo' rubber, but, once this has dried up and perished, it cannot be replaced. Other saddles have a detachable felt panel, called a 'Wykeham' pad. The idea of this was that the rider owned one saddle together with a selection of pads made for different horses, so that the saddle could be put on another horse when the rider changed to a second horse during a day's hunting. Unfortunately it is not possible to add stuffing to these pads once the felt has compressed, or if the pad is wanted for a horse of a different back conformation.

FITTING A SIDE-SADDLE

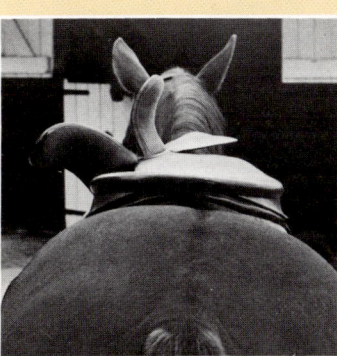

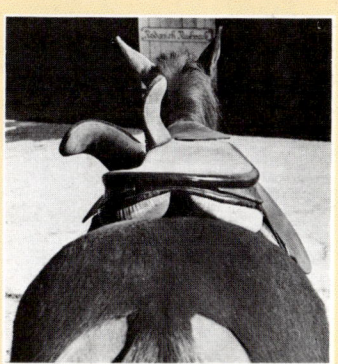

Right: A badly fitting saddle which is already sitting to the left instead of centrally. In use, with a rider on board, this tendency will be exaggerated. **Below:** The rider's weight pulling the saddle over to the left. A saddle fitting as badly as this one is almost certain to cause a sore back.

Right: The same saddle after regulation by an expert saddler. It is now somewhat to the right of the horse's spine but will sit centrally once the rider is in position. **Below:** The saddle fitting correctly and sitting level on the horse's back. Compare this picture with the one on the left.

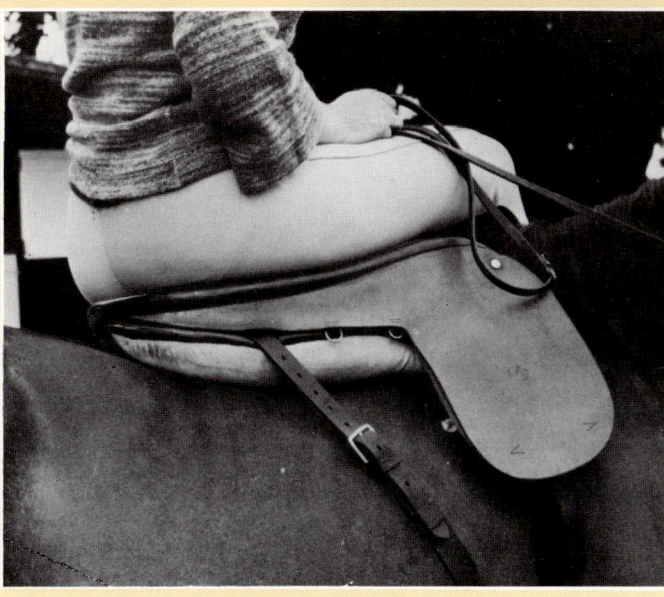

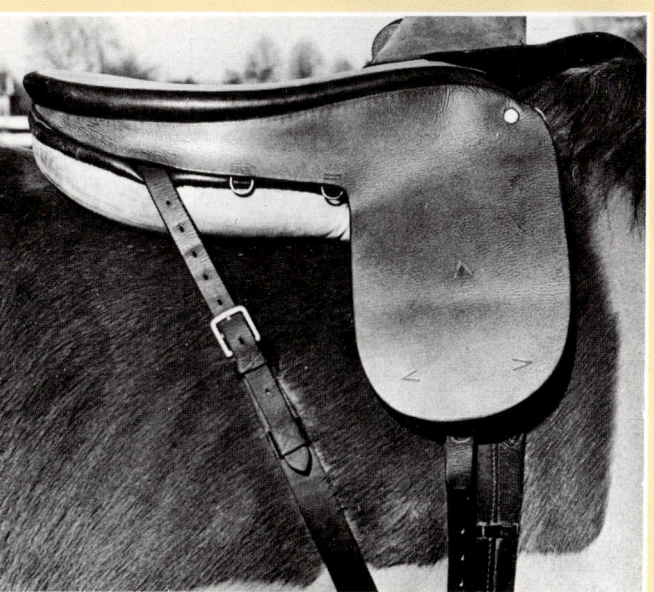

CHAPTER FIVE

Bits, Bridles and Additional Aids

| Bits and Bitting |
| Martingales |
| Nosebands |
| Bridles – Types and Fitting |
| The Western Hackamore System |

The plain double bridle is the hallmark of the schooled horse, and perhaps also of the educated rider. It is the universal bridle for ridden classes in the show ring and for all but the elementary dressage competitions.

CHAPTER FIVE · BITS, BRIDLES AND ADDITIONAL AIDS

Bridling Aids · **Bits and Bitting**

In contrast to the elaborate bitting arrangements of the 19th century—many of which persisted up to the Second World War—the bitting methods of today are mercifully simple. There are two main reasons for this. Firstly, the advancement of equestrian standards has led to a deeper understanding of the theory and practice of riding. Secondly, commercial reasoning has also had its influence in rationalizing the numbers and types of bit available.

In riding today, the emphasis is placed on the engagement of the horse's hindlegs under the body. It is increasingly recognized that the origin of the head carriage lies more with what goes on behind the saddle than in front of it. The bit is seen as an extension of the hand aid, operating, in conjunction with the leg aids and the distribution of the body weight, to effect changes of direction, pace and so on. In this circumstance, the hand is 'suggesting' an appropriate head carriage rather than seeking to impose one by mechanical means centred upon the mouth. As a result the ingenious mechanical contrivances, relying for the most part on a system of levers, which were so much a part of the 19th-century horseman's equipment are no longer relevant to the sort of riding being carried on today.

A *New Method of Bitting Horses*, for instance, as invented and recommended in 1832 by Don Juan Segundo, whose bitting systems were adopted, if only partially, by a number of European cavalry units, is now no more than an interesting study for the equestrian scholar. Segundo had the bits which comprised his system manufactured by Benjamin Latchford, perhaps almost the last of the great British loriners (a maker of bits, spurs and stirrups). Latchford had premises in Upper St Martin's Lane, London, and was the author of a treatise called *The Loriner*. This is little more than a catalogue of Latchford's products, but it included an introduction by the author, as well as Segundo's detailed explanation of his system. This involved numbers of interchangeable cheeks, mouthpieces and curb chains which, in permutation, suited every type of horse, or so it was claimed. It is from Latchford's introduction that the frequently used quotation 'there is a key to every horse's mouth' is taken. In fact, this is an abbreviated version. What Latchford actually wrote was 'the horse's mouth and temper may be compared to a lock, so made that only one key will fit it...'. A far more telling sentence, which is not nearly as well known, reads '... out of every twenty bits I make, nineteen are for men's heads and not more than one really for the horse's head'.

Modern principles
Present-day teaching tends to confine bitting arrangements to the plain snaffle of one sort or another, used often with a drop noseband, and to the double bridle. Outside of this admittedly purist approach, bits of the Pelham group are still to be seen in quite large numbers; gags are certainly not unknown; while, at the present time, there is an increase in the use of the bitless bridle, which is misnamed 'hackamore'.

It is not just contemporary equestrian practice, however, which has led to the reduction in the number of bits available.

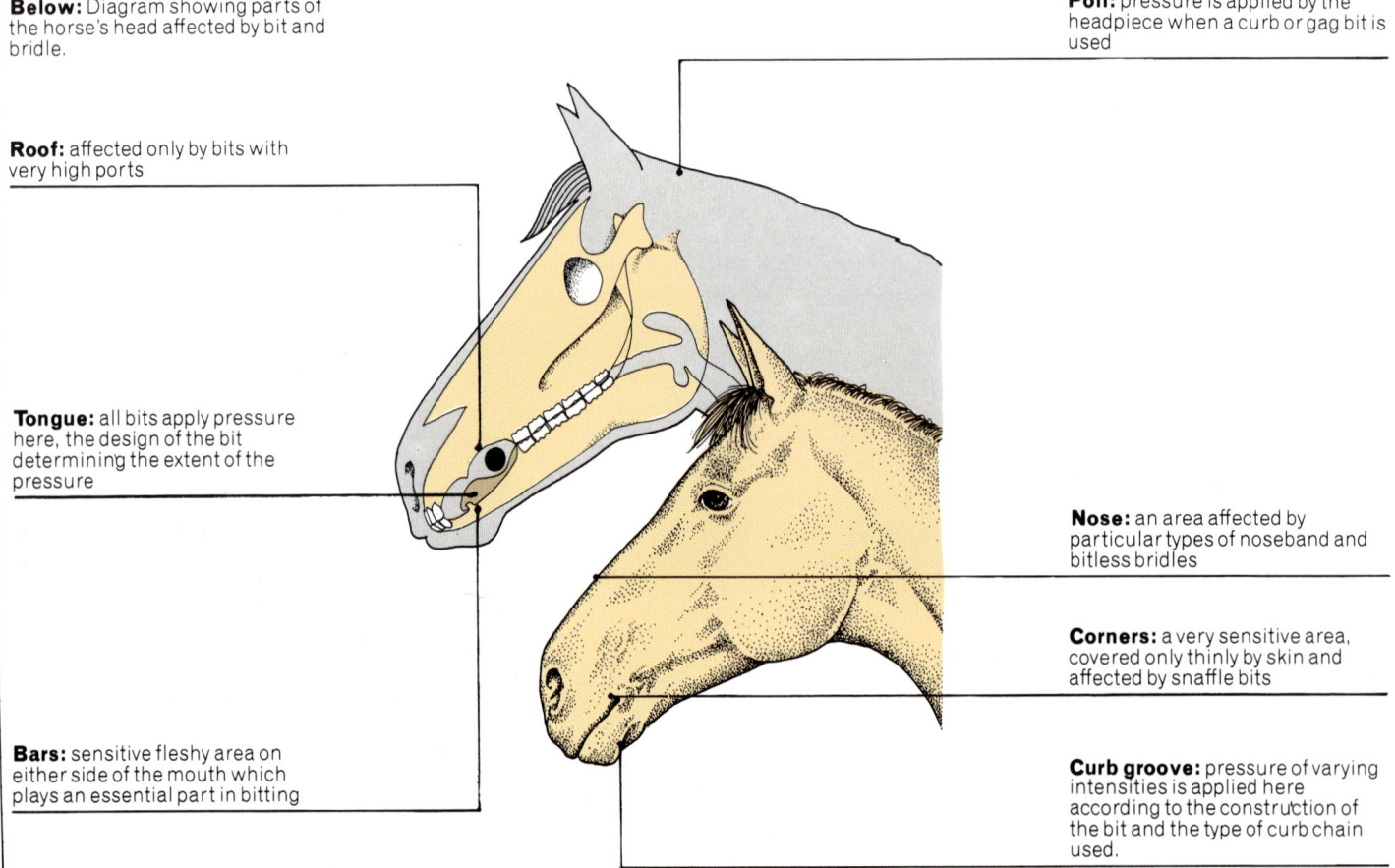

Below: Diagram showing parts of the horse's head affected by bit and bridle.

Roof: affected only by bits with very high ports

Tongue: all bits apply pressure here, the design of the bit determining the extent of the pressure

Bars: sensitive fleshy area on either side of the mouth which plays an essential part in bitting

Poll: pressure is applied by the headpiece when a curb or gag bit is used

Nose: an area affected by particular types of noseband and bitless bridles

Corners: a very sensitive area, covered only thinly by skin and affected by snaffle bits

Curb groove: pressure of varying intensities is applied here according to the construction of the bit and the type of curb chain used.

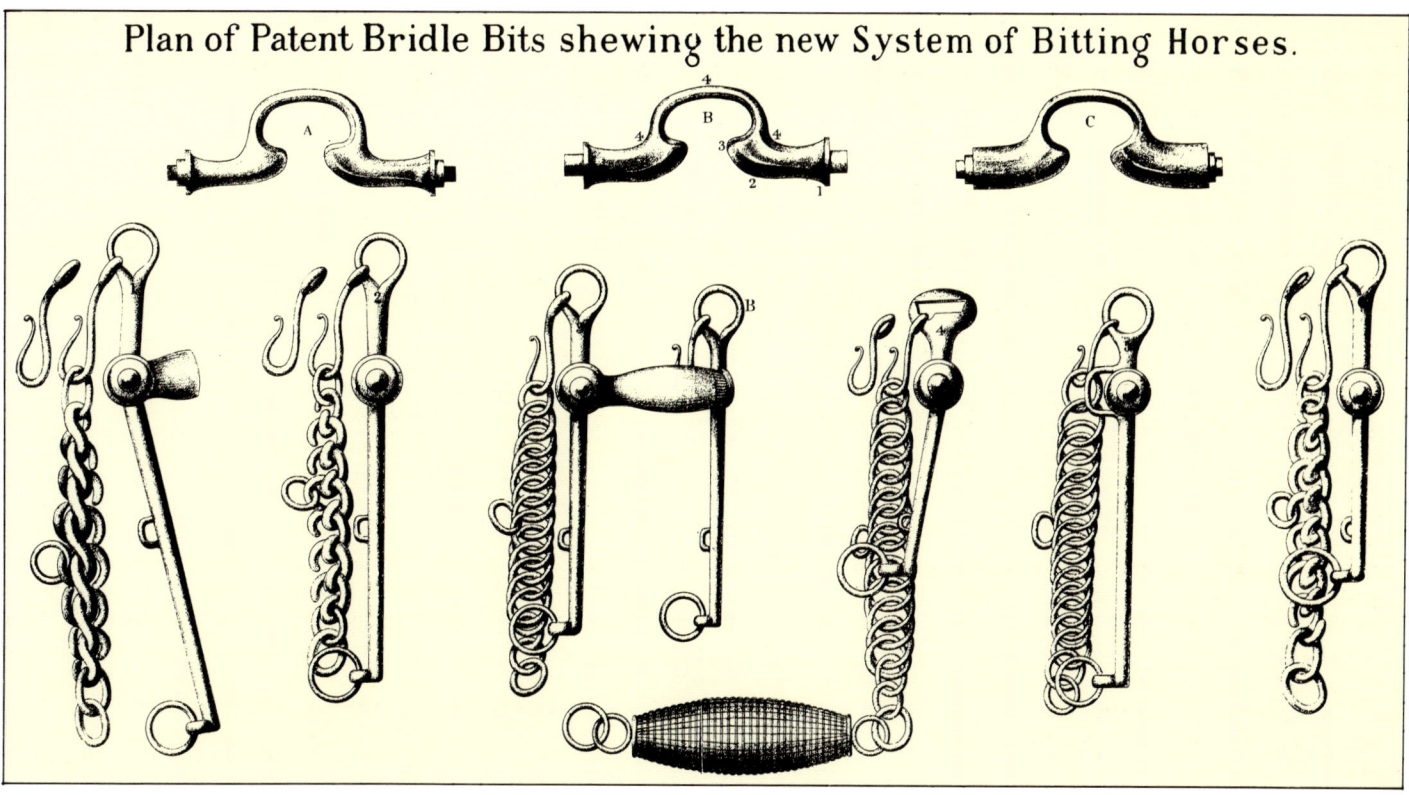

Above: The bits involved in the system of bitting devised by Juan Segundo. Mouthpieces, cheeks and curb chains were interchangeable according to the conformation of the horse's mouth and the way in which the head was carried in relation to the hand. Segundo's treatise was printed in **The Loriner**, published by Benjamin Latchford in 1883.

Less than 20 years ago it was possible to obtain bits in an enormous variety of types and sizes. Indeed, it was still just possible to get a bit hand-forged in stainless steel. The patterns for those bits are probably in existence today, laid away gathering dust on shelves and in corners of the foundries which made them, but it would no longer be practical for them to be produced in small quantities. Today, business sense dictates the manufacture of a minimum number of lines in maximum quantities.

In Britain, there is still a flourishing bit and horse furniture industry carried on in the Midlands, particularly in Walsall. But, in recent years, the largest manufacturers of stainless steel products have closed down their plant and so have a number of smaller concerns. On a smaller scale, Germany continues to produce items of lorinery which are of excellent quality, but are, as a result, expensive. Elsewhere in Europe there exist small pockets of industry to supply the national market, but the most notable influence in the trade is that provided by the countries in the Far East, particularly Korea. Exports of bits and other items of horse equipment from this country take place extensively to the whole of Europe and also to the USA. They are made of stainless steel, are said to be reliable, and can be sold at prices with which few European companies can compete.

The USA's lorinery industry is centred in the western states. It produces the specialist and often very ornate Western 'spade' bits and other similar items of Western riding equipment, including Western saddles. Much of the USA's European-style equipment is manufactured in Europe to special order and exported to the USA.

Principal groupings

In essence there have been no significant innovations in the bitting of horses for some 2,000 years, and even in the 19th century, which must be regarded as the apogee of the loriner's art, each of the multitude of bits produced could be catalogued generally as belonging to one of five bitting groups. Here and there it is possible to discern marriages between groups, with a bit seeming to combine the characteristics of two types, while in other cases a particular characteristic is accentuated in the construction. These, however, are not significant exceptions. The five groups are the snaffle, the Weymouth or double bridle, the Pelham, the gag and those bridles which can be placed in the category described as bitless—a better definition, according to some authorities, would be nose bridles.

The snaffle bridle

The snaffle is held to be the simplest of the groups and, possibly incorrectly, the one which causes the minimum of discomfort to the horse. It is the largest group in terms of type variation and the permutations can indeed be enormous. However, there are distinctive sub-groups formed by differences in the shape of the mouthpiece and the bit rings to which the reins and the bridle cheeks are attached.

The variations in the mouthpiece are between the jointed one and the mullen, or half-moon, mouthpiece which dispenses with the central joint. The bit-rings are either 'loose' rings, running through a hole in the butt end of the mouthpiece, or the rings are 'fixed', as in the eggbutt and most types of 'cheek' snaffle.

The mullen mouthpieces can be metal,

CHAPTER FIVE · BITS, BRIDLES AND ADDITIONAL AIDS

Lorinery, the making of such items as bits and spurs, was for centuries a hand craft, the best bits being carefully hand-forged in steel. Today, of necessity, mass-production methods have been adopted. **Above:** A selection of bits ready for the first finishing stage. **Right:** Patterns for bits.

Top: Nickel, here shown in its molten state, is the other metal used for lorinery. It is stainless but becomes discoloured. It's main disadvantage is that it is a soft metal which can bend in use and is far from being unbreakable.
Left and above: One of the basic materials of bit-making is steel, which is poured in its molten state into the moulds. Modern steel is stainless, but steel used in the 19th century had to be kept clean by the laborious use of materials such as sand and oil.

CHAPTER FIVE · BITS, BRIDLES AND ADDITIONAL AIDS

BITS AND BITTING

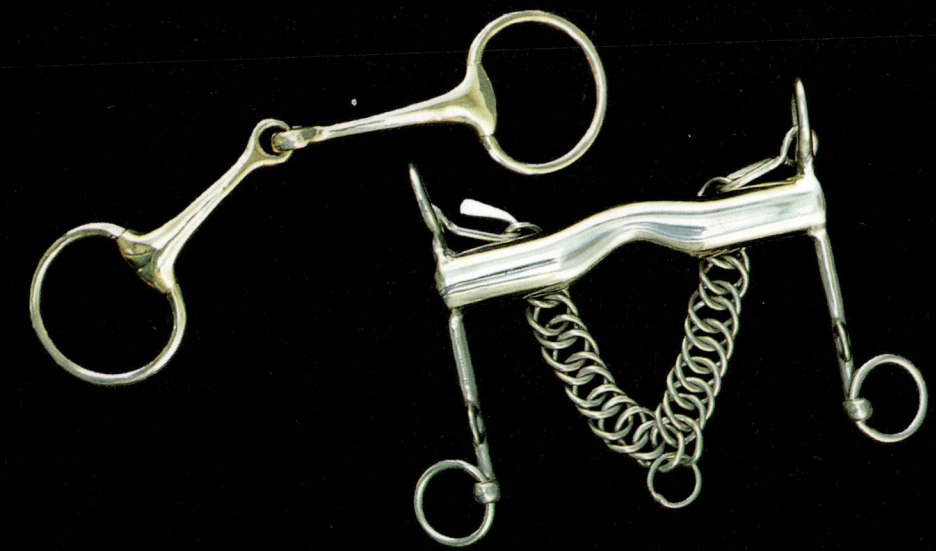

Above: The mouthpiece joints in a batch of eggbutt snaffles being closed by welding. **Far left:** Cleaning out the bit rings and eyes on Pelham and curb bits is a job still done by hand. **Left:** Making curb chains in a Midland foundry. **Top right:** Finishing continues to be a process of hand work at the polishing stage. **Above right:** Bits ready for electro-submersion in an electro-plating tank. **Right:** The finished product, smooth and lightly polished, in stainless steel.

CHAPTER FIVE · BITS, BRIDLES AND ADDITIONAL AIDS

but are more frequently made from vulcanite, nylon or rubber. In the case of the latter, it is essential that the mouthpiece should be fitted with a core of chain, or some other material of great strength, which is attached to the rings on each side. The reason for this precaution is obvious enough.

Usually, the jointed snaffles are made of metal, but they can be covered with either rubber or vulcanite to soften the action. The mildest effect is that of the mullen mouthpiece made in rubber or vulcanite, the former being the softer of the two.

Modern 'loose' rings are usually rounded and are then termed 'wire' rings. Their advantage over the older type of 'flat' ring is that the 'wire' ring passes through a smaller, tighter hole than is possible with the flat type. There is thus less chance of the horse's lips being pinched.

Wire rings also permit the mouthpiece to move in the mouth, making it possible for the horse to play with it with his tongue. Some trainers like their horses to do this, considering that the action produces saliva and thus keeps the mouth 'wet'. With a 'wet' mouth the lower jaw is said to relax more easily in response to the indications made through the bit by the hand. Other trainers take the opposite view, preferring the bit to be 'fixed' so that the movement in the horse's mouth is less exaggerated.

Cheeks on the bit assist the lateral movement of the head—by pressing against one or other side of the face.

The snaffle in action
The action of the snaffle is usually assumed to be an upward one against the corners of the lips, thus encouraging the horse to raise his head. In fact, this is the case only if the head is held low, as might be usual with a young horse, and it would then be quite wrong to attempt to raise the head forcibly with the hands. The head is raised by the rider's legs encouraging a greater engagement of the horse's hindlegs underneath the body; the hands do no more than assist, or give greater emphasis to, the action of the legs.

In truth, the action of the snaffle varies in accordance with the position of the head and in the light of such auxiliaries— a martingale or noseband, for instance— which may be employed to alter or emphasize certain actions of the bit. In the case of a horse with a relatively high neck carriage, whose head is held a little in advance of the vertical, the action of the snaffle is across the bars of the lower jaw, the action being greatly intensified if the mouthpiece is a jointed one.

There are, of course, a number of 'strong' snaffles, the strength being provided by the construction of the mouthpiece. Examples of these are the Magenis (a corruption of MacGuinness), which has rollers set within and across the mouthpiece; bits in which the mouthpieces are fitted with rollers round them; Scorriers,

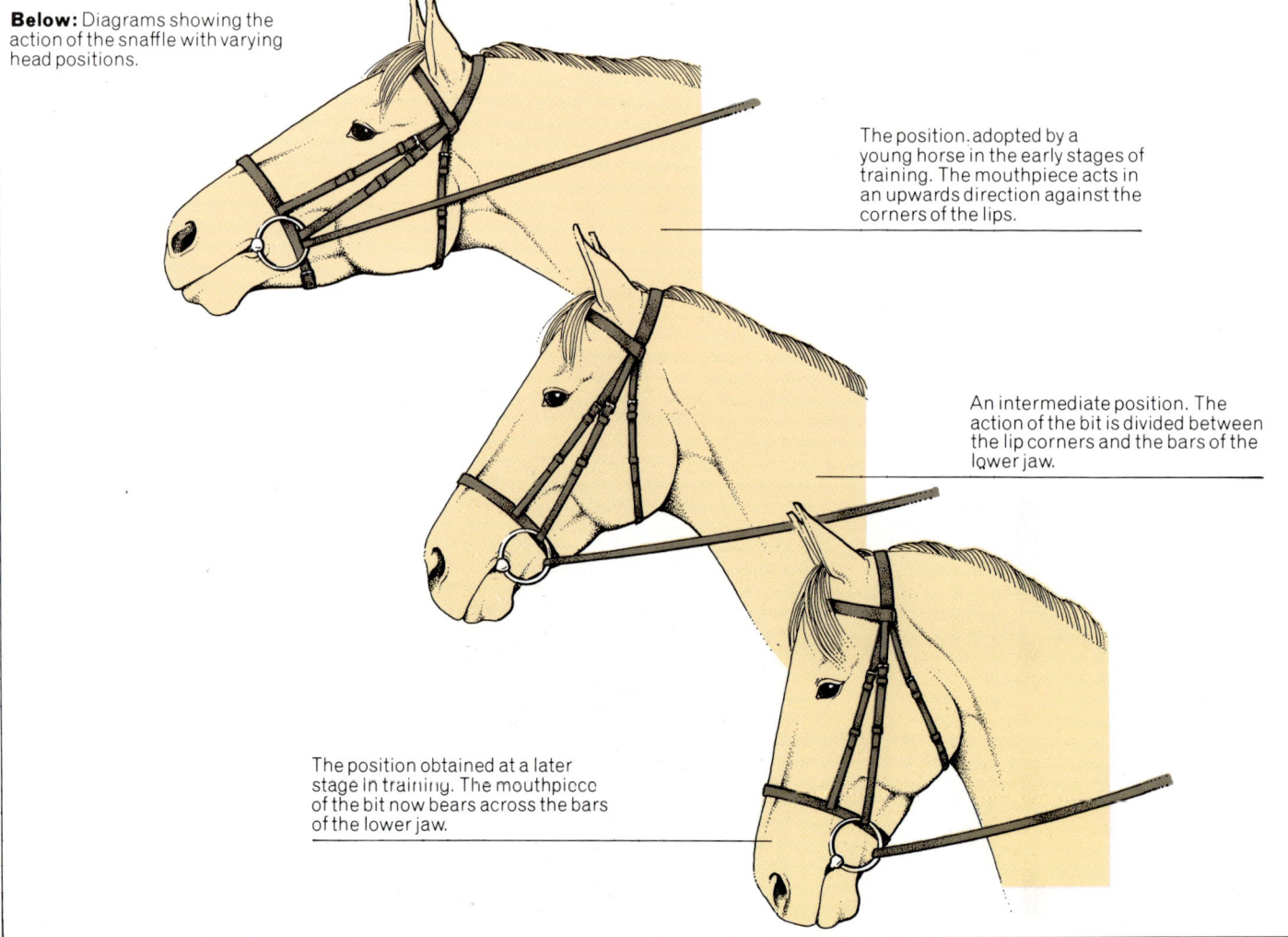

Below: Diagrams showing the action of the snaffle with varying head positions.

The position adopted by a young horse in the early stages of training. The mouthpiece acts in an upwards direction against the corners of the lips.

An intermediate position. The action of the bit is divided between the lip corners and the bars of the lower jaw.

The position obtained at a later stage in training. The mouthpiece of the bit now bears across the bars of the lower jaw.

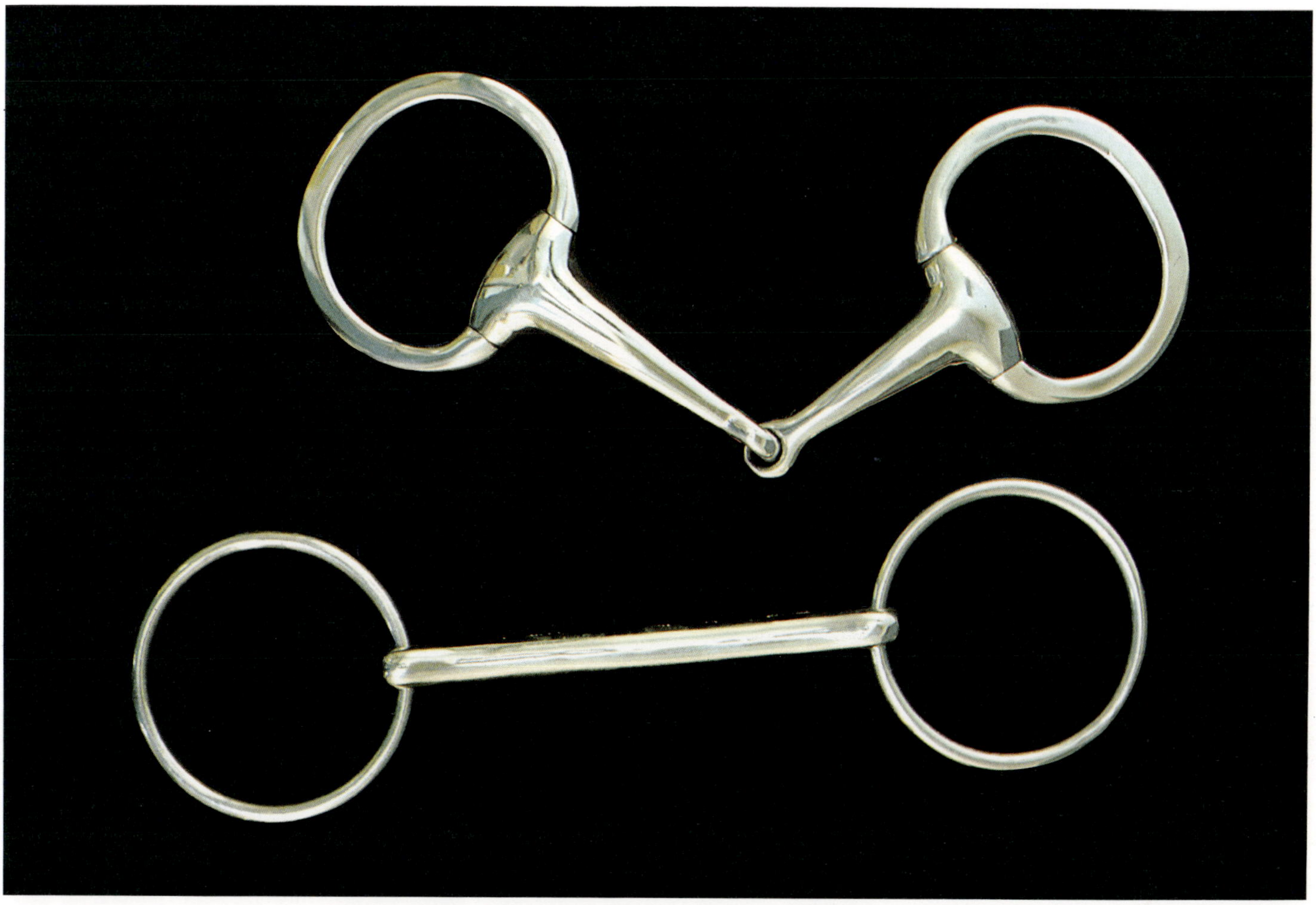

Above: The popular eggbutt snaffle, which obviates pinching of the corners of the lips, and a straight-bar bit, used for stallion or in-hand bridles. **Right:** Detail of a flat ring, a design becoming less evident in bit manufacture. **Below:** Cheek snaffle with loose rings. The top-cheek needs to be secured to the bridle by small retaining straps so that the bit's position is maintained in the mouth.

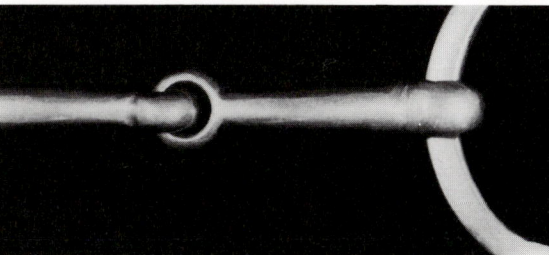

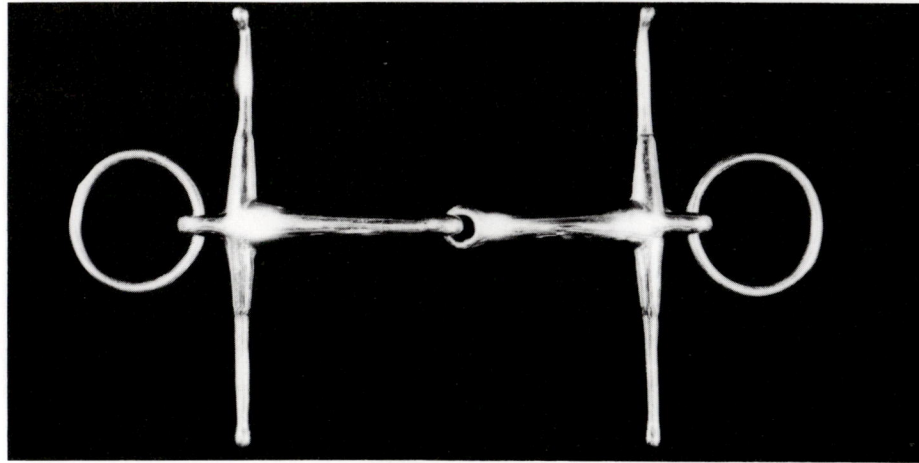

those particularly unpleasant pieces of ironmongery; 'y' or 'w' mouth snaffles, with two mouthpieces, and the somewhat barbaric twisted mouth snaffles.

The double bridle

The double bridle, comprising curb bit and bradoon (a light snaffle bit), goes generally under the name Weymouth, although a century ago there were many similar combinations called by a variety of other names. Today the difference is between a 'slide-cheek' and a 'fixed-cheek' Weymouth. The combination of curb and bradoon, employing a number of forces to achieve its ends, is the most sophisticated of bridles and, in the hands of the accomplished horseman, is probably the most effective one.

The bradoon, fitted in the mouth above the curb bit, does, in this instance, act to raise the head by exerting pressure on the corners of the lips. The curb bit acts upon a number of points in the mouth and on the head to lower the latter and retract the

CHAPTER FIVE · BITS, BRIDLES AND ADDITIONAL AIDS

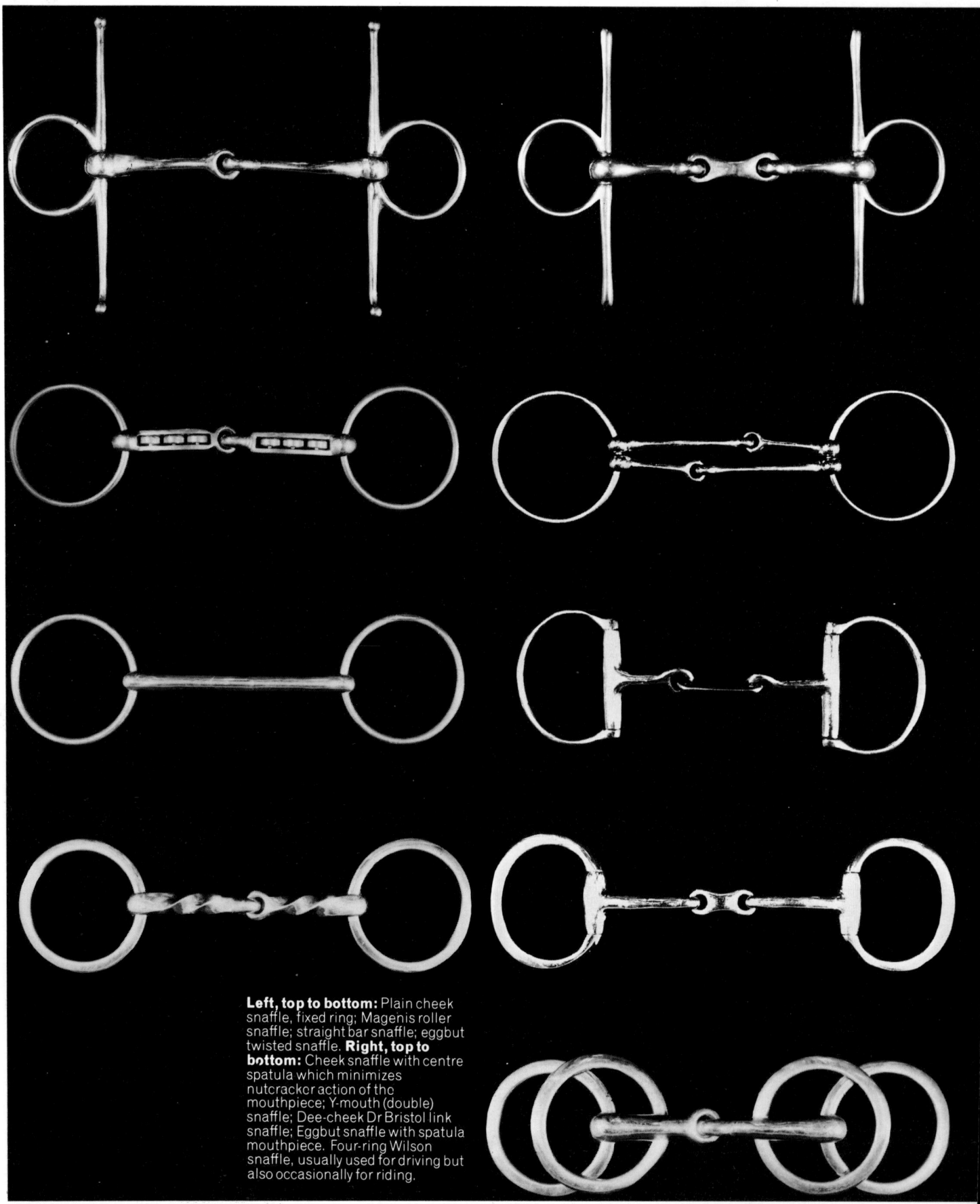

Left, top to bottom: Plain cheek snaffle, fixed ring; Magenis roller snaffle; straight bar snaffle; eggbut twisted snaffle. **Right, top to bottom:** Cheek snaffle with centre spatula which minimizes nutcracker action of the mouthpiece; Y-mouth (double) snaffle; Dee-cheek Dr Bristol link snaffle; Eggbut snaffle with spatula mouthpiece. Four-ring Wilson snaffle, usually used for driving but also occasionally for riding.

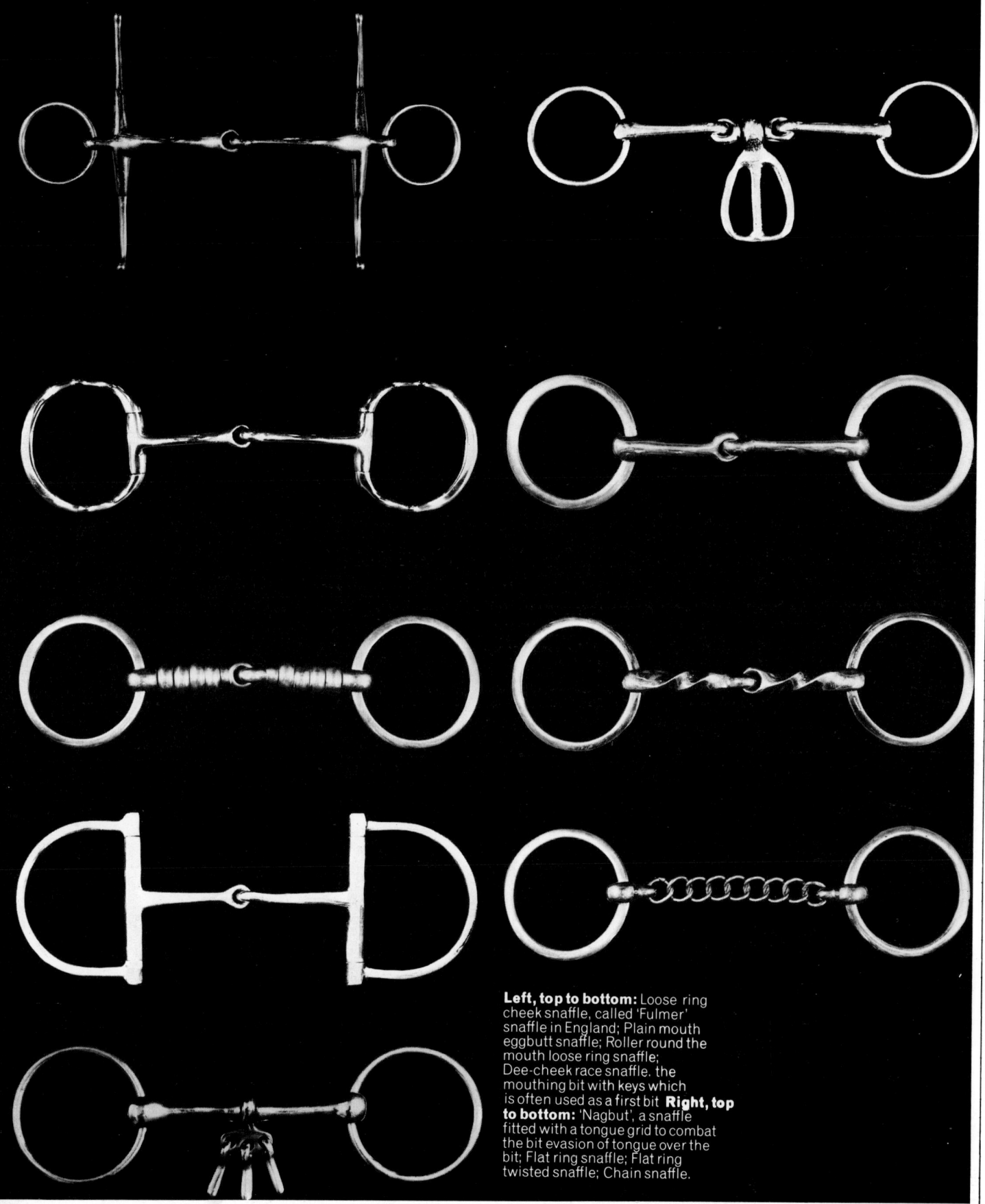

Left, top to bottom: Loose ring cheek snaffle, called 'Fulmer' snaffle in England; Plain mouth eggbutt snaffle; Roller round the mouth loose ring snaffle; Dee-cheek race snaffle. the mouthing bit with keys which is often used as a first bit **Right, top to bottom:** 'Nagbut', a snaffle fitted with a tongue grid to combat the bit evasion of tongue over the bit; Flat ring snaffle; Flat ring twisted snaffle; Chain snaffle.

CHAPTER FIVE · BITS, BRIDLES AND ADDITIONAL AIDS

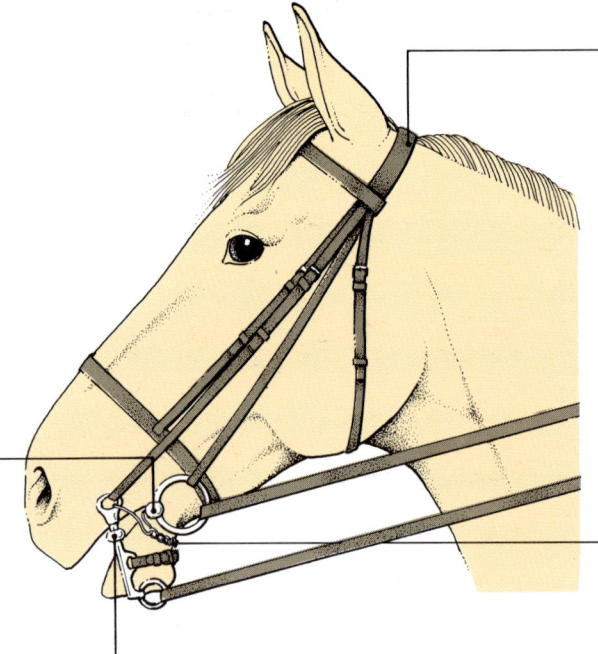

Below: Diagram showing the action of the double bridle, the ultimate aid in assisting the rider to suggest a positioning of the head.

Poll pressure, exerting a downward action, varies according to the length of the cheek above the mouthpiece and is transmitted by the forward movement of the eye of the curb bit.

The bradoon acts to raise the head by a slight upward pressure on the horse's mouth.

The curb chain is also brought into play by movement of the curb bit, causing downward and backward pressure on the horse's jaw.

The curb bit exerts pressure on the bars of the mouth as well as on the curb groove and poll to cause a lowering of the head, retraction of the nose and flexion at poll and lower jaw.

nose, the degree of pressure imposed being governed by the length of the cheek both above and below the mouthpiece. The longer the overall cheek, the greater will be the possible leverage. The length of the cheek above the mouthpiece is important, since upon it depends the extent to which pressure is put on the poll. The longer the cheek above the mouthpiece, the greater will be the poll pressure which can be applied. Poll pressure, which induces a downward action, is transmitted by the forward movement of the eye of the curb bit, through the bridle cheek and thus to the headpiece. This occurs when the bit assumes an angle of about 45° in the mouth and thus causes the eye of the bit to move forwards and downwards. This action also brings into play the curb chain which lies in the curb groove. The tightening of the curb chain produces a downward and backward pressure on the horse's lower jaw.

The pressures on the mouth depend upon the shape of the mouthpiece of the curb bit. In most instances, the mouthpiece is a straight bar, with a port—a raised section—in its centre. The port accommodates the central portion of the tongue, the latter appearing to rise up naturally into this curve. This action stops the tongue from lying over the bars of the mouth (the area of gum between the molar and incisor teeth) and thus prevents the bearing surface of the bit from coming into direct contact with the bars. The action on the bars is a downward one with the direction of the pressure being to the rear.

The shape of the port governs the degree of pressure which can be exerted on the bars. A deep, wide port, allowing more room for the tongue, puts more direct pressure on the bars through the bearing surfaces of the mouthpiece. On the other hand, a mullen mouth bit, which makes no provision for the tongue, puts little pressure directly on the bars because these are then partially covered by the tongue.

The action of the two mouthpieces, the bit and the bradoon, together with the pressures exerted on the poll and curb groove, make this bridle an extremely sensitive instrument. When employed on a schooled horse, it can 'place' the head with greater finesse than is possible with any other bridle in current use.

The 'slide' cheek curb bit which allows movement of the mouthpiece in the mouth itself, is nonetheless probably more severe than the fixed mouthpiece, which permits no such movement. The reason for this is that the slide cheek gives something like an extra ½in of leverage when the bit is brought into play, but, in addition, it is possible for the action of the bit to become uneven if, for any reason, the cheek slides on one side but not on the other.

The Pelham bridle
The Pelham bridle is no more than a curb bit with a loop at the top end to which an extra rein is attached. In its original 17th–18th-century form—long before it got its present name—it probably preceded the independent bradoon and curb bit, being a development of the single curb of the 15th–16th centuries.

Modern attitudes tend to regard the Pelham as the halfway house between the snaffle and double bridle. These have resulted in the bit losing much of its effect and purpose. With a cheek of reasonable length and the original ported mouthpiece, sometimes called a Hartwell mouthpiece, the Pelham can be a very useful bit in the hands of an experienced rider. It is not suitable for a novice.

So, too, can the arched mouth Pelham, which allows even more room for the tongue and therefore greater bearing on the bars. In bits of this shape, where the action is more upon the bars than otherwise (as is the case in the majority of

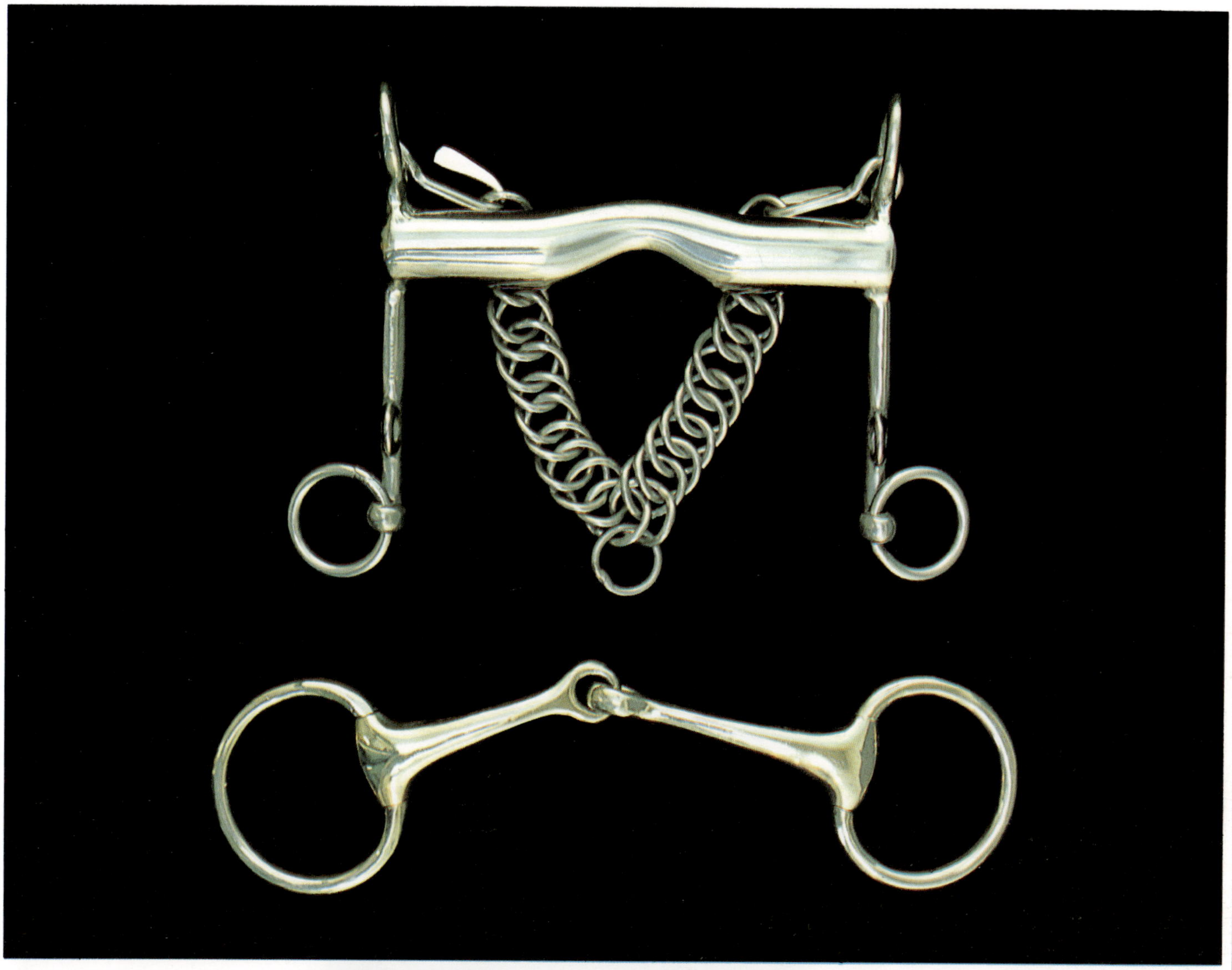

Above: Fixed-cheek Weymouth curb bit with broad mouthpiece and eggbutt bradoon. This type is much favoured for dressage.
Right: The slide-cheek Weymouth bit which can in fact be more severe, and sometimes less satisfactory, than its fixed counterpart in its action.

Below, top to bottom: A selection of curb chains: elastic curb; flat link chain; single link chain; double link chain; jodphur curb chain. more severe, and sometimes less satisfactory, than its fixed counterpart in its action. Curb chains are integral to the functioning of the curb bit, acting on the curb groove as a restraint and also assisting in the relaxation of the lower jaw.

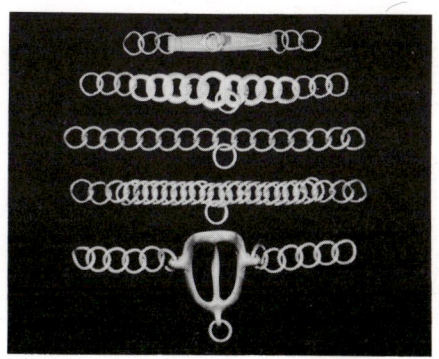

CHAPTER FIVE · BITS, BRIDLES AND ADDITIONAL AIDS

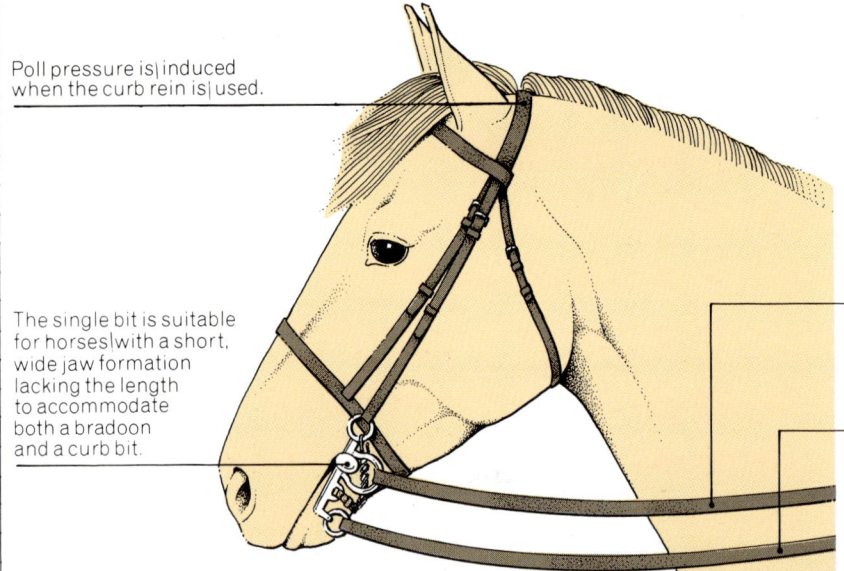

Poll pressure is induced when the curb rein is used.

When the bradoon rein predominates, the action imitates that of the bradoon bit of the double bridle.

The single bit is suitable for horses with a short, wide jaw formation lacking the length to accommodate both a bradoon and a curb bit.

The curb rein imitates the action of the double's curb bit.

Left: The Pelham bridle in position. In essence it seeks to obtain the same result as the double bridle while employing a single mouthpiece. **Below, left:** The little-known SM Pelham is of American origin. The mouthpiece is broad and flat and the cheeks move in a restricted area. **Centre:** The very mild rubber mullen-mouth Pelham. **Right:** The Kimblewick, sometimes known as the Spanish jumping bit, although employing only a single rein is still a member of the Pelham group. **Bottom:** The Scamperdale has the mouthpiece turned back so that the cheek cannot chafe the lip area, a fault with most Pelhams. This bit was the invention of an English horseman, the late Sam Marsh.

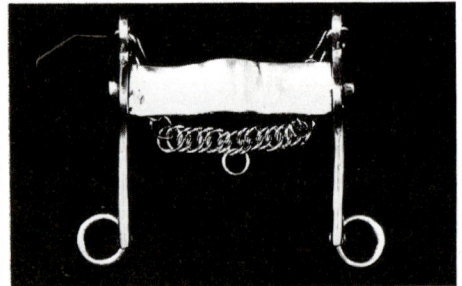
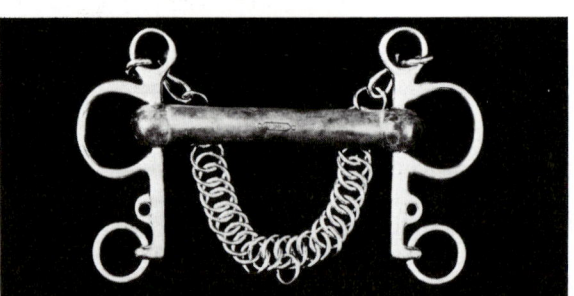
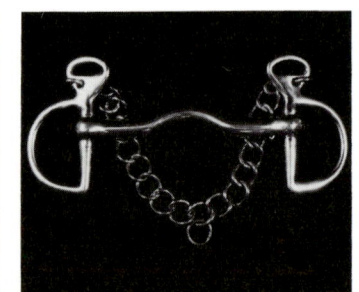

curbs), the pressures are quite clearly defined, even though they can be mitigated by the use of the top (bradoon) rein, which will bring the mouthpiece upwards to the corners of the horse's lips.

For the most part, however, Pelhams are made with mullen mouthpieces and are then sloppy and indefinite in action—this is probably why so many horses manage very well in them. They cannot, however, be regarded in the same light as the double bridle as far as precision is concerned.

The advantage of the Pelham is that it can be used on horses and ponies of cobby type, whose jaw formation is shorter and wider and so cannot accommodate easily the bit and bradoon of the Weymouth. It is also very useful with the Arabian jaw formation, which, though much more refined than the former examples, lacks the requisite length. It is not a suitable bit for the general run of Thoroughbred-type horse, whose jaw formation is for the most part long and narrow. Used on such horses and correctly adjusted sufficiently high in the mouth, the curb chain is bound to rise upwards, out of the curb groove, and rub the virtually unprotected jawbones above.

The shape of the bars in a horse's mouth provide an indication to the sort of bitting arrangement, particularly in regard to the tongue port, which will be most suitable. Sharp, thinly covered bars, often found in Thoroughbred types, are likely to be very sensitive and the horse may not be able to accept direct pressure bearing on them. Conversely, broad, fleshy bars, which are less sensitive, will be better suited to the mouthpiece bearing directly upon them.

Pelhams made with flexible rubber mouthpieces, or with jointed ones, present other curb chain problems, since the chain falls from the curb groove when rein pressure induces the nutcracker action of the mouthpiece. This can be prevented by either adjusting the chain excessively tight in the first instance, or by passing it through the bit rings, and still fastening it tightly. Neither method is considerate.

There are a great many types of Pelham, but one of the most notable—and perhaps unlikely—is the Kimblewick or Spanish Jumping bit. This certainly does not look like a Pelham, because of the short loop cheek to which a single rein is attached. Nonetheless, it has all the curb bit characteristics. Usually, the bit is made with a ported mouth and a square top eye, which increases the poll pressure available. Poll pressure and curb pressure are accomplished by the rein sliding to the bottom of the cheek when the latter acts in response to the movement of the hands. The result is that the horse drops his head, placing the mouth below the hand; in this position he comes more surely under the rider's control.

To ensure that the curb chain stays in position and to make its action more immediate, the chain on these bits is frequently passed through the bit rings.

The gag
The gag bridle, in whatever form it takes, acts primarily to raise the head by lifting up the bit against the corners of the mouth. It achieves this by the bridle cheeks being made of rounded leather, or cord, which pass through two aligned holes at top and bottom of the bit ring before being attached to a rein. It is usual to fix a second rein to the bit, fixing it in the normal way to the bit ring so that it lies above the gag rein. It is then possible, and very advisable, to use the latter only as circumstances dictate, rather than to ride on it continually and so risk reducing its effect by allowing the horse to become familiar and hardened to its action.

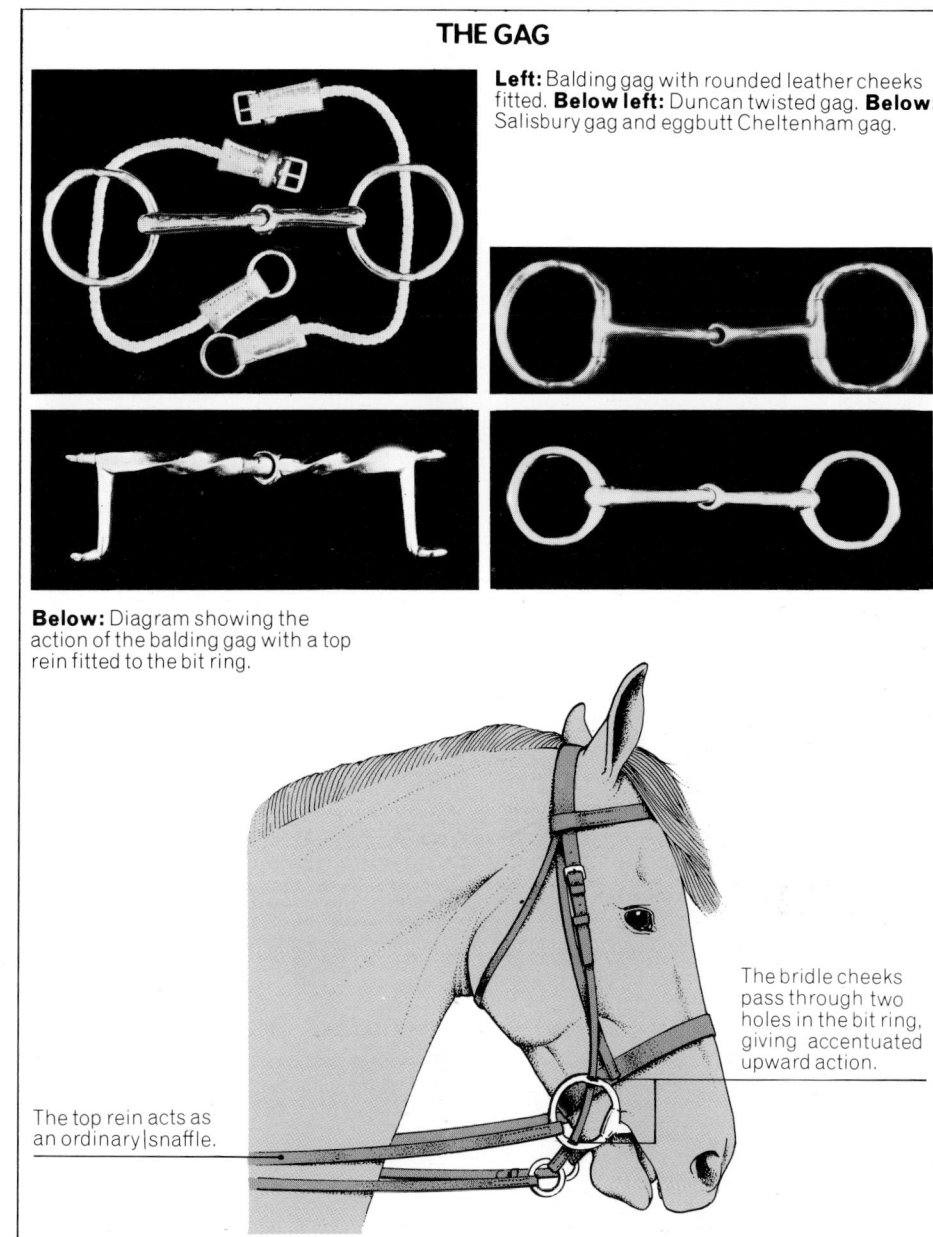

THE GAG

Left: Balding gag with rounded leather cheeks fitted. **Below left:** Duncan twisted gag. **Below:** Salisbury gag and eggbutt Cheltenham gag.

Below: Diagram showing the action of the balding gag with a top rein fitted to the bit ring.

The top rein acts as an ordinary snaffle.

The bridle cheeks pass through two holes in the bit ring, giving accentuated upward action.

Bridling Aids · **Martingales**

All martingales share the common objective of assisting the action of the bit by restraining in one way or another the positioning of the horse's head and neck. In some cases they may go further by accentuating a particular action, or even by altering the character of the bit.

These auxiliaries can be regarded conveniently in two sections. There are those that seek in the simplest ways to prevent the head from being raised out of the control of the hand and those which are intended as serious, long-term schooling aids, designed to affect the whole outline of the young horse or to attempt the correction of that of the older animal. These latter are thus more complicated in both their construction and effect and are discussed in the schooling section. In effect, whether simple or complex, the martingale is an aid to improved balance—although it would not be considered so by the purist.

Simple martingales
The simplest form of martingale is the standing or 'fast' martingale. Essentially this is an adjustable strap attached at one end to the girth between the forelegs and at the other to the rear of a plain, stout cavesson noseband. To keep the strap in place it is fitted with a neckstrap, which can also be used by the rider in case of emergency to keep in place in the saddle.

The martingale prevents the horse, very effectively, from throwing up his head, and, depending on how it is adjusted, places the bit below the hand and acting squarely upon the bars of the lower jaw. Adjusted to a sensible length there is no reason why it should restrict the horse when jumping, since the head and neck are then stretched forwards and downwards—not upwards.

The martingale, in a very much strengthened form, is a virtual essential in the equipment of the polo pony, but sometimes appears as the more colourful *puggaree* martingale. This piece of equipment comes from India. It is, in fact, a length of coloured turban cloth.

Occasionally, in some areas of Western riding, the standing martingale acts directly on the mouth, rather than the nose, being divided at the top end of the strap and the bifurcations being fitted with snap hooks to fasten to the bit. A similar device was once in vogue in Europe.

Running martingales
The running martingale is slightly more complex. Again, this has the central strap divided, the ends of the two branches being fitted with rings through which are passed the reins. When the horse attempts to throw up his head, the action is countered by pressure on the bars of the lower jaw through the bit. The tighter the martingale is adjusted, the greater is the restriction on the position of the head. In theory, it is recommended that the martingale is fitted so that the rings are in line with the wither, but in practical terms the adjustment is usually somewhat tighter. In show jumping, for instance, the rein frequently forms a distinct angle between the mouth and the hand. In both instances the martingales, whether standing or running, alter the action of the snaffle bit, since it must be presumed that without the restraint imposed by them, the horse's head would be held higher, so that the bit would act more upon the corners of the lips than otherwise. Using the martingales, the bit is placed over the bars of the lower jaw, the action being more direct in the case of the running martingale.

Racehorses very often wear a running martingale in which the branches are joined by a triangular-shaped piece of leather. This is called a 'bib' martingale and is fitted as a precaution against an excited horse getting caught up or even

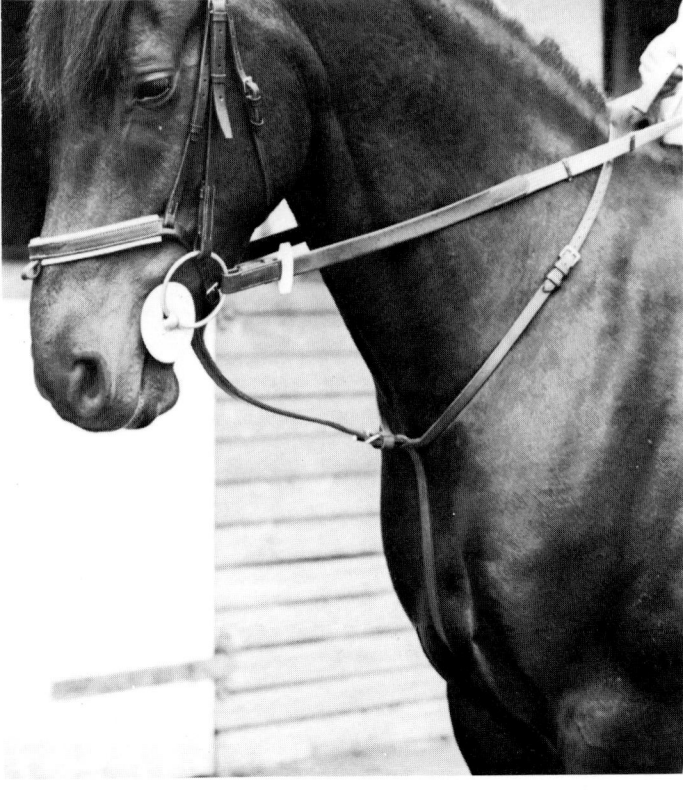
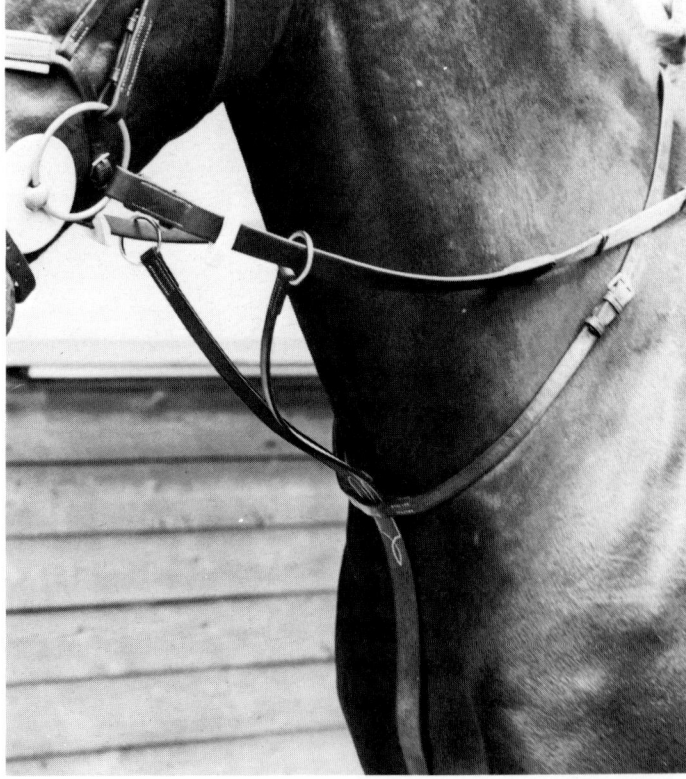

getting his nose between the two branches. Racing trainers also use a small piece of equipment which though called the Irish martingale is an intruder within the martingale family, since it has none of the group's objects or characteristics. It consists of a short strip of leather joining two rings through which the reins are passed and its use has no influence on the head position. Its purpose is to assist the correct direction of the rein pull and to prevent the reins being brought right over the horse's head in the event of a fall.

It is usual to fit 'stops' on the rein with which a running martingale is used. These are shaped pieces of rubber or leather which are slid on to the rein and fit it tightly. Ideally they are positioned some 8in to 10in from the bit. They prevent the rings of the martingale from running too far forward and becoming caught on the bridle in some way, or even caught over one of the horse's teeth.

In theory again, the running martingale should not be used with a double bridle (see preceding section), since the latter, on a schooled horse, provides, without outside assistance, all that is necessary to obtain the required head position and degree of control. In practice, however, the martingale is on occasion used with the bridle. In this instance, it should logically be placed upon the curb rein to assist the lowering of the head which is the purpose of the latter. As often as not, it is to be seen on the bradoon rein, when it becomes a contradiction in terms, and even with both reins passed through the rings. This last may constitute an effective braking system, but makes a nonsense of the reasons why the double bridle is used by riders.

The German rein

Another pattern of martingale much used in show jumping goes under the name of Market Harborough or German rein in Britain, though, in Germany, it is often called an English rein. The rein derives from the more straightforward draw rein which fastens to the girth on either side, then passes through the bit rings back to the rider's hand. Though it is termed a rein, it is much more like a martingale in its action.

The martingale has two strips of leather attached to a ring on the chest and passing through the bit ring to a fastening on the rein. The adjustment is made either with a buckle or by clipping the leather strip to one of three or four small metal dees set on the rein. The action is quite simple. So long as the horse carries his head acceptably, the rein operates in the normal fashion. A downward pressure on the mouth only occurs when the horse throws up the head causing the leather strips to tighten and to pull down on the bit rings.

For the moment, outside of polo, the standing martingale is out of favour, although it is used as a training aid for jumping. The running martingale, however, is widely used in all competitive events, with the natural exception of dressage.

The pulley martingale

The older generations of horsemen and women seem to have given much more thought to bitting than is usual in these days of universal horsemanship based on the snaffle and drop noseband. One older type of running martingale such riders used was the pulley type, in which the rings were attached to a cord which passed through a pulley at the top of the body strap. Its advantage was that in making sharp turns and so on, the horse was allowed to bend his head in the direction of the movement without the kind of restriction on the opposite side of his mouth which is inevitable to some degree with the conventional pattern.

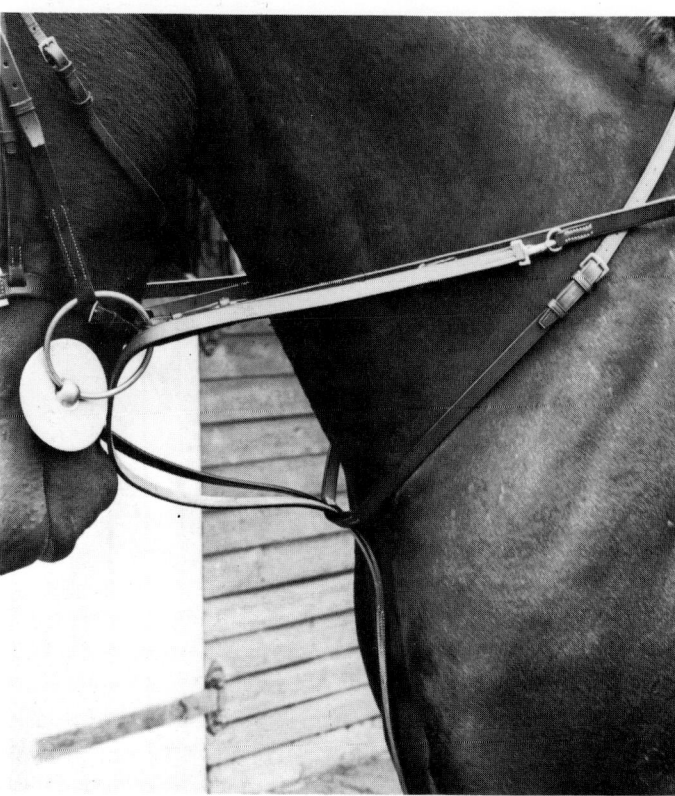

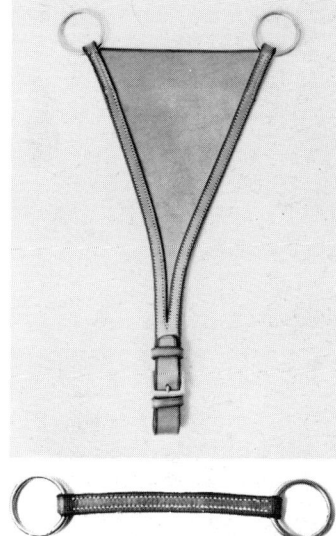

Left to right: Standing, or 'fast', martingale controlling position of head by pressure on the nose; Running martingale, imposing control by pressure on the mouth. The 'stops' in advance of the rings prevent the latter sliding forward and becoming caught on the bridle or over a tooth!; The Market Harborough or German rein (in Germany often called the English rein), which is a much improved version of the old draw rein, the action being brought about when the horse evades by throwing his head above an acceptable level; Bib martingale and (**below**) Irish martingale, and rein stops made from rubber and leather.

CHAPTER FIVE · BITS, BRIDLES AND ADDITIONAL AIDS

Bridling Aids · **Nosebands**

In almost every instance the noseband fulfils some practical function connected with increased control of the horse. The only exception is the plain cavesson noseband which, unless it is used as an anchorage for the standing martingale, serves no more than an aesthetic purpose. In its normal position the cavesson is fitted so that two fingers can be inserted between it and the jawbone. If fitted tightly and a little lower than usual it can partially close the mouth, but not to the same extent as the drop noseband.

The drop noseband
The drop noseband is without doubt the most important type of noseband in the context of modern riding, whether it is being used in the schooling of the horse or in competition. The nosepiece is fitted some 3in above the nostrils, just below the termination of the facial bones. The back strap is then secured under the bit, so as to lie in the curb groove. Positioned in this way and adjusted fairly tightly, the noseband stops the mouth from being opened and, as a result, also prevents the horse from evading the action of the bit in that manner. For the same reason, its use ensures that the bit remains central in the mouth, since the horse cannot slide the bit over to one side or the other.

The pressure of the noseband therefore assists and strengthens the action of the bit. Pressure on the rein is transmitted to the nose as the horse's lower jaw gives to the bit action. In turn such pressure causes the horse to drop his head, allowing the bit to bear across the bars of the lower jaw, in which position it will have the greatest effect. However, it is also the case that the pressure exerted on the nose—if sufficiently strong—can cause a momentary check to the breathing, which will contribute to the dropping of the head.

Variations on the basic drop noseband also exist. One widely-used type is called a 'Flash' noseband, after a jumper who wore it, and another is the Grakle, Figure 8 or 'cross-over' noseband. The former is

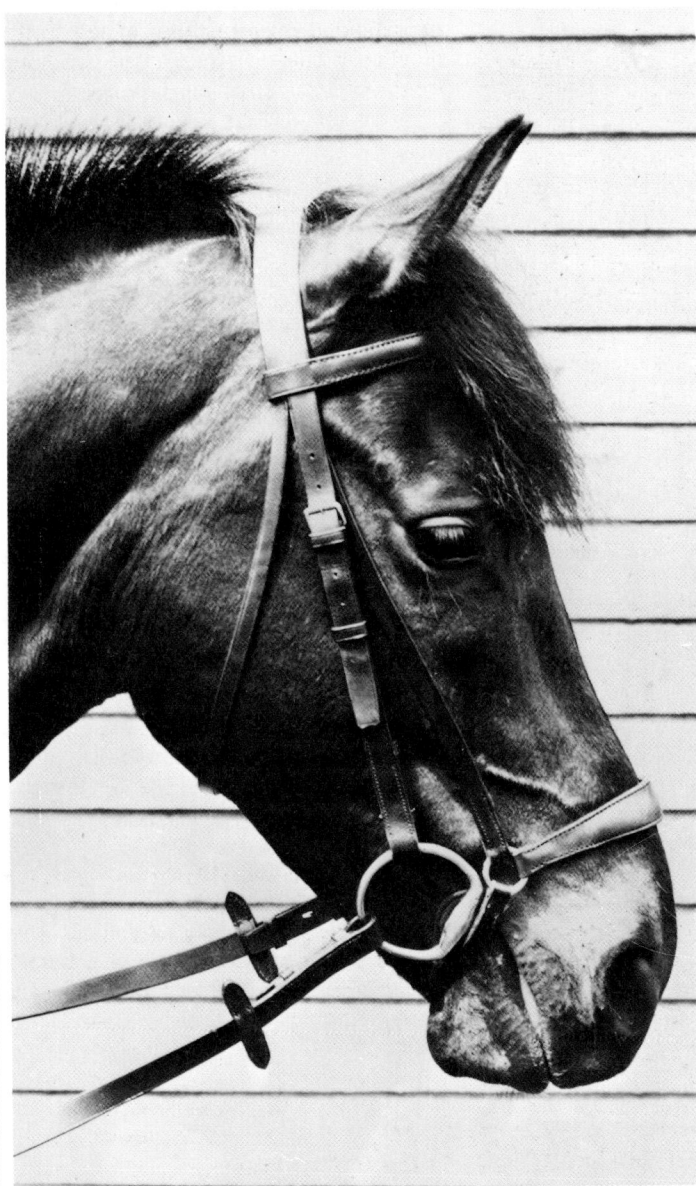

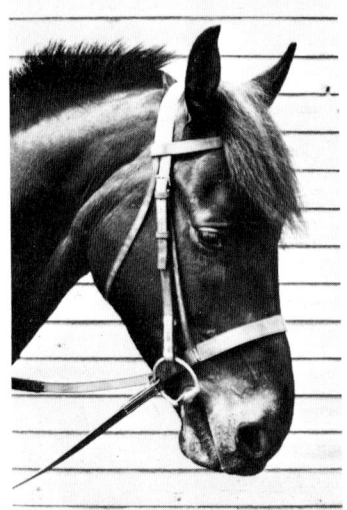

Left: Drop noseband, fastening below the bit, a very common modern bitting arrangement.
Above: Plain cavesson noseband
Above right: Flash noseband.
Right: A raised, show-type noseband with a snaffle bridle.
Opposite, top left: 'Grackle' or Figure 8 noseband. **Top right:** Sheepskin noseband derived from the harness racing shadow noseband. **Bottom left:** Kineton or Puckle noseband. **Bottom right:** Australian racing cheeker.

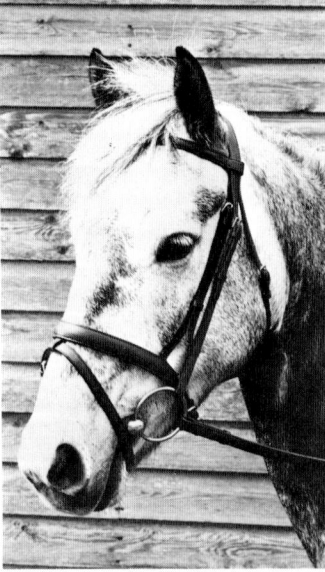

designed for use with a standing martingale, the two crossing straps sewn to the centre of the cavesson, which fasten under the bit, being the means by which the mouth is kept closed. It is not, however, as effective in lowering the head as the straightforward drop, since the point at which pressure is put on the nose is higher than in the true drop noseband. Far less nose pressure can be applied as well.

The Grakle was named after a horse of that name who wore one when he won the British Grand National in 1931. In fact, the Grakle has lost the chief features of its design in recent years and has become merged into the general concept of a cross-over noseband. In its original form, the top strap, fastening above the bit, was carefully shaped, so that it and the lower strap, fastening under the bit, were kept exactly in place; this being assisted by the connecting strap at the rear. Nose pressure was localized at the point of intersection of the straps, but could be adjusted at the headpiece so the point was raised.

The cross-over nosebands are possibly not as precise as the conventional drops, but they are probably more suited to some horses. This is because of their reduced degree of restriction, particularly in relation to the respiration, which make them suitable for the hard-pulling cross-country horse and for the steeplechaser.

The Kineton, or Puckle, noseband goes to the opposite extreme. It has no pretensions to be other than a strong stopping agent for use on very hard-pulling horses. It makes no attempt to close the mouth, the metal loops, fixed behind the bit, transmitting the very considerable pressure which can be obtained directly to the nose by means of the nosepiece which is adjusted both low and fairly tight. The nosepiece is frequently reinforced with a core of light metal.

A noseband popular in racing and other equestrian circles is the sheepskin-covered noseband, which originally was used with harness trotters as an 'anti-shadow' or 'anti-shy' noseband. In the context of the trotting horse the 'shadow roll', as this noseband is termed, has a definite purpose. In conjunction with the characteristic extended nose position of the trotter moving at speed, it prevented the horse from seeing shadows on the track or variations in the surface colour which might cause him to check or break his gait. It has far less to commend it in the context of the riding horse and very little in the context of racing either. No firm opinion, for example, is held as to whether the use of the sheepskin-covered noseband is supposed to encourage a horse to put his head up or down.

The Australian Cheeker

A final, useful piece of equipment is the noseband referred to as an Australian Cheeker, which, for no very good reason, is confined largely to the racing scene. Usually made of rubber, the cheeker fits over the bit rings on either side and then joins into a central strap which runs right up the face and fastens to an attachment on the headpiece of the bridle, right between the horse's ears.

Correctly fitted, the noseband lifts the bit in the mouth, which makes it more difficult for a horse to get his 'tongue over the bit', thus evading its action and causing even more serious trouble by 'swallowing' the tongue. This, however, is not its only effect. For some reason which is still not satisfactorily understood, anything running up the centre of a horse's face exerts some form of psychological restraint and is a very effective ploy to use in the case of hard pullers. In more elaborate forms the system can be seen incorporated into the Rockwell bridle and the Norton Perfection, or Citation; these are bridles of American origin used in racing.

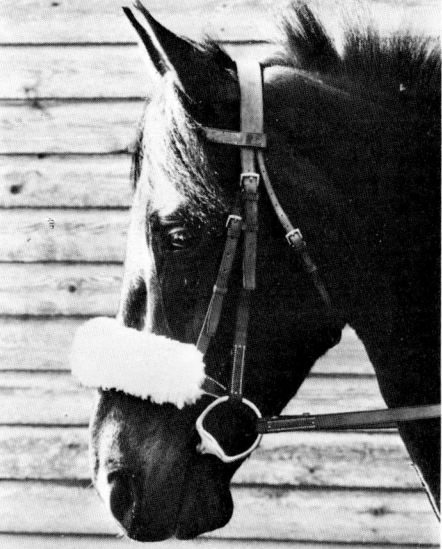

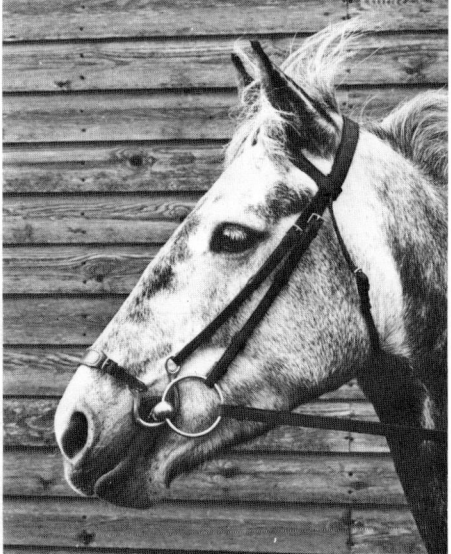

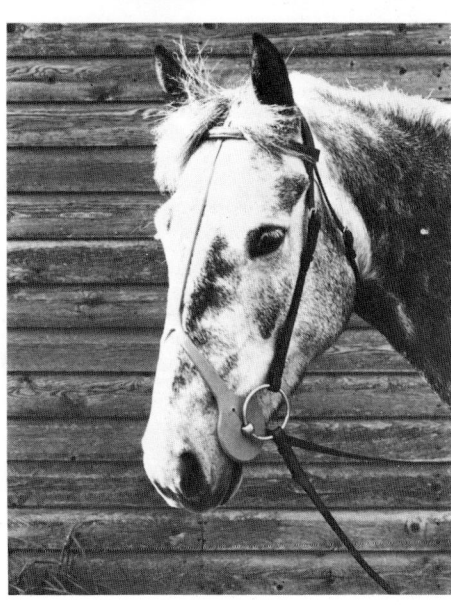

Bridling Aids · Bridles—Types and Fitting

CHAPTER FIVE · BITS, BRIDLES AND ADDITIONAL AIDS

The various parts of the bridle are virtually common to all types, although they may not look the same or employ the same method of fastening.

The head of the bridle, passing over the horse's poll, has attached to it the cheeks to which the bit is secured. The throatlatch (pronounced throatlash) is usually incorporated in the head, though, in some instances, it is a completely separate strap attached to the head by a loop fixed between the horse's ears, as in some American patterns.

Certain types of bridle, however, omit the throatlatch completely. There are, for instance, no throatlatches on the bridles used in the Spanish Riding School in Vienna. The reason for this is that a throatlatch, if it is too tight, can discourage a horse from flexing at the poll, because of the discomfort it would cause. The Spanish School Lipizzaners are, in any case, naturally thick through the jowl and, since

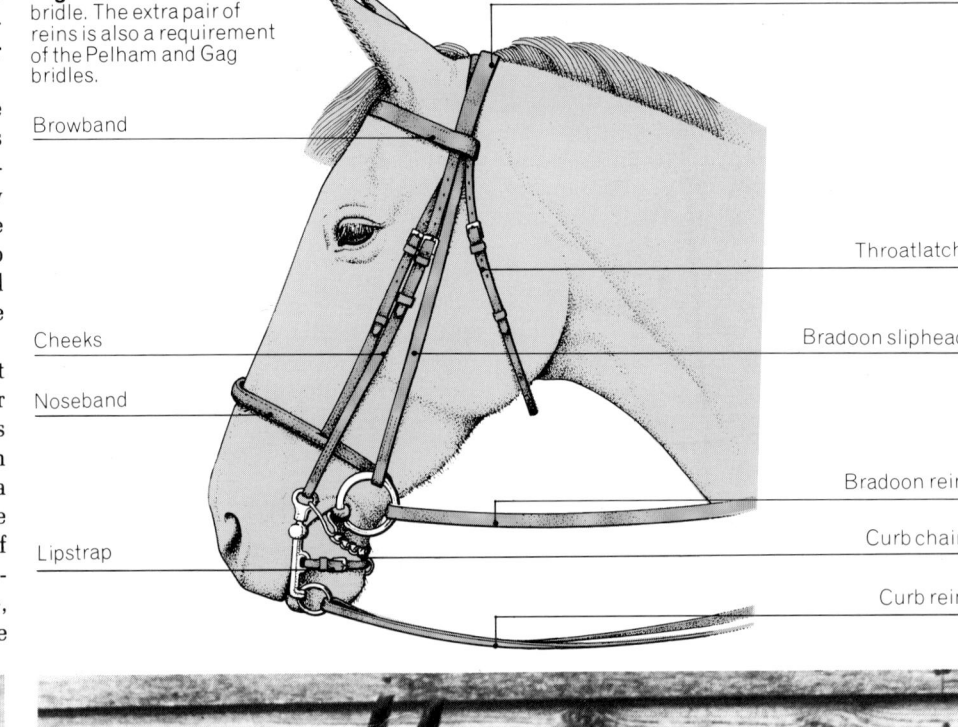

Right: Parts of a double bridle. The extra pair of reins is also a requirement of the Pelham and Gag bridles.

- Browband
- Cheeks
- Noseband
- Lipstrap
- Headpiece
- Throatlatch
- Bradoon sliphead
- Bradoon rein
- Curb chain
- Curb rein

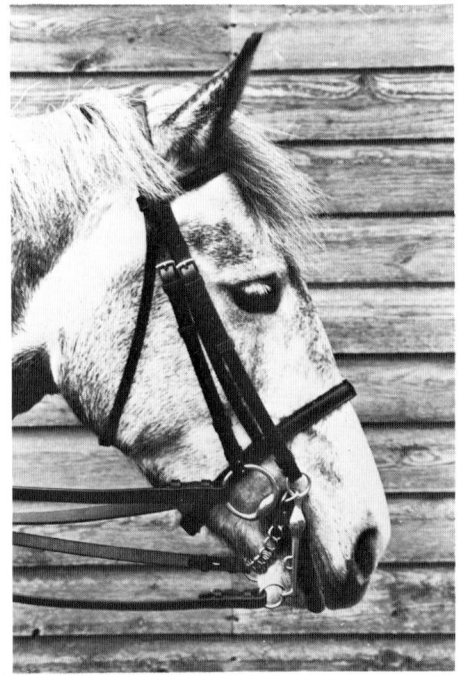

Right: Fine leather, lightweight show bridle with raised and swelled noseband. **Above:** Weymouth bridle in hunting, general purpose weight. Bridles can be attached to bits by sewing, hook studs or, very occasionally, buckles.

BRIDLES – TYPES AND FITTING

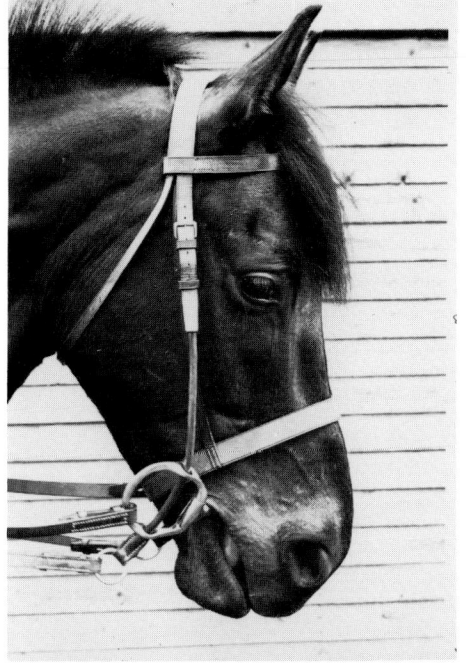

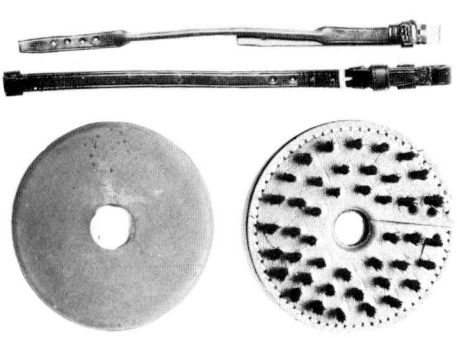

Top, left to right: Gag bridle; Hackamore or bitless bridle; Pelham, which can be converted to a single rein with a leather rounding joining the bradoon and curb rings. **Left:** Hunting snaffle. **Below:** Two types of lipstrap, rounded and flat leather. **Bottom, left:** Rubber cheek guard. **Right:** Brush pricker, used on one side of the bridle to prevent a horse hanging in that direction.

CHAPTER FIVE · BITS, BRIDLES AND ADDITIONAL AIDS

Right: Reins are made in a variety of patterns and materials, usually with a view to giving the rider a better grip, particularly in wet weather or if the rein becomes wet with sweat. **Left to right:** Laced handpart; canvas rein with finger stop; leather plaited rein; nylon plaited rein; plain leather rein; rubber handpart rein.

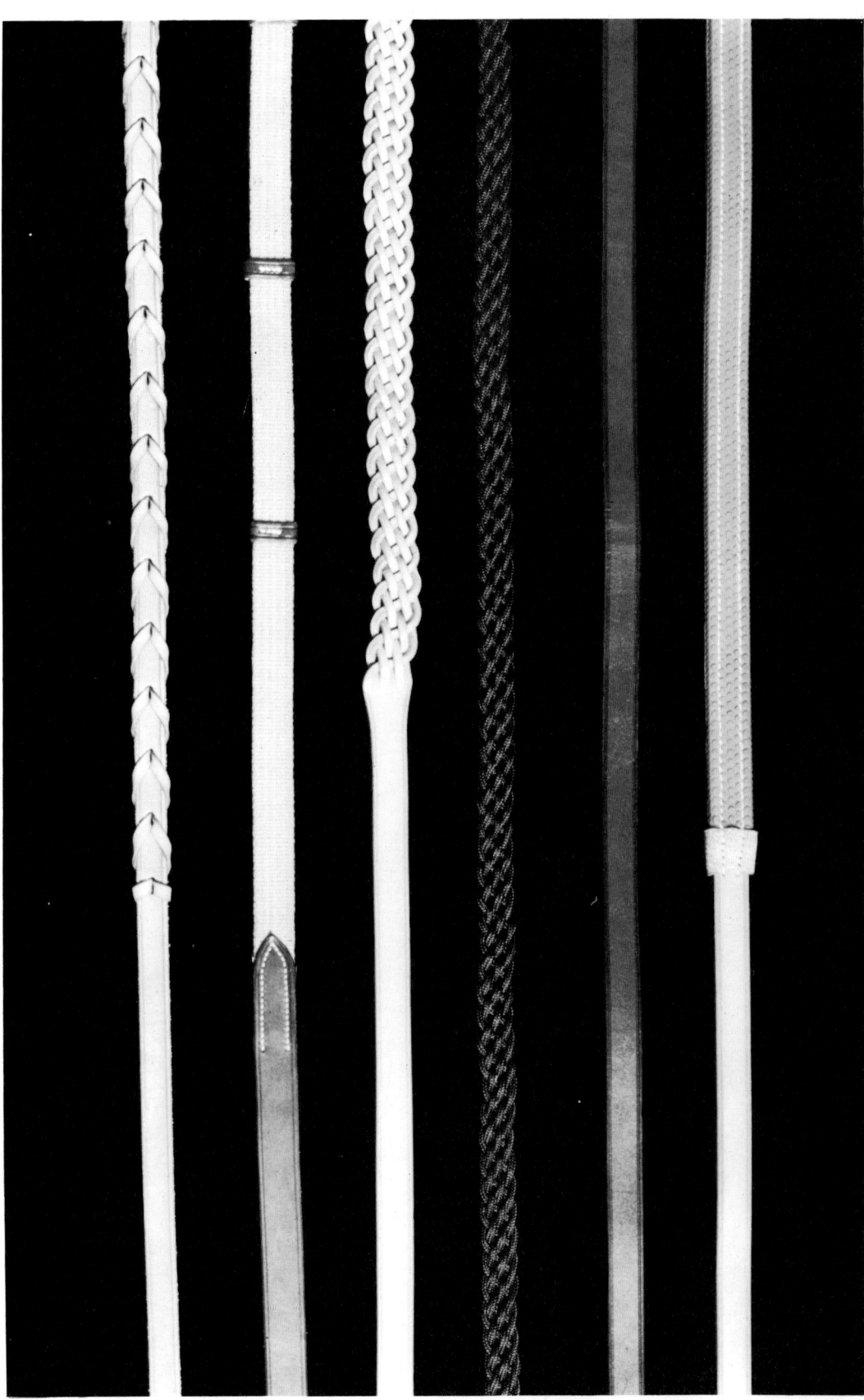

BRIDLES – TYPES AND FITTING

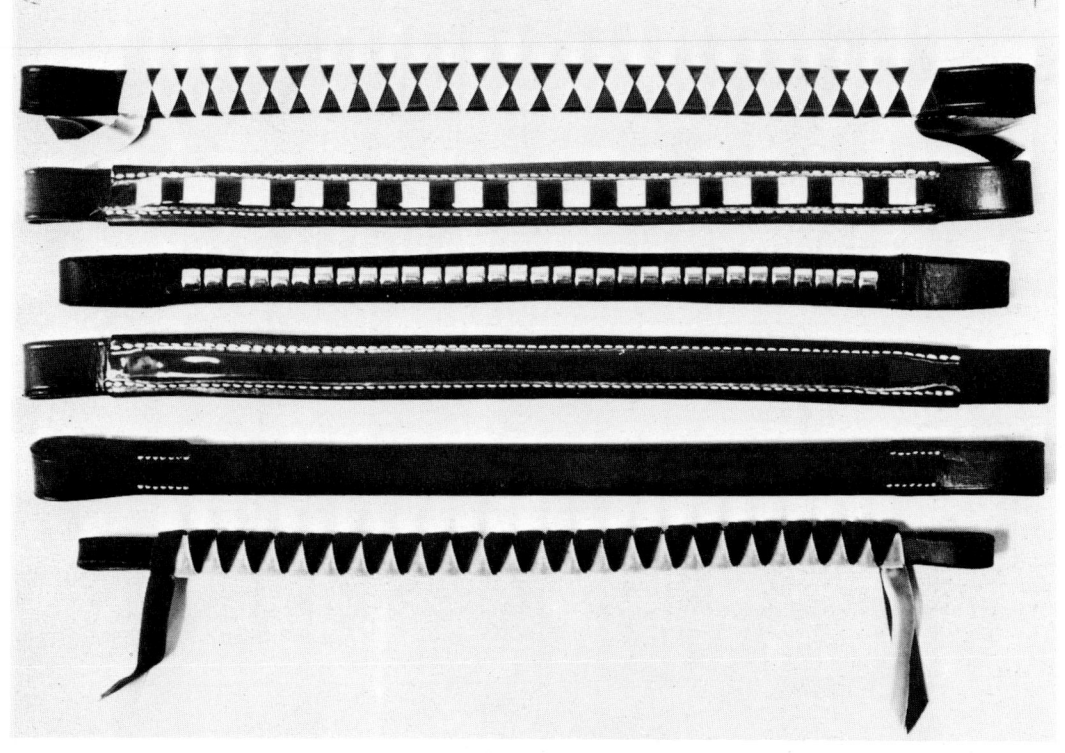

Left: Browbands are available in numerous patterns. Those covered in coloured silk or plastic are usually reserved for show bridles. Brass mounted 'clinker' browbands are for use with in-hand bridles. **Below:** American browbands are considerably more elaborate than the European variety.

they are unlikely to get into situations in which the bridle may be pulled off, there is no need of a throatlatch. Its other purpose is to keep the bridle from coming off in the event of a fall, for instance. A number of Western bridles also dispense with the throatlatch, preferring to keep the bridle in place by a slit passed over either both ears or a single ear.

The browband, or 'front' as it is sometimes known, is fastened by loops to the headpiece and acts to keep the latter from sliding backwards. There is then, in most bridles, but not in all, a noseband and then finally a pair of reins.

Double bridles and Pelhams

The above describes the composition of a snaffle bridle, but, in the case of double bridles and Pelhams, additions are needed. On a double bridle, for instance, there has to to be a sliphead, from which the bradoon is suspended. A sliphead is a strap and one cheekpiece passed through the loops of the browband under the headpiece. The cheek of the sliphead is placed on the off-side so that its buckle matches that of the noseband on the near-side.

In both the double and Pelham bridles, a pair of extra reins is necessary, the curb rein always being the narrower of the two. There is also the addition of a lipstrap, which is attached to the dees halfway down the cheeks of the bit and through the 'fly' (flying) link in the centre of the curb chain. Its purpose is to keep the curb chain in place.

Leather, buckles and reins

The substance of the leather used in manufacture and the width of the component parts varies according to the purpose of the bridle. A show bridle, for instance, will be light and the various straps and reins thin. The noseband may be swelled and hand stitched in a pattern across the nosepiece. Race bridles will be similarly very light, but for their own, different, reasons, while they are always fitted with rubber hand-part reins. Hunting bridles, which must stand up to hard wear, in the rough and tumble of the hunting field, will be necessarily made from heavier leathers.

The bridle may be fastened to the bit or bits in a variety of ways. Though buckles can be used, they are usually considered to be clumsy and 'incorrect'. Hook studs are probably as popular a form of fastening as any other. Loops and toggles are often used on American bridles and many others, but without doubt the neatest method is to sew the bridle to the bit or bits. A sewn bridle has obvious disadvantages. It cannot be dismantled for cleaning purposes and it is difficult to keep the leather nourished and supple where it turns round the bit eyes and rings, and where it becomes worn because of the inevitable friction between the metal and the leather.

The reins again vary, according to the purpose required of them. Most of the various types of reins are designed with the object of giving the rider a better grip in wet weather, when the horse sweats profusely, or when riding a strongly pulling animal.

Plain reins are used almost exclusively for showing activities, but in competition work, reins which afford more grip are the ones most used. Probably the most popular are the reins fitted with a rubber hand-part or, certainly for show jumping, those made of strong web with leather 'finger stops' sewn along their length. Plaited leather reins, or a plain rein laced along its length to give a good grip to the fingers are also very satisfactory, although the former tend to stretch unless the saddler has taken the trouble to 'pre-stretch' his leather before plaiting and making up.

Nylon reins, which were once very popular, now seem to have largely disappeared. These were poor substitutes for the real thing, stretching interminably,

CHAPTER FIVE · BITS, BRIDLES AND ADDITIONAL AIDS

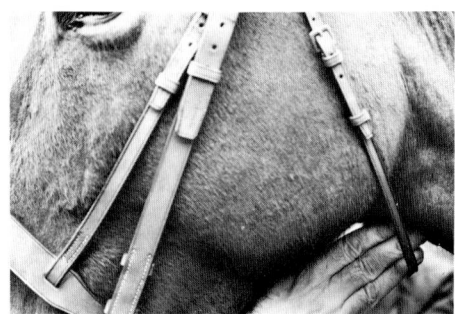

Fitting: The throatlatch must be loose enough to allow flexion of the poll without restriction of the gullet.

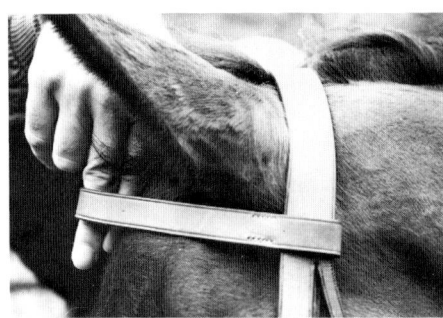

The browband needs to be sufficiently large so that the headpiece is not pulled up against the back of the ears.

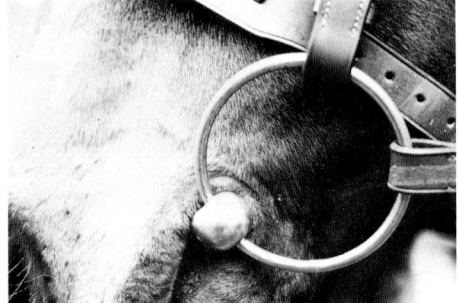

The bit should fit high enough in the mouth to just wrinkle the lips and should project no more than ½ in each side.

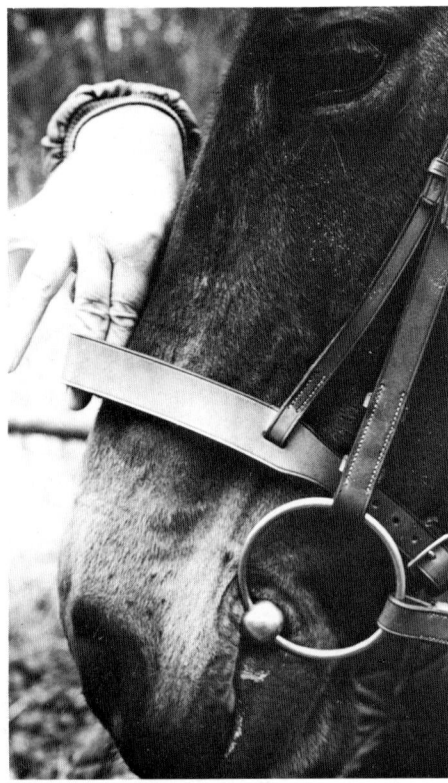

Above: Cavesson nosebands should permit the insertion of two fingers. A more tightly fitting noseband is permissable if a partial closure of the mouth is required. **Right:** A drop noseband fitted with a snaffle bridle, the rear strap sitting below the bit and in the curb groove. The nosepiece is adjusted some 3 in above the nostrils.

becoming slimy in the wet and developing sharp edges when dry.

Fitting the bridle

The fitting of a bridle is as important as the fitting of a saddle but the importance of doing this correctly is frequently not sufficiently recognized.

An over-size snaffle bit, for instance, causes just as much discomfort as one that is too small and so pinches the corners of the horse's mouth. If the bit is both too large and of the jointed variety, its length may bring it into contact with the roof of the mouth at its central joint; it will in any case tend to pull through the mouth so that its action is off centre. The snaffle should project no more than a half inch on either side of the mouth at its extremities, if it is of the type fitted with a loose, wire ring. If it is of the eggbutt or cheek variety, half that distance is sufficient. The same applies to a curb bit or Pelham with a fixed cheek, but the extra quarter inch is needed if the bit has a sliding cheek. In the case of curb bits and Pelhams, it is always advisable to bend the eye of the bit outwards, so that there is no chance of it rubbing against the face.

Both snaffle and Pelham bits need to be adjusted fairly high in the mouth, sufficient to wrinkle the corners of the lips in a little 'smile'. The same applies to the bradoon of a double bridle, the curb bit being fitted a shade lower so as to rest over the bars of the mouth.

When fitted, plain cavesson nosebands should allow the insertion of two fingers beneath them, unless it is intended that they be employed to close the horse's mouth. This second practice is not without risk, since a tight noseband may cause deformities in the growth of the teeth particularly in a young horse.

It should be possible to insert three fingers under the throatlatch, if the horse is to have the ability to flex without discomfort. It is particularly important to ensure that the browband is long enough to prevent it pulling the headpiece against the back of the ears. Nothing is more likely to make a horse become an habitual head-shaker than the irritation of a headpiece pressing uncomfortably against the back of his ears.

Proper and regular cleaning is also vital. Obviously, every part of the bridle should be kept soft, supple and clean if it is to be comfortable in use.

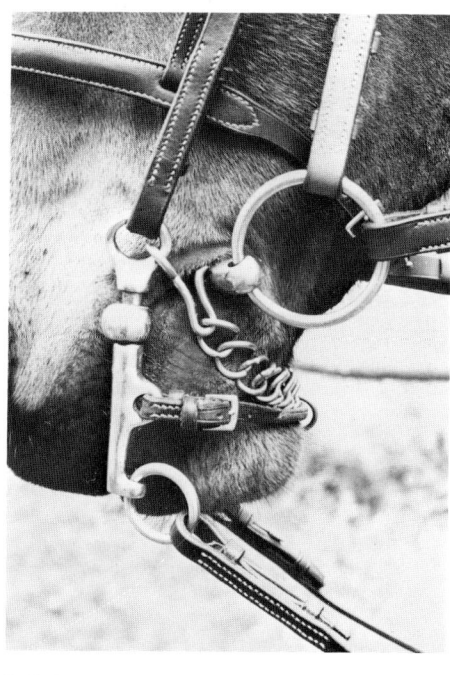

Left: The correct fitting of the double bridle.
Above: Detail showing fastening of the lipstrap to the curb chain.

Bridling Aids · The Western Hackamore System

The ultimate bitting development in the horsemanship of Europe was the curb bit, the most extreme examples of which are the giant-cheeked examples of the Middle Ages. The curb dominated European equestrian thinking and practice for centuries, but in the Middle East there survived a different riding tradition which placed a greater emphasis on control and submission being achieved through pressures concentrated on the nose, rather than the mouth. This tradition extended upwards into the Mediterranean countries, where its influence is still to be seen, as well as in areas further to the east. In countries of the Middle East today, horses are ridden by means of a thick wool rope attached behind the lower jaw to light chains encircling the nose.

A more sophisticated variation on this basic simplicity can be seen in the painting by Henry Bernard Chalon of *George IV's Persian Horses being taken out for exercise* (they are, in fact, Arabian horses), on view in the Tate Gallery, London. In this picture, the action of the bit is assisted materially by the attachment of a light nose chain. The arrangement is remarkably similar to that used on the American cow-pony, though, instead of a nose chain, the American horse wears a light rawhide 'bosal'. The connection, however, is very clear, which is not as surprising as it might at first appear. Further examples can be seen in Italy, where the horses drawing the *fiacres* are driven from a noseband fitted on each side with a ring set on a projecting metal shank to which the reins are attached. The assembly resembles a lungeing cavesson and employs no bit at all.

Origins of the hackamore

The apotheosis of the 'nose school' of riding (as opposed to that which concerns itself primarily with the mouth) came in the period following the Moorish conquest of large parts of the Iberian Peninsula in the 7th and 8th centuries and the long occupation which followed.

The Moors, who at one time threatened to engulf Europe until their decisive defeat by Charles Martel and his knights at Poitiers in AD 720, established a highly sophisticated system of horse schooling based on the use of the sensitive nose area. It employed as a principal element an item termed *la jaquima*, from which the word 'hackamore' is derived. The system was a progression, which culminated in the production of a highly schooled, particularly well-balanced horse. As a result of its training, the horse could perform 'practical dressage' movements—in combat or working with bulls—at full speed on the weight of a floating rein attached to a

Above: 16th-century curb bit of German manufacture. The bit is unusual in the width of its mouthpiece which is also jointed. Provision has been made for the bit to be used as a form of Pelham; there are top rings to which the reins can be attached. **Right:** Henry Bernard Chalon's picture, *George IV's Persian Horses*, from the Tate Gallery, London. The action of the bit is assisted by a light nose chain.

ported curb bit and the indications made by the disposition of the rider's body.

Eight centuries later, the Spanish *conquistadores* took themselves, their culture, their horses and their horselore to the American continent, where horses had been extinct for millions of years. Settling in Mexico and California, which were to become cattle-ranching countries, it was their horse-culture, ideally suited to cattle working, which was to become part of the Western legend. Their equipment and methods, modified and adapted to local needs, gave the world the culture of the Western horseman, which survives and is practised actively today all through the western states of the USA and on into Canada.

The true hackamore

In Europe, 'hackamore' often is used mistakenly to describe a bitless-type bridle, usually fitted with metal cheekpieces. The true hackamore largely consists of a heavy braided rawhide noseband, the shape of a *Réal* tennis racquet, with a large knot at the end which lies under the horse's chin. The noseband itself is called a bosal and is fitted to the horse by means of a lightweight latigo headstall. This may be slit at an appropriate point so that it can be kept in place by passing it over an ear, or may be made more secure by the addition of a browband, a *cavesada*.

The hackamore is completed by the addition of a rope made from mane hair, which is called the *mecate* and usually by a *fiador*, made from the same material or sometimes from cotton. The *mecate* is attached to the heel knot by a system of 'wraps' to produce a delicately balanced and sophisticated control device, the heavy rope reins and the heel knot combining to act as a counterweight to the substantial nosepiece. The *fiador* is used as a throatlatch and adjusted short enough to prevent the heel knot from bumping annoyingly against the lower jaw as the horse moves.

The hackamore is adjusted so that the nosepiece of the heavy bosal lies at least 2in above the ending of the nose cartilage, the cheeks sloping downward to the curb groove, behind and below which lies the heel knot. The cheeks of the bosal are scarcely in contact with the horse; at rest the hackamore barely touches the nose, so well is it balanced. The extent of the pressure that can be applied is determined by the number of 'wraps' taken with the *mecate* round the heel knot. Only when the hand is raised and the bosal tipped into contact is a momentary restraint put on the nose which causes the horse to retract the head. Directional changes, which, in common with all movements,

Left: An Arab horse wearing a fairly powerful curb bit of Turkish design which was most probably introduced via a system employing a nose-chain. **Below:** The finished Western horse executing the difficult sliding halt in a Western curb bit, but with the rein in a virtually looped position.

CHAPTER FIVE · BITS, BRIDLES AND ADDITIONAL AIDS

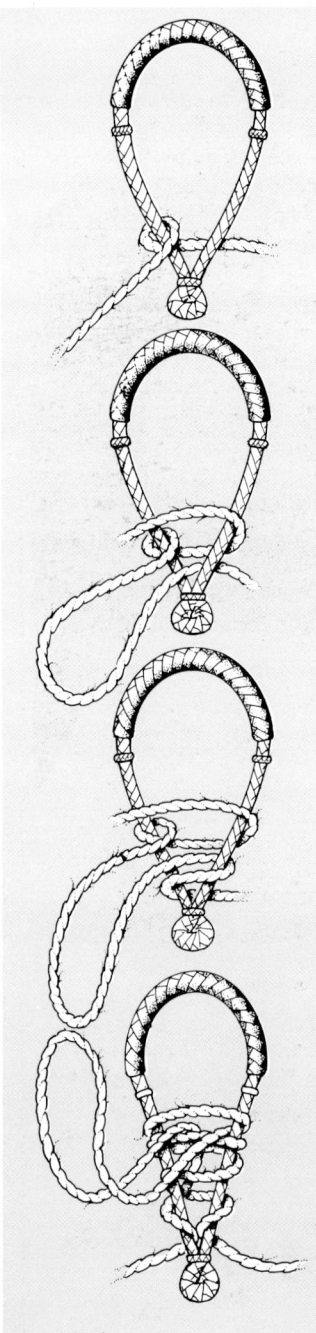

Above: The method employed to attach the **mecate** to the heel knot of the **bosal** in a series of wraps. The rope reins (**mecate**) and the heel knot act as a counterweight to the substantial nosepiece. **Right:** The **bosal** fitted to the horse by the **latigo** headstall. It is so balanced as to lie clear of nose and jawbones whilst the horse maintains a steady and correctly positioned head carriage.

THE WESTERN HACKAMORE SYSTEM

Above: The parts of the hackamore including the **fiador**, the throat-latch which prevents the heel knot from bumping annoyingly against the lower jaw.

Below: The rawhide **bosal**, the woven **mecate** and the simple **latigo** headstall which combine to make the hackamore.

THE CURB BIT

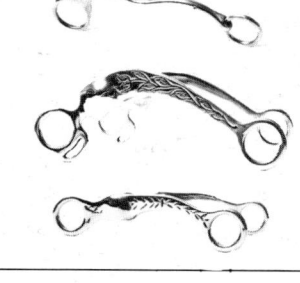

Above: The Western curb bit which is the last stage in the Californian system of bridling. In the trained Western horse it is sufficient to maintain contact with the mouth by the weight of the rein alone. **Left:** A selection of Western curb bits including one with 'pistol' cheeks.

are taught first at the walk, are made by a rein pull outwards to the side required, supported by the opposite rein being laid on the neck. At all times the low-held hands operate on the act-and-yield principle—the hand acting to obtain the movement and yielding the moment the latter becomes evident. The action of the bosal on the nose teaches the horse to 'tuck in' or flex the head and neck, while the heavy heel knot acts in opposition to this when Necessary to ensure that it is impossible for him to evade the pressure on his nose by means of over-bending.

From hackamore to bit

Initially, the hackamore is used with both hands, but, as the horse's schooling progresses, the reins are used in one hand only. The fully schooled hackamore horse can carry out all the movements required of him in a state of constant balance and at high speed. He can make the sudden stops, the pivots (the equivalent of the dressage pirouette, though not the same movement), the turns and the rein-backs all on a looping rein and without his mouth ever being touched. The final stage is the graduation from the hackamore to the bit, usually, but not always, a fairly long-cheeked, high-ported curb (the port is the inverted U in the mouthpiece which allows room for the tongue and permits the bearing surface of the bit to rest directly on the bars). This transition is a gradual one, made with the help of a much

CHAPTER FIVE · BITS, BRIDLES AND ADDITIONAL AIDS

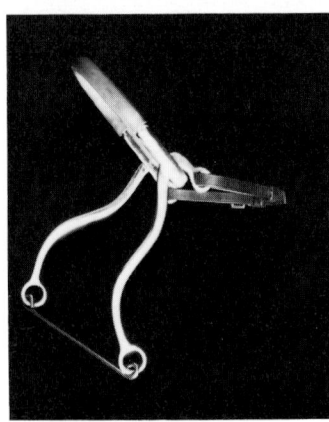

Top and right: Two variations of the bitless bridle, misnamed hackamore, now in general use. Both achieve their object by putting pressure on the nose. The sheepskin padding on the nose and rear strap is to prevent chafing. It is also necessary to vary the fitting frequently to avoid callousing the nose. **Above:** Another bitless bridle, acting as a form of curb on the nose and employing a single rein.

THE WESTERN HACKAMORE SYSTEM

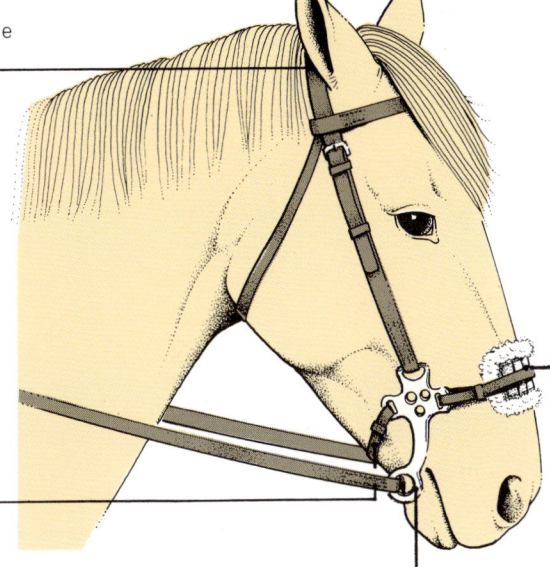

Below: This diagram shows the action of the European hackamore

A little pressure is exerted on the poll by the headpiece.

The tight back strap also exerts pressure and should be well padded.

The longer the cheekpiece, to which noseband and backstrap are fastened, the more severe the action.

Pressure is exerted by a tightly fastened noseband. Care should be taken that it comes above the ending of the nose cartilage.

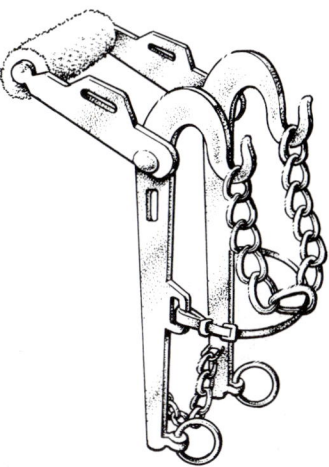

Above: The William Stone Bitless Pelham. It is relatively sophisticated and is used with two reins.

lighter hackamore fitted with a pair of very light rein ropes. It is often known as a two-rein bosal. In the final stages, control passes to the bit, the latter being supported by a bosal of the very lightest proportions acting independently without reins.

The finished Western horse is ridden in a light curb bit bridle without a bosal or noseband of any sort, and a floating, or looping, rein, which exerts no more than a minimal contact on the mouth. Sometimes the reins are weighted by the addition of small decorative pieces of metal, but the ideal is for the horse to ride on the weight of a plain ¼in rawhide rein!

The European hackamore

The European equivalent of the hackamore is the variety of bitless-type bridles, deriving from the hackamore system. Of these, the best known is Blair's pattern. This bridle consists of the usual type of headpiece, a noseband, a curb, or back strap, and a pair of long metal cheeks to which the last two items are attached. Control is effected by exerting pressure on the nose and on the back strap embracing the lower jaw, the potential severity of the action being dependent upon the length of the cheek. Since nosepiece and back strap must be adjusted tightly to be effective, both must be soft and well-padded. The nosepiece should rest, as in the case of the bosal, above the ending of the nose cartilage, so as not to restrict the breathing, and its position needs to be altered continually if the nose is not to become calloused.

Contrary to the general view, the bitless bridle is not suitable for novice use, since a novice could do far more damage with it than with a metal bit. Nor will it produce sudden and miraculous results. It is the precision tool of the expert horseman with of a pair of delicate hands. Ideally, it, too, should operate from a floating rein, changes of direction being made by carrying the required rein outwards and combining that action with a shift of the body weight in the same direction. Less severe and often effective on a horse whose mouth, for whatever reason, precludes the use of a bit, are the far shorter cheeked bitless bridles, but they have little in common with the hackamore system.

An interesting bitless bridle is that perfected by William Stone, a loriner in Walsall, Britain, who worked for many years with the firm of Matthew Harvey Ltd. It is called the W S Bitless Pelham and it, or something very similar, is still available on the market today. The bridle employs two reins—hence the term 'Pelham'—the top rein acting on the nose and the lower one on the curb groove by means of a curb chain. The metal cheeks of the bridle, which are comparatively short, move independently and thus allow a certain finesse in the action which is not found in other patterns in current use.

The advantages of the hackamore system are obvious enough in the schooling of polo ponies, for instance, but perhaps less so in regard to the modern, competitive horse-world. This is considered to be unfortunate by many, because there is much to commend to the present-day rider in this older and infinitely skilful school of riding.

CHAPTER SIX

Driving and Farm Harness

Present Day
Whips
Trotting Equipment
The Farm Horse

A pair of work horses in farm harness with Scottish pattern peaked collars. The horse was the dominant factor in agriculture over the centuries.

CHAPTER SIX · DRIVING HARNESS

Driving Harness · **Present Day**

The driving harness of today is being produced, as it has been for centuries, to a large variety of designs, shapes and sizes to suit different requirements. Some basic factors have remained the same—the best harness is made of either black or brown leather—but, in certain instances, new substances have come into use alongside traditional ones. Materials such as plain webbing, plastic coated webbing, canvas and buffalo hide are now used for some modern exercise harness, while rivets take the place of stitches on some sets. The harness furniture—that is, buckles and so on—can be made of brass, nickel or other white metal, or it can be silver-plated. Gold-plated furniture is fashionable in parts of Australia for exhibition purposes.

Showing harness
The most popular harness for showing in private driving classes is made of black leather with patent trim on the blinkers, collar, saddle, false martingale front and face drop. Brass furniture is favoured. The

HISTORICAL ACCOUTREMENTS

Above: Accessories certainly not in evidence today: a sun bonnet; black silk bridle front for periods of mourning; decorative French flowers for horses' heads.

PRESENT DAY

Left: Single harness turnout to a four-wheeled vehicle at a driving meet. This light, black harness is plain and functional but very smart.

CHAPTER SIX · DRIVING HARNESS

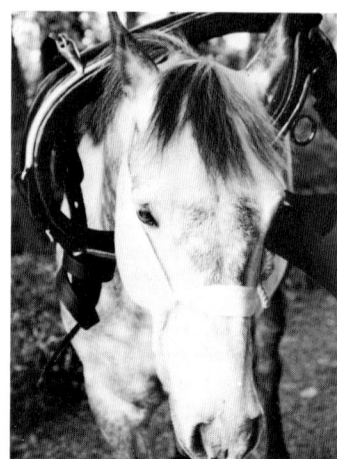
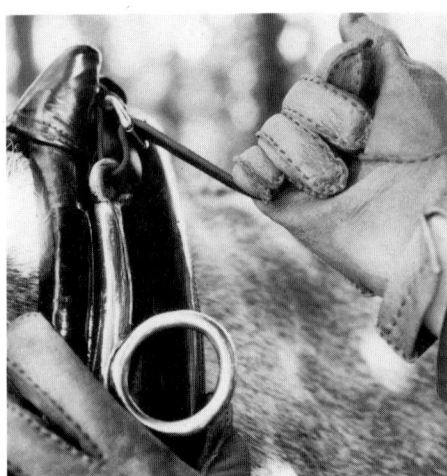
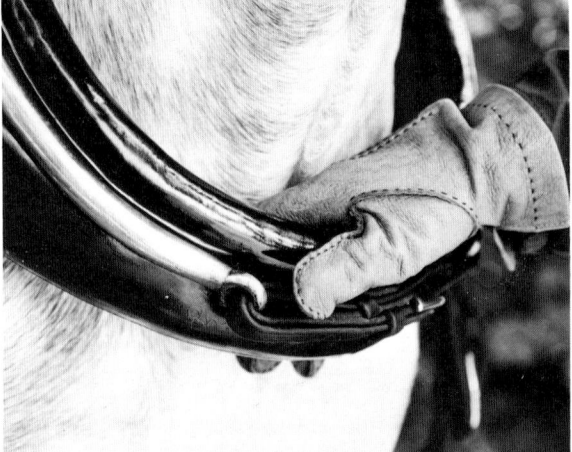

harness itself is as light and elegant as it is practical. Two layers of fine quality leather are painstakingly joined by rows of hand stitching wherever possible. Such parts as the girth, belly band, loin strap and crupper have buckling adjustment on both sides so that perfect uniformity is obtained throughout the set.

Designs are broadly similar to those which were used 100 years ago, although some modern materials have been introduced. Some harness makers, for instance, now use fibreglass, instead of metal plates, for the winkers. As a result the winkers hold their shape better and do not rust. Saddle trees are now sometimes built with laminated wood to give them additional strength. Solid wood is more liable to crack and split and is more susceptible to woodworm, which dislike the glues that are used with laminated trees. Most modern patent leather is finished with polyurethane, which makes it very durable and less likely to crack. It is not, however, as easy for the harness maker to work as it is reluctant to mould and difficult to finish on the edges.

Single harness

Different types of harness are necessary for a single, pair, tandem and team. A set of single harness is designed for one horse to work between the shafts of a two- or four-wheeled vehicle. It consists of a bridle, collar, saddle, reins and a multiplicity of additional components. These can amount to as many as 35 separate items when the set is taken apart for cleaning.

When harnessing a single horse, the collar is always the first item. There is a strong superstition amongst driving people which holds that there will be an accident if any other part of the harness is put on first. This belief probably originated in the days of serious coaching, when teams were harnessed in great haste. The collar and hames were put on with the false martingale buckled round the collar. Then, when the pad went on, the martingale could be threaded through the girth as it was buckled. This was quicker than putting the pad on and girthing it before putting on the collar and martingale, because the girth would then have to be undone again to take the martingale. This coaching practice has remained a part of the technique to the present day.

When putting on the collar, great care must be taken to stretch it slightly sideways, so that it is not forced over the animal's eyes. It should then be left upside down on the horse's neck while the hames are put into place in the groove between the fore- and afterwales. The top hame strap should now be buckled to fasten the hames lightly on to the collar. The latter can then be turned around, at the windpipe, and pushed down into position against the shoulders where it should fit comfortably. The top hame strap must now be tightened, so that the hames fit firmly into place. They should lie well into the groove so that there is no danger of them coming out.

The fit of the collar is also extremely

Opposite: Stages in putting on the collar. **Top, left to right:** The collar, turned upside down, is put over the head; hames are fitted to the collar while the latter is still reversed; collar turned round with the lie of the mane. **Bottom, left to right:** Hame strap tightened; check to see that it is possible to pass the hand between the bottom of the collar and the base of the neck; check to see that a flat hand can be inserted between collar and neck. **Right:** If it is not possible to find a properly-fitting collar, a breast collar is a satisfactory substitute and is easy to fit.

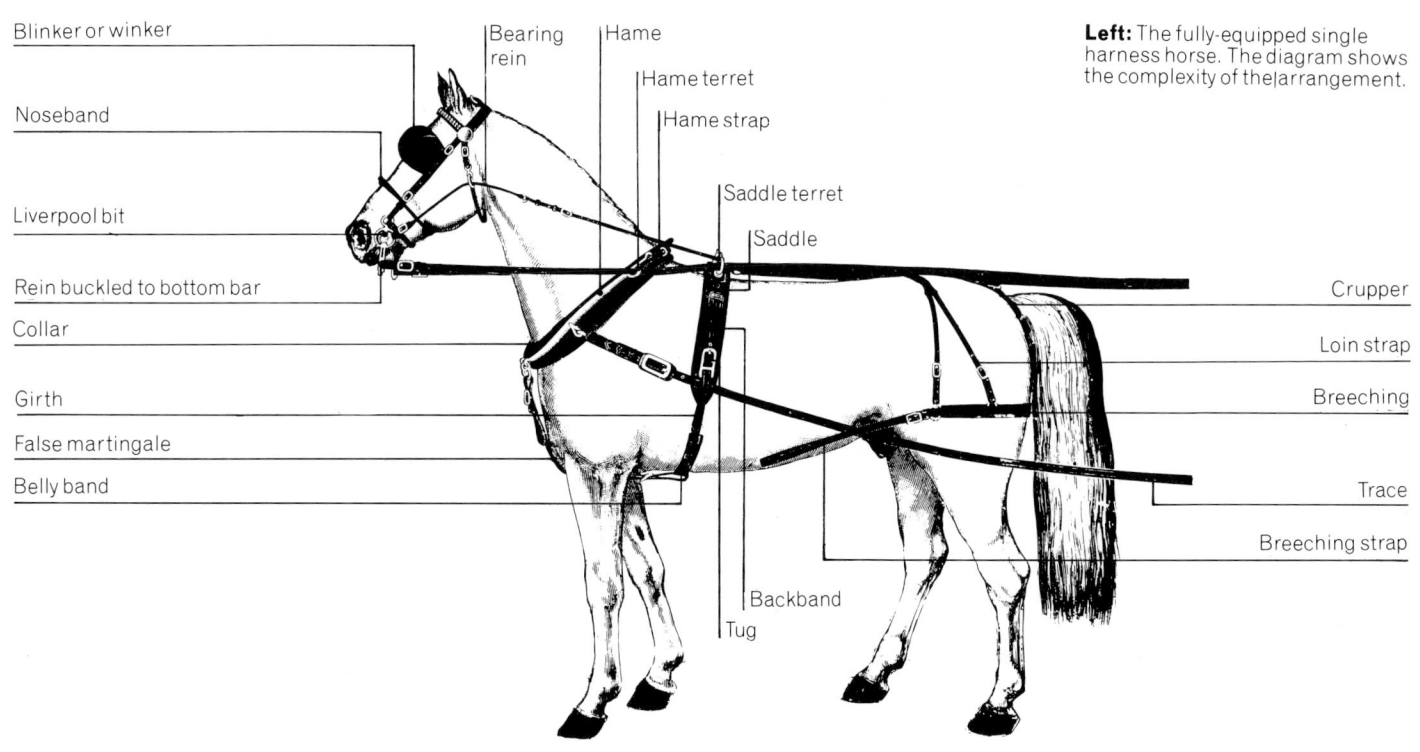

Left: The fully-equipped single harness horse. The diagram shows the complexity of the arrangement.

Right: The saddle is built on a tree which, as in the case of the riding saddle, must fit the horse's back comfortably. **Below:** Placing the saddle in position on the back. It is most important, both from the point of view of looks and of the horse's comfort, that the saddle is not placed too far forward on the back.

important. There should be adequate room at the side to permit the flat of the hand to lie between the horse's neck and the collar, while there must be enough space at the bottom to allow the whole hand to pass freely between the base of the collar and the bottom of the neck. A collar which is too wide will rock from side to side. One which is too narrow will pinch. One which is too deep will ride upwards, whilst one which is too shallow will press against the windpipe. It can be very difficult indeed to find a collar which fits the horse properly. One which does not fit will probably gall the horse and make him sore. This, understandably, can lead to reluctance to work and may result in severe problems.

If it proves impossible to find a collar that fits correctly, it is better to use a breast collar, rather than compromise. A breast collar can be adjusted at the neckpiece to fit any horse or pony within a range of a hand (4in) or more. More importantly, it can be made to fit narrow, wide, muscular or scraggy necks; finding different collars for a horse whose neck changes shape and size, according to the time of the year and the amount of grass consumed, can be wearying. The breast collar itself should be fitted to the animal in question so that it lies below the windpipe and above the point of the shoulder.

The traces are buckled to the hame tug buckles if a full collar is used or to the tug buckles on the breast part of a breast collar if that is employed. Traces are generally made of two layers of leather which are stitched with four rows of stitching. Hand stitching is preferable, although this is naturally far more expensive than

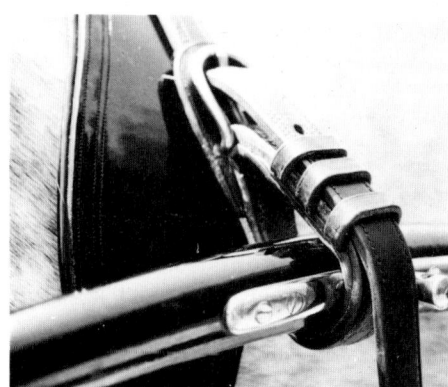

Positioning the shaft tug: The shaft tug in position against the tug stop or safe. The tugs are buckled onto the backband, which must take the weight of the vehicle if necessary.

Connecting the traces to the vehicle: The traces are attached firmly to the vehicle by hooking them over an open-ended loop known as a trace hook.

Attaching the breeching strap: The breeching strap is buckled round the shaft and the traces and also through the breeching dee which is found on the shaft.

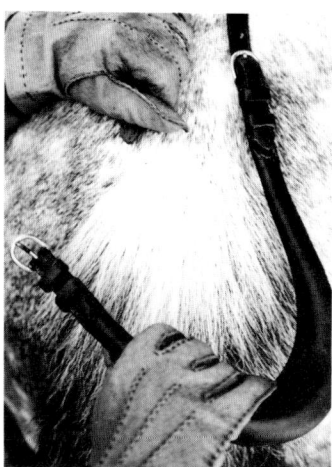

Left: When fitting the crupper, the tail is folded carefully at the base of the dock and threaded through as shown. **Above:** The crupper dock is sometimes sewn to the crupper back strap, but buckles instead of stitches facilitate fitting and adjustment.

machine stitching. The advantage of the former is that if one stitch gets worn and breaks, the stitches will not run, as can happen with machine stitching.

A layer of leather lying under the hame tug buckle, known as a safe, saves trace wear from the buckle. It is cheaper to renew safes than to replace a pair of traces.

If a false martingale is used, it should be buckled around the collar and lower hame strap or hame chain. Its purpose, with a single horse, is to hold the collar down. Large moving horses, with big fronts and sloping shoulders, will tilt the collar upwards when they are in action.

The saddle's additions of backband, tugs, crupper and breeching are added separately and the completed assembly is put on next. It is important that the tree of the saddle fits the contours of the animal's back. Too narrow a tree will pinch the horse, while one which is too wide will press down on the horse's spine and make him sore. There should be adequate padding so that the horse can take the weight of the vehicle, if it becomes unbalanced for any reason. The backband is threaded through a slot in the saddle. The backband is normally made of double leather with four rows of stitching, similar to that of the traces. Its strength is essential as it may have to hold the weight of the vehicle through the tugs and shafts, both in going down hill, if the breeching is not tight enough, or if the balance of the vehicle is at fault.

The shaft tugs, which should have safes behind them, are buckled on to the backband. The terrets, which hold the reins in position, are screwed into threaded sockets in the saddle tree. The crupper back strap is passed through a dee at the back of the saddle. The point is then threaded back through its floating keeper before being buckled. The crupper dock, which is usually filled with linseed and well-oiled to keep it soft, is sometimes sewn to the crupper back strap, and is sometimes attached by one or two buckles to make it easier to put on the horse. The loin strap of the breeching is passed through the slot in the back strap of the crupper, and the seat of the breeching is buckled to the 10in strap on each side. The shaft straps are attached to rings at each end of the breeching seat, while the point should be passed through the keeper by the buckle in order to hold the strap on the ring.

The complete saddle unit should be placed on the middle of the horse's back. The tail is then folded at the base of the dock to take the crupper, like darning wool going through a needle. The crupper must then be carefully placed in position under the top of the dock, taking care to get all the hairs out from under the crupper. The breeching seat is left hanging loosely against the horse's hindquarters. It should be adjusted so that it lies below the widest and above the narrowest part of the quarters. The saddle should then be lifted up and put down in a position the same as that of a stable roller. Novices tend to place the saddle too far forward. Not only does this make the horse look long, but the faulty positioning can give the animal a sore back and girth galls. The girth can now be buckled, taking up the false martingale. The belly band is passed through the loop on the girth. This prevents it from sliding back towards the belly.

The reins are put on next. It is best if these are made of brown leather, since reins with black leather hand-parts tend to leave their dye on the driver's gloves and apron. The reins are threaded through the saddle terrets and hame terrets (or breast collar terrets, if fitted) with enough left at the head end to buckle to the bit. The

CHAPTER SIX · DRIVING HARNESS

Top: The reins are passed through the saddle terrets. **Above:** They are then passed through the hame terrets (or breast collar terrets, if fitted). **Right:** The loose rein ends are folded neatly into the off-side saddle terret so that they can be picked up easily by the driver when he mounts the vehicle.

loose, hand end should be folded into the offside saddle terret in such a way that it can be easily picked up for mounting.

The bridle is always put on last and should be fitted as carefully as a riding bridle. The browband must be of the correct size; one that is too short, for instance, will pull the headpiece against the ears and cause considerable discomfort. It is held in place on the headpiece by two rosettes, which are not purely for decoration. They are secured on to the browband by a dee at the back and the points of the headpiece are threaded down through the browband loop on either side of the rosette dee. This prevents the browband from rising upwards and keeps the blinkers close to the sides of the horse's face so that he cannot see backwards. The blinkers are permanently fixed to the cheeks of the bridle, the tops being held in place with stays coming from the centre of the headpiece. The noseband must fit correctly and should lie close to the nose so that the cheekpieces which are threaded down through slots in the noseband, and up through keepers on the outside, hang straight down the side of the horse's head. This again ensures blinkers kept in place.

Liverpool bits are most commonly used for single private driving. They have the advantage of providing a large range of positions for the reins allowing the bit to be used with greater or less severity. When the reins are buckled to the ring, or plain cheek, the action is that of a straight bar snaffle. Increasing degrees of curb action can be obtained as the reins are buckled lower down the cheeks, the bottom bar giving the greatest leverage on the curb chain. In this position the greatest degree of pressure is exerted on the horse's poll, through the eye of the bit, and also on the bars of the mouth by the mouthpiece.

Tandem harness

Tandem harness is much the same as that for the shaft horse but with some necessary modifications. Basically, a set of tandem harness is made up from a set of single harness, with modifications for the shaft horse and a set of tandem leader harness.

The saddle terrets are divided by a horizontal roller bar so that the wheel and lead reins are separated. The hame tug buckles have protrusions at the lower sides with slots into which the lead trace spring cockeyes are buckled, and the bridle has rosettes with terrets to take the

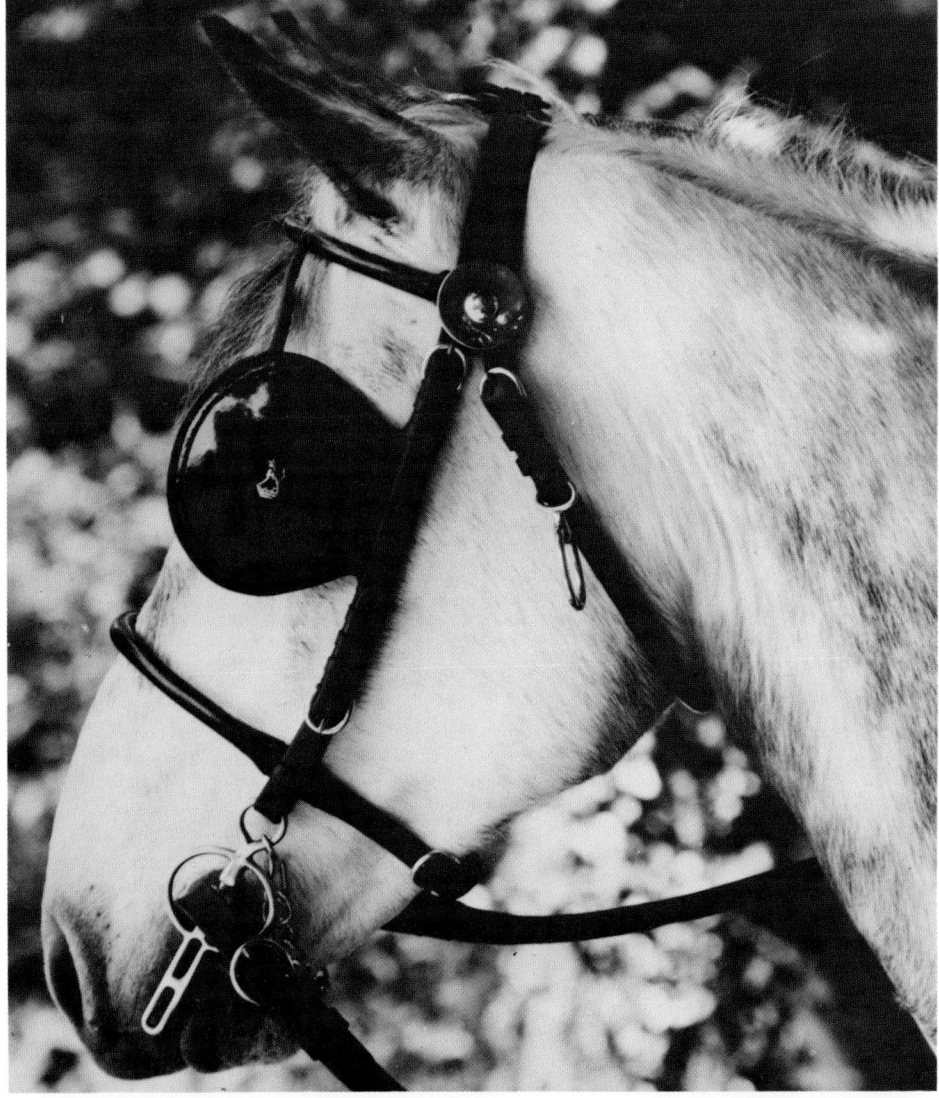
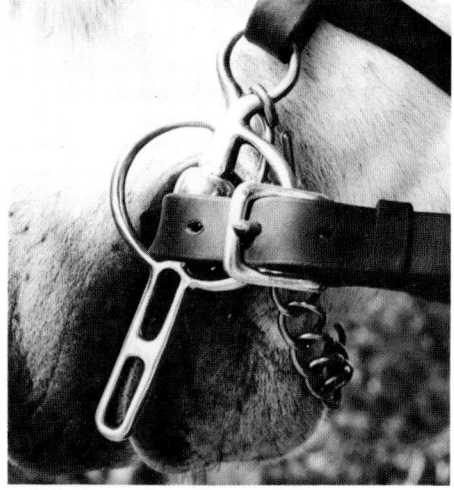

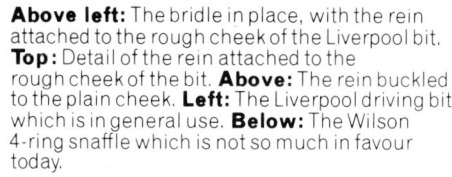
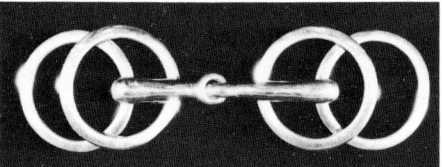

Above left: The bridle in place, with the rein attached to the rough cheek of the Liverpool bit. **Top:** Detail of the rein attached to the rough cheek of the bit. **Above:** The rein buckled to the plain cheek. **Left:** The Liverpool driving bit which is in general use. **Below:** The Wilson 4-ring snaffle which is not so much in favour today.

CHAPTER SIX · DRIVING HARNESS

Right: Tandem leader in breast-collar harness. **Below, left to right:** Leader's saddle terret (also used for single and pair); hame terret (without dividing bar) shows the leader's rein lying above the terret and the wheeler's passing through; tandem wheeler's saddle terret; tandem wheeler's terret with leader's rein on top of the bar and wheeler's below. **Bottom:** 19th-century tandem harness which is an engraving from an American catalogue.

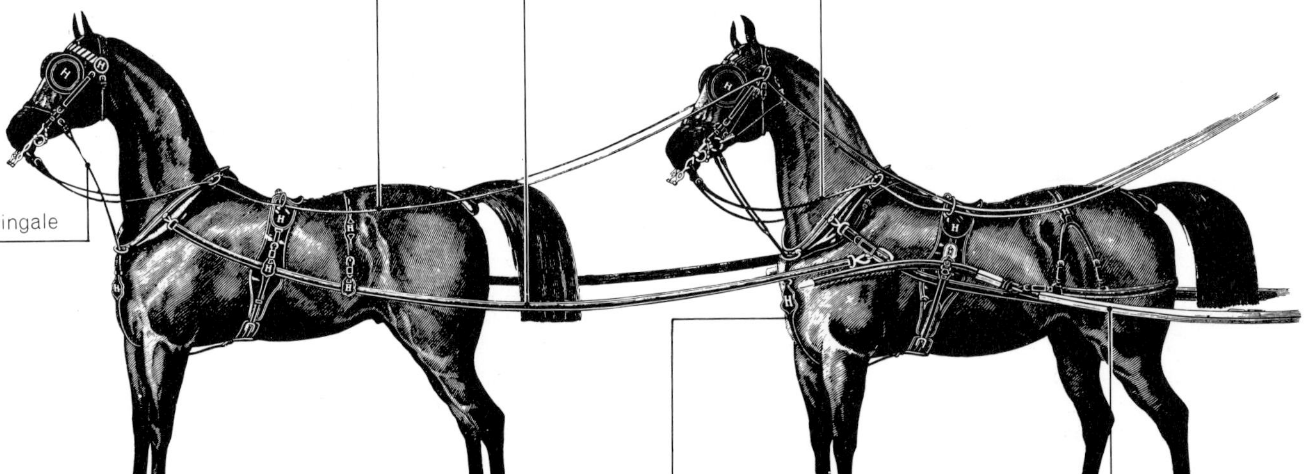

Leader's reins | Leader's trace | Wheeler's reins

Martingale

False martingale | Wheeler's trace

156

Above: A modern tandem turnout at the British Lowther Three-Day Driving trials in 1975. It sets a splendid example in style and elegance, with black leather harness, and brass furniture.

leader's reins. It is also a good idea to have an additional strap in the form of an extra throatlatch to hold the bridle to the wheeler's head if the leader should come round suddenly. This can easily be made by putting an extended loop on the back of the browband. A strap with a buckle is put through the loop and passed over the horse's head before going down through the other browband loop. The strap is then passed through a double loop which is secured to the back of the noseband. It can be buckled far tighter than an ordinary throatlatch, because the pressure is put on the horse's cheeks instead of on his throat. As a result the horse will be more comfortable, more inclined and more able to flex at the poll. It is essential to use a bar bit in a tandem harness to prevent the leader's reins from getting caught inextricably in the cheeks. If this happens, the leader is pulled round and the result is that the driver is left helpless.

The leader can wear either a breast or a full collar, but, unless tandem bars are used, the leader's traces must be longer than usual traces and are passed through loops on the sides of the saddle. This latter matches that which is on the shaft horse in shape, but it has no slot through the top since there is no backband. The belly band points are threaded through dees on the lower sides of the traces. A false belly band is buckled to these and then passed through a loop at the back of the girth, whilst the traces are held up, at the back, by a trace bearer. This should be of the martingale type, so that there are no points

CHAPTER SIX · DRIVING HARNESS

Below: Tandem wheeler's bridle showing the extended loop on the noseband, the additional throatlatch, a bar bit and leading eye terrets to take the leader's reins. **Right:** Bridle with Buxton pattern driving bit with the rein fastened to the middle bar.

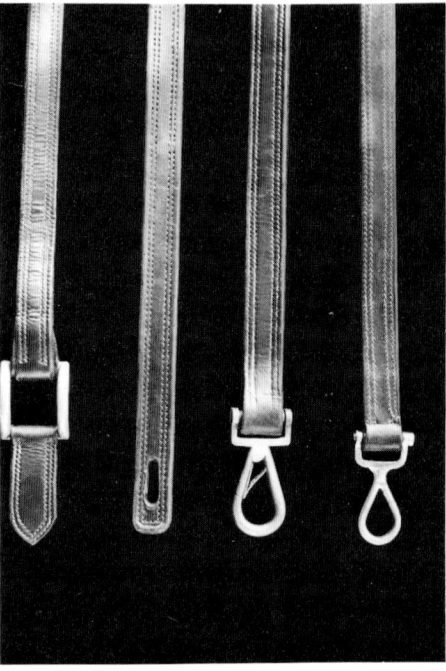

Above, left to right: A variety of trace ends. Pair, with link through which the trace passes to make a loop; single with a crew hole; tandem with spring cock-eye; team leader with cock-eye.

of leather under which the lead reins can get caught. For the same reason, the leader should wear a martingale-type crupper.

Pair harness

Pair harness has the same bridles and collars as single harness, but the hames are different. The bottom eyes, in this instance, are joined by a kidney-shaped link which has a floating ring on the lower side. It is on this that the pole strap is buckled. Breast collars have a dee at the front for the same purpose. The hame tug in pair harness is longer than that on single harness, so that the buckle lies level with the pad. This buckle differs from that used in single harness in that it has a dee both above the buckle and below it. A short strap with a small buckle is sewn to the top dee and is fastened to a point strap coming down from a dee on the pad. A point strap, sewn to the lower dee on the tug buckle, is used to attach the false belly band. The pads used for pair work are very light because they do not have to take any weight, their purpose being as a securing point.

In putting a set of pair harness on the horses, the collars, hames and false martingales go on first, and the pads next. It is best to buckle the hame tug buckle tugs to the points on the pad dees on both sides before putting on the cruppers, so as to prevent the pads from falling to the ground; the latter are then girthed with the false martingales threaded through. The false belly band should be buckled next after it has been passed through the false martingale. The traces should be passed through the trace carriers and thrown over the horses' backs in preparation for putting to, with the outer trace lying on top of the inner one. The trace ends for pair harness are usually designed to go round roller bolts on the splinter bar, some of which are made with a curving square metal link at the end through which the trace is passed to form a loop, whilst others have a quick-release system of two metal fittings, while still more have a simple loop at their end. Those which are used with swingle trees, which are necessary when breast collars are worn, have crew holes at their ends. The breeching is buckled into the hame tug buckle alongside the trace on each side. When the vehicle runs onwards in going down a hill, or stopping, the pole goes forward, the weight being transmitted to the pole straps pulling on the bottoms of the collars, which, in turn, are held down by the false martingales. Unavoidably, a certain amount of pressure is taken on the top of the horses' necks through their collars. If breeching is worn, this tightens around the quarters as the hame tug buckles go forward.

The reins are the next items to be fitted. The draught rein, which is the continuous one, with about 11 holes punched in the centre to which the coupling rein is buckled, goes on the outside of each horse. It is passed through the pad and hame terrets in preparation for buckling to the bit. The coupling rein is passed through the inner pad and hame terrets. The secret of successful pair driving lies mainly in the adjustment of the coupling rein buckles. They must be fitted in such a way that both horses work evenly in their collars with their heads straight.

The bridles are then put on and the draught reins are buckled to the outer sides of each bit with the coupling reins

PRESENT DAY

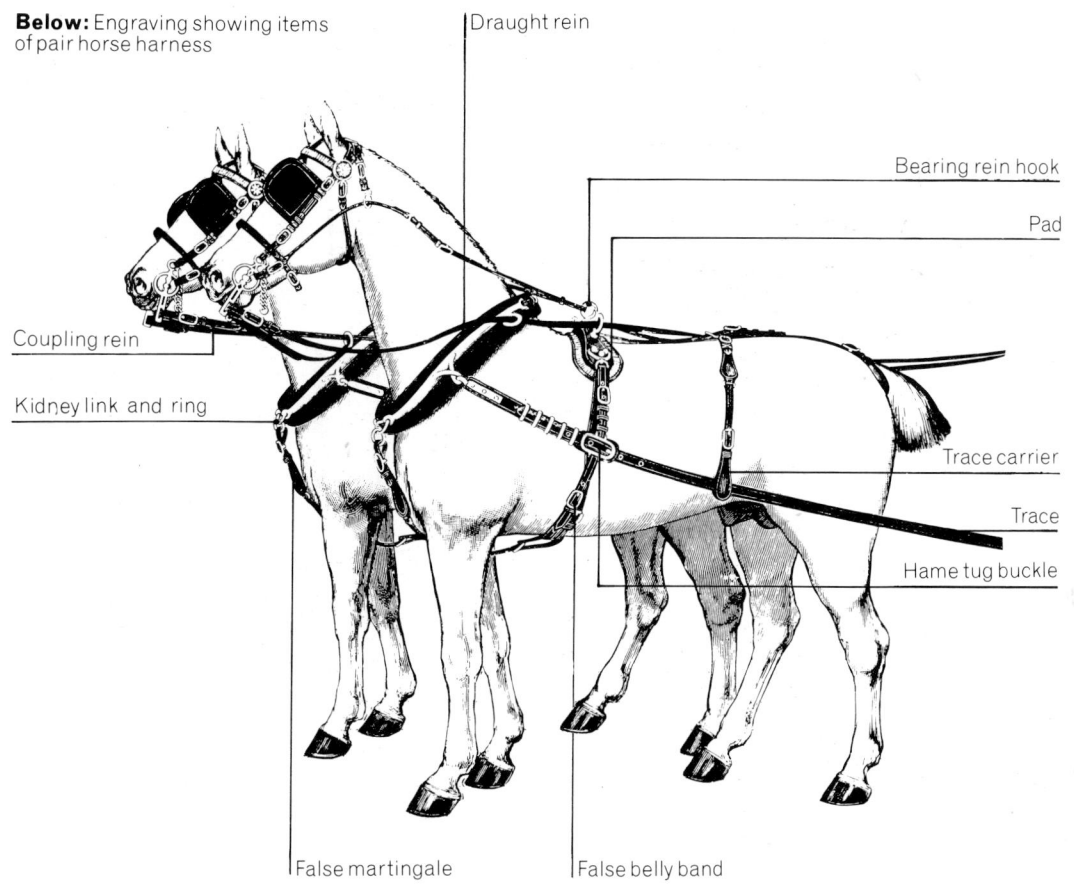

Below: Engraving showing items of pair horse harness

- Draught rein
- Bearing rein hook
- Pad
- Trace carrier
- Trace
- Hame tug buckle
- Coupling rein
- Kidney link and ring
- False martingale
- False belly band

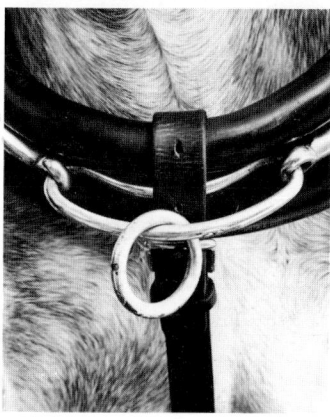

Left: Pair horse harness. **Top:** Pair horse pad showing the hame tug buckle. This buckle lies level with the pad and has a dee both above and below it. **Above:** Pair horse hames showing the kidney-shaped linking and false martingale.

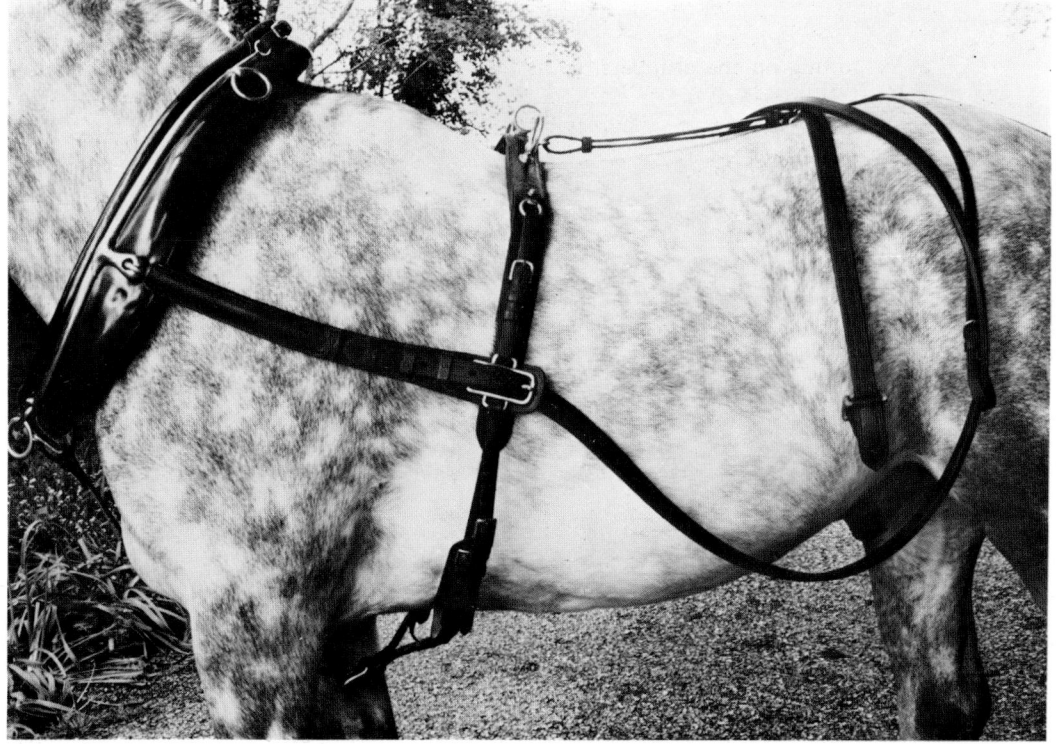

CHAPTER SIX · DRIVING HARNESS

Opposite: George Bowman driving a splendidly turned out four horse tandem. Yesterday's commonplace means of transport has become one of the more specialist forms of horsemanship.
Above: A well turned out pair of bays.
Right: The larger horse shows are ideal places to see a variety of types of harness. This example of the unusual Unicorn harness was photographed at the Royal Windsor Horse Show.

being passed round the backs of the nosebands with the rein points secured in their keepers. They are then ready to be put across to their partners when the horses are put to the vehicle. Traditionally, pairs are driven in bar bits to prevent the coupling reins from getting caught in the cheeks. However, there is the grave danger of long-cheeked bar bits, on small ponies, becoming caught on the pole head. This can result in broken bridles and cause even more problems.

Team harness
Team harness is similar in many ways to pair harness. The leaders wear pair

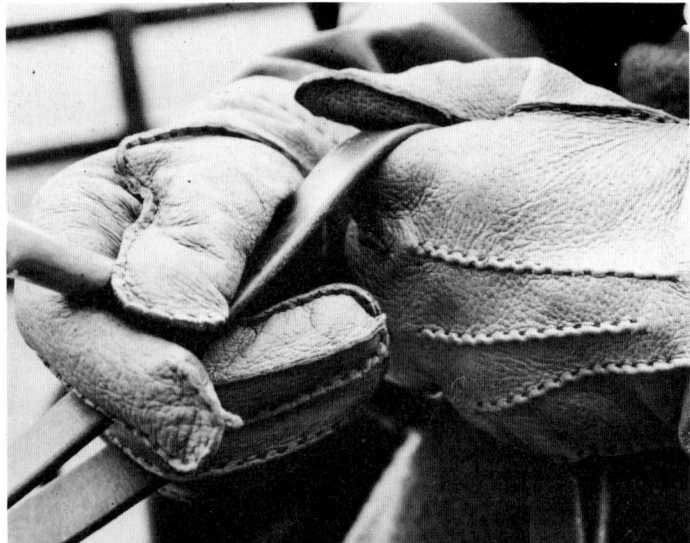

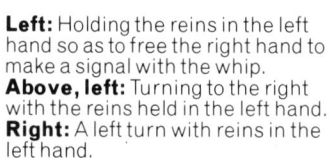

Left: Holding the reins in the left hand so as to free the right hand to make a signal with the whip.
Above, left: Turning to the right with the reins held in the left hand.
Right: A left turn with reins in the left hand.

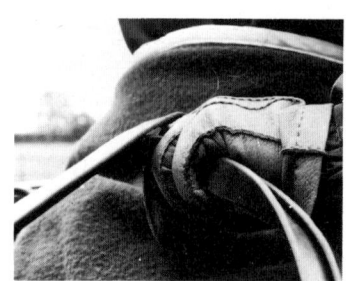

Left: Reins and whip held correctly for single and pair driving. The right hand is supporting the left.
Above, left: Position of the hands in making a turn to the right.
Right: Position for making a turn to the left.

harness but have no breeching as there is no pole. Very often, the leaders wear trace carriers and then traces usually have metal cockeyes at their ends which hook over the lead bars. False martingales, however, are not always worn by leaders. The reins are the same as for a pair except that the draught reins are longer so that they will reach back to the driver. The wheeler harness is similar to that of pair but with modifications. The bridles have leading eye terrets on the outer rosettes to carry the leaders' reins and the pads have central terrets through which the reins are passed.

Unicorn harness
Unicorn harness is a slightly different arrangement of team harness, employed when a unicorn—two wheelers and one leader—is being driven. It is made up from team wheeler harness with the bridle terrets put on the inner sides, as the reins run centrally from the single leader who wears one side of a set of lead harness. Tandem leader reins are best for this purpose, but if these are not available, then team lead reins, with the coupling reins off, can be used.

Handling reins and whip
The handling of the reins and whip follows the same principles, irrespective of whether one, two, three or four horses are being driven. As far as the reins are concerned, the only difference is of number; there are two reins in the hand with a single and a pair, whilst with a tandem, a unicorn or a team there are four reins.

For single and pair driving, the two reins are held in the left hand with the nearside rein lying over the index finger and the offside rein lying below the middle finger. They are secured in position by the finger tips against the palm. The right hand, in which the whip is held at all times, is placed on the reins in front of the left hand. The left rein lies over the middle finger and the right rein lies below the third finger. The right hand is then in a position to assist the left in turns and in pulling up. The left hand remains as an 'anchor' hand.

A turn to the right is made by increasing the pressure on the offside rein with the right hand, whilst making sure that the index finger is not still pressing on the

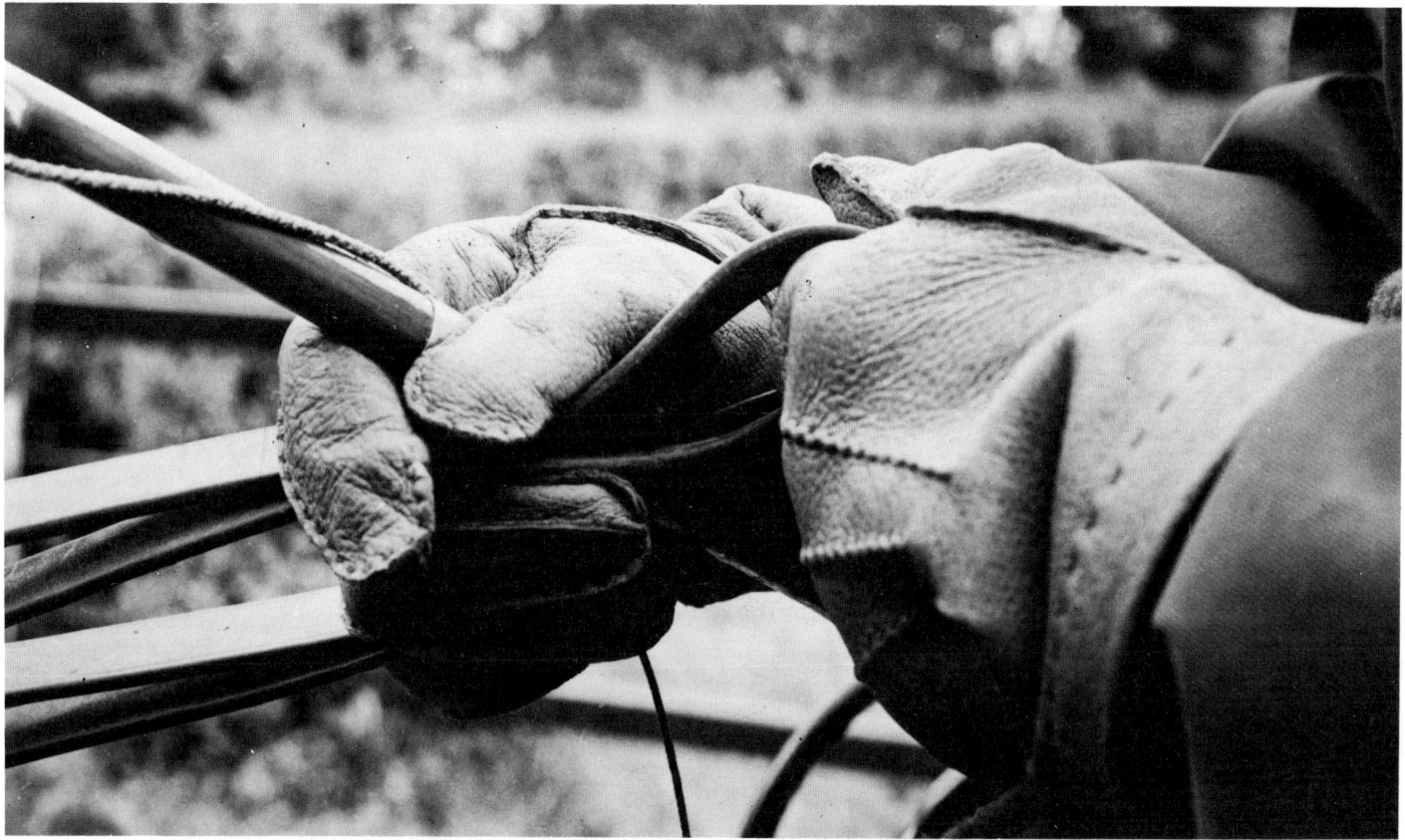

Above: Method of holding reins and whip when driving tandem, team or unicorn. **Far left:** The hands initiating a gentle turn to the right. **Left:** Making a gentle right hand turn.

nearside rein. At the same time the left hand can be turned slightly, so that the palm lies uppermost and the nearside rein is slackened in consequence.

A turn to the left is made by putting pressure on the underside of the nearside rein with the right hand. The left hand can be turned slightly with the knuckles facing uppermost to slacken the offside rein.

If additional pressure is needed, it can be gained by bringing the left hand towards the right hip for a left turn and towards the left hip for a right turn, thus increasing the contact on the desired rein and loosening the opposite one. The reins are shortened by either sliding the right hand forward and following up with the left hand or by grasping the reins with the right hand, held behind the left, and sliding the latter forward the desired amount.

For tandem, unicorn and team driving the four reins are held in the left hand. The near lead rein lies over the index finger. The off lead rein goes under the index finger. The near wheel rein lies under the off lead rein on top of the middle finger and the off wheel rein goes under the middle finger. The right hand is placed with the middle and third fingers separating the nearside and offside reins, in front of the left hand. Simple, wide, turns to the left and right are made, as with a single or pair, by bringing the horses round as one with both left or right reins as desired. Tight turns are much more difficult, as it is essential to prevent the shaft horses, or wheelers, from cutting across the corner in an attempt to follow the leader by a shorter route. If this is allowed to happen the vehicle will inevitably become caught on whatever may be in the way. Therefore, it is important to oppose the wheeler adequately before asking the leader to turn.

It is often necessary to take a loop in the relevant rein with a unicorn or team, but lighter opposition with a tandem is usually adequate. Then, when the leader has begun to come round, the opposition rein can be released to allow the wheeler to follow him.

The whip is held at all times between the index finger and thumb of the right hand. It should lie at an angle of 45° across the thumb muscle. One which is held at the wrong angle is likely to get caught in the wheel or it could touch the horse's quarters by mistake.

Driving Harness · Whips

The driving whip is an essential piece of equipment for the driver of any horse-drawn vehicle. Its function is to urge on or correct the horse and its careful use adds to driving safety. It is to some extent, also a staff of office, the driver being known traditionally as the Whip. The aid should be carried at all times when on the move, held lightly but firmly in the right hand in such a fashion that the fingers of that hand are free to assist the left hand with the reins when necessary. An approximate angle of 45° forward and a similar angle upwards should be maintained so that the whip is ready for use without putting the passenger's hat at risk. Whilst a sharp stroke is occasionally necessary a light touch between collar and pad is often sufficient. The whip, however, should not be used whilst the whip hand is on the reins because of the resultant jerk on the horse's mouth.

Signals to other road users are also made with the whip. Held vertically aloft it indicates slowing down or stopping. A similar position with a circular movement of the point followed by a horizontal gesture to right or left indicates a turn in that direction. When not in horse-drawn company it is probably prudent to use motoring hand signals so as not to confuse motorists whose knowledge of horses can be extremely limited.

Types of whip

In the main, there are two traditional types of driving whips still in use and the survival of so many, a number having been made around the turn of the century, testifies to their popularity and quality. Firstly, there is the Dealer's whip, or 'dropthong', and secondly the Coach, Carriage or Gig whip, sometimes called the 'bow-top'.

The Dealer's whip, both flexible and enduring, lacks the reach, balance and elegance of the Coach whip, but it has withstood the test of time for commercial and general use. Such whips were familiar pieces of equipment at the fairs and similar gatherings depicted by the British painter Sir Alfred Munnings and described by the writer George Borrow.

The stock of the whip, in the best examples, had a whalebone core or lining about ¼in square, whilst the less expensive types, which are still made today, were lined with spring-steel wire. In both cases, the lining is enclosed within split cane to provide taper and substance and covered, by means of a machine, with woven waxed thread. This ingenious and unlikely combination of materials produced a stock as resilient as it was strong, but today as a result of the restrictions on the slaughter of whales, the whalebone-lined type is no longer made.

The hand-part of a Dealer's whip is sometimes leather-covered with white metal mounts at top and bottom, stamped or engraved with an attractively florid design. The occasional absence of a normal stitched seam on the underside of the leather hand-part may puzzle post-war drivers, but it was thus because it was made from a calf's tail pulled over the stock! The four-plait thong of split horsehide was secured to the stock by means of a loop or keeper from which it hung down (hence the name 'dropthong').

A longer-stocked version of this whip with a very short rawhide thong was also produced for heavy horse teams. The bottom of the butt mount (or cap) was usually sealed with a Victorian copper coin and the thread-covered cane stock deco-

Left: A selection of ornamented Victorian whips, the mounts being of silver, brass and gilt. The parasol driving whip belonged to Queen Victoria. **Above:** Detail of an elaborate turquoise-studded whip butt. Whips of the Victorian period were frequently intricately decorated. **Opposite, left to right:** A selection of driving whips. Drop throng dealer's whip; holly pony driving whip; gig size holly whip; gig size braided cane driving whip; pair horse size whip also of braided cane.

rated with closely spaced brass collars, or ferrules.

Whilst this whip is well suited for its original purpose—modern hybrid versions serving well enough for exercising or informal occasions—the 'dropthong' type should not be used at any event where a stylish appearance is required.

The Coach whip is the whip for the elegant well-appointed private turnout and discrimination is needed in its selection. The whip must suit the driver, the horse and the vehicle—in short, the whole turnout. An important factor in selection is that of utility. The ideal is to have a light whip with sufficient reach for the job and for it to be well-balanced. There has to be a limit so far as weight is concerned, as a wet 12ft thong swishing through the air cannot be carried on a twig. The point of balance should be just above the collar of the hand-part and is achieved by tapering the body and sometimes counter-weighting the stock. Examination of the hand-part of an old whip will sometimes reveal a quantity of lead-foil wrapped around under the leather so as to fix the balance.

Specialist whips and decoration

As far as standard whips are concerned, the achievement of a satisfactory end product can be more or less assured. When, however, a screw-jointed or dog-leg whip is required—or a custom-made whip of unusual design—then much preliminary work has to be done until the whip comes to life, as it were, with an easy balance in the hand and increasing flexibility towards the top of the stock.

Various woods are used for the stock, the most usual being holly and blackthorn, but other woods are occasionally substituted, such as hickory, bamboo, greenheart, yew, and, very rarely, solid whalebone. It is probable that the finest quality whips, and the greatest number, were produced around the turn of the century, when the fashion in design was to make things look like something else. Ivory hand-parts were, for example, sometimes decorated with a pattern of wood knots and a simulated wood grain. Some manufacturers went even further and produced a type of celluloid which, posing as ivory, was also moulded to resemble knotty wood.

Many of the old whips described today as 'ivory-handled' are, in fact, made from a composition which has the even, opaque, and yellowish tinge of dairy cream, but lacks the slight translucence and the subtle graining of ivory. An infallible test is to file off a little powder and sniff—no genuine elephant's tusk smells strongly of camphor.

Whip maintenance

Whips are subjected to much misuse. They are walked on, run over, leaned up against corners, caught up in tug-buckles or roadside bushes, picked up and 'cracked' by non-drivers or left in whip-holders and pushed, to their detriment, under coach-house lintels as the vehicle is being housed.

The most usual damage to a whip is a cracked or broken stock, a broken thong or crippled quills. When quills are badly bent or broken, it is almost certain that the whalebone or cane core will also be damaged. Replacement of this with renewal of quills and the whipping necessary to refix the thong is difficult, but a neat and effective repair can be made by leaving the original work alone and, with adhesive, fitting a pair of short goosequill splints on each side of the thong, at the site of the break, and whipping, or binding, the whole tightly with black thread. The alternative is to fit an entirely new thong.

The bow-top thong, which nowadays is six-plait at the thicker end reducing to four-plait at the thin end, usually gets broken at the latter part, where splicing is difficult. A knot is ugly and catches up in use, so the best repair method is to taper off the broken ends, overlap them by an inch, moisten with adhesive and whip tightly with matching cotton.

The elegant bow which distinguishes the Carriage whip is formed by the curved whalebone or cane core, which will revert to its original straightness if it is allowed to do so. It is therefore essential when the whip is not in use to keep the bow part of the thong curved round a 'whip-reel' (or can about 4in diameter—the base of a saddle-soap tin makes an excellent reel).

This treatment is only effective if the thong is in the correct position—that is, with the end of the cross-threading at 3 o'clock on the reel. This position on an average thong will bring the tip of the core (which may be felt with the fingers) to about 12 or 1 o'clock. The thong must be prevented from slipping round the reel by securing the thin end with a loop of string tied to a nail.

Driving Harness · **Trotting Equipment**

TROTTING EQUIPMENT

Harness racing, the racing of trotters and pacers, is a highly specialized sport. The basic item of equipment is breast harness. This consists of a breast collar, traces, a saddle and girth, plus a bridle fitted with long driving reins. The collar itself is a broad leather strap that passes round the horse's breast and is supported by another strap fitted over the shoulders. Long leather straps, called traces, run back from each side of the breast collar and are fastened to the shafts of the sulky, which the animal draws and the jockey sits.

The saddle sits in the normal place behind the withers; it usually has a pad or towel placed underneath it to prevent chafing. It is girthed, in the normal way around the horse's belly. To prevent it riding forward, a crupper may be fitted around the horse's tail and attached to the rear of the saddle by means of a back strap. Fitted to either side of the saddle are small leather loops, known as shaft tugs, through which the shafts are passed and which support their weight. Each shaft is inserted into a shaft thimble (also known as a point strap), a thimble-shaped device which fits over the end of each shaft and is connected to the side of the saddle by a strap. Point straps control the positioning of the sulky and prevent it from riding forward, too close behind the quarters.

The traces, which enable the horse to pull the sulky, are slotted through leather loops, specially positioned on the inside of the shafts, and attached to hooks set on the inside of the rear of each shaft. On either side of the girth is a strong strap called a wrap strap or tie down. Each of these is wound round the corresponding shaft and fastened with a buckle. These straps must be properly adjusted to hold the shafts firmly in place.

The driving bridle and bits
The basic driving bridle is open—that is, not fitted with blinkers—and consists of a headpiece, throatlatch, browband, cheekpieces, noseband (known in the USA as a head halter), snaffle bit and reins, or lines, which pass through rings, or terrets, on the saddle and then back to the driver's hand.

Driving bits come in two main varieties—the jointed and the unjointed

Left: The exhilarating sport of trotting, which is immensely popular in America, Australia and the Continent of Europe but has only a comparatively small following in Britain.

CHAPTER SIX · DRIVING HARNESS

snaffle. A leather- or rubber-covered mouthpiece and rubber bit guards are frequently used to prevent soring of the mouth and cheeks, while special bits are employed for schooling young horses. Since the young horse takes time to develop his balance and steering, there is a tendency for him to lean to one side or the other, thus pulling the bit through his mouth. This soon leads to soreness. To guard against this, a youngster is usually schooled in a special colt-breaking bit. This has a strap attached to the rings which fastens under the chin and is also fitted with large leather cheekpieces to guard against chafing. One variety of colt-breaking bit, the Frisco June, has the chin strap built in as an integral part of the bit; others have detachable straps.

Keeping a straight course
It is a prime requisite for harness racers to hold their heads absolutely straight in front of them. If a horse does not do this, he will not only be unable to achieve his maximum speed, but also will almost certainly strike into and injure himself when moving at racing pace. Various devices have been invented to cope with the problem of the horse who persistently leans to one side or the other. One is the side-lining bit which has an extension—a steel bar 2 to 4in long and about ¼in in diameter—protruding from one side. The rein fastens to a ring at the end of the extension. The extra leverage this arrangement produces is often sufficient to keep the horse straight.

For horses who tend to pull on either side at different stages of a race, the slip-mouth side-lining bit is the answer. Here the straight, leather-covered mouthpiece is hollow, with a bar running through it and protruding on either side of the horse's mouth. The bit automatically adjusts to extend on one side or the other, depending which is favoured.

Another device for keeping the head straight is the head pole, a small pole running alongside the neck and head from the saddle to the noseband. Head poles are telescopic, so that they can be adjusted to exactly the length required. The pole is attached to the saddle by a strap running from the terret, through a slit in the pole, to the overcheck hook, which is positioned on top of the saddle pad. The front of the pole fastens to a ring on the noseband. Even with this arrangement, some horses still find it possible to lean in a little towards the pole. To discourage this, a small rubber ball or a burr—a length of leather studded with little rivets—can be fitted around the pole where it runs alongside the neck. The poles can be fitted on either side of the neck, or on both, depending on the idiosyncracies of the particular horse.

Some horses object to the presence of a head pole, so an alternative means of straightening the head has to be employed. One way is to fit a burr, appropriately

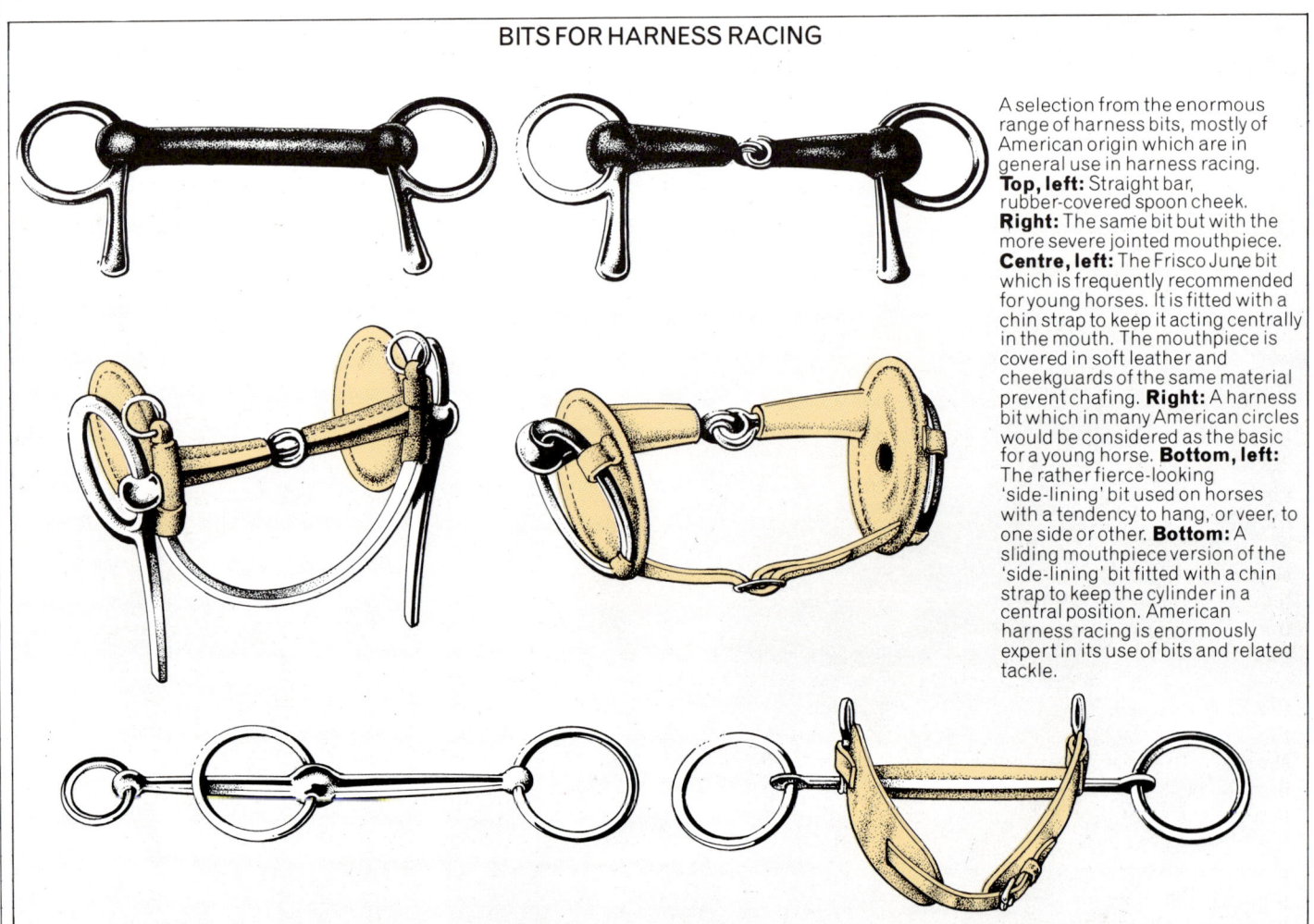

BITS FOR HARNESS RACING

A selection from the enormous range of harness bits, mostly of American origin which are in general use in harness racing.
Top, left: Straight bar, rubber-covered spoon cheek.
Right: The same bit but with the more severe jointed mouthpiece.
Centre, left: The Frisco June bit which is frequently recommended for young horses. It is fitted with a chin strap to keep it acting centrally in the mouth. The mouthpiece is covered in soft leather and cheekguards of the same material prevent chafing. **Right:** A harness bit which in many American circles would be considered as the basic for a young horse. **Bottom, left:** The rather fierce-looking 'side-lining' bit used on horses with a tendency to hang, or veer, to one side or other. **Bottom:** A sliding mouthpiece version of the 'side-lining' bit fitted with a chin strap to keep the cylinder in a central position. American harness racing is enormously expert in its use of bits and related tackle.

Above: Using a head pole on an American pacer. (Pacers move their legs in lateral pairs while trotters use diagonal pairs.) The head pole is a salutary aid in keeping the horse straight. Poles can be fitted on one side of the neck or on both as necessary and can be reinforced with a burr. **Right:** Yet another piece of American equipment designed to keep a horse running straight. This is the Murphy blind which can be adjusted to counteract a tendency to hold the head on one side. In this instance, the horse holds his head to the left and the blind is therefore fitted over the right eye.

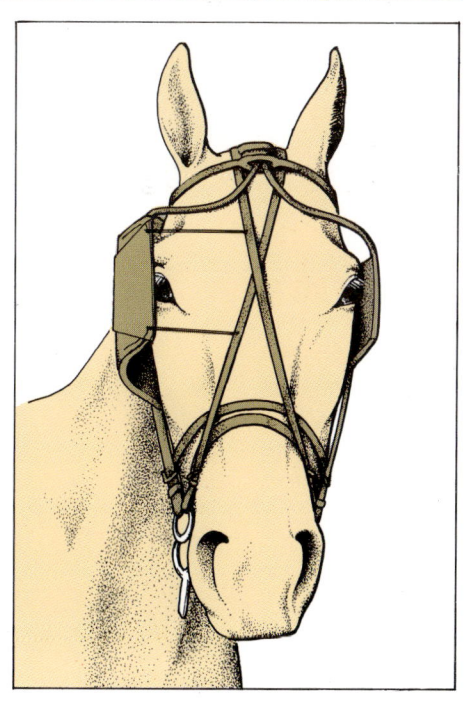

positioned, to the rein, another is to use a Murphy blind, a type of blinker. Some drivers prefer a blind to a pole in any case, since it is less cumbersome. The Murphy blind, named after the notable American trainer and driver Thomas W Murphy, is a piece of stiff leather that fits on to the cheekpiece of the bridle. It is shaped so that it cups inwards slightly at the front of the eye. The principle of operation is simple; with a horse who turns his head to the left, the blind is fitted on the right, so that too acute a turn of the head will bring the blind in front of the right eye, thus obscuring his vision. A horse quickly appreciates that if he keeps his head straight he can see straight ahead perfectly well, but that if he turns it his vision will be obscured.

Shadow rolls and hobbles

Other items in common use on harness horses, particularly pacers, are shadow rolls and hobbles. The shadow roll is basically a sheepskin-covered noseband, fitted so that a horse can see straight ahead but cannot look down at the ground immediately in front of him. It is used on horses who have a tendency to shy at shadows, marks on the tracks, bits of paper and so on. Pacers are particularly prone to spookiness, something which, it is believed, is the result of their wearing hobbles. Because they do not have free use

CHAPTER SIX · DRIVING HARNESS

A SELECTION OF SHADOW ROLLS

  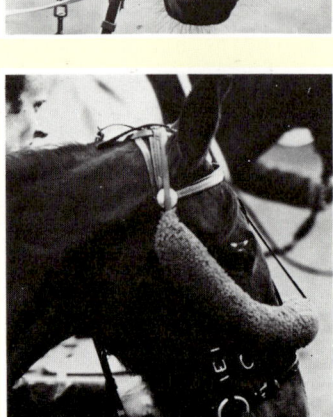

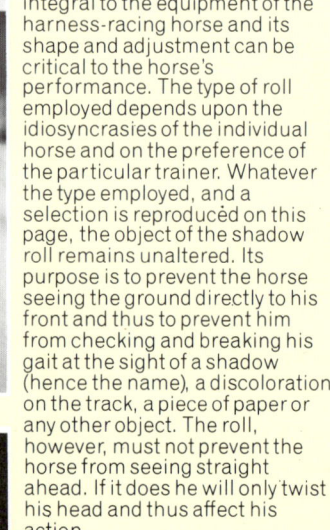

The shadow roll is virtually integral to the equipment of the harness-racing horse and its shape and adjustment can be critical to the horse's performance. The type of roll employed depends upon the idiosyncrasies of the individual horse and on the preference of the particular trainer. Whatever the type employed, and a selection is reproduced on this page, the object of the shadow roll remains unaltered. Its purpose is to prevent the horse seeing the ground directly to his front and thus to prevent him from checking and breaking his gait at the sight of a shadow (hence the name), a discoloration on the track, a piece of paper or any other object. The roll, however, must not prevent the horse from seeing straight ahead. If it does he will only twist his head and thus affect his action.

of their legs they seem to be much more fearful of stepping in a hole or of tripping up than are other horses. As a result, they are likely to shy violently at real or imagined objects on the ground, something which is extremely dangerous when they are racing alongside other sulkies. There are various designs of shadow roll, all of which fit across the nose below the eyes, buckling under the jaw. They must be adjusted with great care, so as not to obstruct the horse's vital forward vision.

Hobbles are used on pacers to keep them steady and enable them to maintain their lateral gait. The traditional material used was leather, but nowadays lightweight plastic and nylon are frequently substituted. Hobbles are adjustable straps fitted with padded loops at each end. One loop encircles the front leg and the other the hindleg on the same side of the animal. At the front and back of each leg loop is a vertical strap which fits on to a set of four hobble hangers. The front hangers on each side pass up over the neck just in front of the withers—the rear ones rest on the horse's quarters, either side of the tail— joining up and fastening to the back strap some way in front of the top of the dock. The two centre hangers are also fastened to the back strap, the forward one immediately behind the saddle and the rear one a little in front of the hips.

Alternatively, the two centre hangers can be replaced by a single one which divides halfway down the horse's sides into a Y shape. Although this arrangement looks neater, it can cause chafing.

The fit of hobbles is critical and must be constantly corrected, since the straps stretch with use. If they are suspended too high, they will restrict the action of the muscles at the top of the legs; if they are too tight, they will prevent a horse extending properly and will tire his legs; if they are too loose, a horse that is used to them may start to roll about in his gait as he seeks their support.

Cross hobbles, which, as their name suggests, are fitted from one foreleg to the opposite hindleg, used to be employed on trotters to prevent them from breaking into a faster pace, but their use has considerably declined, probably because of their tendency to make a horse hit his knees and shins. Half hobbles can be used on both trotters and pacers. These are made of two loops joined by rope which runs through a pulley. Although they can be employed either on the front or the hindlegs, they are most usually seen on the front legs of a trotter. The pulley is positioned under the horse's belly just behind the girth and is kept in place by means of two straps attached at right angles to the shafts. Two further straps prevent the pulley from riding forward. It is difficult to maintain the desired tension and, therefore, the desired effect of half hobbles because of the tendency of the vehicle to move forward a bit when the horse begins to take a strong hold.

Coping with pulling

A great many harness racers are inclined to hot up in excitement and pull. Various

Below: Many harness horses pull quite strongly and to counteract this difficulty an overcheck or check rein is used. This will prevent the horse lowering his head below a certain level and becoming out of full control.

CHAPTER SIX · DRIVING HARNESS

COPING WITH PULLING

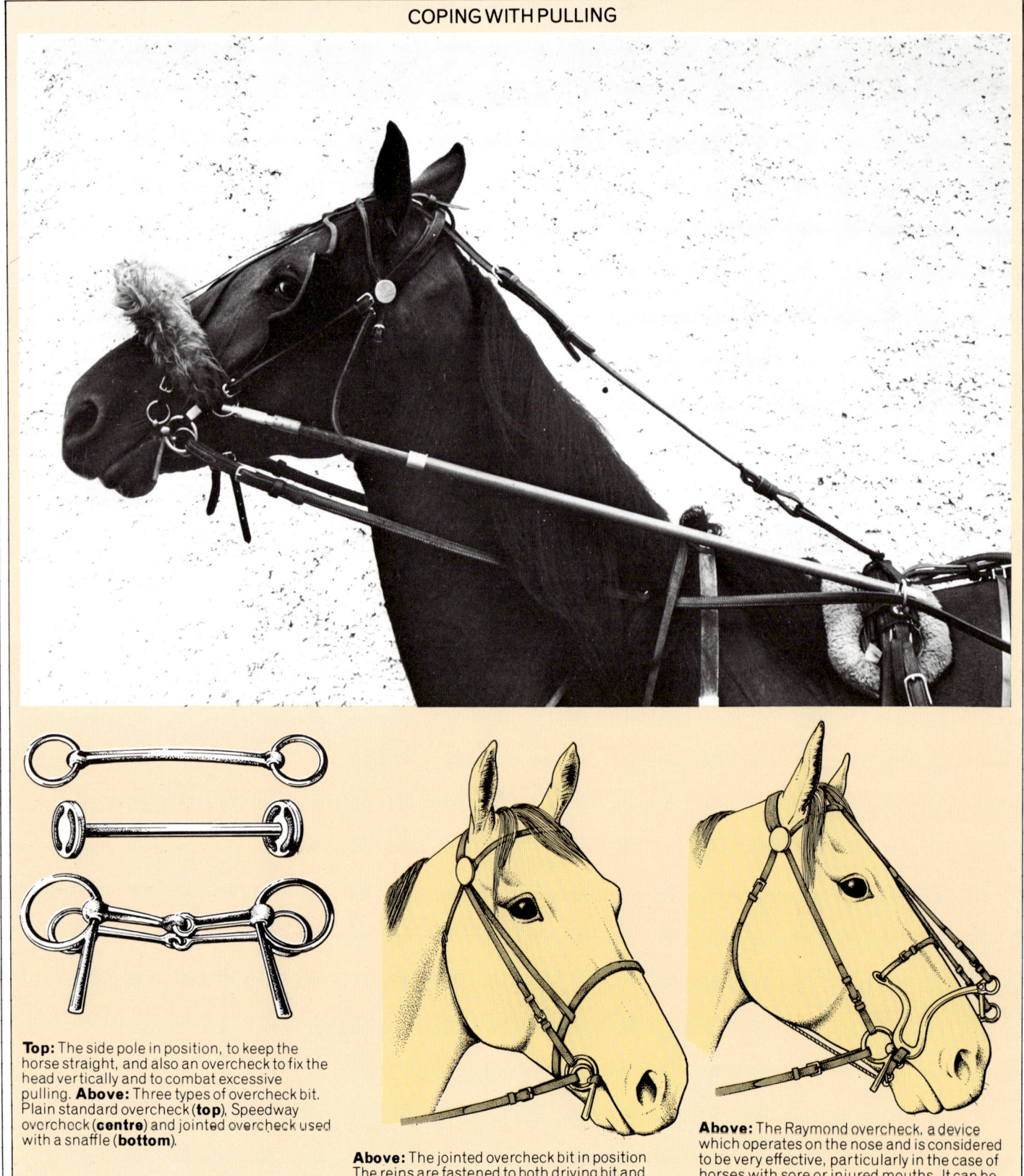

Top: The side pole in position, to keep the horse straight, and also an overcheck to fix the head vertically and to combat excessive pulling. **Above:** Three types of overcheck bit. Plain standard overcheck (**top**), Speedway overcheck (**centre**) and jointed overcheck used with a snaffle (**bottom**).

Above: The jointed overcheck bit in position The reins are fastened to both driving bit and overcheck; the bridle head to the driving bit only. This constitutes a fairly mild restraint.

Above: The Raymond overcheck, a device which operates on the nose and is considered to be very effective, particularly in the case of horses with sore or injured mouths. It can be kept in place either with a chinstrap or a curb chain.

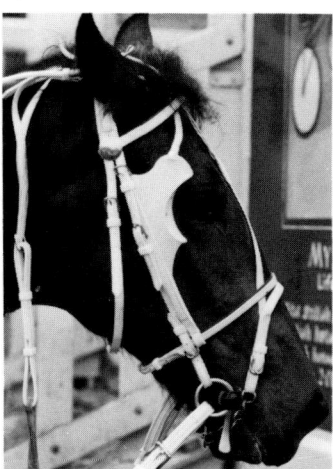

Far left: Blinkers are used to restrict the horse's lateral and rear vision and to concentrate his attention to the front. This form of closed bridle allows good forward vision and some lateral vision also.
Left: The modified 'Kant-See-Back' type of blinker, which is less restrictive.
Right: Full protection for the legs and heels is given by bell boots, ankle boots and knee boots.

ingenious devices have been invented to cope with this, including the jointed overcheck bit, the lip cord and the overcheck or check rein. A jointed overcheck bit is simply a second jointed snaffle, used in conjunction with the usual driving bit. The reins are fastened through the rings of both the driving and overcheck bits; the extra pressure exerted on the mouth is often sufficient to control a mild puller.

The lip cord is much more severe. This is a cord fitted around the top gums below the upper lip, behind the mouthpiece of the bit and out at the corners of the mouth, fastening under the chin. It is an effective deterrent to a pulling horse, but it requires a very light hand; otherwise the mouth might be damaged.

The overcheck or check rein is more common. The rein is a strip of leather that runs from the saddle, to which it is attached by a hook, up over the horse's neck where it divides into two. Each strap passes through a separate loop provided in the headpiece of the bridle and runs between the ears and down the front of the face, fastening to each side of a check bit or chin strap. The overcheck is used to prevent a horse lowering his head below a certain level, ensuring that it stays at a height where he can be most easily controlled and where he can use himself to best advantage.

Further controls

Horses with basically good head carriage who just occasionally pull down with their heads at moments of excitement—perhaps before the start of a race—or those who have particularly light mouths can be fitted with a simple chin strap, which has a ring at each end to which the overcheck buckles. The chin strap is usually connected to the throatlatch by a strap running under the jaw. This ensures that the chin strap stays in the correct position. When a chin strap is insufficient to control the position of the head an overcheck bit is used. The basic bit is a straight piece of metal with small rings at either end, but there are many variations, some of which are quite severe and only suitable for horses who are otherwise uncontrollable. An overcheck bit can also be used in conjunction with a chin strap, an arrangement which will help to keep a horse's mouth closed. In this case, a bit called a Speedway is usually employed, since it has special slots into which the chin strap can be fitted.

A horse who persistently puts his head down can be fitted with one of the many leverage devices on the market, such as the Raymond overcheck. This may look clumsy, but it is most effective. The equipment is somewhat like a sophisticated version of the chin strap, since it employs no bit. It works by lifting the chin and at the same time pressing down on the nose. Many horses seem to perform better in it than in an overcheck bit.

Other additions to the harness racer's wardrobe include standing and running martingales and various nosebands, including the figure-of-eight and a version of the drop noseband. Some horses, particularly those inclined to be lazy or lacking in concentration, are fitted with closed bridles—that is, bridles with blinkers. The latter come in a great variety of shapes and sizes, but they share the same basic principle—to concentrate the horse's attention to the front.

A horse who tends to swing his quarters over towards one shaft or the other can be fitted with a gaiting strap or gaiting pole. It runs parallel to the horse's body from the tip of the shaft back to the crosspiece or arch of the sulky and acts on the quarters in the same way that a head pole acts on the neck and head.

Boots for protection

Finally there is a large selection of boots designed to protect various parts of the racer's limbs. Trotters often strike their elbows with their feet; to guard against this special elbow boots are fitted to cover the vulnerable area. Knee boots are most often used on pacers, who are prone to striking the inside of the knee with the opposite forefoot. Both elbow and knee boots are fitted with suspenders.

There are many other forms of boot designed to protect the shins, ankles and coronets, all of which can be injured when a horse is moving at high speed. Trotters tend to need shin boots and scalpers behind and quarter boots in front, while pacers normally need tendon and pacing quarter boots in front.

Quarter boots are designed to protect the heels and coronets of the front feet at the rear or both the rear and the inside. They are usually made of felt or leather. Many pacers need this type of boot because of their tendency to cross-fire—that is to hit the front foot with the opposite hind foot.

Scalpers are similar to rubber overreach or bell boots and are pulled on over the foot. The front part curves upwards to give protection to the coronet and the area above it. They are used on horses who are prone to speedy cutting and on passing-gaited trotters, horses whose hindlegs pass outside their front legs.

CHAPTER SIX · DRIVING HARNESS

Harnessing a trotter. **Right:** The first fitting is a light halter. **Far right:** The crupper being placed in position. **Below, left:** Pad, backstrap, etc in place. **Centre:** Putting on the bridle. **Right:** The bridle correctly adjusted and the breast girth in position.

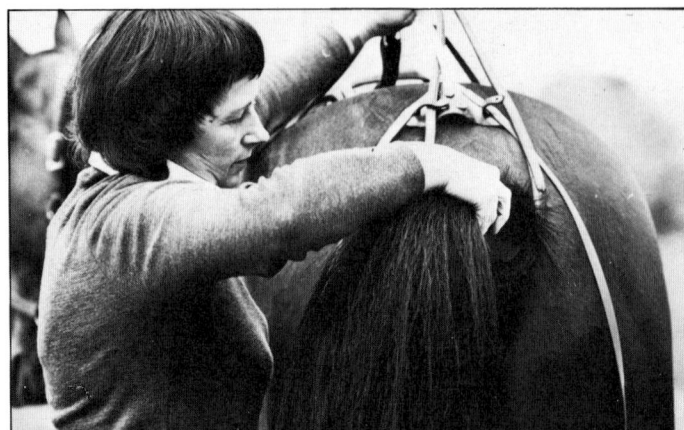
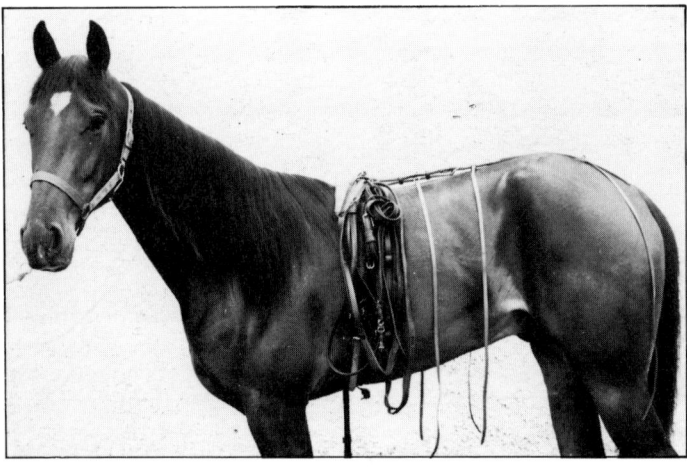
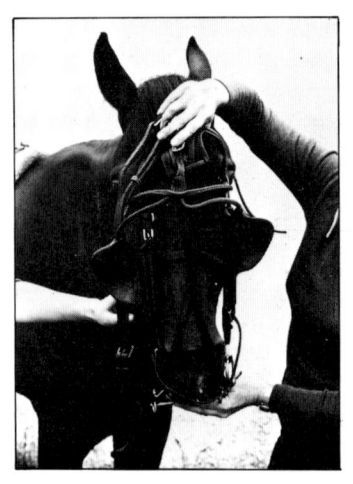

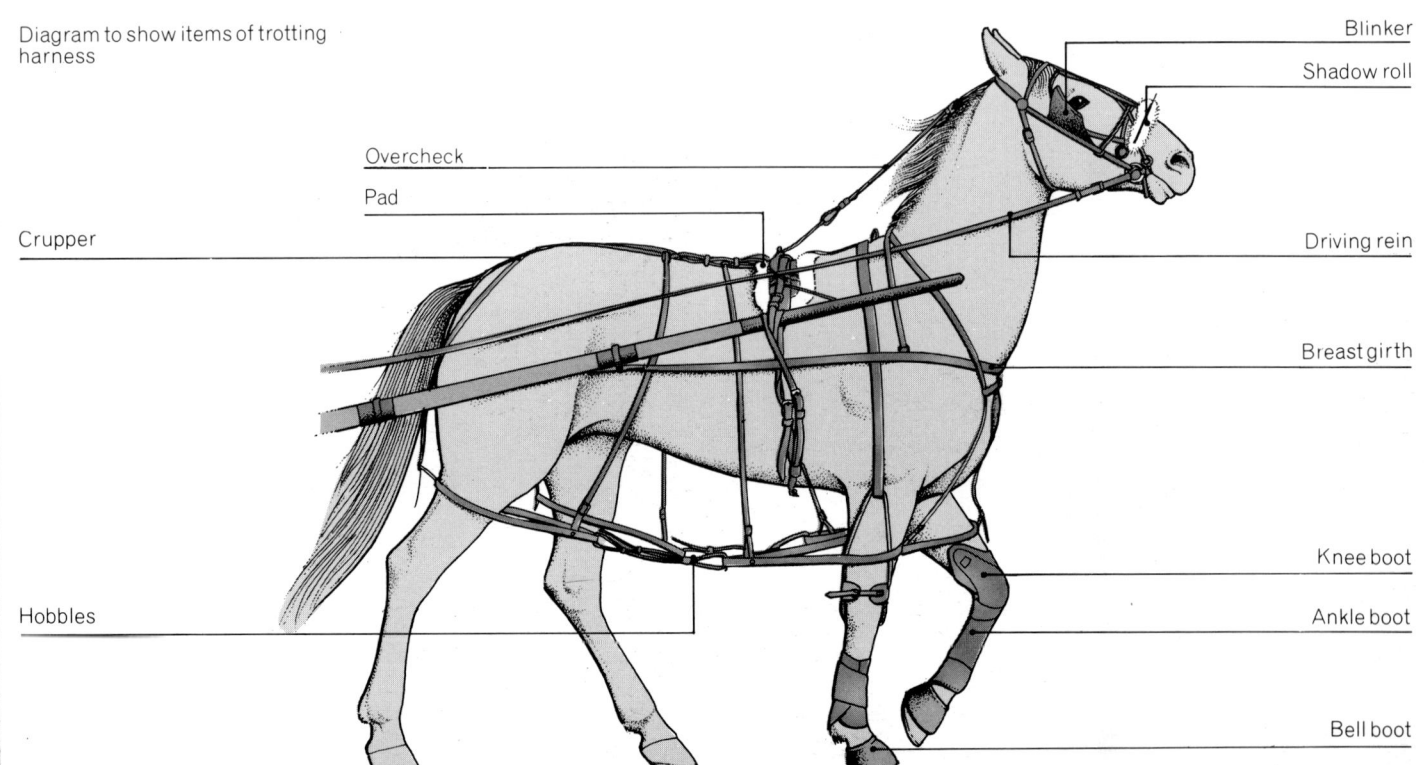

Diagram to show items of trotting harness

TROTTING EQUIPMENT

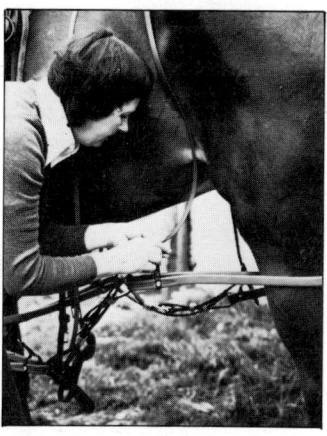
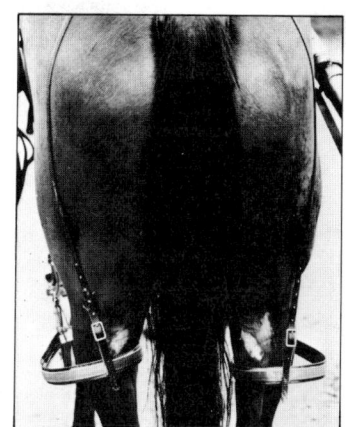

Far left: Getting the horse to step into the hobbles. **Centre left:** Connecting and adjusting the hobble straps. **Left:** Rear view of the hobbles hanging equally and adjusted correctly. **Below, left:** The harness fitted and the horse ready for putting to. **Centre:** Detail of shaft holder. **Right:** Detail of pad/shaft fastening.

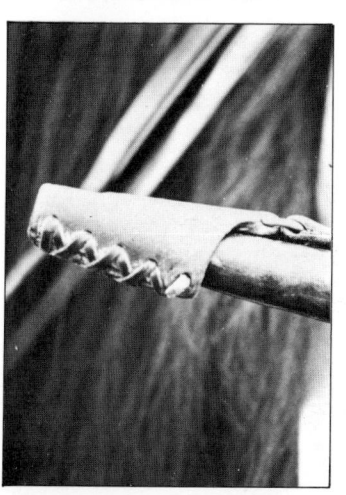

Left: The harness pacer in racing harness with booted forelegs, hoobles, light shadow roll, closed bridle and overcheck. The harness racing trainer takes infinite pains with the correct bitting of his charges and the minute adjustment of each part of the harness.

CHAPTER SIX · DRIVING HARNESS

Driving · **Farm Harness**

When horses were first domesticated by man some 3,000 years ago, their small stature made them more suitable for pulling some sort of vehicle or load than for carrying a rider. Since the ox had already been successfully pressed into service as a draught animal it seemed natural enough for the horse to be utilized for the same purpose.

In practice, however, this was not as simple as it sounds in theory, since the horse's conformation differs a good deal from that of the ox. The latter was attached to a vehicle by means of a simple wooden yoke, which rested on top of the beast's shoulders—an arrangement which worked admirably and is still to be seen in many parts of the world where agriculture has yet to be mechanized. The structure of a horse's shoulders, however, makes it not only difficult to secure a yoke, but the method of haulage required is actually detrimental to the animal's pulling ability. The only way to keep a yoke in place on a horse was to employ some form of neck strap which, as soon as the horse began to pull against a heavy load, had the undesirable effect of putting undue pressure on the windpipe.

The first farm horses
In the course of time, breast harness was developed, which was a considerable im-

FARM HARNESS

action of the shoulders and can also ride up and exert pressure on the windpipe.

Because of the imperfections of early harnessing devices, therefore, the horse was, of necessity, restricted to pulling light loads, such as chariots. Then, when the horse had grown large enough to carry man into battle, his use as a draught animal dwindled, leaving the ox to its traditional role. It was not for many centuries that widespread use of the horse on the land occurred and, even then, this varied from area to area and depended on many factors.

Available evidence points to Scandinavia as the first area to use horses as farm animals. The most likely reason for this development was the invention of the collar, a piece of equipment which revolutionized draught work just as the coming of the stirrup revolutionized riding itself. Although it is possible that the nomads of

There is a tradition of decorated horse displays throughout Europe and at some horse shows classes are held for the best-decorated horse. **Above:** An English Shire horse. **Left:** A Scottish Clydesdale, wearing a very good example of a Scottish peaked collar. **Far left:** A pair of highly-ornamented German horses wearng the collars peculiar to the Bavarian area from which they come as well as such accessories as bells and ear caps. The muzzles have a purely practical purpose and prevent the horse from biting or eating.

CHAPTER SIX · DRIVING HARNESS

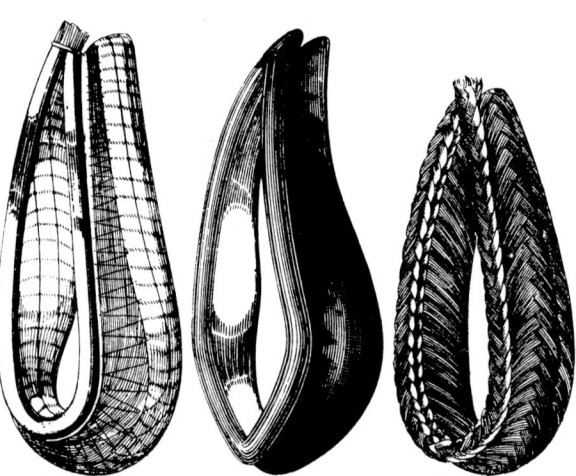

Far left: Reproduction of a page from the illuminated Apocalypse of Trèves (c. 880 AD) which shows a horse collar of the period. **Left:** Three collars, the illustrations taken from a trade catalogue of the early 1900s. They are (**left to right**) a bodied country cart collar, a piped van collar and a straw-woven segg or plough collar.

Central Asia used collars, the earliest tangible evidence for their introduction lies in the frames of metal collars unearthed from Swedish tombs of the middle and late years of the 9th century AD. Towards the end of that century King Alfred of Wessex, writing of voyages to the north, expressed surprise that in northern Norway the horse was used for ploughing, while a picture of a horse collar exists from about the same period in the illuminated *Apocalypse* of Trèves (c.880).

The link with Scandinavia is apparent in England, too. The earliest instances of the horse being used as a farm animal there occur in the eastern counties, areas which most felt the influence of the Vikings and other north European invaders. Although there seems as yet to have been no organized breeding of horses specifically for agricultural work, by the time of the 12th century there was an increase in their use on the land. However, it was not until Tudor times that the horse began to share with the ox the job of pulling wagons and ploughing the land. The changeover from ox to horse power was thus a very slow one, spanning a period of several centuries. Only as the weight-carrying war horse became obsolete in its original field, did farmers begin to appreciate their tractive powers and, additionally, the advantages of breeding horses of a certain type to carry out specific tasks. One such example is the Suffolk, bred in the East Anglian region of England and ideally suited to working the area's heavy clay soil.

The working collar
The item of equipment which enabled the horse to become the agricultural worker *par excellence* of the 18th and 19th centuries, especially in Europe and the USA, was the final version of the collar. As can be seen from paintings and various other records of the day, it and the other items of horse harness have changed little since those dates.

A collar is made of a tube of leather, called a forewale, which is stuffed with straw until it is stiff. The body, known as the afterwale, consists of padding made from stout woollen cloth filled with rye straw, with leather side pieces to protect it from weather and wear. The design is planned to avoid putting pressure on the windpipe and the withers; horses who are particularly prone to choking can be fitted with a special variant as a further precaution. This is made with a pipe, a device which is placed in the forewale at the stuffing stage, so changing the shape of the collar slightly. To ensure a good fit, the collar is made narrow at the top and wide at the bottom to correspond with the shape of the horse. However, because the collar must be passed over the horse's head, which is small at the lower end and broad at the top, it is necessary to put the collar over the horse's head upside down and to turn it round once it is on the neck.

Horses who are head-shy may be fitted with an open-topped collar, a regional design, confined mainly to south-west Britain and Ireland. This, as the name suggests, is not closed at the top but can be pulled open and slid over the neck. This, however, is not wholly satisfactory, since, with constant use, it tends to lose its rigidity and is then liable to produce shoulder sores. Over the years, many other types of 'improved' collars have been tried—pneumatic (with air instead of stuffing), elastic steel, collars stuffed with cork and ones with removable, washable linings—but none has succeeded in replacing the basic model.

The implement to be pulled is attached by chains to the hames, a rigid frame which fits round the collar. Hames used always to be made of wood—either ash or beech—but, by the end of the 19th century, iron hames had largely superseded wooden ones. Today, this process has gone one stage further, with steel. The hames are fastened together at the top by a strap, or leather thongs, and usually by a chain and hook at the bottom.

The draught bridle
The other essential piece of equipment is the bridle, which, in principle, is the same as that of a riding horse, with a headpiece, throatlatch, cheekpieces and a bit (usually a simple snaffle). In some areas, nosebands are used; in others they are not. Some horsemen, too, favour blinkers, while others are opposed to their use. Blinkers probably derive from the days of horse armour, when protective devices were worn to save the horse's eyes from injury during combat. The chief justification for their use on a farm horse is that they prevent his catching sight of the implement he is pulling and taking fright. However, since most young horses are trained without blinkers and many older ones can be seen working calmly in 'open'—that is, blinkerless—bridles, it seems likely that blinkers are something of an anachronism. Many people, however, still favour them. Blinkers can be made in different ways. It

is possible, though wasteful, to cut the blinker and the cheekpiece of the bridle from one piece of hide. However, it is more usual to cut the blinkers and the cheekpieces separately and then stitch them together.

Leather reins are usually used for driving with cart harness and rope 'lines' with plough harness. In addition, the horse may wear a shorter rein fastened to the bit rings and hooked over the hames. This is a useful device which acts like a mild bearing rein, stopping the horse from putting his head down to graze while at work.

Harness types

Equipped with the basic essentials of bridle and collar, the farm horse is worked in one of three types of harness—cart harness, plough harness or trace harness. Cart harness is used with all vehicles or implements equipped with shafts. These include a variety of wagons and carts, as well as some horse-drawn hoes and rollers and one or two other devices, such as manure spreaders. In order to work in shafts, the horse must be fitted with the usual collar and bridle, with long leather reins, plus a pad, or saddle, and breeching.

The cart pad or saddle is made on a tree of elm or beech, consisting of two boards fixed either side of a grooved arch. It occupies the same position on a horse's back as a riding saddle and is secured in a similar manner by means of a girth. A strap is fastened to the front of the pad and secured to the collar, thus guarding against any backward movement of the pad. This item of equipment is known as a meeter strap.

In bad weather a piece of stout leather called a housen may be attached to the collar and positioned so that it bridges the gap between the collar and the pad, the idea being to prevent rain from running between the horse's shoulder and his collar. In most areas, however, the housen is no longer used.

To stop the pad riding forward, the horse may be equipped with a crupper, a padded leather loop which passes under

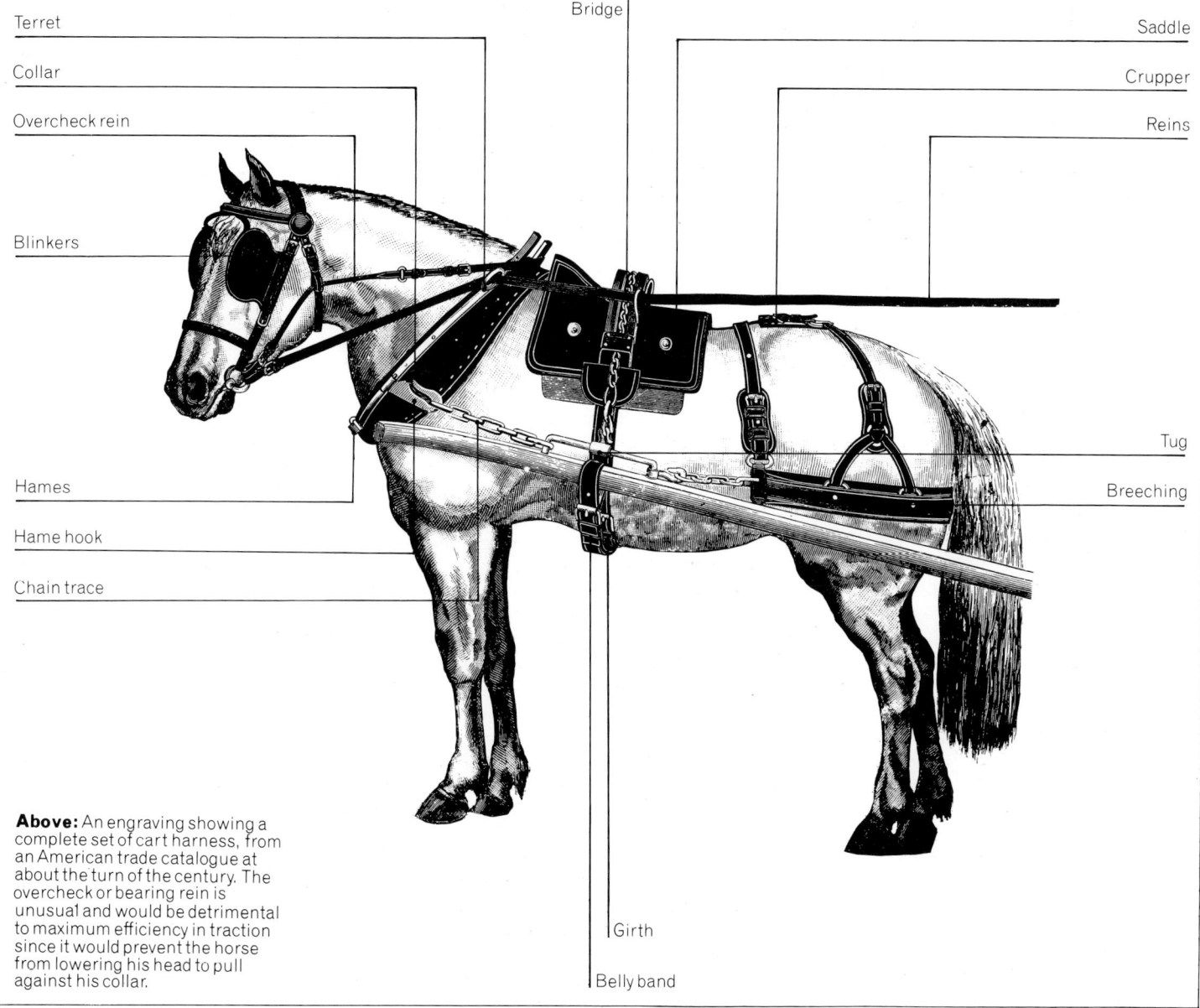

Above: An engraving showing a complete set of cart harness, from an American trade catalogue at about the turn of the century. The overcheck or bearing rein is unusual and would be detrimental to maximum efficiency in traction since it would prevent the horse from lowering his head to pull against his collar.

CHAPTER SIX · DRIVING HARNESS

Right and opposite: These illustrations show the stages followed when harnessing a cart horse. The collar is always put on first and upside down so that it passes easily over the head, being turned into place at the thinnest part of the neck. Apart from the logic of beginning at the front and working backwards, there is an element of superstition in the practice and no horseman would put on the saddle before the collar. Once the collar is in position the hames are put on and fastened with the small hame strap. The driving reins are put on last and looped over the near side hame preparatory to the horse being put to.

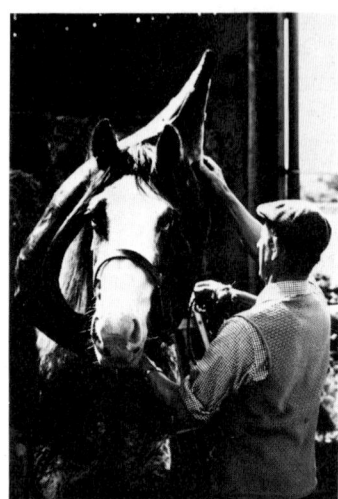

the dock and is kept in place by means of a broad leather strap attached to the rear of the collar. However, such a precaution is not usually necessary and the tail loop is often dispensed with, the back strap being retained merely to suspend vertical hip straps and breeching.

The purpose of the pad is to support the back chain, or ridger. This chain passes over the horse's back and is attached to both shafts, thus keeping them at the correct elevation for easy forward movement. In the case of a two-wheeled vehicle the horse supports a portion of its weight, but when a four-wheeled vehicle is used the ridger merely takes the weight of the shafts. The deep groove on the upper side of the pad houses the ridger when it is in position, the ends being attached by hooks to a metal ridger bar fitted to the top edge of each shaft.

The shafts of a vehicle are attached to the horse's collar by means of strong chains known as tugs. It is important to ensure that, when in position, the offside and nearside tugs are of equal length or the horse will not be able to pull effectively. Forward movement of the vehicle is effected by the horse leaning into his collar and exerting a pull on the shafts via the tugs.

Sometimes, it may be necessary for the horse to back the vehicle. This is where the device known as breeching comes into play. Breeching consists of a broad band of leather which passes round the hindquarters and is suspended from the crupper strap by vertical hip and loin straps. Chains are used to fasten the ends of the breeching band to a bar on each shaft. By pushing back against the breeching a horse can put a cart into reverse or help to steady a load when travelling downhill.

An additional strap or rope may be attached to each shaft, passing under the horse's body. This is a belly band; it is not fastened tightly under the horse's belly like a girth but is left fairly loose. Its role is to help prevent the vehicle tipping backwards, should it become tail-heavy for any reason. The weight of the horse's body counteracts the upward swing of the shafts.

Sometimes a strap is passed between the horse's forelegs and attached to the girth at one end and at the other to the collar. This, the martingale, is often decorated with horse brasses. The latter ornaments are believed to be of pagan origin and legend has it that they are efficacious in bringing good fortune.

The process of harnessing a horse to a cart or other shafted vehicle is termed shutting in. Collar, bridle, pad and breeching are fitted on the horse. He is then lined up square with the shafts of the vehicle and backed between them. Once the horse is correctly positioned, the shafts can be lifted and held in the raised position by one of the tugs while the ridger, breeching chains and second tug are all fastened.

When removing a horse from shafts—

FARM HARNESS

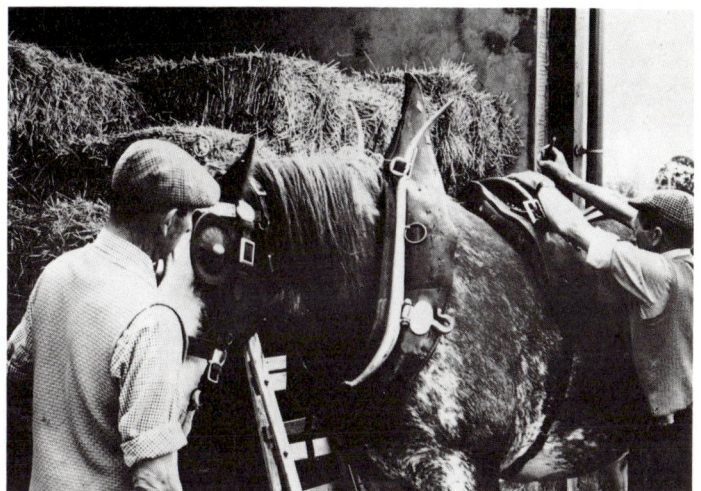

Left: A Shire in cart harness and ready to move off. The hame strap, keeping the hames on the collar, can be seen clearly at the top of the latter. When the size of the Shire is considered (some of them measure 18 hh and may weigh nearly a ton), and the weight of a loaded vehicle, the necessity for harness of the greatest strength is appreciated.

CHAPTER SIX · DRIVING HARNESS

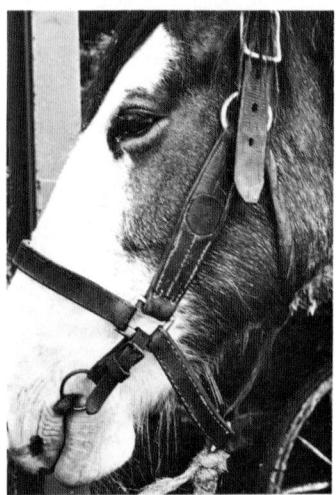

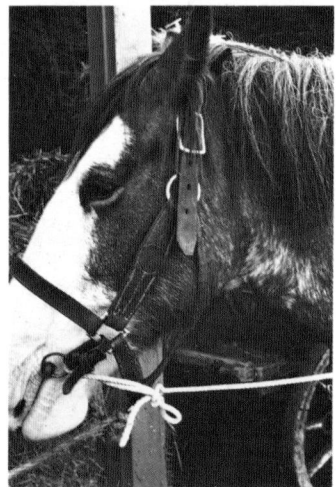

Above and left: Detailed illustrations of plough harness, in which such items as breeching are unnecessary and cord plough lines are used in place of the leather driving reins in a cart harness. These lines are secured to the open bridle (no blinkers) by means of a ploughman's knot, illustrated left. **Opposite:** A Shire in single plough harness. This time the horse is wearing a blinkered bridle.

shutting out—the breeching is unfastened first, followed by the tugs and finally the ridger. After this, the shafts can be lowered to the ground and the horse led forward and clear of the vehicle.

Plough harness
Plough harness, also known as chain harness or sling gear, is employed for implements such as ploughs and harrows. The horse wears a bridle and collar as for cart harness, but dispenses with the pad and breeching. The traces, or chains, which are used to pull the implement are attached to the hames of the horse's collar, one on either side, the other ends being fastened to either end of a piece of metal or wood called, variously, a whipple-tree, a swing-tree or a billet. This must be long enough to ensure that the chains do not touch the horse's sides, otherwise galling will occur. The whipple-tree is attached by means of a chain and hook to the implement.

Various devices are employed for supporting the weight of the chains and preventing the horse stepping on them when they are slack. Sometimes a backband is used. This is fitted in the same place as the pad; no girth is necessary, however, since the downward pull of the chains keeps it in place. Hip straps, suspended from the crupper strap, are also used as an alternative way of performing the same function as the backband.

When two horses are harnessed abreast, each horse's traces are fastened to separate whipple-trees. These are attached by chains to the ends of another whipple-tree, which in turn, are chained to the implement. Things become more complicated when three or more horses are used, since the combination of whipple-trees has to be calculated carefully. Various combinations of whipple-trees and compensating whipple-trees can be used for such teams, care being taken to ensure that the leverage is the same on each side of the implement. When unhitched from the

whipple-trees the chains are hooked up on to the hames.

When working two or more horses abreast it is usual to employ couples, made of leather, rope or chain. These are fastened from one horse's bridle to the next, preventing a horse moving too far in front of, or away from, his neighbour.

The reins
The reins used for ploughing, harrowing etc are usually made of rope and are termed lines. Because there is a danger of lines of the necessary length becoming entangled with the horse's harness, some means must be employed to keep them clear. How this is done is largely a matter of individual preference. One method is to pass the lines through rings on either side of the hames; another is to suspend two rings on lengths of cord—one on either side of the horse's quarters—the cords being attached to the crupper strap. The lines are passed through these rings and thence to the driver's hands. The lines are held one in each hand and the driver walks behind the implement along the mark left by the last bout—each trip across a field is known as a bout.

When not in use the lines are neatly wound up to prevent tangling and hung on the end of the hame. One method is to take the two leather straps which fasten the lines to the bit rings in one hand and wind the doubled line round the wrists in a figure of eight holding it rather like a skein of wool. To finish it off neatly, the spare end of the line—that is, the looped end—is wound several times around the centre of the coiled line, passed through one of the loops in the figure of eight and then hung.

Harnessing variations
When working on heavy ground it may be necessary to use three or more horses and there are a variety of ways of harnessing them to the implement. One is the unicorn method, where two horses are yoked

CHAPTER SIX · DRIVING HARNESS

Above: Drawing a harrow in conventional harness. **Right:** Detail of the swingle tree which acts to direct the pull and to prevent the horses becoming entangled in the chains and implements.

FARM HARNESS

Above: A team of four Shires at work in the harvest field and wearing traditional English harness. **Left:** An American engraving of horses in tandem showing clearly the wheel and lead harness.

abreast, and the third placed between, but in front of, the pair and attached to the whipple-tree by a long chain called a soam. In some regions three horses are sometimes yoked in what is termed Bodkin fashion, the third horse being placed in front of the furrow horse of a pair. For exceptionally heavy implements, four horses can be yoked abreast, but this is impossible where ploughing is concerned, since they would ruin the farrow. Where heavy ground warrants it, either two pairs are yoked one in front of the other, or four horses are used in line.

An implement fitted with a pole requires a pair of horses to draw it, one on either side of the pole. Basically the harness is the same as chain harness, but with the addition of a broad leather collar or neck strap, which is fitted to the front of the collar and supports the front end of the pole.

Trace harness

A trace horse is sometimes needed to help a single horse pull a heavy load, particularly when steep hills have to be negotiated. In this instance the lead horse wears a collar and bridle and usually a backband and crupper. Long chain traces are attached to the collar of the trace horse, the other ends being fastened to hooks on the underside of the shafts. The backband and hip straps take the weight of these chains, with a spreader—a bar of wood or metal—placed between the chains behind the horse's quarters to keep them apart and prevent them from chafing his sides. To prevent the horizontal pull of the cart traces pulling the collar up so that it presses on the windpipe, a belly band can be fitted to the traces slightly forward of the backband. An implement like a plough does not present this problem, since its pull is downward.

CHAPTER SEVEN

Training Aids

Schooling Equipment
Breaking Equipment

Long-reining is one of the methods which may be employed in the breaking of a horse.

Training Aids · Schooling

CHAPTER SEVEN · TRAINING AIDS

The equipment employed in the training of horses differs in various parts of the world according to the horse culture that has developed and been passed from generation to generation in the particular areas. In some instances, the equipment is simple and the methods employed are forceful in comparison with those practised in other countries. In California, for instance, hobbles are part of many a horse-trainer's gear; while the methods used there may seem rough to European eyes, they are nonetheless quick, effective and long-lasting. European methods are without doubt the most sophisticated, but whether the horse appreciates them any more than the systems practised in the western states of America is something that Californians may feel entitled to question.

There is naturally a difference between training horses and schooling them. Horse-breakers, like the Americans Rarey and Sample from whom 'Professor' Sydney Galvayne, the celebrated Victorian horse-master, learnt his trade, were more tamers than trainers. Much of the assortment of tackle used by them to subdue the recalcitrant horse is not relevant to the present day.

The specialist artificial aids described here can be and are used for the schooling of the competition horse. Such aids are designed to equip the horse physically for the various competitive disciplines by developing the muscular formations correctly and perfecting the animal's balance. They are also used in the re-schooling of horses which have been incorrectly developed in respect of the muscle formations, and whose potential cannot be fully realized as a result.

The side-rein
The simplest of the items used in schooling in order to improve the overall carriage, in particular that of the head and neck, is the side-rein. This is fastened from the mouth to either a body roller or to the saddle girth. At the Spanish Riding School in Vienna, the side-reins are plain leather straps unadorned by any additional elastic or rubber insets and this practice has a large following.

However, probably just as many trainers use side-reins inset with a rubber ring, or a strip of strong elastic. The idea is that the resilience given to the rein by the elastic or rubber allows it to 'give' to the movement of the head, makes it easier on the mouth and is altogether less restrictive. It is an attractive theory but there are sound arguments against it as well.

Supporters of the plain leather side-rein point out that the elasticated rein not only contributes to an unsteady head position but can also encourage the horse to evade the bit by going behind it. In other words, instead of seeking contact with the bit, the horse brings his nose back so as to avoid the pressure. It is thought that the continual give and take of the strong elastic or rubber gets the horse into the habit of dropping the bit. Both types of rein are, however, used generally in schooling, whether the horse is being worked on the lunge or under saddle. Their use materially assists the trainer in the fixing of the head position; when used with a rider in the saddle, they also assist the effective action of the bit.

The draw rein
Almost as simple, though not accepted so universally, is the draw rein, which was the invention of the British master, the Duke of Newcastle (1592–1676), who used it from a padded cavesson and not from the bit.

The basic draw rein is fastened to the saddle girth, then passes back through the bit rings to the rider's hand. Obviously, such a rein has a very considerable influence on the position of the head and makes it very easy for the rider to 'draw' in his horse's nose. There are some variations in the use of the rein nonetheless. Even more leverage can be obtained, for instance, if the rein is fitted to the girth between the forelegs before passing to the hand via the bit rings.

Another form of rein is that fastened to the girth (or between the forelegs) and then taken upwards to pulleys set each side of the bridle, on a line with the browband, and from thence through the bit rings to the hands. This arrangement is similar to that of the French Chambon, but it is not really suited to mounted schooling, since it often causes the very resistances and evasions it seeks to avoid. It is possible to dispense with the pulleys and the attachments to the girth, placing the rein over the poll and passing it through the loops on the browband down to the bit rings and then to the hand. In these instances the action of the rein differs to that of the ordinary draw or running rein, since it exerts a downward influence on the poll (hopefully, encouraging flexion in this area). In addition, it causes a retraction of the nose through the bit pressure.

Above: The simple side rein running from bit to girth. This helps a trainer to obtain a steady head position, which can be more or less fixed by adjusting the rein's length. By fixing the head position, it also assists the effective action of the bit.

SCHOOLING

Above: Usually a draw rein is fastened from the girth and comes to the rider's hand through the bit rings. This is an alternative way of lowering the poll, dispensing with the attachment to the girth. **Right:** The French Chambon, a training device used to induce a lowering of the head and neck accompanied by a raising of the base of the neck. This will result in a rounded top line and greater engagement of the hocks under the body.

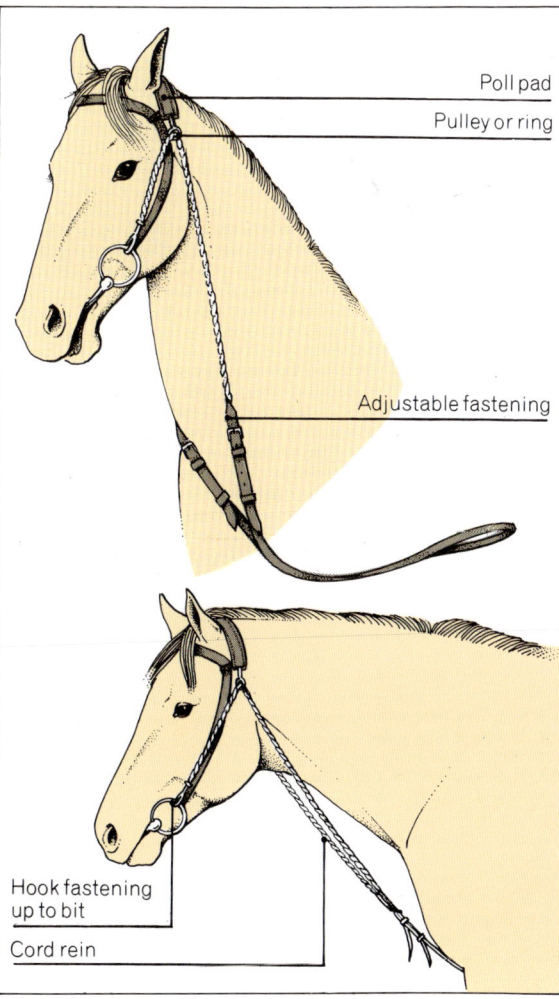

- Poll pad
- Pulley or ring
- Adjustable fastening
- Hook fastening up to bit
- Cord rein

Those who use a rein in this last fashion claim that its use makes it possible to be more precise in holding the head position and that there is less chance of the horse evading the bit by overbending.

The Chambon

More sophisticated and with more far reaching effects upon the horse as a whole is the Chambon. Unlike the various draw rein arrangements which act upon the front end of the horse, the Chambon is designed to influence the whole of the horse's body and is used only when the horse is being worked loose in a confined area.

The Chambon tackle consists of a body roller, to which the martingale is attached between the forelegs in the usual way. At the breast, the martingale divides into two branches, considerable adjustment being possible just above the point of division. The 'branches', usually cords, pass through rings either side of a felt poll pad, and then fasten to the bit. With the Chambon in position, it is impossible for the horse to raise his head unduly. The device is tightened gradually, the result being that the horse learns to move with a lowered head and neck, which is the one position in which he can be entirely comfortable.

The effect of the Chambon, once the horse learns to move at the short, balanced trot which characterizes this schooling device, is to raise the base of the neck, exercising and developing the muscles of the back and loins so that the former becomes rounded and in full use. In this position the shoulder will be unrestricted in its movement and the hindlegs will be increasingly engaged as the hock, stifle and hip joints begin to work to full capacity. This is the outline which is sought by every trainer who takes the pains to produce a young horse in the right 'form' or shape, with the muscles and joints correctly developed so that the structure is as near to 'mechanical' perfection as possible. When that is achieved, the horse is then capable of realizing his full potential.

The de Gogue

As a development of the Chambon, allowing the trainer to continue and improve upon the work established by that martingale, there is the de Gogue device, perfected by the Frenchman Rene de Gogue and named after him. In fact, it is not an

CHAPTER SEVEN · TRAINING AIDS

over-exaggeration to regard the de Gogue as a schooling system in its own right, rather than merely a training aid.

The device can be used in two positions, with an extra rein direct from bit to hand being employed as required. The 'independent' position, in which the horse is first worked loose, obtains its results in a somewhat different manner to the Chambon; in addition the equipment produces greater refinement, in the wider ranging effects which it is capable of bringing about.

The martingale forms a triangle comprising the poll, mouth and base of the neck, the three points of major resistances in the unschooled, or badly schooled, horse. Within the confines imposed by those three points of restraint, the horse can carry his head comfortably in the lowered position required. When the muscles have been built up and made supple and the horse is moving freely and energetically in the correct manner, further adjustments can be made so as to bring the nose inwards and increase the flexion at the poll. The horse cannot become over-bent because of the stops fitted to the rein below the small pulley on the poll pad.

The next stage is to establish ridden work. The de Gogue is fitted in its independent position, a rein being attached to the bit in the normal manner. The final stage is reached when the rein is attached directly to the cords, or lengths of rounded leather, which pass from the base of the neck, via the poll through the bit rings. With the martingale in this position, the horse can be schooled on the flat or over fences and can be ridden in competition. The arrangement gives the rider the maximum amount of control for the expenditure of the minimum effort, whilst the horse can perform with the greatest degree of athleticism of which he is capable. This, in brief, is the claim made for the de Gogue system and it has numerous adherents to bear witness to its efficacy.

Controversial methods

The difficulty faced by trainers attempting the introduction of schooling methods relying upon 'artificial' training aids is the almost certain antagonism their efforts will provoke amongst the riding 'establishment' which controls, for better or worse, national equestrian policies. It is not necessarily that the 'establishment' is narrow in its outlook or unduly entrenched in its views; in most instances, however, the 'establishment' is forced to be the champion of orthodoxy if only for the general good of the riding population it serves. It therefore feels bound to condemn much corrective equipment as offering 'short cuts' and to support the purist

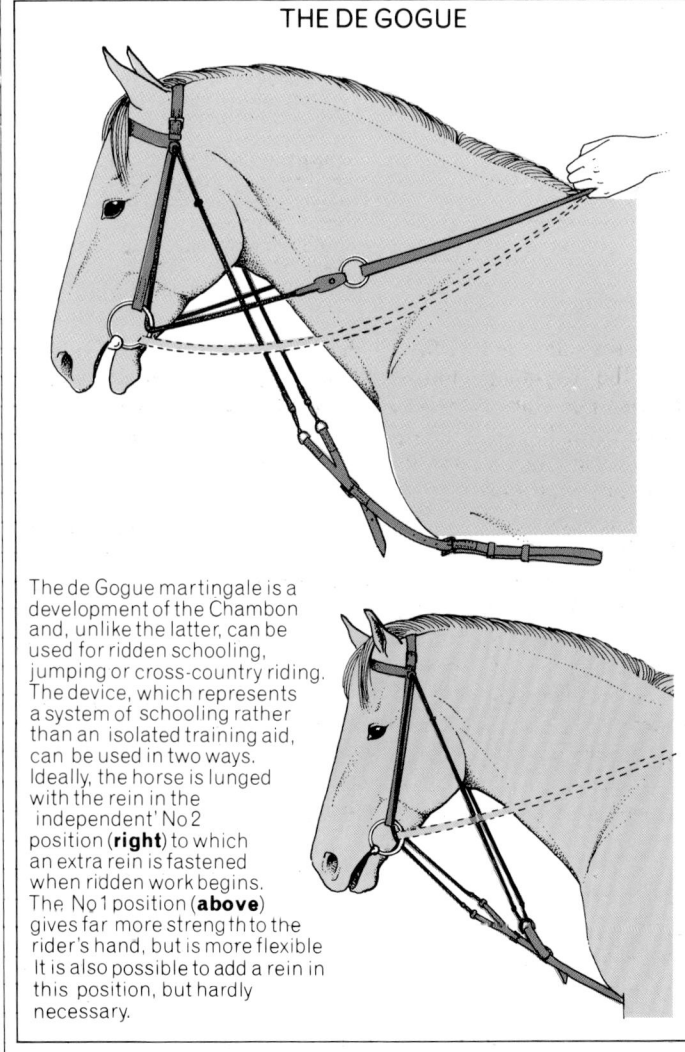

THE DE GOGUE

The de Gogue martingale is a development of the Chambon and, unlike the latter, can be used for ridden schooling, jumping or cross-country riding. The device, which represents a system of schooling rather than an isolated training aid, can be used in two ways. Ideally, the horse is lunged with the rein in the independent' No 2 position (**right**) to which an extra rein is fastened when ridden work begins. The No 1 position (**above**) gives far more strength to the rider's hand, but is more flexible. It is also possible to add a rein in this position, but hardly necessary.

Above: The Abbot-Davies Balancing Rein. Its object is to develop the muscles of the back and hindlegs by raising the base of the neck. Initially, a connection is made from the tail to the mouth between the forelegs, the action on the mouth being initiated by an ingenious spring and pulley arrangement. In the latter stages of schooling, however, the rein is fastened from the girth to the mouth.

concept by offering counsels of perfection in the methods employed to school horses. The prospects for argument are endless

In Europe, France, the most logical of the horse nations, is possibly the country most receptive to new ideas; Britain, on the other hand, with less general understanding of the classical principles involved in schooling the competition horse, but having possibly a greater reservoir of potential talent than any other country, is probably the most conservative in its acceptance of innovatory equipment.

At no time has the British 'establishment' acknowledged, let alone accepted, the usefulness of the Chambon and de Gogue, although a number of trainers and top-class competitors use the devices. Not surprisingly, therefore, the riding 'establishment' reacted strongly to the aggressive promotion of an advanced schooling aid launched into the equestrian market in 1977. This was the Abbot-Davies Balancing Rein, perfected by Peter Abbot-Davies, and it was to cause a considerable controversy.

The Abbot-Davies Rein is the ultimate descendant of the *rienda de vencer* (rein to conquer), as the draw or running rein is aptly termed in the Castilian tongue. That it should have horrified the traditionalists is understandable, since it involves, in one of its uses, the tying of the horse's tail to his head, the connection being made from the tail and thence between hind- and forelegs to the mouth where an arrangement of springs and pulleys was said to mitigate shortcomings in the rider's hands.

The rein can be used in three positions—attached from mouth to tail, from mouth to girth and from the mouth to behind the ears. The object is to develop the muscles, the rounding of the top line and the effective engagement of the hocks in a relatively short period of time without causing resistance. The mouth to tail position is, in fact, used only initially and then only occasionally, the second position being the one in which the horse is worked. The ultimate aim is for the horse to be ridden in a simple snaffle whilst retaining the rounded outline, suppleness and obedience which have been established by the use of the balancing rein.

The Abbot-Davies Rein made use of a principle known to horsemen for over 2,000 years, though it has never been a part of orthodox training systems. The aim was to adapt to modern usage and then

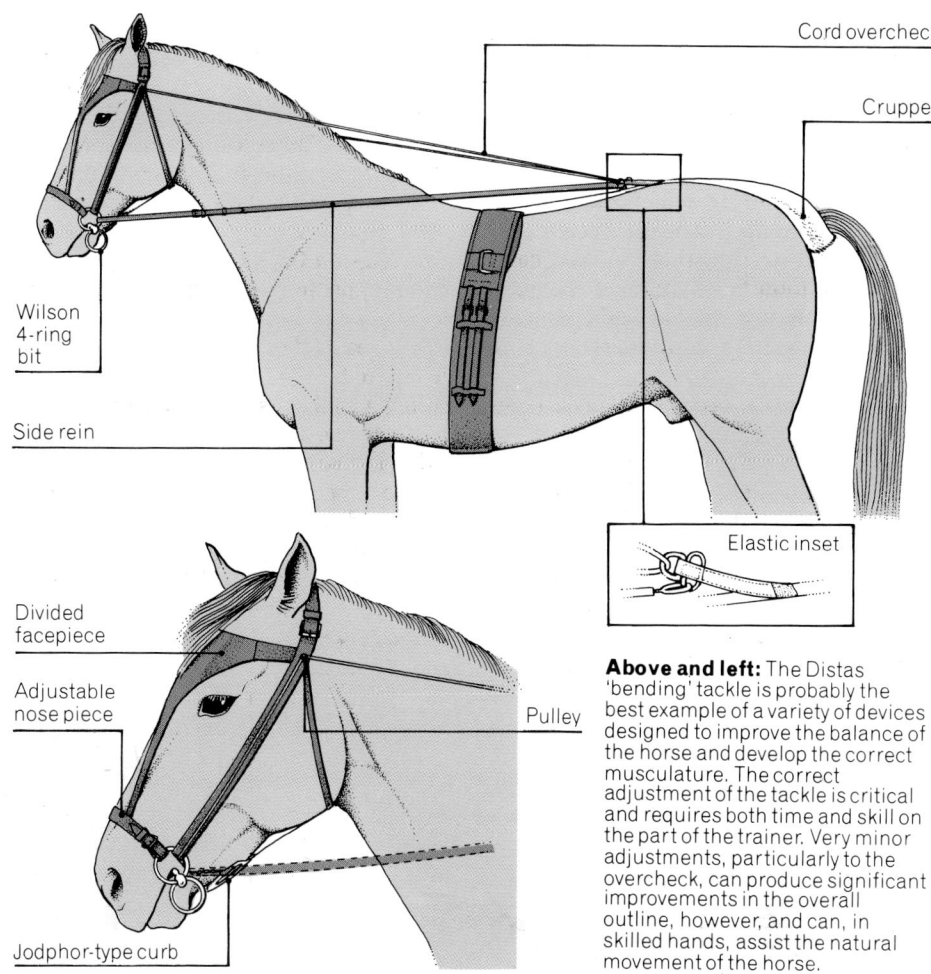

Above and left: The Distas 'bending' tackle is probably the best example of a variety of devices designed to improve the balance of the horse and develop the correct musculature. The correct adjustment of the tackle is critical and requires both time and skill on the part of the trainer. Very minor adjustments, particularly to the overcheck, can produce significant improvements in the overall outline, however, and can, in skilled hands, assist the natural movement of the horse.

attempt to perfect the 'Rameses rein', depicted on the temple of the Egyptian Pharaoh Rameses III at Medinet Habu. Rameses used the rein on chariot horses and the practice persisted amongst horse people down the centuries, although the principles involved were not always completely understood. It is a fact, nonetheless, that horses will submit easily to a 'tail-rein'; certainly Sydney Galvayne's systems were founded largely on the involvement of the tail as a method of producing tractability in the most unpromising material. To what extent, however, the Abbot-Davies Balancing Rein can be accounted as a success is problematical. It has certainly not found general acceptance.

The Distas bending tackle
There have always been specialist tackles designed to produce the better moving, better balanced horse. One good example is the equipment known to an older generation of horsemen in both Britain and the USA as the Distas bending tackle. This, too, employed the tail; in this instance, however, the tail was connected to the mouth along the top of the back which, on the face of it, would seem to produce an opposite result to the one desired.

The tackle employed a four-ring bit, with a nosepiece fastened to the inside rings. The side-reins, joining the crupper by an elastic inset on the croup, were attached to the inside bit rings so that the pressure was taken on the nose and not by the mouth. The position of the head was then finalized by adjusting a cord overcheck attached to a broad Jodhphor polo curb (which lay between the jawbones), so as to raise the head to the position required.

The operation of the tackle required experience, but in skilful hands remarkable and quite unexpected results were obtained. This was particularly the case with show ponies, whose small riders were not sufficiently strong to school the ponies effectively from the saddle.

Training Aids · Breaking

The equipment used today in breaking the horse to saddle (or harness) is relatively simple—more so now, indeed, than previously when the device known as the 'dumb jockey' was much in vogue. This was a body roller fitted with crossed gutta-percha arms to which the reins were fastened, the arms being provided with rein attachment points at a number of levels. A crupper was also used together with side-reins, overchecks and so on to truss the horse, like a chicken, into the required position. The animal was frequently left for quite long periods in the stable with the tackle in place.

Basic equipment

Today, the basic requirements are a lunge cavesson, the modern descendant of the somewhat fearsome device invented by Grisone in the 16th century, a lunge rein, lunge whip, breaking bridle and roller. There are, however, other interesting additional items—some of which are perhaps less well-known to modern horsemen—as well as the long-reining equipment which varies according to the school of thought. The first essential is suitable equipment for lungeing the horse. The object of lungeing is to improve balance, build muscle and make it supple and to teach the very necessary habits of obedience and discipline.

A lunge cavesson can be of either one pattern or the other, but all will provide a ring on the metal noseplate to which the lunge rein can be fitted. Many cavessons have three rings on the noseplate for those who prefer to lunge from an inside ring, rather than directly from the nose. The two side rings can also be used for side-reins, but a better arrangement is to use the side-reins from dees placed at the ends of the noseplate. The advantage of the device is that it gives the trainer far greater control over his pupil than if he were to attempt lungeing from a headcollar. In any case, the latter is easily pulled across the face and could therefore damage an eye.

For preference a lunge rein should be made of tubular web—not rope, which burns if pulled through the hands. It should be between 18ft and 35ft in length and have a buckle fastening mounted on a swivel to allow the necessary movement of the rein.

The whip, which is used as an extension of the trainer's arm to encourage the horse to go forward and to indicate to him to keep out on the circle, needs to have a thong which is long enough to be able to touch the horse if absolutely necessary. It also needs to be light in weight. Modern whips made from fibreglass are a great improvement on the older type whips in this respect.

An early example of the schooling device which came to be known as a 'dumb jockey' in action at the Spanish Riding School, Vienna.

The choice of the first bit for a young horse is a matter of personal preference. The traditional mounting bit is the key bit (either a straight bar or a jointed one), the loose keys encouraging the horse to mouth and make saliva. However, many modern trainers first mouth a young horse with a plain mullen-mouth rubber snaffle. The argument for this is that, since they do not want horses to be continually throwing their heads about as they play with the bit, it is better to start as they mean to go on.

The breaking roller acts as a prelude to the saddle and also provides a convenient place to which side-reins may be fastened in the secondary stage of training. The best rollers are without doubt those made in two parts, so that the adjustment can be made on both sides. It is also advisable to have the forward edge of the girth portion shaped to the rear away from the elbow and bound with soft padding. Dees sewn at intervals on each side for the attachment of side-reins allow the latter to be placed at different heights. These may also be used when long-reining is introduced, the reins being passed through the lower pair of rings.

Whether there is an advantage in having side-reins crossed at the wither and fastening to buckles on the top of the roller pads is debatable, but this fitting used to be very much a traditional feature. Most trainers, however, agree that a crupper is a necessary item. It holds the roller in place and seems to help the horse to make use of his loins in balancing himself. Well-made, good old-fashioned cruppers had the dock stuffed with linseed so that the body heat kept it always soft and supple.

Long-reins and long-reining

Long-reins need to be as light as possible, so as not to put too much weight on the mouth. The old-fashioned tapered plough lines serve this purpose extremely well, but there is the danger of burns if the rope is pulled through the hands. Long-reining is not necessarily carried out with a roller. Trainers in Britain often prefer to long-rein with a saddle on the back, the reins being passed through the stirrups, whilst Danish trainers achieve an enviable standard using a driving pad, the reins passing through the terrets and the outside one being held across the back.

The logical French use a driving collar and a roller fitted with dees halfway down its sides. The reins pass through the collar terrets, then drop downwards, so that they pass through the roller dees before going back to the hands. The trainer stands directly behind the horse and is thus able to assist in 'the body advancing towards the head'. This method of placing the horse firmly on the bit is a more advanced form of training.

Other items

These are the conventional articles of equipment. Though they may differ in detail from one place to another, all are generally used. There are, however, other devices which are less well-known. They belong perhaps to an older school of horsemen, such as Rarey and Galvayne, and have their origin in far older cultures than theirs. Indeed, some of them echo the 'Rameses rein' which so fascinated the modern British authority, Peter Abbot-Davies.

Sydney Galvayne is still famous for his system of establishing horses' ages by examination of their teeth; Galvayne's

LUNGEING TECHNIQUES

Right: A lungeing cavesson correctly fitted to the horse, with the lunge rein fitted with a swivel fastening to the central nose ring. **Far right:** A cavesson fitted with side-rings to which side-reins can be attached, or from which the horse can be lunged if the trainer follows the practice of lungeing from the inside ring. **Below:** A long lunge whip is an essential part of schooling equipment.

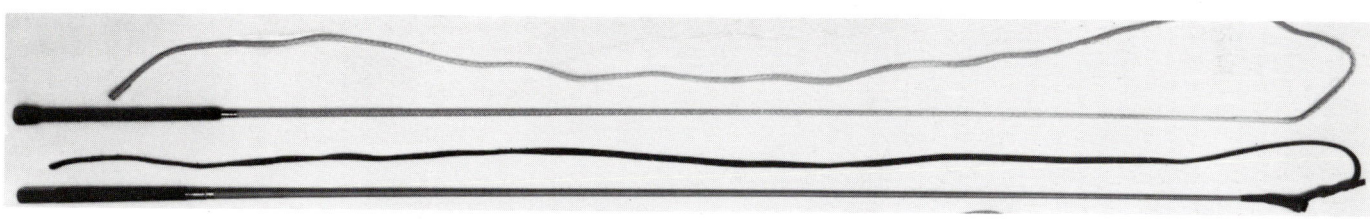

Above: A young horse during an early lesson on the lunge. Initially, the trainer often employs an assistant to lead the horse around the circle until he understands what is required. The trainer 'leads' with the rein in his left hand and the whip held point down behind him.

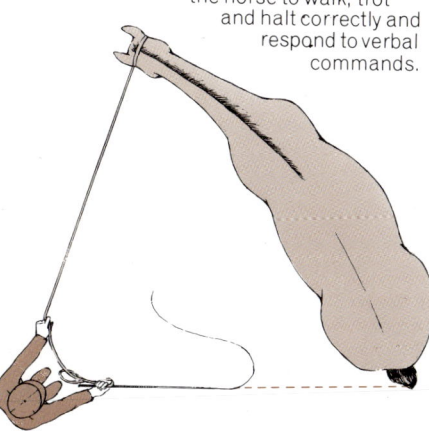

Below: The diagram shows the correct positioning of the trainer in relation to his pupil. Here, the horse is circling left on the lunge. The trainer stands a little behind the shoulder controlling the head with his left hand and maintaining impulsion through the presence of the lunge whip. The aim is to get the horse to walk, trot and halt correctly and respond to verbal commands.

Groove, the convenient brown mark which extends down the teeth as the horse grows older, is named after him. His early career is obscure, but he nonetheless acquired an enviable reputation for himself when he came to England in 1884. His purpose in making the journey was to demonstrate his 'new, humane and scientific system' of horse-breaking and training; so well did he succeed in this that in 1887, the year of Queen Victoria's Golden Jubilee, he appeared at Balmoral to show his skill before the queen.

Exactly where Galvayne discovered his system is not known. Galvayne's real name was Osborn and, although an Australian, he came to England from America, where he had been employed by the American tamer 'Professor' Sample. He changed his name on arrival in England and it could be that his methods were those of his former master, who, it is suggested, may have been the author of the celebrated system of ageing horses by their teeth which Galvayne claimed as his own. Another authority, Major Barrowcliff-Ellis, an officer in the Indian army during British rule, attributed the system he practised to a German named Lichtwark who settled in Australia in 1865. This, too,

CHAPTER SEVEN · TRAINING AIDS

Left: The horse in long reins in accordance with the English fashion. There are other, more sophisticated methods of long-reining, such as the Danish method, the classical style employed by the Spanish Riding School and the French way using a harness collar. However, the English style is satisfactory for the limited objectives required.

could have been the inspiration for Galvayne's methods.

Galvayne based his system on a collection of ropes and surcingles. This may seem slightly rough and ready, even mechanically forceful, and is certainly poles apart from the orthodox approach of today. The essence of Galvayne's system, however, was very sound—it was, in fact, based on a psychological force being applied by a mechanical one.

The first step was the 'Galvayning' of the horse, with the horse's head being tied to his tail. The horse was then 'gentled' by the third hand, a wooden pole with a 'blob' or egg-shaped pad on the end. This pole was passed all over the horse until he would accept it, and the handling that followed, with complete equanimity.

Galvayne's simple rope harnesses frequently employed the tail of the horse, as, for instance, with his simple device to cure horses who persistently ran back against their headcollars. A similar arrangement is illustrated and described in 'The Conquest of the Horse' (1947), by the French cavalry officer and international show jumper Yves Benoist-Gironière. The tail was also used in Galvayne's leading tackle. This piece of equipment is still used in Australia and is extremely useful if dealing with a horse who is unwilling to enter a trailer or box.

The Barnum rein

A piece of equipment certainly known to Rarey, Galvayne, Jesse Beary and others, as well as to Yves Benoist-Gironière, was the Barnum rein. This is named after the Barnum of circus fame, but there is evidence to show that a similar device was known in Mexico and South America in much earlier times, so it may well have been, as so much else, part of the ancient Iberian horse-culture.

The Barnum is designed to assert the trainer's authority over a difficult or unruly horse and its object is to teach a salutary lesson in obedience. The rein is fitted with a rubber bit and a soft cotton rope. When the horse plays up, the rein is pulled tight. The animal may fight for a moment but inevitably he will give up, usually very suddenly, and come towards his trainer who quickly releases the tight cord. The trainer is thus associated with the relief of the discomfort.

Benoist-Gironière states that the 'obsession of the point of resistance' is broken and the habit of straining against the rein or refusing to be led is cured for ever by the use of the device. He also summarized most tellingly the effect of this type of device in a quotation from another great French horseman, Gustave le Bon: 'So long as there has been no struggle the horse cannot be totally convinced of his rider's authority. Only this struggle will convince him, and it is far better that it should take place at the start rather than later on. As soon as it is over, the animal will be disciplined and once he is disciplined in one respect, he will easily be so for all others. The battle is won, and from now on we need have recourse to nothing but kindness ... a kindness which is quiet but never weak.'

Though such devices may seem out of place to the riders and trainers of today, it should not be forgotten that they have an essential place in equestrian history. Whatever is practised today is no more than a small part in a progression that began with the first horsemen and is the result of the knowledge that has been accumulated gradually by a succession of riders and trainers over the centuries.

BREAKING EQUIPMENT

Right: The Barnun schooling rein may be of more ancient origin than the name suggests. Should the horse attempt to run back or break away, the rein is pulled tight and the rubber bit rises uncomfortably high in the mouth. It is held that the Barnum asserts the trainer's authority over an unruly horse very effectively and without the risk of injuring the animal.

Below: A selection of the simple rope harnesses employed by the trainer 'Professor' Sydney Galvayne on the principle of a psychological force being applied by a mechanical one. Galvayne made much use of the tail in subjugating difficult horses and his system of leading (**below right**) by applying pressure on the dock is very effective. The pole in the centre illustration was used to gentle the horse, the 'blob' end being passed over the body while the horse was secured by having his head tied to his tail.

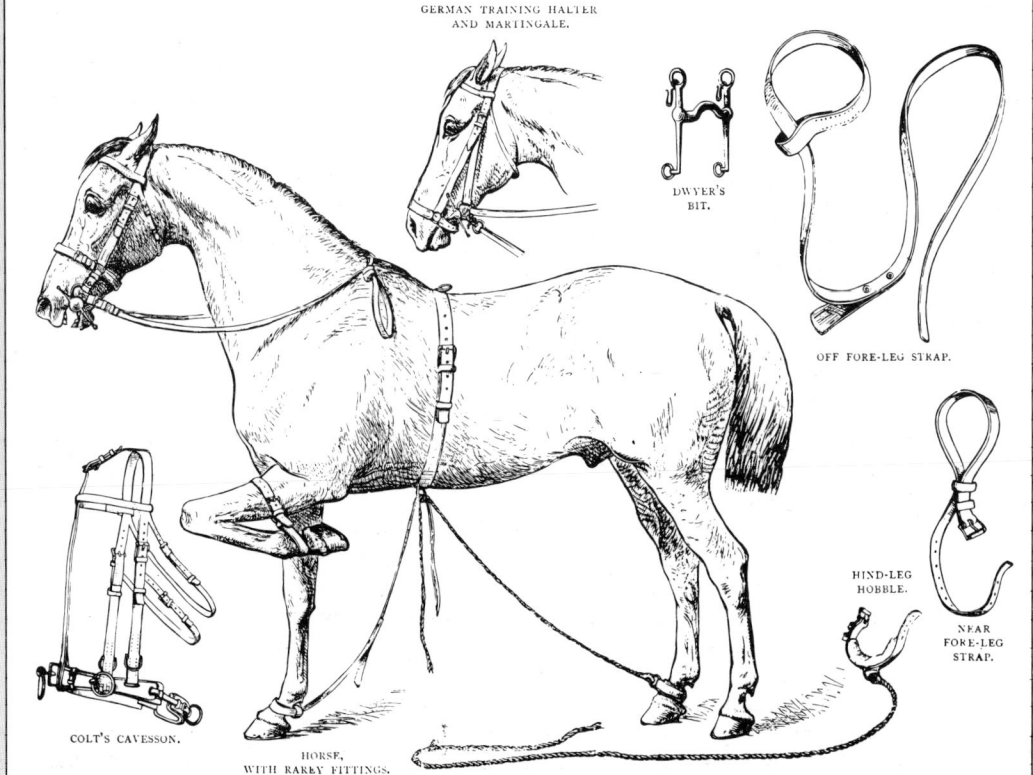

Left: Rarey, possibly the most famous of Victorian horse-tamers, specialised in difficult subjects which he subdued by tying up legs, throwing the horse and so on. The practice of strapping up a foreleg on a horse who objects to being shod, clipped or given veterinary treatment is still in use today. The German training halter shows the use of the drop noseband which was generally employed in Europe during this period, but was not much used in England.

CHAPTER EIGHT

The Well Equipped Stable

Tools and Fittings
Grooming
Tack Cleaning
At Home in the Horsebox
Show Tack
At Stud
Rugs and Travelling Dress
Bandages and Boots

Equipment in the stable is not confined to the horse's box. It involves also rugs, bandages and boots, grooming equipment and, if there are young horses or breeding stock, in-hand and service equipment.

CHAPTER EIGHT · THE WELL-EQUIPPED STABLE

Stable Equipment · **Tools and Fittings**

Stable tools and fittings are an essential part of any horseman's equipment list. Even if a horse or pony is kept at grass all year round, he will have to be brought into the stable at times—to be fed, groomed and tacked up, for instance. A basic kit of stable tools is therefore vital, while, if the animal is kept stabled, further stable fittings will also be necessary.

In the latter case, a loose box, with a properly fastening door, is an essential item. The door should be made in two halves, with a bolt at the top of the lower door on the outside and a 'kick-over' fastening at the bottom for extra security, should the horse be prone to escaping. The upper half of the door is usually kept open to allow air to circulate freely and the animal to see out; should, however, the animal tend to weave—that is, lean over the door and wave his head from side to side whilst shifting the weight from one foreleg to the other—or should, for instance, birds fly into the box and take the animal's feed, then it may be useful to have a wire mesh top door made to size and fitted. The windows, usually one on the same side as the door and another at the back of the box, are normally either of the louvre type or may be of plain glass with bars or wire mesh fitted across the inside, so that the horse would find it difficult to break the glass should he hit it.

The chief fitting in any box is always a manger. The best place for this is across one corner. Mangers are made of either galvanized metal or heavy-duty plastic, the latter being more satisfactory since it can be taken out easily to be thoroughly cleaned. A plastic manger, too, cannot be easily broken, although it may possibly be chewed harmlessly at the edges. Clean, fresh water is an obvious necessity and should be available at all times, except when the horse is hot after exercise. It can be provided in one or two heavy-duty plastic buckets, according to how much water the particular horse drinks. These have largely replaced the heavy wooden painted and galvanized metal stable buckets, since the plastic variety is easier to manage as well as being cheaper to purchase. Large stables often employ self-filling water containers, since these are

Above: A swing-over safety bar at the bottom of the stable door is a necessary and important additional fastening. **Left:** This airy box has a louvred window, fitted with bars; a corner feed manger; a haynet secured to a strong ring and a water bucket set in a wall fitting so that it cannot be knocked over. Fresh water has to be freely available at all times – except if a horse is 'heated' after exercise when the amount of water must be carefully controlled – so the bucket must be kept full if an automatic water trough is not available. The box itself should be strongly built of good quality materials to keep it warm and draught-free and should be large enough to allow the horse freedom of movement. As a rough guide, 12ft square is probably the optimum size, rising to 13ft square for horses over 16 hands high. The floor must be hard-wearing, non-absorbent and slip-proof. It should also slope slightly, so that urine can drain away easily.

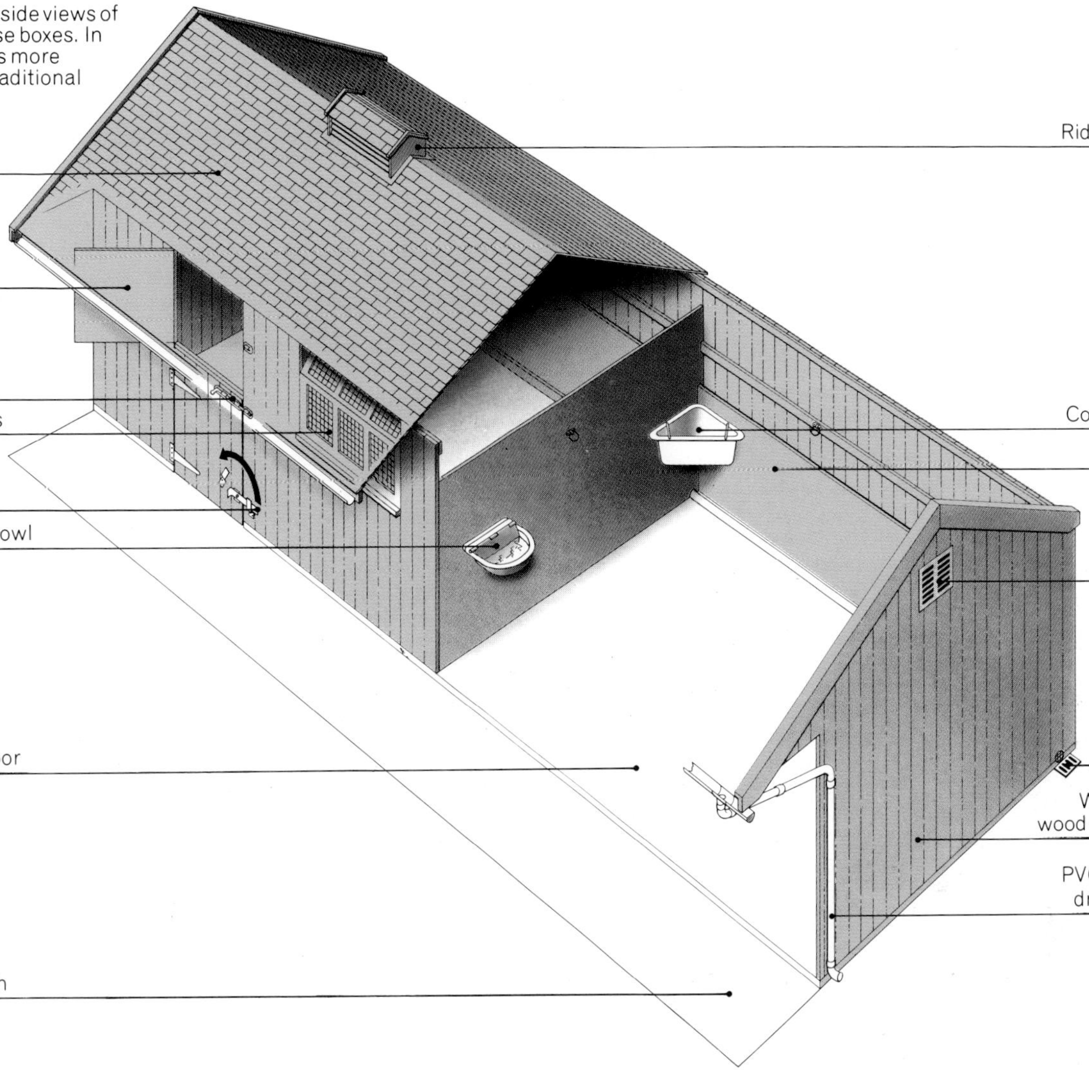

Right: Inside and outside views of two well-planned loose boxes. In the USA, however, it is more common to find the traditional stalls.

- Sloping tiled roof
- Stable half-doors
- Draw bolt
- Metal window guards
- Kick bolt
- Self-filling drinking bowl
- Non-slip concrete floor
- Concrete access path
- Ridge ventilator
- Corner manger
- Kick board
- Louvred ventilator
- Drainage channel
- Weatherproof wood construction
- PVC gutters and drainage pipes

obviously time- and labour-saving, but it is not generally worthwhile going to the expense of having them fitted in small one- or two-horse stables.

Two further items should be provided in the stable. First, there should be a metal ring fixed fairly high up on the wall, from which can be hung a hay net (a nylon or tarred heavy string net with a drawstring round the top in which the horse is given his ration of hay so that it can be eaten without being wasted). Secondly, there should be a salt or mineral lick holder fixed at, or slightly above, manger height.

A selection of stable tools will be needed in order to keep the stable clean and tidy. The box will have to be 'mucked out' each morning if the horse is stabled. This involves using either a two-pronged pitch fork or a four-pronged stable fork to sort out the wet and soiled bedding from the clean straw. The latter is then put to one side of the box and the floor swept clean with the aid of a stiff bristled yard broom. The dirty bedding is picked up with a shovel, put in a wheelbarrow and wheeled to the muck heap for eventual disposal. Alternatively, the muck can be put on a 'muck sheet'. A feed sack split down one side to make a large flat area of sacking makes a good one; alternatively, there is now a plastic variety on the market called a 'humper dumper', the contents of which are disposed of in the same way. From time to time during the day the piles of droppings with which a stabled horse is bound to litter his bed should be removed with the aid of a skip—a shallow rubber or basketwork container—and again removed to the muck heap. The procedure is known as 'skipping out'.

Above: Essential equipment for mucking out. On the wall, a stable fork, a rake for boxes laid with wood shavings or peat, a shovel and a broom. In the foreground, a barrow and a muck skip for collecting droppings.

CHAPTER EIGHT · THE WELL-EQUIPPED STABLE

Stable Equipment · **Tack Cleaning**

Ideally, saddlery should be cleaned each time it is used; at the least, it should be given a quick cleaning, with a thorough one once a week. If the leather is allowed to dry out, it will become brittle. **Right:** The necessary equipment. This consists of 1. Chamois leather; 2. Dandy brush; 3. Saddle soap; 4. Round sponge for soaping; 5. Flat sponge; 6. Bucket of tepid water; 7. Two cloths, one for polishing; 8. Metal polish; 9. Two stable rubbers.

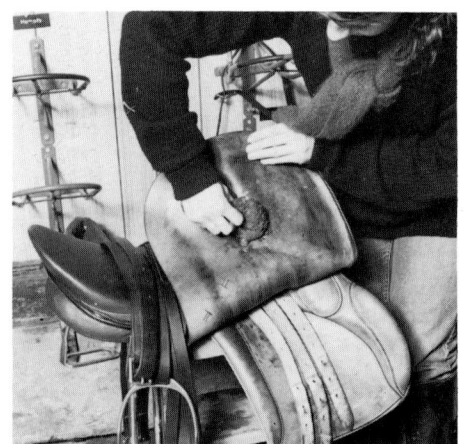

Cleaning a saddle: 1. The lining of the saddle is washed with a damp sponge. Only leather-lined saddles should be washed like this.

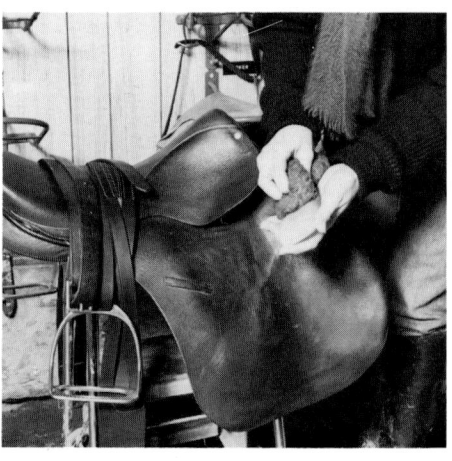

2. Applying saddle soap to the seat. Care must be taken not to over-wet the leather, or water may seep into the stuffing.

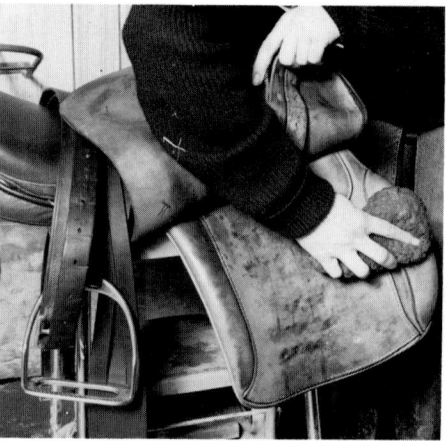

3. Cleaning under the flap. This area attracts dirt and sweat, so it needs a thorough cleaning with a damp sponge.

4. Rubbing over the seat and flaps with a damp sponge. The areas are dried with a chamois leather to remove surplus soap.

5. Washing the girth straps. These should be checked thoroughly for wear, since they are vital to the rider's safety.

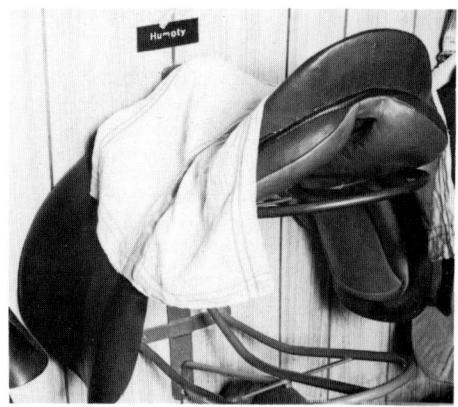

6. After polishing the saddle, it is replaced on its bracket or saddle horse and covered with a stable rubber.

TACK CLEANING

CLEANING BRIDLES AND BITS

1. A dismantled bridle, consisting of reins, snaffle bit, noseband, headpiece, browband and cheekpieces.

2. Rubbing down the reins with a damp cloth. All leather parts should be cleaned similarly and then dried.

3. If the bridle is fitted with metal rings or studs, these should be cleaned with metal polish.

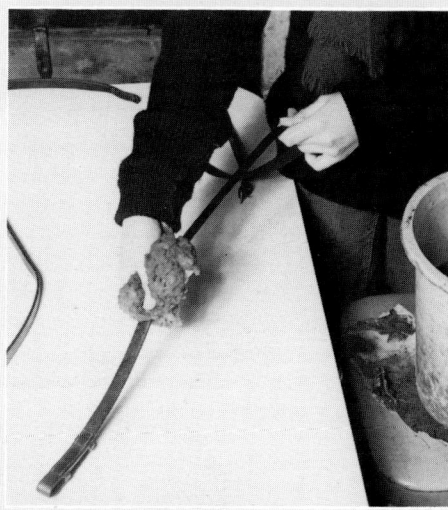
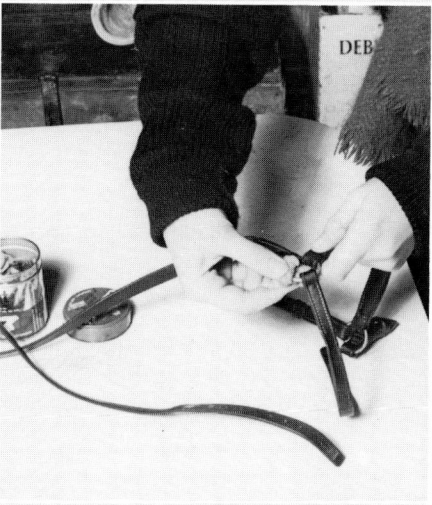

4. Washing the bit thoroughly to remove all traces of stains and saliva.

5. The rings of the bit – not the mouthpiece – should be polished with metal polish.

6. The final polishing. The bridle is then re-assembled and hung up ready for use.

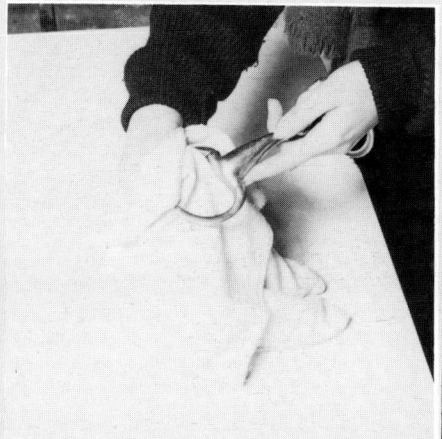

7. Cleaning the girth. The method varies – webbing is brushed and scrubbed, nylon and string scrubbed.

8. Cleaning the stirrup leather. This is done in the same way as the saddle, checks being made for wear.

9. Cleaning the stirrup irons. After the dirt has been removed, the irons should be cleaned with metal polish.

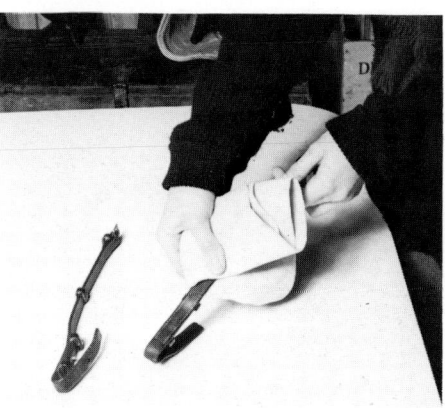
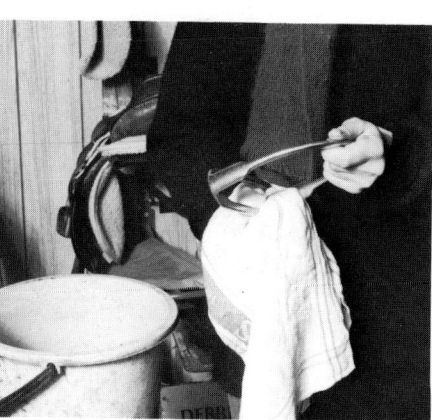

CHAPTER EIGHT · THE WELL-EQUIPPED STABLE

Stable Equipment · **Grooming**

As well as improving a horse's appearance, grooming is essential to maintain the animal's health and general well-being. A basic grooming kit is therefore an essential purchase; this should consist of at least eight basic items, with more being added as necessary.

The basic kit
The basic grooming kit should consist of a metal hoofpick, a dandy brush, a body brush, a metal curry comb, a water brush, a stable rubber, two sponges and a metal mane comb. The hoofpick is used, as its name implies, for picking out the feet. There are two types—the traditional rigid variety or a folding model. The dandy brush has long stiff bristles, now frequently made of nylon but traditionally of whalebone or Mexican whisk. This is used for brushing dry mud and sweat off the horse's body and legs. The body brush has short, soft bristles and is used in conjunction with the metal curry comb to remove grease and dust from the horse's coat and head. The comb, in fact, is never used on the animal; it merely serves as an aid to cleaning the body brush. The brush should also be used to remove any tangles from the mane and tail.

The water brush is made of soft bristles attached to a wooden, boat-shaped back. It is used damp on the mane, tail and the horse's coat after body brushing to take off any surface dust and add a shine. The stable rubber is a linen cloth, similar to a tea towel. It is rubbed over the entire horse to give a final polish, while the sponges—one for cleaning the eyes and nose and the other for the dock – are also then used. The mane comb is for combing the mane.

There is, however, an important difference in the amount of grooming that should be given to a grass-kept horse, as opposed to the amount required by a stable-kept animal. A horse living out will probably only need his feet picking out regularly and his coat brushing over with

Right: Grooming and trimming equipment. 1. Plastic-toothed curry comb (for use on horse); 2. Water brush; 3. Dandy brush; 4. 'Cactus' horse-polishing cloth; 5. Metal curry comb (for cleaning brushes); 6. Stable rubber; 7. Hoof oil brush; 8. Hoof oil; 9. Sponge; 10. Mane comb; 11. Coarse mane comb; 12. Hoofpick; 13. Curved blade trimming scissors; 14. Wisping pad; 15. German-pattern body brush; 16. Brush grooming glove; 17. Rubber edge sweat scraper; 18. Brass double-handed sweat scraper. **Inset left:** Portable electric, vacuum-type horse groomer. **Inset right:** Electric clipping machine. The chief point of grooming is to keep the horse clean, massage the skin and tone up the muscles. It falls into three stages, each of which is carried out at a different time of day. Quartering is normally done first thing in the morning, before exercise. Strapping – the thorough grooming – follows exercise, after the horse has cooled down. 'Setting fair' is the last grooming of the day. Clipping is done for comfort and smartness. In the winter, the thicker coat the horse grows for protection against the cold can lead to excessive sweating during exercise if it is left unclipped.

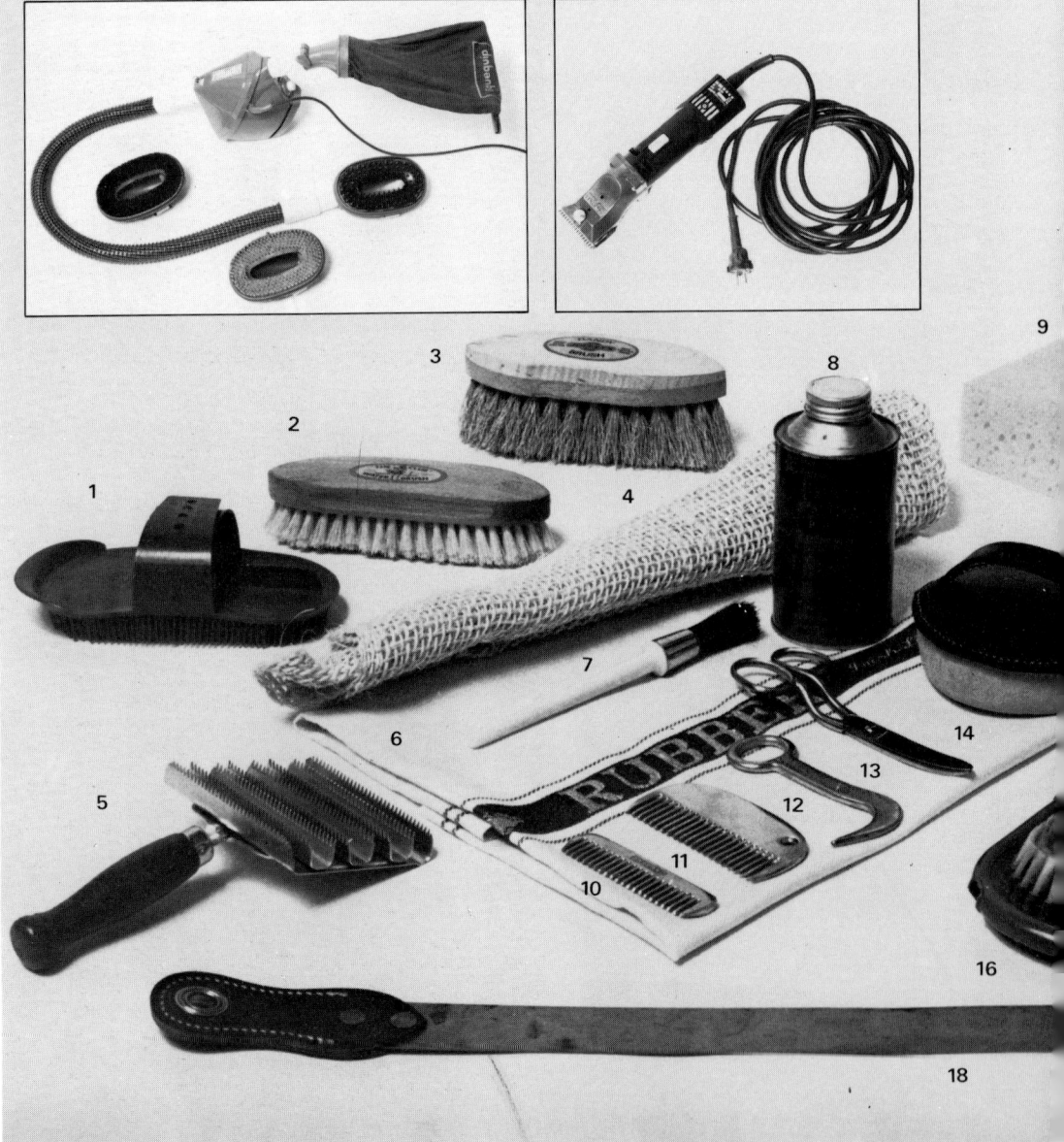

the dandy brush. If too much grease is removed from a grass-kept horse's coat, he is likely to catch a chill. Two further items of equipment are useful. A rubber, or plastic, curry comb—an oval-shaped tool, with rubber or plastic teeth and a hand strap across its back—can be used to remove dry mud; it can also be used to stimulate the skin. A cactus cloth, a large piece of sackcloth, is a useful aid for removing dry mud and sweat. It can be used all over the body even on a horse which has been clipped out. When used damp, the cloth gives shine to the coat.

Another extra item, which can benefit both stabled and field-kept horses, is a wisp. This is made from a rope of lightly woven hay taken from the feed, or proprietary models can be purchased. These are oval-shaped leather pads, stuffed with hay. The wisp should be dampened and then slapped down only on the neck, shoulders and quarters of the horse. Its use helps to develop the muscles and stimulates the circulation, as well as producing a shine on the coat.

Mud and sweat call for special procedures. If a horse's feet are extremely muddy, they can be scrubbed out carefully with a scrubbing brush. As this tends to remove the natural oils and so can cause cracked heels if done too frequently, the heels must be dried thoroughly afterwards. Hoof oil should be used to prevent cracking and to give a shine.

If the horse is sweating profusely, he will need washing down with a sponge. The excess water is then removed with a sweat scraper. This is a curved instrument with thick rubber on one edge for removing water from the more bony areas and metal on the other to remove surplus moisture from the body. An alternative tool consists of a long thin piece of curved metal, with handles on either end, while a wash/grooming mitt is also on the market. This is made of rubber, with rubber teeth on one side and bristles on the other.

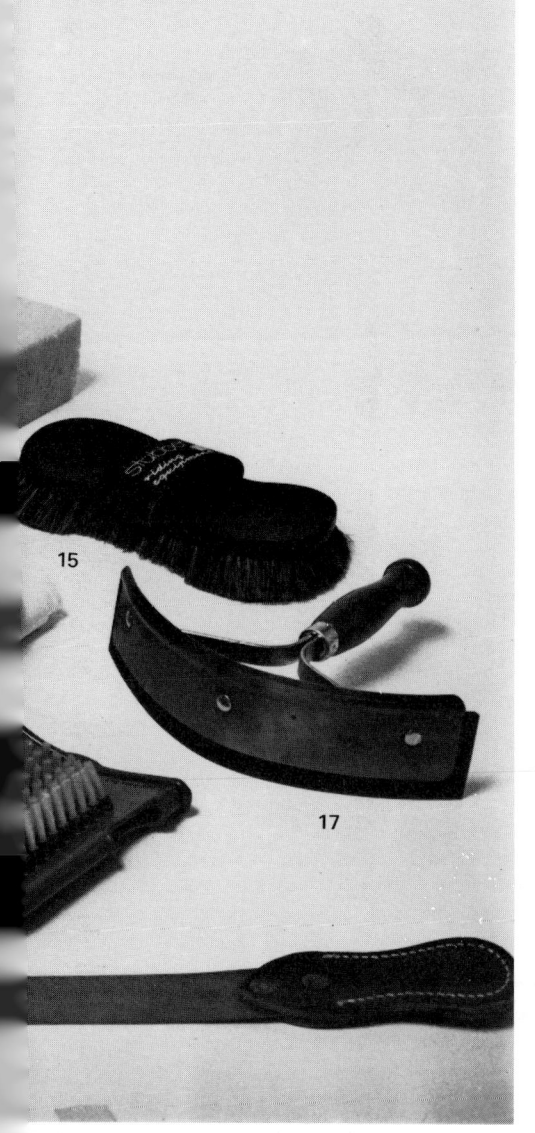

Left: A groom in the stable of King Ashurbanipal of Assyria attending to his horse and adopting a stance that would have the approval of modern instructors. **Below:** An early American grooming machine of the late 19th century in action. The brush revolved at the rate of 500 to 600 times per minute and was driven either manually, through a system of belts, pulleys and counterweights, or by a small gas engine. It was claimed that 'so searching and vigorous is its action that a perfect cloud of dust is raised from the horse's skin'.

CHAPTER EIGHT · THE WELL-EQUIPPED STABLE

Stable Equipment · **At Home in the Horsebox**

Right: Some of the items of equipment that would be needed at a show and which the experienced horseman would check before setting out. 1. Complete bridle with martingale (if worn); 2. Saddle with mountings and numnah (if worn); 3. Filled haynet; 4. Rug; 5. Grooming kit; 6. Hoof oil and brush; 7. Veterinary box and scissors; 8. Water bucket. **Below:** Horse box with side-ramp loading. The main reason for a horse showing reluctance to enter a box is usually its fear of the noise of its hooves on the ramp. This can be overcome by putting down some straw or sacking to deaden the sound.

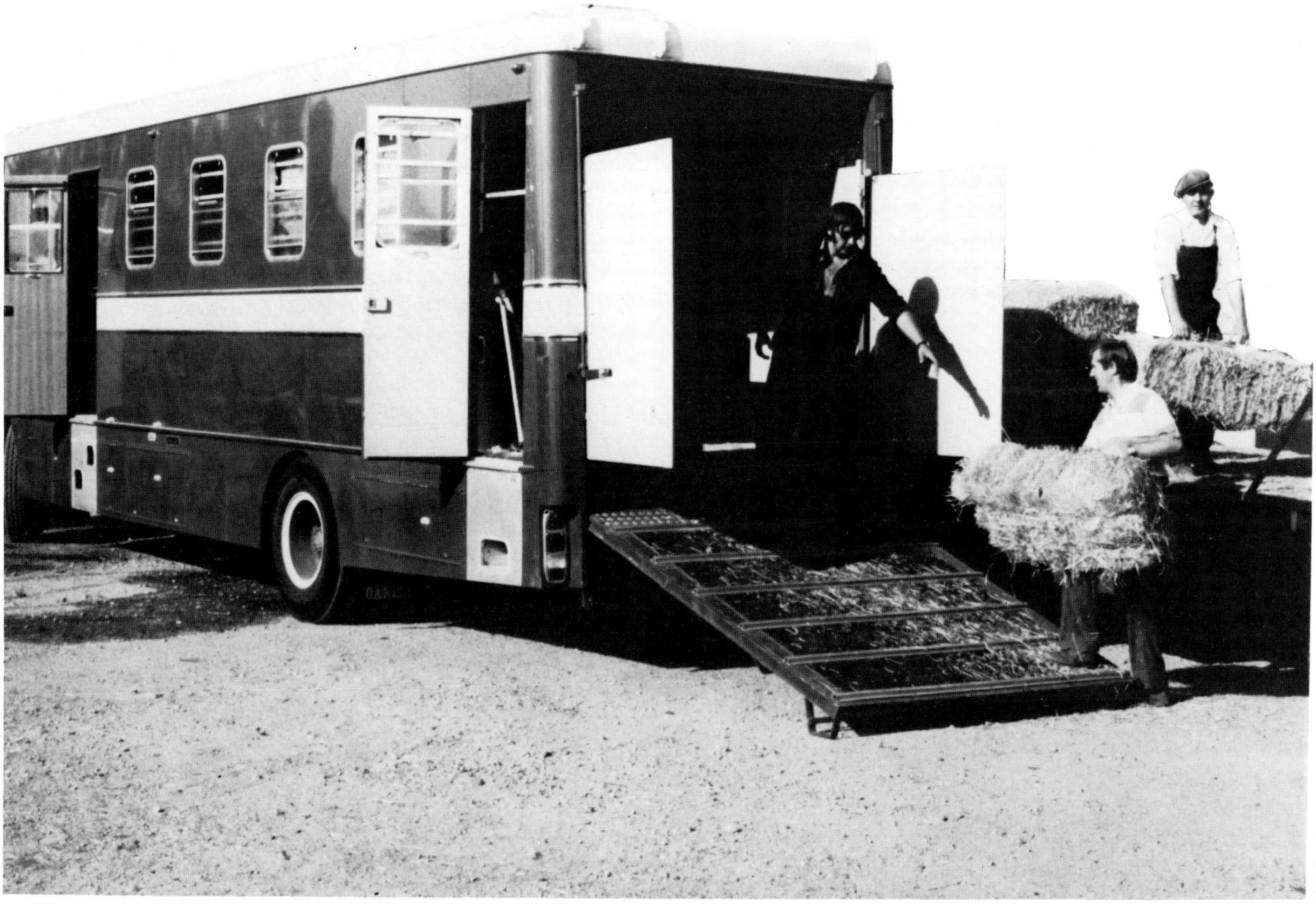

AT HOME IN THE HORSEBOX

Above: A professional's horsebox. The box shown here belongs to David Broome, one of Britain's leading show-jumpers. As well as accommodating the horses, their fodder and saddlery, it is also equipped with living quarters for the rider and his grooms. Show-jumping riders spend the summer season – and part of the winter, too – travelling from one show to the next, so a box of these proportions is not luxury but a necessity. **Below:** The one- or two-horse amateur owner whose travelling is limited can manage extremely well with the simplest form of horse transport, the trailer, which can be towed by either a car or a Land Rover-type vehicle.

205

CHAPTER EIGHT · THE WELL-EQUIPPED STABLE

Stable Equipment · Show Tack

Tack for the show ring is a specialist area. It was once intensely conservative, but is now very much more progressive both in outlook and in the various items of equipment employed. Credit for this change of heart is due largely to the increasing internationalism of horse affairs, which gives greater opportunities for show ring fashions and, indeed, methods of presentation to be seen outside the country of their origin.

In Britain, for instance, the show rings, which were once firmly entrenched in established conventions, have been influenced by visitors from the Continent, and the USA, whose equipment and mode of presentation contribute to a bravura that at one time would have appeared almost immoral to British eyes. Only the handlers of the Welsh breeds can match, and on occasions surpass, the turnout of the Continental exhibitors and the sense of theatre displayed by their American counterparts. The former, unlike their bowler-hatted British counterparts, often appear bareheaded in white shirts and trousers with running shoes to match; the Americans, on the other hand, affect a show costume somewhat similar to the waistcoat turnout of the pool player with the addition of a cheeky soft hat. Both, particularly the American handlers, carry long show whips (like dressage whips) with which they perform a continuous *pas de deux*, gyrating and dipping in their efforts to present their charges before the judge to the best possible advantage.

Elegant and functional

The most elegant pieces of show gear are, without doubt, those employed by the exhibitors of Arabian horses. The opportunities for in-hand or halter class tack are necessarily restricted, but the light rolled leather show bridles or halters, often discreetly ornamented, used by the Arabian handlers set off the beautiful heads of their charges to perfection. The origin of these expertly-made pieces of headgear is American, for, in the USA, far more attention seems to be given to the business of showing a horse effectively. The great majority of American halter class entries are shown in these excellent halters, designed specifically for the purpose.

Stallions shown in hand wear a special type of bridle, with a purpose-designed bit, while in Britain yearling colts are often led in hand from a ring bit fitted with mouthing keys. Somewhat more severe is the Chifney bit, often described as an 'anti-rearing' bit. Like its inventor the conceited 18th-century trainer, Sam Chifney (1753–1807), it is hardly intelligent.

Stallions of some breeds—particularly those of the British native pony breeds but many others as well—are often shown in a roller and a crupper, the roller being fitted with a side-rein on the offside to keep the horse straight, in the required outline and under better control. Brood mares of riding breeds, with or without a foal at foot, are frequently shown in riding bridles, the custom being to show them in a double bridle. In instances where a horse is shown with a bit in its mouth, the method of leading employed is crucial. It is possible to lead from the bit using a

Below: Horse equipped for an American halter class. Similar tackle can be seen in many European countries, excluding Britain.

SHOW TACK

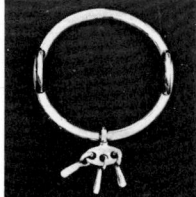
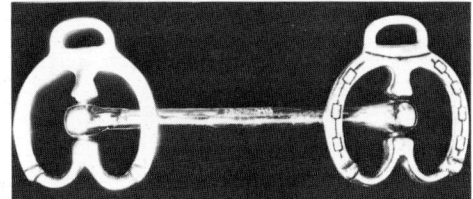

Top: A Haflinger stallion being shown in Britain is wearing full stallion tackle of roller, crupper and off-side side rein. The somewhat un-English bridle is perhaps a concession to the pony's land of origin. **Above left:** A light Arabian show bridle made of rolled leather. **Centre:** A similar bridle using a running chain instead of a rear strap to give greater control. **Right:** English-type stallion show bridle with coupling attached to the bit rings. **Right top:** Yearling bit ring with mouthing keys and the shaped 'anti-rear' Chifney bit. **Right below:** Horseshoe cheek pony stallion bit, the same as that worn by the Haflinger pony opposite. The horseshoe is a symbol of virility and fertility in horse peoples' folklore.

chain or leather couple, or a lead rein fitted with what is known as a Y-couple, which will ensure that the animal is controlled with an even pressure from both rings of the bit. Possibly the best way of leading is provided by a 3-way couple, which has a centre attachment fastening to the rear of the halter or bridle and thus allows the handler to exert the restraining pressure on the poll as well as the mouth.

The ring type bits are of interest, since they must certainly be derived from those early ring bits of North Africa, the area in which this particular construction originated. It is certainly not found elsewhere.

CHAPTER EIGHT · THE WELL-EQUIPPED STABLE

Stable Equipment · **At Stud**

Relatively little equipment is required for stud purposes, beyond the items necessary to control the stallion and to protect him against a mare who may kick during the mating process.

The stallion has to be under control both when being led in the vicinity of mares and during the performance of his stud duties. At most studs, a strong stallion bridle is used; this, by tradition, is brass-mounted. The bridle is of particular importance, since a stallion will quickly come to associate it with the act of covering a mare and will be aroused sexually by it being fitted. The bit employed is usually a straight bar metal one, which may have a twisted mouthpiece so that its effect is slightly sharper than normal. A strong, leather lead, somewhat longer than usual, is also necessary. This can be fitted with a stout length of brass chain with a strong snap hook.

Twitches and hobbles

Slightly more equipment is necessary for the mare. A twitch is usually regarded as being essential to keep the mare still and to discourage her from kicking at the stallion. A twitch is a device which causes enough discomfort to distract the animal from whatever operation is being performed—whether this is covering, clipping or shoeing—and, by concentrating the animal's attention on the discomfort, causes it to submit and stand still.

The simplest form of twitch is a length of wood 12in to 14in long, in which a hole has been bored so as to be able to pass through it a loop of cord. The cord is then placed around the upper lip and the stick twisted until the cord is tight. The stick can then either be held or poked back through the sidepiece of a headcollar. A chain can also be used as a twitch. It can be passed through the mouth and pulled tight—a relatively mild use—or it can be passed under the upper lip so that it bears tightly on the gums above the incisor teeth, when it will act as a restraint.

At some studs mares are hobbled, so that they cannot kick. The hobbles on the

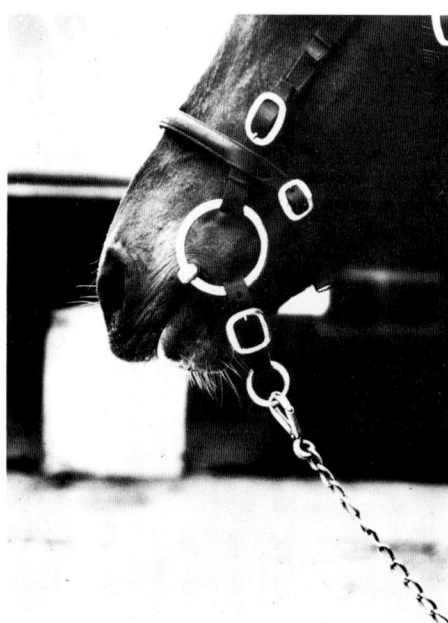

Left: A brass-mounted stallion bridle with chain lead. **Above top:** A straight bar stallion bit. **Below:** A stallion bridle with a lead couple connecting the bit rings. The stud equipment for stallions falls into two categories – equipment to control the horse and that to protect him during serving.

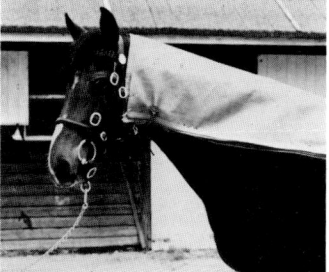
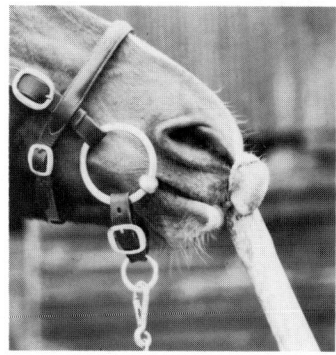
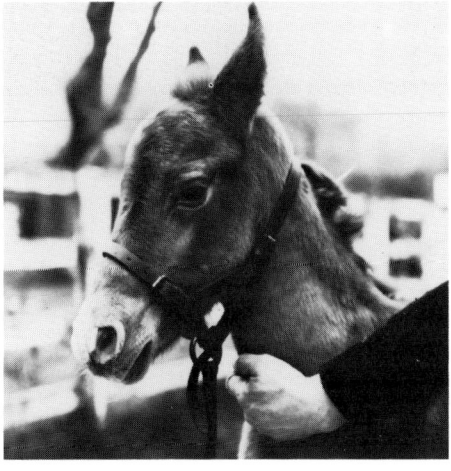

Left: Service hobbles are used as a precaution against the mare kicking the stallion as the latter attempts to serve her. **Right, top:** Thick service boots of felt. These are fitted to the mare's hind feet as another safeguard against her kicking. **Centre:** A neck cover which will prevent the stallion biting the mare's neck during a service. **Bottom:** A simple cord twitch applied to the nose to restrain an excitable or unruly horse. **Bottom left:** The standard type of foal slip which can be made in soft leather, web or even in nylon.

hind feet are fitted with a central strap, which passes forward between the forelegs and culminates in a neck strap. Often such hobbles are fitted with a quick-release device in case of emergency. Sometimes a thick strap is used to fasten up a foreleg, which is a common method of control. Many studs, however, prefer to rely on a pair of 'kicking' boots made from very thick felt and to dispense with hobbles and leg straps.

A tail bandage is almost always put on a mare who is to be served, so that her tail hairs will not cut the stallion's organ, while nervous mares can be fitted with a pair of blinkers, so that they cannot see the stallion's approach. These are often extremely effective.

Some stallions, when they have mounted the mare will bite her neck, in front of the withers, quite severely. To protect the mare from these love bites, she can be provided with a harness collar, which the stallion can bite, or a thick rope 'necklace'.

Foals are nearly always provided with a headcollar of the 'Dutch slip' pattern, which is easier to put on than other varieties and is easy to adjust. Such headcollars are made from either soft, tubular web or supple leather and are fitted with a lead tag.

CHAPTER EIGHT · THE WELL-EQUIPPED STABLE

Stable Equipment · Rugs and Travelling Dress

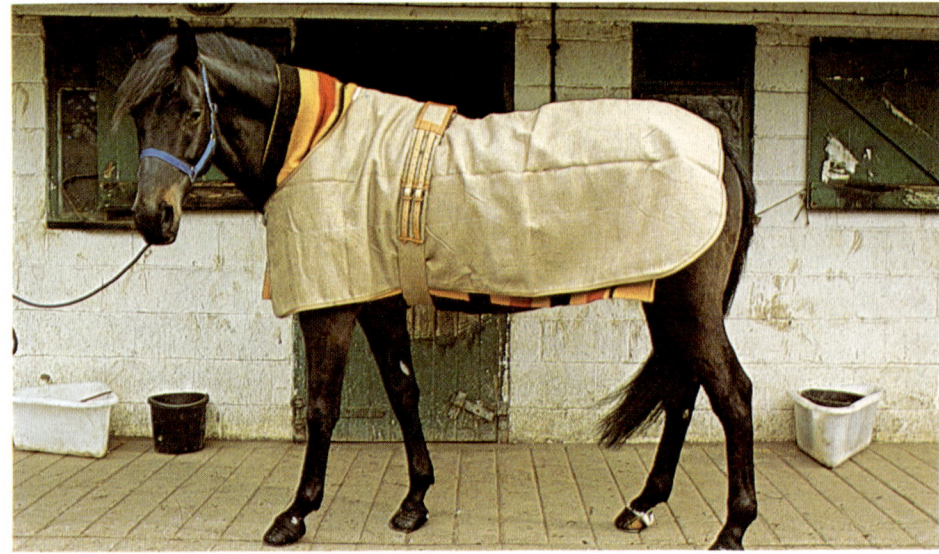

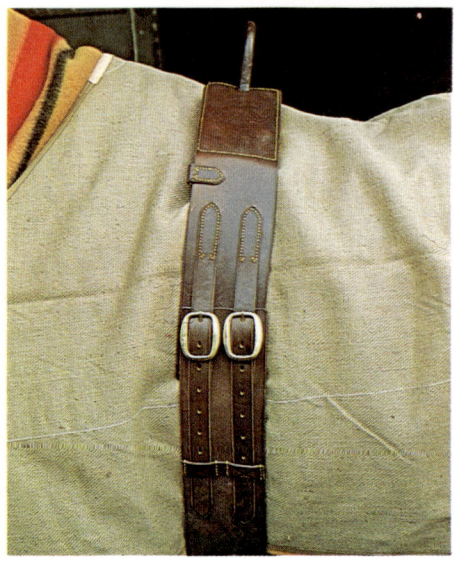

If a horse is worked during the winter, he will normally need clipping to avoid excessive sweating. The corollary of this is that his natural coat must be replaced by an artificial one, if he is not to catch cold. Winter stable rugs exist for this purpose and come in a number of varieties. The traditional pattern, made of jute or finely-woven canvas and fully lined with a grey wool mixture blanketing, is probably the most successful. The rug is kept in place by a leather buckle fastening at the chest and either by a jute surcingle, attached to the rug, a plain leather roller or an anti-cast roller. The last is an adaptation of the ordinary leather roller, being fitted with a metal arch which goes over the horse's spine. It prevents the horse rolling over in his box and perhaps getting cast—that is, unable to get up unaided.

For added warmth, a 'pure new wool' Witney blanket can be placed underneath the rug. These blankets are traditionally fawn in colour, with black, red and blue stripes at either end. They weigh approximately 8lb. Lighter-weight blankets, made of 'all wool' as opposed to 'pure new wool' in similar, but brighter, colours, are also on the market, plus grey or brown wool and fibre mixture varieties.

An anti-sweat sheet, similar to a string vest, can also be used under the night rug for extra warmth. The sheet, made of cotton mesh, creates air pockets next to the body to insulate the horse against extremes of heat or cold. Its normal use is with a sweaty horse. For best results, it should be put on the hot animal next to the skin, with a day rug or summer sheet on top of it, to prevent the horse getting chilled.

Other rug varieties

Recently, a range of nylon quilted rugs, similar to the human anorak, have been introduced. Most are made of nylon with polyester filling, with either a brushed nylon or cotton lining. They are extremely light and warm at the same time. These rugs are again kept in place by a surcingle or roller, with a nylon and metal fastening at the chest.

An alternative method of fastening is particularly popular in the USA. Here, the rug is fastened at the front with a chrome box clasp, with a cross-surcingle, designed on stress engineering principles, to keep the rug in place. The two webbing straps sewn on the rug equalize the tension by

Top left: A horse ready for travelling, wearing a headcollar, wool day rug, roller, tail guard, knee caps, hock caps and protective bandages. **Above:** A jute night rug worn over a striped under-blanket and secured by a body roller. **Left:** Leather stable roller fitted with anti-cast hoop. **Top right:** Mesh anti-sweat rug. **Centre right:** Linen/cotton summer sheet with fillet string and light surcingle. **Right:** Striped blanketing, originally used by the Hudson Bay Company for trading with the North American Indians, is traditional to the horse clothing industry.

RUGS AND TRAVELLING DRESS

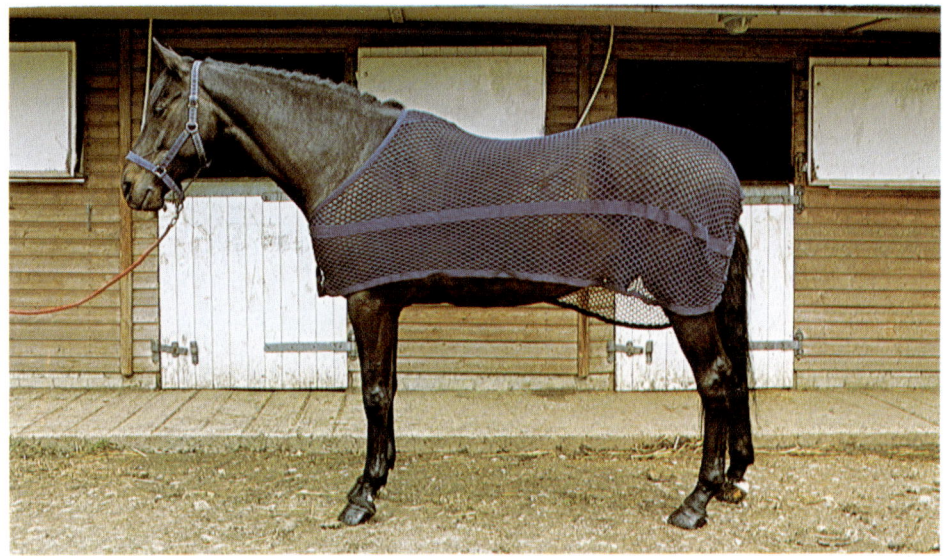

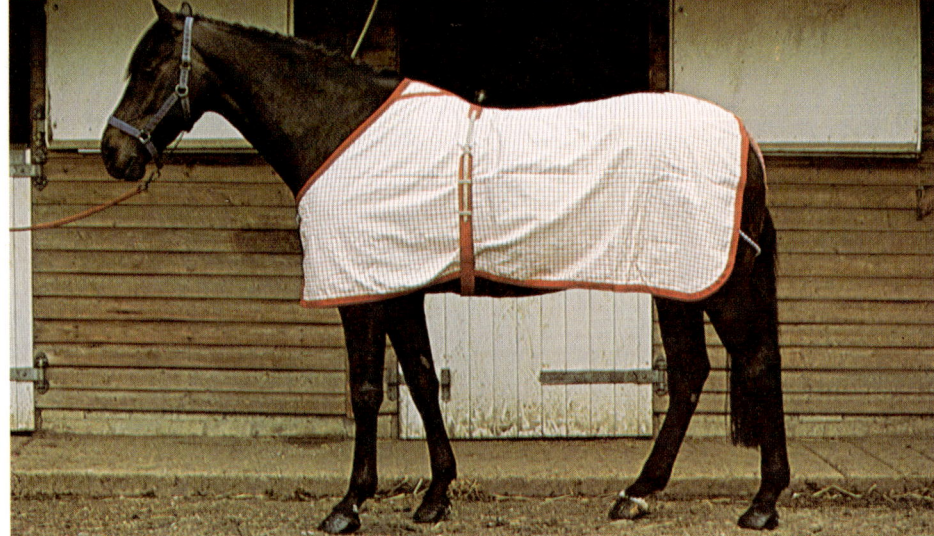

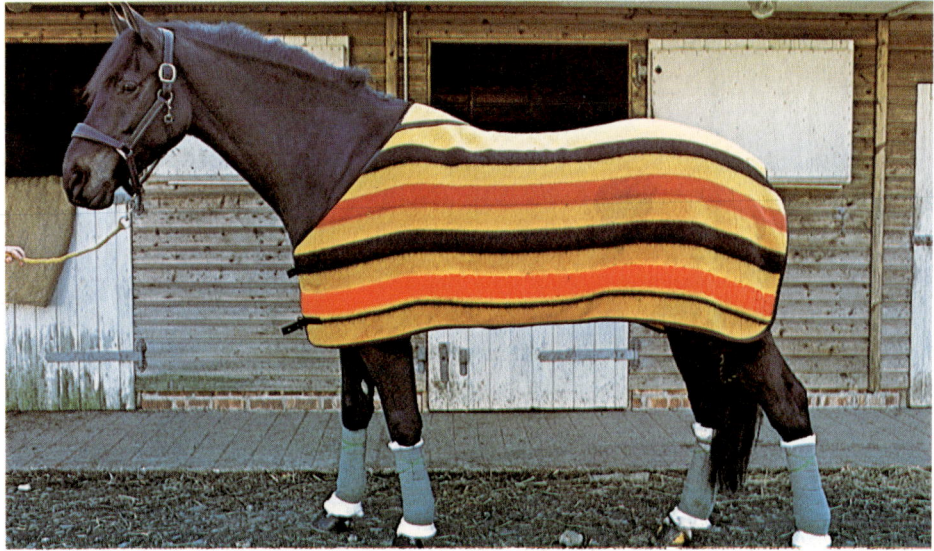

starting from the points of each shoulder and crossing under the horse in the normal roller position to the top of the hindquarters.

A new rug, made of a very light fabric called Thermatextron, has a similar cross-surcingle fastening. Laboratory tests have demonstrated that this fabric has a higher degree of thermal insulation than any other. It also absorbs less moisture.

Both these factors mean that the heat generated by the horse's body is conserved. For the maximum benefit, the rug should be worn next to the skin. It can be put over a wet or sweating horse, the damp evaporating through the fabric.

A further type of rug with cross-surcingle fastenings is known as a 'banner blanket'. It is made of triple thickness woven acrylic fabric and keeps horses warm and the dampness out, even in the cold US winters for which it was designed.

All purpose rugs
For horses living out in winter, or for those which have been clipped and are turned out for a few hours a day, a New Zealand rug is necessary. An extremely long-established and well-tried rug in Europe is made by the Emston Saddlery Co, who first introduced it in 1928. It is made from dark fawn waterproof canvas with a heavy wool check lining, the rug being generously cut to allow freedom of movement. It is fastened by a leather buckle at the chest and adjustable leather hindleg straps, with spring hooks. Because the rug is full, it will stay in position with the aid of a surcingle even if the horse rolls, provided that it has been fitted correctly in the first instance.

Another rug of this type, kept in place with similar fastenings, is made of 18oz proofed flax material and is lined with 50 per cent wool blanketing. Like canvas, the flax allows the skin to breathe. A useful additional fitting is a matching neck cover, which is extremely handy in really cold weather. It is fastened to the rug by leather buckles at the neck and continues up to the horse's ears. It is secured around the throat by three more buckles.

Several rugs known as 'turnout' or 'all purpose' are available, the idea being, as the name implies, that they serve the dual purpose of stable rug and New Zealand rug. One example, originating in Australia, is called the Lancer turnout rug. Its

CHAPTER EIGHT · THE WELL-EQUIPPED STABLE

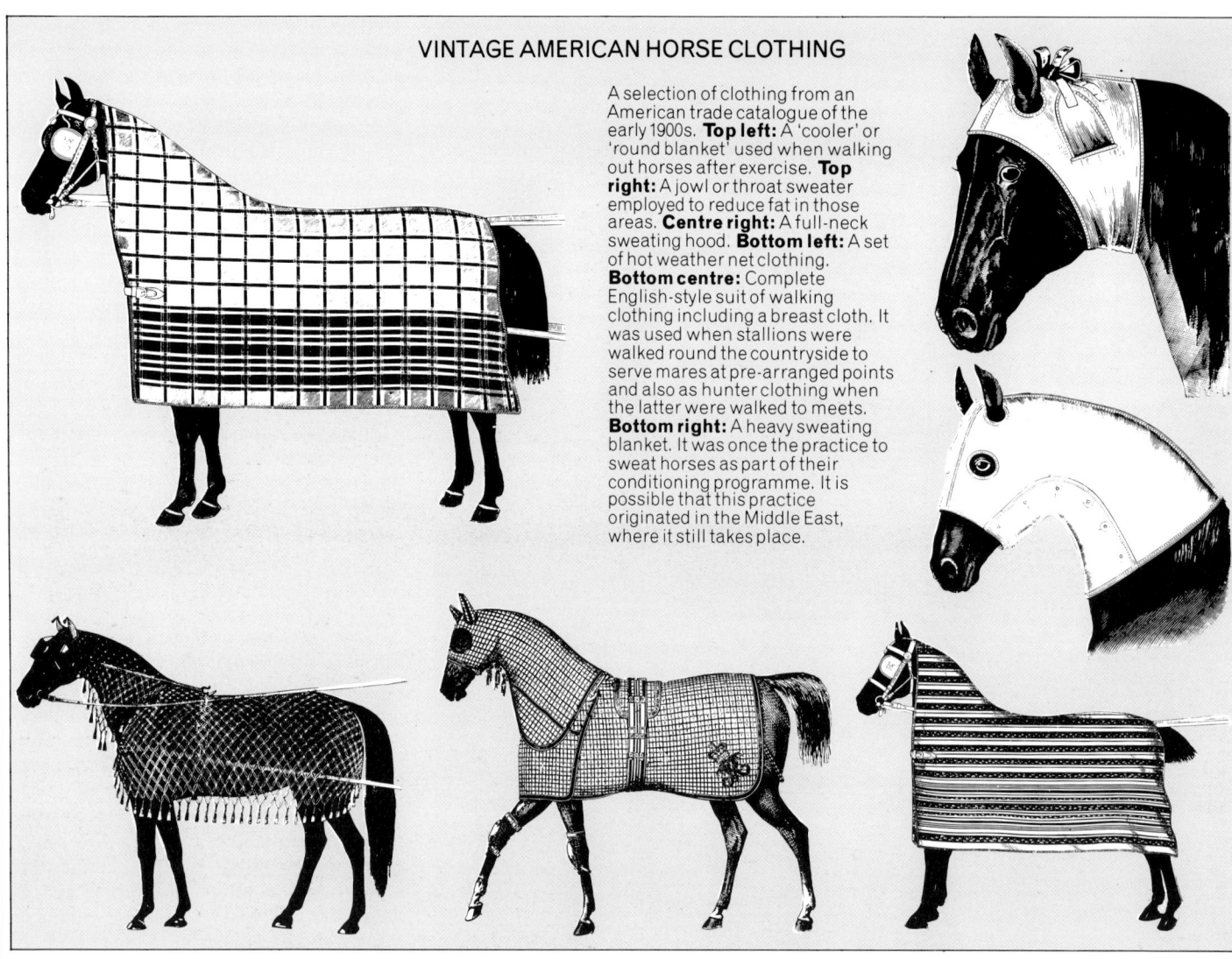

VINTAGE AMERICAN HORSE CLOTHING

A selection of clothing from an American trade catalogue of the early 1900s. **Top left:** A 'cooler' or 'round blanket' used when walking out horses after exercise. **Top right:** A jowl or throat sweater employed to reduce fat in those areas. **Centre right:** A full-neck sweating hood. **Bottom left:** A set of hot weather net clothing. **Bottom centre:** Complete English-style suit of walking clothing including a breast cloth. It was used when stallions were walked round the countryside to serve mares at pre-arranged points and also as hunter clothing when the latter were walked to meets. **Bottom right:** A heavy sweating blanket. It was once the practice to sweat horses as part of their conditioning programme. It is possible that this practice originated in the Middle East, where it still takes place.

makers claim that it can be used as a stable or New Zealand rug, since it is lightweight, made of strong nylon with a fleece lining, and is sufficiently waterproof to withstand heavy rain. Suppliers, however, are reluctant to guarantee any nylon rug as completely waterproof.

Another dual purpose rug is produced by a company specializing in parachuting and marine equipment. It is made from a new, lightweight and strong synthetic material, which, manufacturers claim, is waterproof, since all the seams have been treated with a special sealant. An additional feature is a detachable clip-in blanket lining, made of acrylic fibre pile.

Day and exercise rugs

A day rug is a useful addition to the horse's wardrobe for smart stable wear or for travelling. The best are made of heavyweight pure wool and bound in livery cloth; a cheaper variety is made of wool mixture and bound in cotton braid. All are fastened with a leather buckle at the chest and with a fillet string for greater security. A fillet string is a strip of plaited cotton braid, usually in two contrasting colours, which goes up under the tail in order to prevent the rug being blown up in the wind and generally to keep it in place. The rugs are used usually with a roller, often of the same colour webbing and binding as the rug. The summer rug is called a summer sheet. This is made of cotton and traditionally has a navy and red check pattern on a white background. Other colours, however, are available.

In cold weather, clipped, thin-skinned horses may require some additional protection for warmth when out at exercise. Wool exercise rugs of striped blanketing serve this purpose. The rug is worn under the saddle, stretching a little in front of it and back over the horse's loins. Similar exercise/quarter sheets, made of polyurethane-coated nylon, can be used in addition to, or instead of, the woollen sheets in foul weather. To keep the saddle dry, they can be placed over it and kept in position by a surcingle. Rain sheets are another useful item. They can be used on their own, or as an outer skin over another rug. They are made of unlined waterproof bri-nylon, with a cotton wither pad and with loops for a fillet string and chest fastening. They are very convenient protection for both horse and rider when caught in a sudden downpour.

Dress for travelling

In addition to a day rug or summer sheet a horse must certainly be properly dressed for travelling to avoid the risk of injury in transit. The horse should be equipped with a leather or nylon headcollar, with a rope attached to secure him to a ring in the trailer or box. The tail should be bandaged down as far as the bottom of the dock with an elasticated tail bandage, a tail guard of either leather or wool being fitted over this. These are kept in place with tapes or Velcro fastenings on wool guards or two straps and buckles on leather ones. A long leather strap at the top of the guard is secured by a return buckle and strap to the roller. The purpose of the guard is to prevent a horse from rubbing the tail hairs raw, should he acquire the habit of sitting heavily against the back of the trailer. Various types of bandage, hock caps, knee caps and boots are also required.

It is unusual, but nevertheless possible, for a horse to throw his head up when entering a trailer, banging and possibly cutting himself at the poll. To prevent this, there are several kinds of poll guard on the market. Two, made of soft well-padded leather and leather-covered foam rubber respectively, slot over the headpiece of the headcollar. The first goes horizontally along the headpiece, while the second runs vertically between the ears from the headpiece to the browband on the headcollar. Probably the most satisfactory device—especially for a horse travelling by air—is the skull cap. This is made of leather and covers the whole poll area, having three leather loops, which slot on to the headpiece, and holes for the ears.

Above: Full travelling equipment, including leg guards fitted with Velcro fastenings. The head collar is fitted with a poll guard to protect the poll. **Right:** A tailguard in position over the tail bandage.

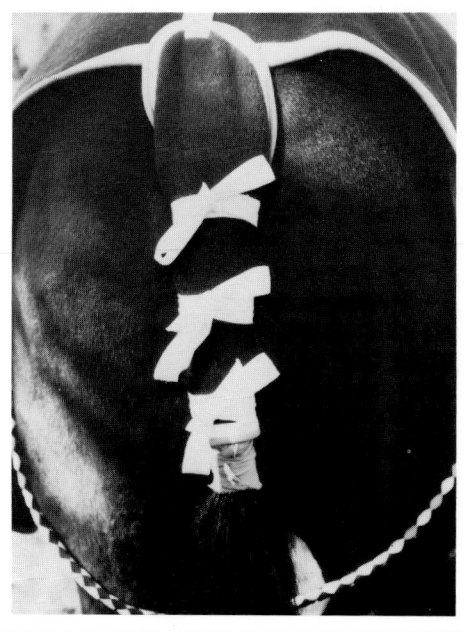

Right: An American sheet employing two surcingles. **Far right:** Another American pattern using twin crossing surcingles. This is probably the most efficient rug fastening of all. **Below left:** An example of the quilted nylon rugs, of which there are a number of makes. **Centre:** A waterproof sheet. **Right:** This rug is made of Thermotextron and constructed on an advanced insulation theory. It is extremely effective. **Bottom, left to right:** Two types of waterproof New Zealand rugs secured by leg straps, cross-surcingle Australian rug of extra warm material and a striped blanket exercise sheet.

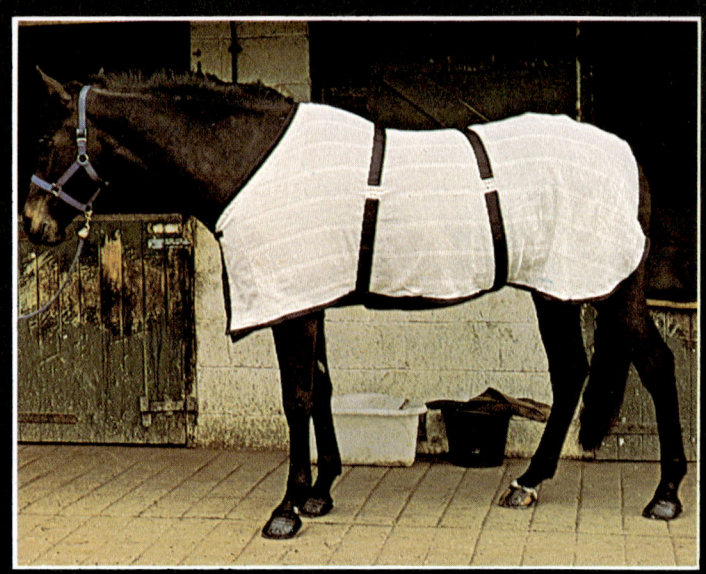
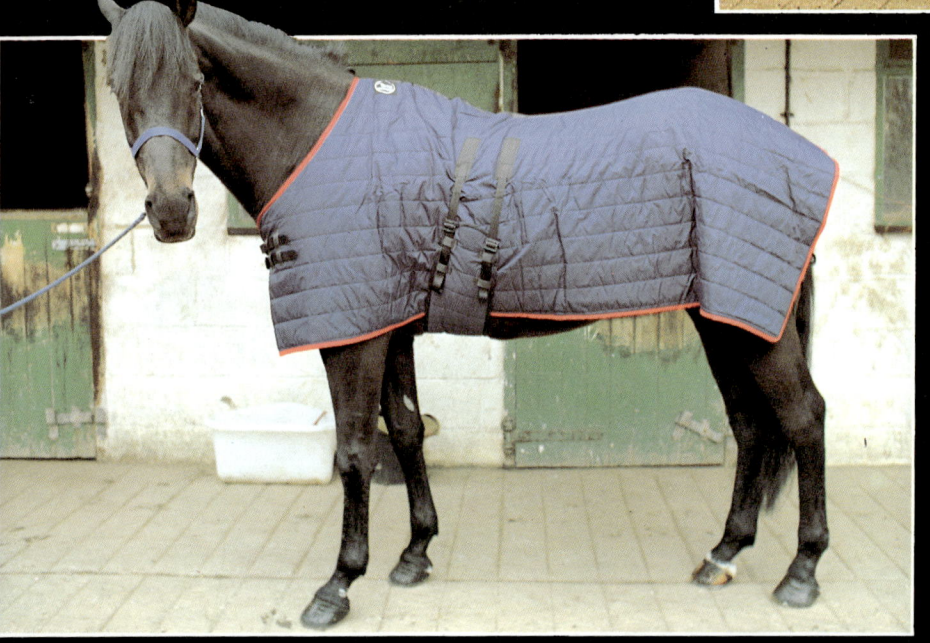
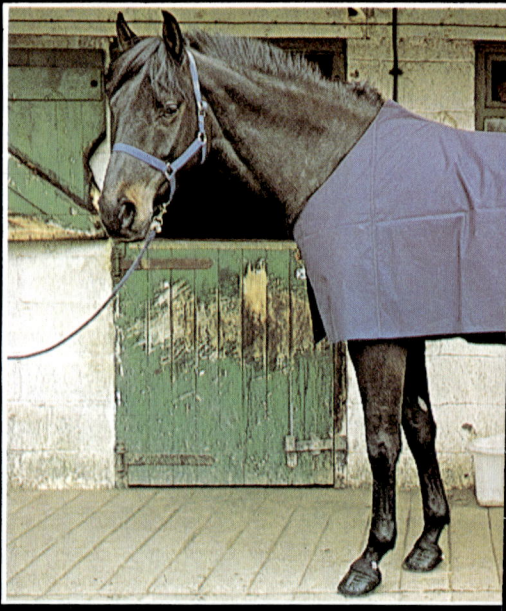
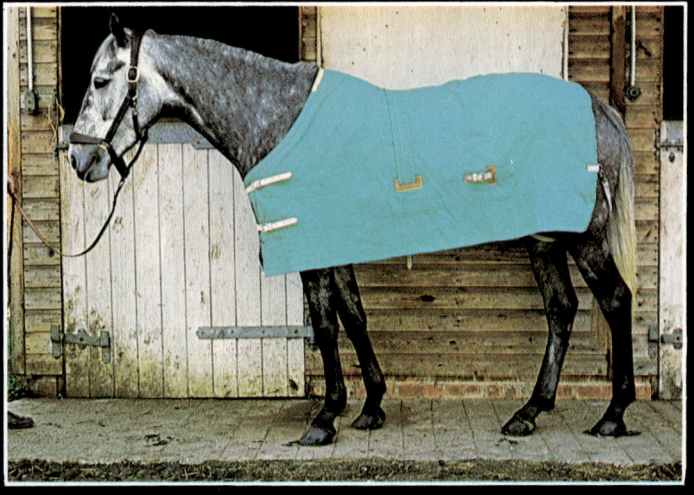
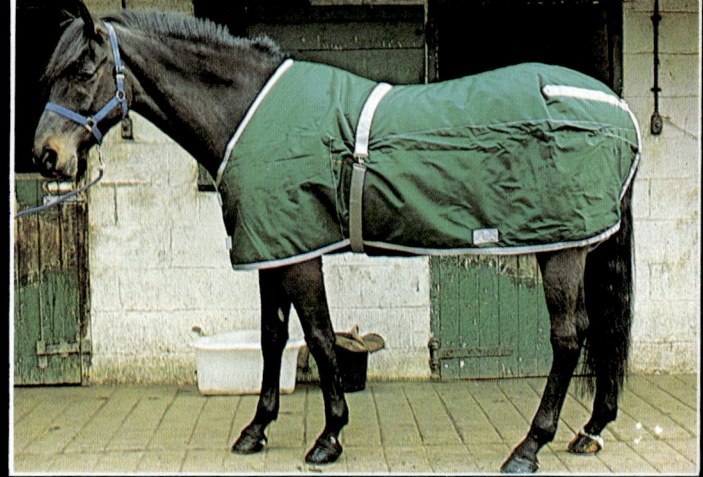

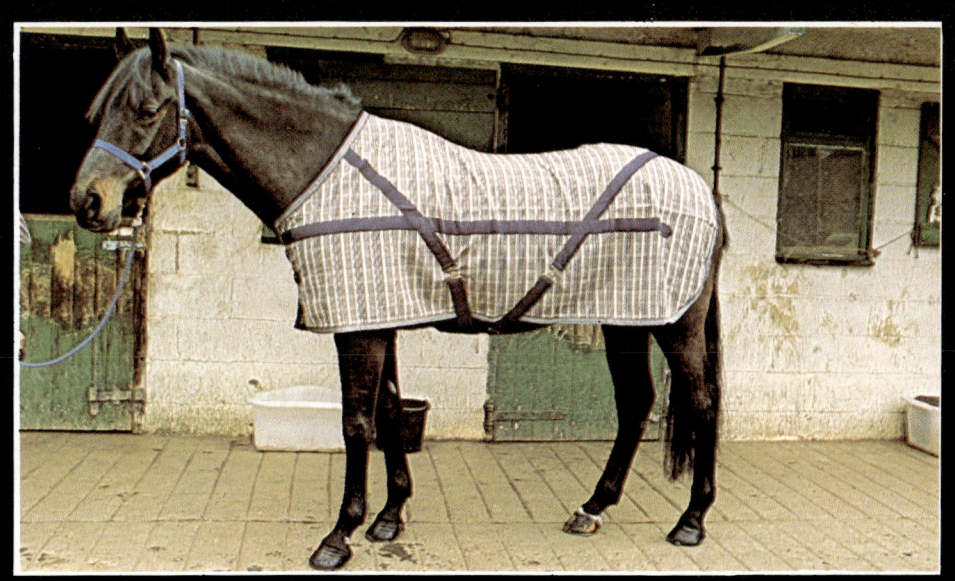

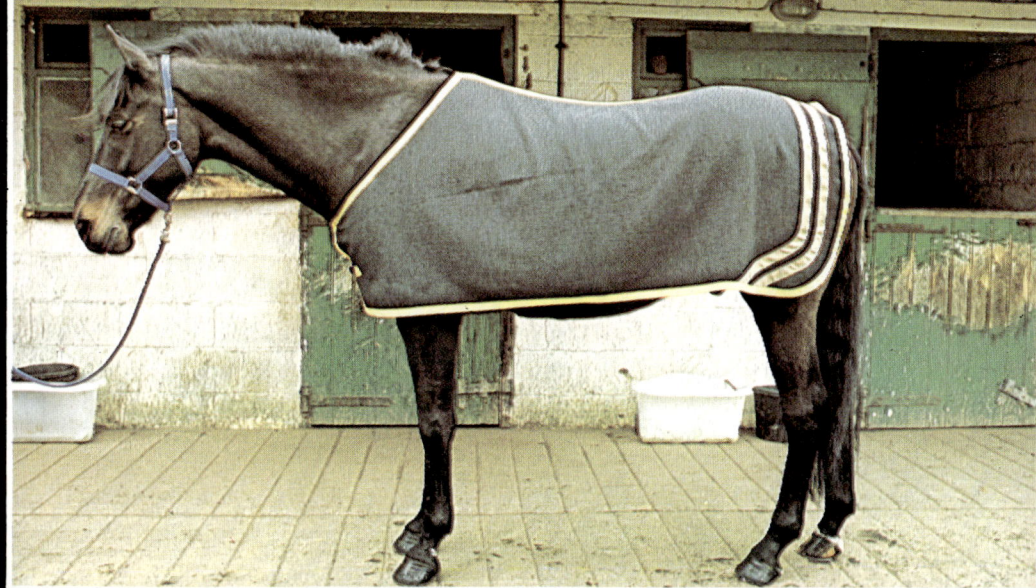
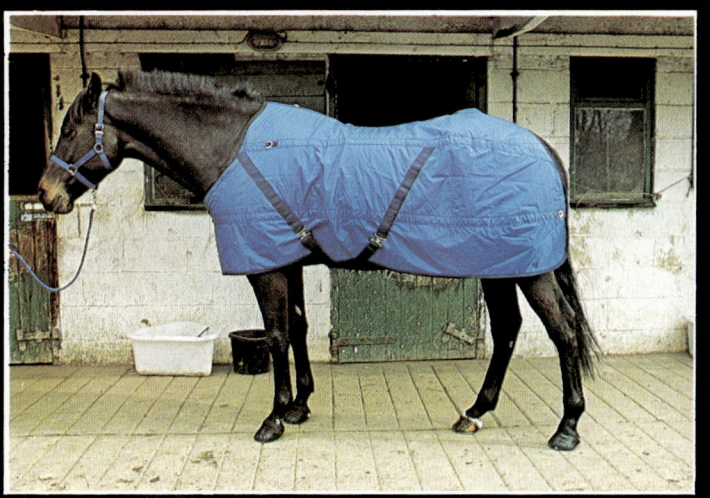
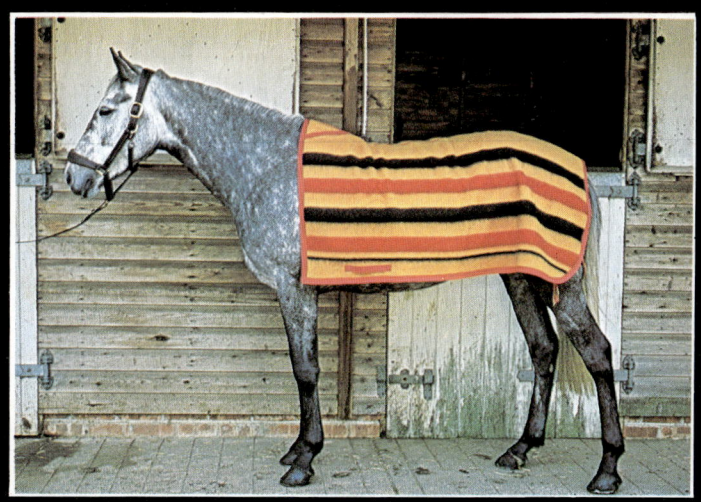

Stable Equipment · Bandages and Boots

Horses wear bandages for a number of reasons. Principally, bandages are used to protect the horse's tail and legs when travelling; to prevent injury to the limbs, should the horse knock himself in the field or when being ridden; as a support for the tendons during exercise; to keep the horse warm in the stable; and to hold dressings in place when veterinary treatment is required.

The type of tail bandage commonly used is made of a strip of elastic crepe, about 8ft long and 3in wide. This is bound around the tail to keep the hair flat and in place. Such a bandage should always be worn during travelling to prevent the horse breaking his tail hairs, if he rubs his tail on the back of a trailer or against the side of a box. The tail hair should be dampened before the bandage is applied; the bandage itself, however, should not be wetted, as it might otherwise shrink when in place causing both discomfort to the horse and damage to the tail. It should be wound around the tail, from the top down to the end of the dock, and then up again for a few inches before being secured.

The same 3in-wide crepe bandages are also used as exercise bandages to support the tendons. Here, they are usually worn over a layer of Gamgee tissue, thick cotton wool, pads of cotton, felt, or other similar material. Such bandages are applied at the top of the cannon bone under the knee and extend down to above the fetlock joint. The tapes of the bandage are fastened securely on the outside of the cannon bone with a knot. Bandages fastened on the inside of the leg are more likely to come undone while the horse is working, since the knot can be caught by a blow from the opposite leg.

The purpose of the bandages is to help in absorbing concussion and to ensure that the pressure ridges, which could damage the tendons, are evened out. When used on horses taking part in strenuous activity, such as competing across country, show jumping, or hunting, it is advisable either to sew the bandages in place after tying the tapes, or bind them round with surgical tape. This ensures that the bandage will not come undone, while, if surgical tape is used, this will also supply a waterproof covering.

Support must be given to each pair of legs, if it is to be effective—that is, both forelegs have to be bandaged, or both hindlegs. The horse can be bandaged all round if this is considered necessary.

Crepe bandages can also be used to keep dressings in place, or as a cold water bandage for sprains and swellings. A type of proprietary elastic sock can also be used for this purpose. Another recent innovation is the 'self stick' variety of crepe bandage. Its use removes the necessity of using tapes.

Woollen stable bandages, approximately 5in wide and 8ft long, are particularly useful for keeping a stabled horse warm in winter and protecting the legs of horses in a box or trailer. In the second case, it is particularly important to ensure that the bandage and its padding comes down well over the coronet, thus affording protection to the heel. Gamgee or similar padding is again used, though, in the case of some bandages, this is unnecessary. This type is made of thick, padded wool, with stockinette at each end.

The bandages are applied between the knee or hock and continue down over the fetlock joint, this affording more warmth

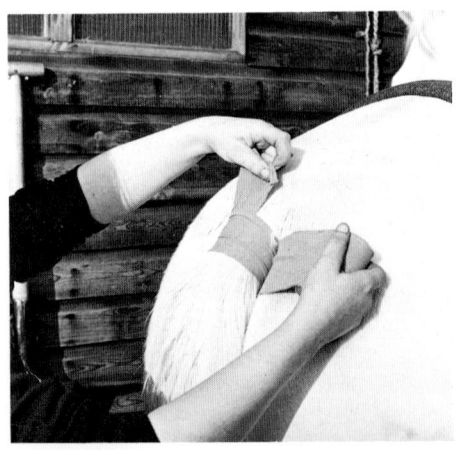
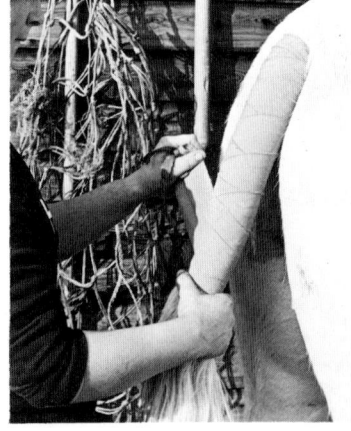
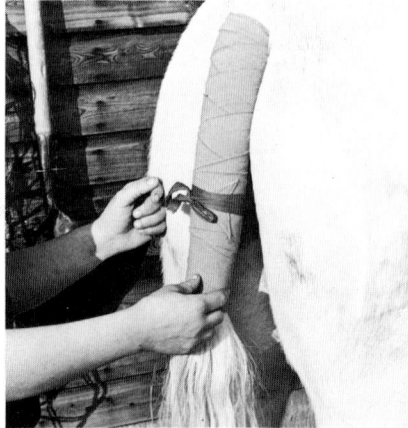
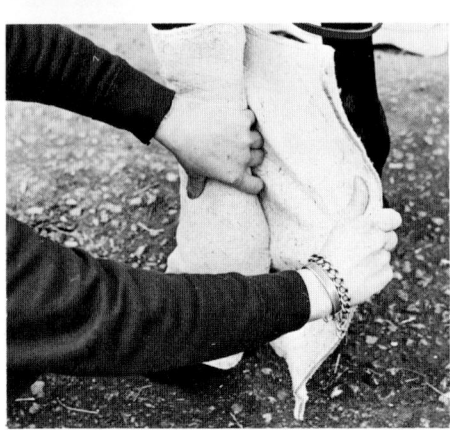
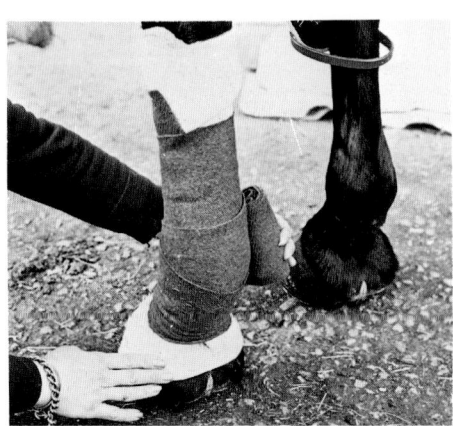
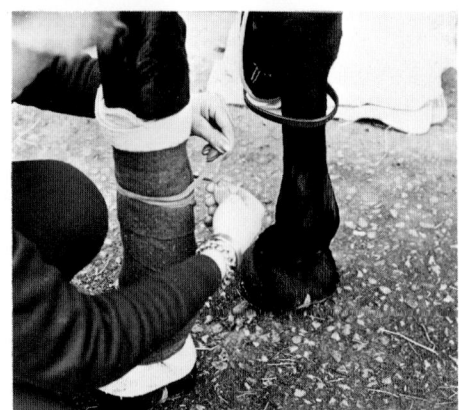

BANDAGES AND BOOTS

Right: This showjumper is bandaged in front for protection and support, the bandage being firmly secured by a wrapping of surgical tape. The tape covering also protects the bandages from the consequences of being immersed in water, which can cause the bandage to shrink and become uncomfortably tight. It is for this reason, as well as for that of security, that surgical tape is so frequently used in the sport of eventing.

Left top: The stages involved in putting on a tail bandage. The end of the bandage is held against the tail and turned once to secure it. The process continues evenly down the tail, stopping just short of the last bone. The remaining bandage is wound upwards and secured, the tail being bent into the most comfortable position. The bandage shapes the tail and keeps the hairs in place. **Left bottom:** Leg bandages being put on for wear in the stable or when travelling. The bandage, wound over the fetlock joint, is put on over a layer of Gamgee tissue or a felt pad. Not only do they give protection against blows; they also keep the extremities warm.

Right: Exercise or working bandages in position. These are used to give support to the lower limbs and do not cover the fetlock joint. **Far right:** Travelling bandages, covering the joint, worn with protective hock boots.

CHAPTER EIGHT · THE WELL-EQUIPPED STABLE

Top row: Side view of knee caps; travelling hock boot, knee caps and boots; skeleton knee caps, used for exercise or jumping; hind brushing boots. **Middle row:** Foreleg brushing boots; a pattern of felt brushing boot, which also gives protection to the rear of the joint; the classic tendon support boot; a German-pattern tendon boot, made of plastic; a single-strap fetlock brushing boot of felt with blocked leather cup and a similar boot which is slightly longer.
Bottom row: A very good leather boot, lined with strong foam plastic to protect the inside of the legs and encompass the joint; the cup fetlock boot, lined with foam plastic, originally introduced by Count Robert Orssich to Britain and the basic, but very effective, brushing ring.

BANDAGES AND BOOTS

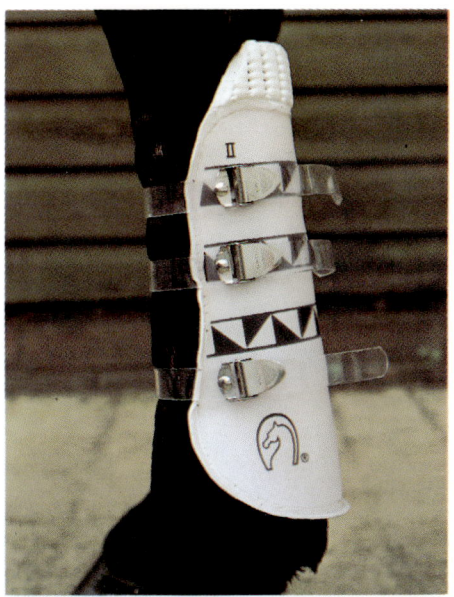

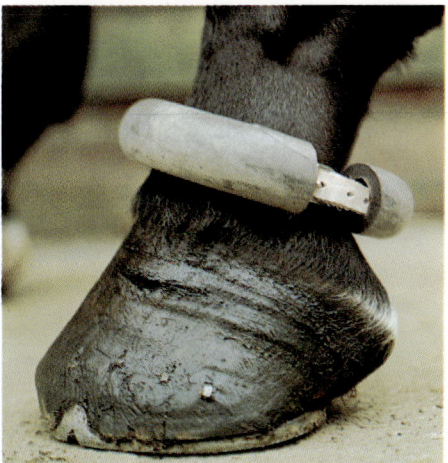

and protection than exercise bandages. They are fastened with strips of Velcro (as in the case of the padded bandages described above), or tapes. Velcro strips are quick and easy to apply, but their use can present a problem. The noise of the Velcro being unfastened can startle a young or nervous horse and care should be taken accordingly. If tapes are used, they should again be fastened on the outside of the cannon bone.

Boots and pads

There are many varieties of protective boot on the market. These range from plastic boots, used for travelling, to the various leather ones used to protect the horse against injury during exercise or in competition. Plastic travelling boots, lined with a thick layer of foam and fastened with Velcro, are quick and easy to put on and give considerable protection to the lower parts of the leg, provided they are secured far down enough to cover the coronet. Their disadvantage is that they tend to split easily, but they are far less trouble to apply than bandages.

The demands of travelling also entail providing protection for knees and hocks. Knee caps and hock boots are therefore a necessity. Knee caps consist of a thick woollen or canvas square, bound around

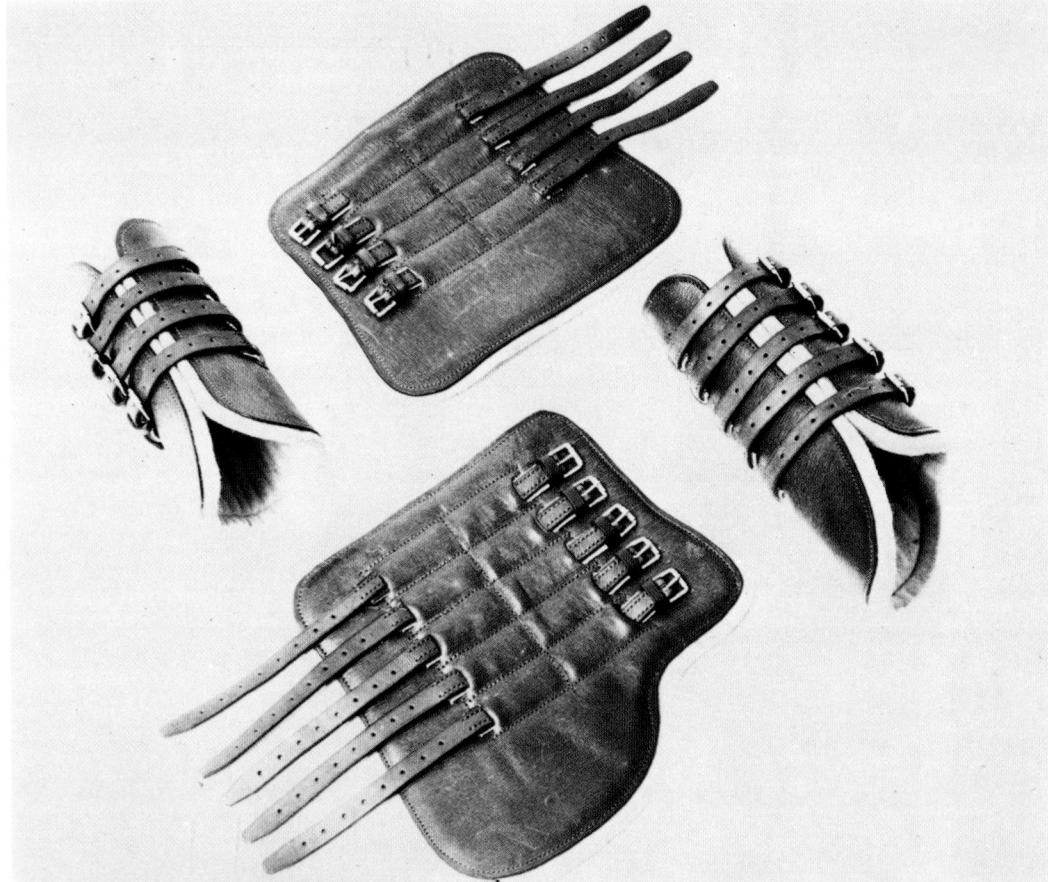

Above: Coronet boots, giving protection against blows or treads. **Left:** A selection of felt-lined polo boots giving overall protection and support to the legs. **Below:** A pair of foreleg polo boots in position.

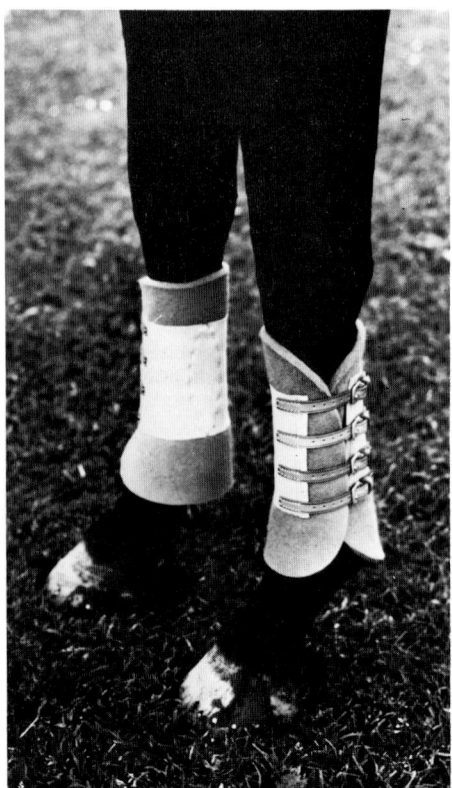

the edges, to which is fixed a shaped disc of leather, which covers the knee itself. The device is fixed in place by a padded leather strap, fastened tightly with a buckle just above the knee, and another one fastened loosely under it. The arrangement facilitates easy movement of the knee joint. A 'Skeleton' pattern knee cap is also available. As the name implies, this provides a more open form of protection, without the surrounding cloth.

Both types of knee cap can be used during exercising, the 'Skeleton' variety being designed for this very purpose. They are particularly valuable when riding on hard surfaces, especially if the horse is prone to tripping. They are also used when schooling young horses over fences, since their use can prevent the serious injuries which might otherwise occur if a young horse hits a fence hard.

Hock boots serve the same purpose as knee caps. They are used for protection when travelling and in the stable, if a horse has developed the bad habit of kicking against the stable wall. They can be made of leather, felt or wood, with a strong reinforcement over the point of the hock enveloping the whole joint. They are shaped to fit closely, fastening with a leather strap, sometimes set on elastic, above and below the hock.

As far as travelling is concerned, a relatively new product has been introduced, which claims to do the job of conventional hock boots, knee caps and bandages. This is an overall 'leg protector', made of PVC and lined with fur fabric and thus combining the function of both boot and bandage. Reinforced in the joint areas, the protectors have Velcro fastenings.

Brushing and over-reaching

One of the commonest equine injuries is that caused by brushing—that is, knocking one fetlock against the other. Several types of boot have been designed to counteract this faulty action. The simplest is probably the Yorkshire boot, an oblong piece of felt or bandage with a tape sewn horizontally across the centre. It is tied just above the fetlock, the upper part of the boot then being folded over to form a double thickness. A felt, or leather, cup boot, straight

Left: Overreach or bell boots, which protect the heel of the forelegs from blows made by the hindfeet. The pattern on the left has a fastening which facilitates the fitting and removal of the boot.

along the top and shaped to cover the inside of the fetlock joint, can also be used. Another simple device is a hollow ring of thick rubber, with a leather strap fixed through it. This fastens with a buckle just below the joint.

A more sophisticated boot is made of felt, boxcloth or woollen material, with a wide strip of leather running down the centre. It is much longer than the other types of boot, being fastened just below the knee and continuing down over the fetlock. It is then secured by four or five straps along the outside of the cannon bone, an arrangement which has the advantage of giving the tendon some support.

The disadvantage of the woollen variety is that they tend to collect mud, water and grit. The boxcloth and leather types are lighter and easier to keep in good order. However, boxcloth is now both expensive and difficult to find.

Tendon boots are used in the case of weak tendons. This can occur possibly when a horse is coming back into work after breaking down, or in the case of high over-reach. The latter, striking the back of the foreleg with the toe of the hind foot, is potentially dangerous, since it is possible to damage the tendon severely, or even cut through it. The boots are shaped to the leg and made of boxcloth or leather, with added protection down the back to cover the tendon area. They are fastened, from just below the knee to the fetlock, by means of four leather straps on the outside of the cannon.

The heel boot is used on horses, which, when doing fast work, bring their heel down into contact with the ground. They extend over the heel and are shaped to fit around it. All such boots are now available in plastic, as well as more traditional materials; although plastic is not as strong, it can be easily kept clean.

Horses—particularly when jumping—are also more likely to over-reach low down in the heel region than in the tendon area. Bell-shaped rubber over-reach boots are an effective preventative against such injury. Their rubber construction makes them sufficiently flexible to pull over the hoof, but they fit fairly tightly below the fetlock. In heavy going, however, there is the risk of them turning inside out, while they can prove difficult to pull over a large hoof. To lessen this problem, the boots can be fitted with various forms of strap fastening if necessary.

Show jumpers, hurdlers and steeplechasers are all prone to rapping their shins and various boots have been produced to lessen the risk of injury. They are similar in design to tendon boots, the difference being that the protective padding is at the front, over the shin area, and not the rear. Polo ponies, however, are probably the most likely to suffer leg injuries and therefore need the greatest leg protection. Polo boots, of thick felt covered with leather and with the option of a coronet extension to save treading, are virtually *de rigueur* on the polo field. They also give a degree of support to the tendons. Foreleg boots fasten with four straps—these are usually set on elastic—while hind boots fasten with five, since they are necessarily longer. This difference in fastening is usual with most boots covering the leg as opposed to just the joint.

CHAPTER NINE

Ceremonial Trappings

The long tradition of decoration, military and mythological.

Britain's Household Cavalry, the Queen's personal guards, provide an integral part of British ceremonial, attending the Royal family on all state occasions.

Ceremonial Trappings

CHAPTER NINE · CEREMONIAL TRAPPINGS

From the start of man's association with the horse, display and decoration have been a virtually integral part of the relationship. There are two main traditions, one linked to demands of war and the other to the more indefinite areas of custom, myth and ritual.

In India, for instance, at the time of the feast of Dasshera, horses are garlanded and colour applied to their feet and heads as part of this religious festival. Similarly in the east, the horse bearing a bridegroom to a wedding is extravagantly caparisoned in honour of the occasion. In the west, the harness of heavy horses is frequently decorated with brasses. Though considered as decoration today, these owe their origins to something far deeper than mere display. In their various forms and designs, horse brasses are good luck charms, often deriving from pagan beliefs. They were thought to combat the effects of an 'evil eye'. The eastern counterpart is the necklet or anklet of coloured silks or wool, worn for good luck by racehorses and humble tonga ponies alike.

In the past, too, horses have been deified. There have also been times when the horse was considered the most acceptable of sacrifices and the creature most worthy to accompany a noble or royal master to the tomb. Such horses were buried with the accoutrements befitting the station of the late owners. Such trappings, in fact, were the owner's badges or rank, an aspect which often persists in the ceremonial saddlery of today.

Mogul saddles of northern India, for instance, are sometimes decorated with as many as seven yak tails. This practice originated with the Mongols; under Genghis Khan, the *orkhons* (leaders) of the *tumans* (divisions) of the great Mongol horde used a standard adorned with yak tails to mark the position of their horse-borne headquarters in battle. In time, this insignia of authority was transferred to the saddles of high-ranking officers.

Survival on ice

The finest surviving examples of regalia of the early horse peoples are those from the Siberian tombs of Pazyryk. The finds are not only important in themselves; since it is from Central Asia that all subsequent horse cultures derive, the debt extends to much of ceremonial saddlery,

Right: The decoration of working horses is of long standing. Farm horses were turned out in a colourful way for market days, braided and plentifully adorned with horse brasses. Harvest time was also an occasion for decking the horses out in every possible sort of finery. The tradition survives to the present day in show ring classes and in public parades.

CHAPTER NINE · CEREMONIAL TRAPPINGS

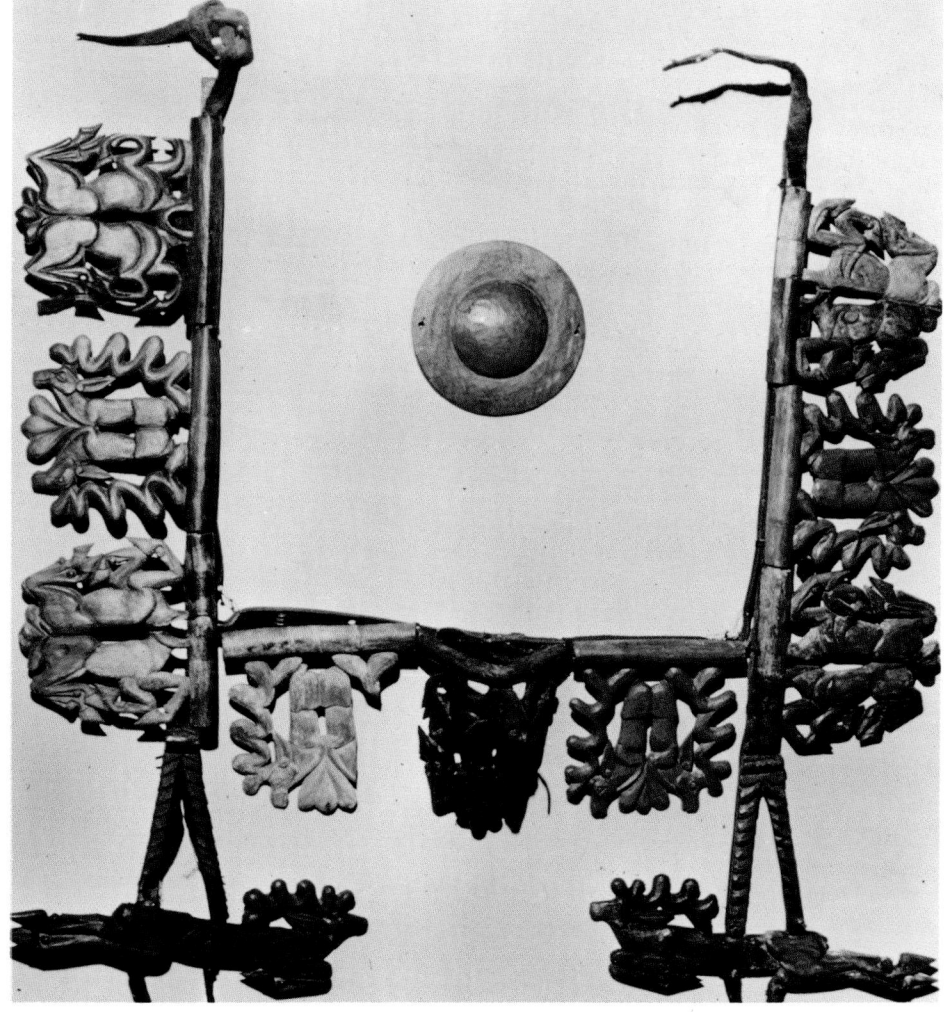

Left: Ornamented bridle from the Pazyryk tombs (5th-4th century BC) in the Hermitage Museum collection, Leningrad. **Above:** Carved moufflon heads used as saddle ornamentation, also from the Pazyryk tombs.

as well as the more utilitarian items of saddlery and horse equipment.

The tombs, situated high in the Altai Mountains of western Siberia, were first opened in 1929 by Dr S I Rudenko, a curator of the Hermitage Museum, Leningrad, the last one—Kurgan (barrow) 5—being explored in 1948, after the Second World War. Because of the climatic conditions peculiar to the area, the contents had been frozen in a bed of ice and thus preserved for over 2000 years.

The probable date when these once nomadic, but then settled, horse people were buried is around 423 BC. Who they were is unknown, but they were obviously of high rank, possessing much wealth, What is very clear is that they belonged to an extremely sophisticated horse culture, in which the ceremonial apparelling of horses in items of leather and cloth, most sumptuously embroidered in gold and silver, was a highly-developed skill.

Rudenko himself suggested that these people were the inheritors of a tradition of horse husbandry that might have extended back to about 3000 BC, when their ancestors gave up reindeer in favour of horses.

The equipment found in the tombs was varied and gorgeous. It included, for instance, magnificently embroidered 'saddle' pads of felt and leather, with intricate appliqué designs. One pad fitted on each side of the horse's spine, joined front and rear by a wooden arch. The assemblage was kept in place by a form of belly girth, a breast plate and a sort of breeching passed around the quarters. The early form of military shabraque incorporated into this elaborate piece of equipment was decorated with pictures of birds, beasts and mythical monsters and studded with gold and silver.

Bridles, similarly decorated and of remarkably modern design, were also found on the horses, which were naturally preserved by the ice exactly as they had been at the moment of death. Much ingenuity had been expended on the mane and tail. The former was hogged—a natural development for a race of horse archers, since a flowing mane would obstruct the drawing of a bow. It was provided with a most elaborate case. The tail was also encased in an embroidered sheath, the lower end being plaited and worked with coloured fibres and thongs. Today, tail cases can still be seen at the classical riding schools of Saumur and Vienna and mane covers are in use in Asia and other parts of the east. In addition, the custom of plaiting manes and even tails for special events is commonplace in many regions of the world.

Possibly the most remarkable decoration was the face mask. This could have been a pattern for the medieval chamfron, but for the animals which it simulated. When in place, the mask transformed the head into that of a reindeer, a bird, or beast of prey. The effect was not only to make the horse more impressive, or terrifying, but also taller. Similar devices in the shape of plumes and other head decorations have been used for the same purpose down through the centuries.

The military tradition

Nevertheless, saddlery developed for military use has been the principal factor in the development of ceremonial equipment. This equipment was not entirely the result of what might appear to be the horseman's superficial need for bright display. It was also based on practical

CHAPTER NINE · CEREMONIAL TRAPPINGS

necessities, at least in theory. Flattering uniforms, richly decorated, and accoutrements which distinguished one unit from another were undeniable morale boosters for the rank-and-file, as well as providing easily recognizable badges of rank for the officers. The effect of gaily caparisoned bodies of mounted men also had an influence upon enemy infantry standing in stubborn ranks with feet planted in inches of cold penetrating mud.

The very early horse soldiers, such as the Assyrians, fully appreciated the advantages to be gained from impressive accoutrements. Assyrian bridles were richly decorated and studded, as were their chariot fittings. Such equipment was by no means an idle extravagance. The metal decorations were strong enough to withstand a blow from a sword, while the magnificent collars and necklaces also provided positive protection.

In modern terms, however, the military saddlery from which today's ceremonial equipment derives, has a dual origin. One important influence was the saddle used by the medieval knights. It could be argued that the world's military saddles are simplified, cut-down and improved versions of these. This, however, would be an over-simplification, since another influence came from the Mongol warriors and the two combined to affect the whole course of equestrian evolution.

The mercenary pioneers

There is little doubt that the pioneers of the military saddle were the Hungarians. Not only did their designs have the greatest influence on the cavalry of Europe, but also on that of the USA. It is possible, too, that the sartorial example of their dashing hussars set the pattern for innumerable European cavalry regiments.

Hungarian horsemanship contained much that was eastern, or Asian, in concept. There had been for centuries a regular trade in Oriental horses, on which the Hungarian cavalry was almost entirely mounted. In fact as well as by reputation, the Hungarians were Europe's light cavalrymen *par excellence*, following the traditional pattern of eastern and Asian horsemen. Similarly, they adapted the high-peaked Oriental saddle, which held the rider high off the horse's back, merging its design into the less sophisticated, but earlier, Mongol-type saddle, which was well established in eastern Europe.

The Hungarian example deeply influenced some of the chief military thinkers of the day. Surprisingly enough, these were frequently mercenaries. European armies had traditionally employed mercenary troops of other nationalities. Such officers were the true professionals of the day, making deep studies of warfare and acquiring an exceptional level of competence. In this respect, they were excep-

CHAPTER NINE · CEREMONIAL TRAPPINGS

Left: Russian saddle at the Royal Mews, London. It shows a pronounced Asian influence and it is interesting to note that the cushion-shaped seat is not dissimilar from that used by the Argentine **gaucho**. **Above:** The same saddle with its woven covering of Eastern design. This cover could double as a mat on which to sit or as protection from the cold.

tions to the general rule. Many cavalry officers looked upon their commissions as no more than an agreeable pastime suitable for gentlemen. Although dashing, some were positively incompetent.

The mercenary was largely a European phenomenon and there a high proportion was of Anglo-Irish descent. Celebrated mercenary officers included MacMahon, who became a Marshal of France and President of the Third Republic; O'Dwyer, who served in the Austrian cavalry; and Nolan, who served with the Hungarians. The last was arguably one of Europe's most advanced cavalry thinkers and his death at Balaclava in 1854 ended what might have been a remarkable military career, had he been able to win acceptance from the conservative establishment.

It was largely due to the detailed studies of experts of this sort that the prototype of a near-universal military saddle came into being. Both O'Dwyer and Nolan went into print to explain their theories and the former, in his 'On Seats and Saddles, Bits and Bitting, Draught and Harness', published in the mid-1800s, provided a clear exposition of the Hungarian light cavalry saddle. This consisted of two wood bars, suitably reinforced, which lay on either side of the spine, being placed over a blanket or numnah. The bars were joined front and rear by arches, between which was stretched the bearing strap. This, in

Opposite: Detail of an embroidered saddle cloth from the Pazyryk tombs. **Right:** Another Russian saddle from the Royal Mews collection, which was presented to Queen Elizabeth II by the Russian statesman Nikita Khrushchev. Eastern in concept, the covering is heavy woven silk.

CHAPTER NINE · CEREMONIAL TRAPPINGS

Above: A magnificently worked ceremonial saddle from the Royal Mews, London which is fitted with ornamented holsters. **Above left:** An officer's saddle from the same collection with pouches in place over the front arch.

turn, was laced to each bar. The saddle's beauty was that it not only held the rider well clear of the horse's back, but, by adjusting the laces, it could also be fitted to the conformation of the individual trooper, so he was made to sit centrally.

O'Dwyer commented: 'It is just as necessary, or more so, to make the saddle fit the man's seat as to make his coat or boots fit his body or feet; and this is done, after careful observation of the seat, by shortening or lengthening the bearing strap of the seat, or by altering the lacings, till the seat comes right of itself, when you don't need to correct it in the riding school.'

Such consideration for the rider was not

CHAPTER NINE · CEREMONIAL TRAPPINGS

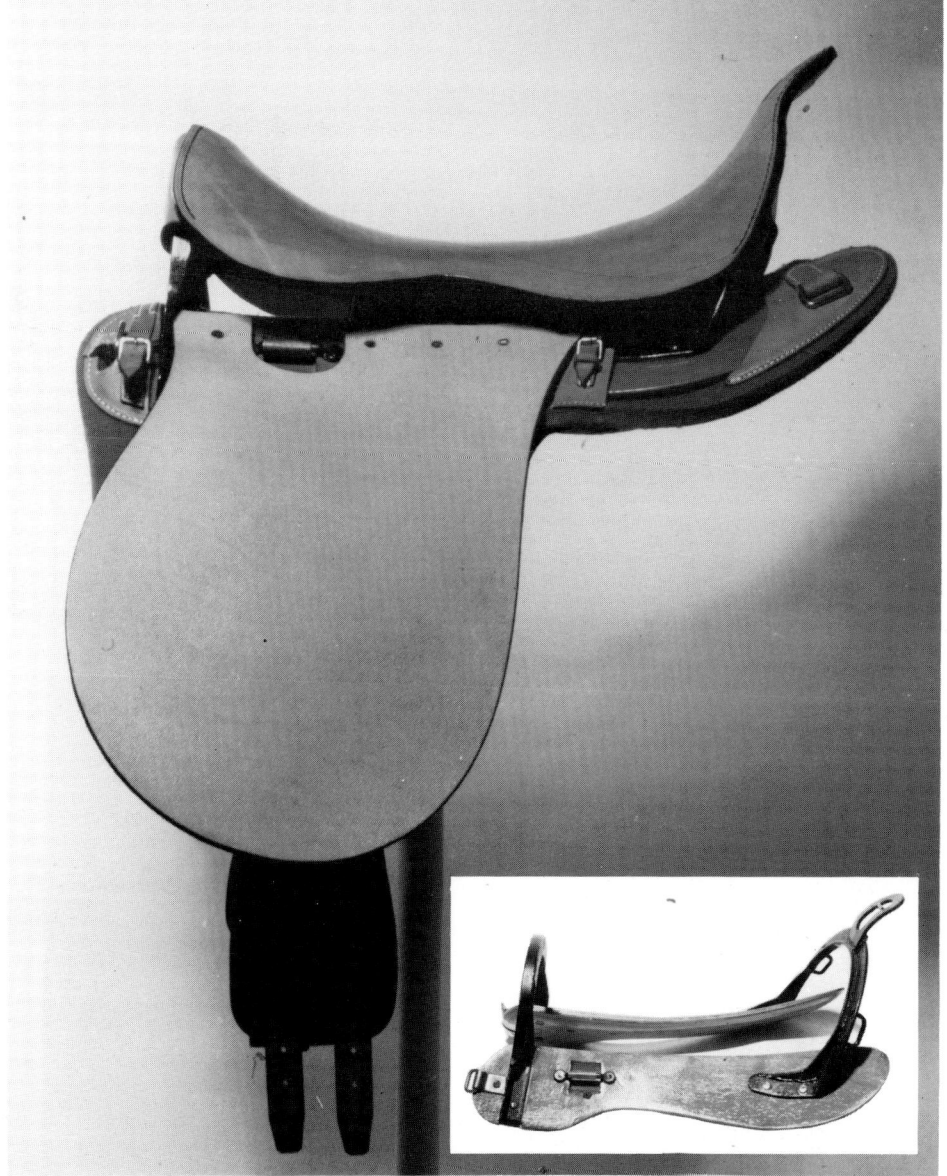

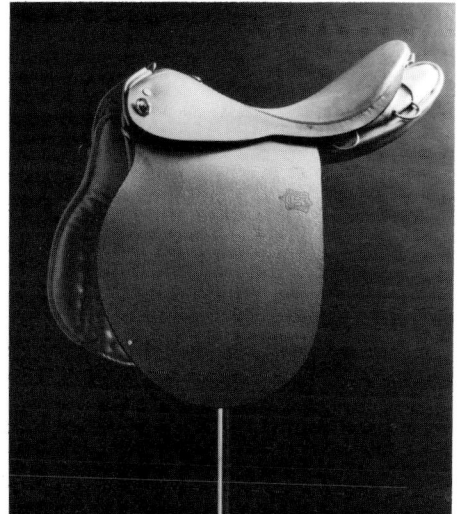

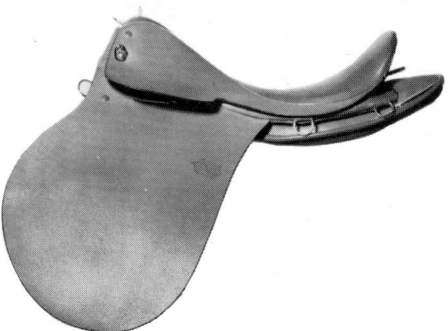

Left: The British Army Universal pattern saddle, developed following the Crimean War and first known as the Nolan saddle. It had its origins in the Hungarian cavalry saddle. **Inset:** The tree, an infinitely practical item which was easily maintained. **Top:** Modern version of the army officer's saddle, recommended for such activities as trekking and long distance riding. **Above:** A modern saddle made for police work which follows the same basic military pattern.

as much in evidence elsewhere, as most of the European derivatives had no such means of adjustment, but the Hungarian principles were followed nonetheless. Following the Crimean War, much attention was given to saddle design. In Britain, the result was the Universal Pattern Saddle (first known as the Nolan saddle), which survives in its essentials today, despite numerous and inevitable modifications. Though other European saddles varied in detail, they followed the same basic form for the most part.

The UP weighed 15lb. It had panels that could be adjusted to fit any back, either with or without the folded blanket or numnah. The dipped seat positioned the rider centrally well above the back, while the stirrup bars were positioned so as to allow the use of a shorter leather if the need arose. It was fitted with an assortment of buckles and slits for the attachment of extraneous gear, while it could be repaired easily—the basic repair kit was a piece of twine, a knife and a screwdriver. Just as important, it had a regulation life of between eight and 14 years, though usually it was serviceable after as much as 30 years of use.

The UP was the trooper's saddle. In almost every other army, except for the US cavalry, officers preferred to use the conventional type of English hunting saddle, possibly with individually designed fittings for attaching various pieces of equipment. Such saddles, though, were not as hard-wearing as the UP; in arduous conditions, they could become unserviceable after as little as a year.

The pack saddle

Almost as important as the riding saddle was the pack saddle, for armies depended upon pack transport for the movement of supplies well into the 1900s. Again, the British version, known as the Universal Purpose Pack Saddle, had the same basic pattern as that used throughout Europe. The saddle was really no more than a pair of side bars joined by a strong metal front and rear arch, to which were fitted hooks

CHAPTER NINE · CEREMONIAL TRAPPINGS

Left: This richly embroidered saddle is to be seen at the Royal Mews, London. It is of Iberian origin and close to the **Selle Royale** in design. The heavy stirrup irons are a relic of the long Moorish occupation of the peninsular.
Right: A North African, or Arabian, saddle from the same collection. Both are reminiscent of the much earlier saddles of the Middle Ages.

for attaching the load. The bars were fitted with large, well-stuffed, square panels, covered with either serge or linen. The whole was kept in place by two girths, a surcingle, crupper, breastplate and breeching. Frequently, mules were preferred to horses, since their relatively long and straight backs were better suited to the saddle's construction.

Bridles and bitting
Most 19th-century armies employed a type of Pelham bridle, that is, one operating a single mouthpiece with two pairs of reins. Nolan had produced just such a bridle in the years prior to the Crimea, incorporating with it a headcollar which doubled as a noseband. This was an attempt to suit the equipment to the standard of riding, for cavalry recruits were by no means good horsemen. The standard of riding in Napoleon's cavalry at Waterloo (1815), for instance, was extremely low; indeed, for many years afterwards, there would have been no more than a handful of troopers who could have persuaded their horse to leave the ranks and act independently of their comrades.

Bitting under such circumstances was a matter of prime concern, particularly in regiments obsessed with uniformity of appearance in men and horses. The Spanish authority Don Juan Segundo devoted much time and no little ingenuity to his 'Complete System of Bitting,' which involved the interchange of mouthpieces, cheeks, curb chains and so on in accordance with the construction of the horse's mouth, plus the general conforma-

CHAPTER NINE · CEREMONIAL TRAPPINGS

tion of the head and neck. It was probably the British, however, who came up with the most satisfactory solution.

This was the Army Universal Pelham. The angled cheek of this bit permitted the use of a single rein in one of three positions. For a light-mouthed horse, the rein was fastened to the top ring; for an average mouth, on the centre slot; and for a hard one, on the third slot.

Ceremonial saddlery

Though ceremonial saddlery reached the peaks of extravagance in the 19th century, it was not, in fact, much more than an adaptation of that used in the field. Indeed, for some time, there was little, if any, difference between the two.

The most impressive item of cavalry furniture was the shabraque, ornamented in gold and silver lace and embroidered to show the regimental crest, or, in the case of general officers, the rank of the rider. Laid over the saddle, with its shape varying considerably from one regiment to another, the officer's version was usually lined with moleskin and the trooper's with leather or rawhide.

The housing was scarcely less eyecatching, even though it lacked the dramatic rake of the shabraque. The general tendency was for it to be a more rectangular shaped cloth, covering the horse's back behind the saddle, but it was often as beautifully worked and coloured. The essential difference between the two was that, whereas the shabraque was laid over the saddle, the housing was laid, or joined, under it to connect with the weapon

231

CHAPTER NINE · CEREMONIAL TRAPPINGS

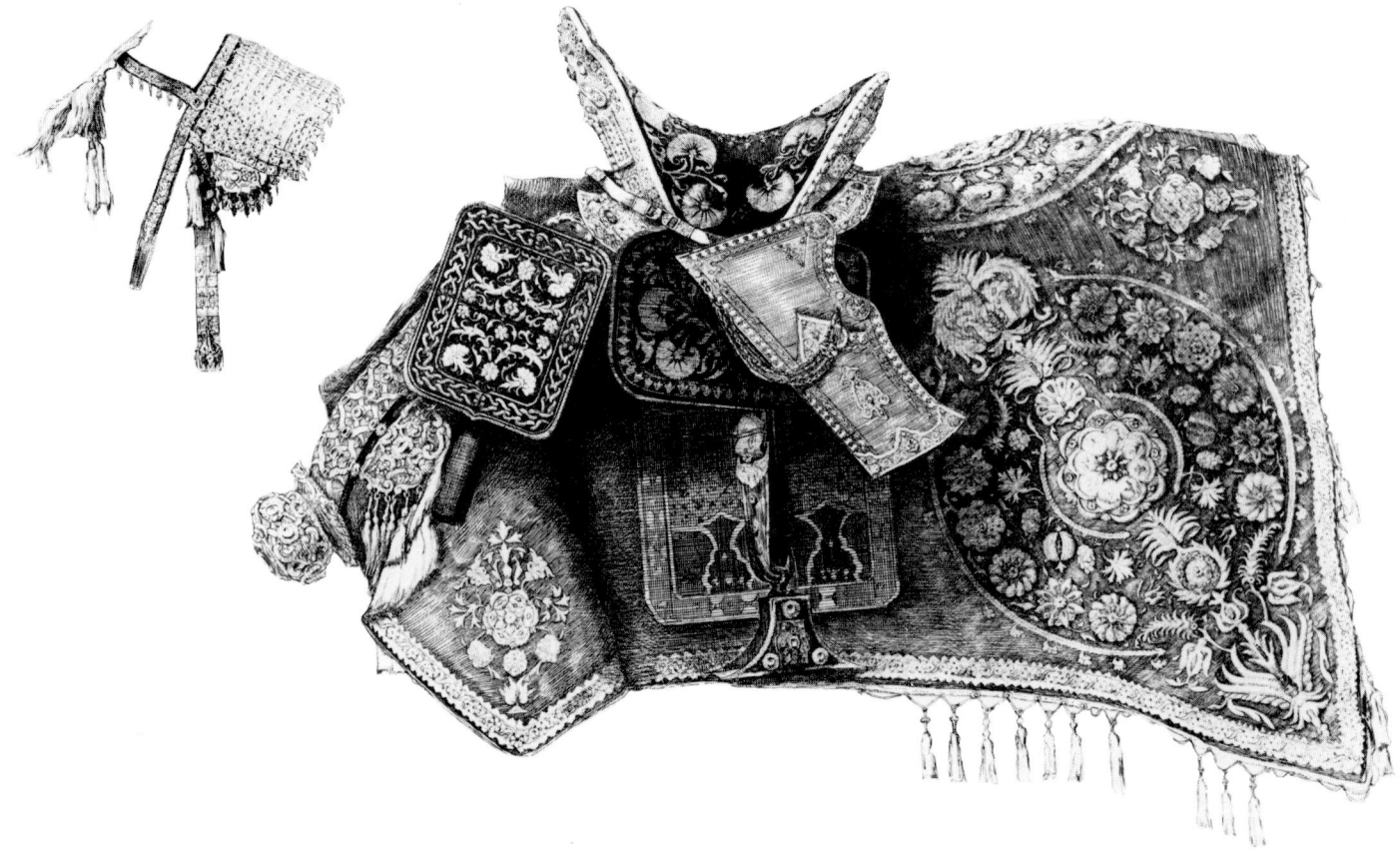

Above: Polish saddle, mountings and bridle of the 17th century. The Poles had an Eastern connection and their cavalry made much use of Arabian horses. The influence is evident in this superb example of a ceremonial saddle. **Left:** The saddle and accoutrements, from the Royal Mews collection, made for King Christian IV of Denmark on the occasion of his son's marriage in 1634.

coverings to the front of the pommel.

These fur-covered holsters (also called caps or flounces) were first in evidence when firearms were introduced to the cavalry proper in the early 18th century. They were only replaced by similarly covered wallets just before the Crimea to carry pistols, carbines and similar weapons. None of these coverings was of much practical value.

Traditionally, hussar officers laid leopard or cheetah skins (troopers used sheep skins) to cover the shabraque from pommel to cantle. This gave them a more secure seat than they would have enjoyed on the slippery leather of the saddle when riding in the then fashionably long manner. Both shabraque and skin were secured by an ornate surcingle.

A contemporary description of a 'furnished' British officer's charger of around 1860 gives a fascinating glimpse of the grandeur of ceremonial cavalry trappings of the period. 'The shabraque is of fine blue cloth made to fit the seat of the saddle, with a hole to let the cantle through. It is ornamented with two rows of gold lace all round, with 'V.R.' and an Imperial crown embroidered in gold upon

the front corners. The hind corners, or points, have the Prince of Wales feathers with motto surmounted by an Imperial crown; under that a scroll, with 'The Prince of Wales Own' on it, and a '10' in the centre; below that, at the extreme point, the letter 'H'; the whole handsomely embroidered in gold and silver. The shabraque is lined with strong fustian enamelled gold cloth and leather at the wearing points, and made up with straps, loops and strings where required. With this a cheetah skin is used, cut to regulation shape to cover the cloak (rolled) and valise, edged all around with cloth and gold fringe; these together are used for review and dress purposes. The surcingle buckles over the whole. For marching order, an entire cheetah skin is used—the head, paws and tail being stuffed soft; the head has a false tongue and glass eyes and is tied on the crupper, a hole being cut in the shoulder of the skin to let the cantle through and two holes over the holsters, the forelegs hanging on both sides. The hind legs hang on each

CHAPTER NINE · CEREMONIAL TRAPPINGS

Top left: Gericault's exciting picture shows the officer's accoutrements to perfection, in particular the leopard skin shabraque and the bridle. **Above:** French cavalryman of the late 19th century in marching order. **Left:** Officer's charger, Royal Horse Artillery 1890.

side in front and are tied to the breastplate straps. The tail hangs loosely on the near side of the neck, the whole also secured by the surcingle. On all occasions, the troopers use a shabraque, with woollen embroidery and lace with a black lamb-skin seat kept in place by the surcingle.'

Small wonder that one officer of the regiment described above was not amused when he was caught in the rain while on sovereign's escort duty between London and Windsor. His own uniform, as well as his charger's trappings, was ruined and he had no option but to have everything replaced, paying from his own pocket.

Finally, there was the valise. This was an oval or square cloth case, worn behind the saddle with the centre hollowed out to keep it off the back of the horse. It would bear an abbreviated regimental title and it held spare clothing, cleaning materials and the like. By the end of the 19th century, however, it had been largely replaced by the more practical saddlebag.

Ceremonial bridles retained the metal covered headpiece, originally a guard against a sword cut, and were often fitted with a chain replacing the leather rein in the first part of its length. This, too, was a preventative measure against the rein being cut and the rider being unable to control his mount as a result. Bits bore bosses bearing the regimental crest, or, in the case of general officers, bosses indicating the rider's rank.

The US tradition

Across the Atlantic, the US cavalry was unfettered by the conventions of Europe. It used practical saddlery suited to its method of operation and disdained, almost entirely, any sort of ceremonial trappings along European lines.

The US saddle was the McClellan, brought from Hungary in its original form by the future General George B McClellan in 1858. It remained in service until 1940. It was a simple saddle worn over a blanket, the two pads joined by the arches and the seat made from a piece of stretched rawhide. The stirrups were shaped wooden ones, following Western convention, while the girth was often of the Western type. The whole thing was very light—in this respect, it scored heavily

233

Top: The saddle pad and terrets from a set of State Coach driving harness. It is made of red Moroccan leather, with elaborate gold mouldings. **Above:** The complete set of harness, except of course for the bridle. Elaborately decorated harness of this type makes quite a weight for the horse even before he starts to pull the coach.

CHAPTER NINE · CEREMONIAL TRAPPINGS

Far left: Detail of the hames and the decorative boss on a set of harness worn only by horses pulling a carriage carrying H.M. the Queen. **Left:** The saddle pad and terret from this same set of harness. **Below:** The harness ready for use in the procession for the celebration of the silver wedding of H.M. the Queen. All these photographs were taken at the Royal Mews, London.

CHAPTER NINE · CEREMONIAL TRAPPINGS

over its European counterparts—but it was a saddle for horsemen. In this respect, the USA was more fortunate than Europe, for its cavalrymen were certainly better and more experienced riders.

Though the US cavalry tended to eschew the fripperies of ceremonial, this was certainly not the case with its chief opponents—the American Indians. The latter had an innate love of colour and decoration. Clearly the pattern for the early Indian saddles was set by the saddles used by the Spanish explorers, but, given this, it is also evident that the Indians developed them to accord with their intricate and colourful art forms.

The Indians produced two distinct types of saddle—a pad saddle and one made on a wooden frame, which was usually, but not always, a woman's saddle. The pad was a skin bag divided so as to lie on either side of the spine and filled with grass. It was kept in place by a girth and fitted with stirrups set centrally. The stirrups were made from shaped pieces of willow wood. Such a saddle was an ideal

Top: An Indian artist's view of Custer's last stand at the Little Big Horn. The cavalry horses galloping away from the battle show the simplicity of the McClellan saddles to perfection. **Above:** The US Army McClellan saddle which was brought from Hungary and adapted by General George B. McClellan in 1858. It remained in use until 1940. It was a very light saddle but not particularly comfortable other than for experienced horsemen.

tool for horse stealing, since, when emptied of its stuffing it weighed very little and could be rolled up easily. The frame saddle, made of wood or antler horn, resembled the Hungarian cavalry saddle, or, more particularly, the saddles found in the Pasyryk tombs.

Saddle clothes and saddles were frequently ornately decorated in beadwork and, sometimes, with coloured porcupine quills. Often, there were fringes of buckskin hanging from intricately fashioned discs. The Cree, in particular, specialized in beautifully worked quill cruppers, which lay over the whole of the back, falling well down the flanks. Horses were given coats of paint, like their warriors.

Surprisingly enough, these saddles bear a remarkable resemblance to the saddles made by primitive peoples across the world. Such equipment once again demonstrates the universal nature of the development of horse culture and horse equipment. It also serves to demonstrate how the horse has always been essential in the development of human civilization.

CHAPTER NINE · CEREMONIAL TRAPPINGS

Left: The Alamo saddle, presented to H.M. the Queen by the film actor John Wayne and displayed at the Royal Mews, London.

237

CHAPTER TEN

Riding Dress

Clothes Ancient and Modern
Whips and Spurs

Scarlet is the traditional colour of the hunting field, probably originating in livery dress. The cap, as opposed to other forms of headwear, was at one time the prerogative of the Master and his hunt servants, later being extended to farmers over whose land hounds hunted. Today the custom is 'more honoured in the breach than in observance...' and caps are worn generally by ladies and children and in frequent cases by men.

Riding Dress · Ancient and Modern

The first surviving illustrations of men riding animals which can be positively identified as horses are generally accepted as being those found in the tomb of the Egyptian Pharaoh Horenhab (14th century BC). It is thus in this distant epoch that the development of riding clothes began.

Tunics and bare legs

The tomb paintings show Egyptians riding virtually naked. This is not exceptionally surprising considering the country's climate, the fact that during the early days of Egyptian civilization the lower orders went about entirely naked and that, even under later dynasties, man's clothing remained flimsy. The basic male garment was a simple loin cloth or a short skirt made of linen or cotton; members of the upper classes wore a long transparent garment over this. The riders' clothes reflected this general flimsiness of dress, while, since there was as yet no such thing as a saddle, there was no great need to protect the legs from chafing. Indeed, in a hot climate the skin would probably have given as good a grip as was possible.

As late as the time of the Greek general and historian Xenophon (c. 430–350 BC), whose treatise on horsemanship includes a description of clothes and equipment for the cavalryman, decorative vases and plates still depicted youths on horseback riding naked. However, except for one brief period of bare-legged horsemanship among some North American Indian tribes after the re-introduction of the horse into that continent during the 16th century AD, the trend down the ages has been for horsemen of all races and nations to cover themselves with a combination of protective and decorative clothing, using whatever materials were available and reflecting, to a great extent, the style of their local, everyday costume.

Among the earliest of the great horse peoples were the Assyrians, who lived in what is now the northern part of Iraq. Their riding outfit consisted simply of a long tunic, which covered the whole of the upper body and upper arms, was belted around the waist and finished just above the knees. Bas reliefs from the 9th and 8th centuries BC show that both mounted Assyrian civilians hunting wild animals and cavalry riding into battle wore this tunic. But whereas the civilians are usually shown bare-headed, the warriors often sport conical helmets and, in some cases, calf-length boots.

The demands of war

As soon as men began to ride horses into battle, they must have become aware of the need for some sort of protection. The mass of available pictorial evidence, ranging from coins and medals depicting kings on horseback to the greatest works of art—mosaics, statues, friezes, illuminated manuscripts, tapestries and paintings—bears witness to the number and variety of the various forms of armour which evolved in different regions.

Xenophon wisely emphasized the need for protection coupled with comfort and ease of movement, while at the same time taking into account man's love of ornamentation. He recommended that the cuirass, that part of the armour which covers the chest, abdomen and back, be made to fit the body, with: 'a covering rising out of the cuirass itself to fit the neck. This will at once be an ornament; and if it is made as it should be, it will cover the rider's face when he pleases as far as the nose.' This neck-protecting device was probably of eastern origin, observed by Xenophon during his period of service in his Persian campaign.

The head was protected by a helmet made, like the cuirass, of metal. This gave protection to both head and face. Flexible flaps of metal-covered felt or leather protected the groin and hips and also the right part of the body, which was exposed when

Right: An Assyrian, wearing a form of skirt, the coolest item of clothing in a hot climate, and also some form of protection on the legs.

CLOTHES ANCIENT AND MODERN

Far left: The basic simplicity of the early horseman, who rides quite naked. Greek horsemen of Xenophon's time rode either entirely naked or with no more than minimal clothing. **Left:** This bronze of a warrior of 550 BC shows some of the very earliest armour. The rider wears a helmet and what appears to be a pair of armour shorts. His legs, however, are bare, perhaps to give him a better grip on his horse. **Below:** Alexander the Great is also skirted (possibly with cloth or even leather drawers underneath) and wears high ankle boots.

the sword arm was raised. Greaves of metal-covered leather or felt were worn on the legs below the knee, while Xenophon also recommended the use of a similar device on the right arm. For the left or rein arm he favoured a piece of equipment known simply as 'the arm' to cover the shoulder, arm and elbow. Top-boots of **leather gave protection to feet and shins.**

Even in Xenophon's day, scale armour, made of small pieces of metal fixed to felt (which gave greater freedom of movement than plate armour) was not unknown. The Parthenon frieze, completed around 440 BC, depicts a rider wearing a combination of plate and scale armour.

As far as protection was concerned, the basic requirements of the mounted soldier scarcely varied down the centuries. The style of armour underwent many changes, however, reaching its zenith of complexity during the 15th and 16th centuries when knights were covered from head to foot in elaborately decorated metal suits—their horses also being armoured.

Clothes to suit the climate

When not engaged in combat, the Greek cavalryman wore a simple outfit and this was the accepted garb for the civilian riders of the day. This consisted of a short cloak known as a *chlamys*, which covered both the front and back of the body and was kept in place by means of a buckle fastened over one shoulder, high boots and a broad-brimmed hat.

Because of the mild climate of their country, the ancient Greeks, like the Egyptians before them, favoured loose garments of light cloth. In this respect, again like the Egyptians, riding clothes reflected ordinary everyday dress. Climate was a

CHAPTER TEN · RIDING DRESS

major influence in the development of riding clothes throughout the world, as evidenced by the clothes of the inhabitants of a country whose climate, terrain and lifestyle could scarcely be in greater contrast to those of the Mediterranean.

The ancient nomadic tribes of Siberia dressed to suit the cold weather of their northern homeland, whether on or off their horses. Although modern industrial man considers trousers the most suitable garment for the male form and the skirt for that of the female, in earlier times such matters were governed more by climate than by gender. The skirt was, and still is, the coolest thing to wear in hot climates—it is still traditional male dress in many eastern countries—while trousers were the best form of protection against the icy blasts of the far north.

Not surprisingly, therefore, excavations in the High Altai of Siberia have revealed that, while the Greeks wore skirts, the nomadic Siberian horseman of 2,500 years ago wore a loose tunic, belted at the waist, over baggy trousers tucked into short, pliable boots, which were strapped at the ankle. The outfit gave him overall protection against the extremes of the winter months. Climate and natural resources also governed which materials were available, so that garments of felt and woven hemp fibre were here the order of the day. Decoration was not neglected. It consisted of open-work applied designs in leather or felt, animals and birds being favourite motifs. The mounted nomads, their horses arrayed in decorative saddlery and exotic head-dresses, must have made an impressive sight.

Another notable race of horsemen were the Scythians, who lived much further south and prospered during the times of the Greek and Roman civilizations. They also adopted tunic and trousers as their basic riding clothes, as did the dreaded Huns of Central Asia and their great adversaries, the Chinese.

Breeches and boots

The Romans relied less on horses than the Greeks, the core of their armies being the courageous infantryman of their legions. It was not until quite late in the history of the Roman Empire that it proved necessary to increase the numbers of their cavalry significantly in order to repel attacks from their enemies—particularly those on the eastern frontiers, who had always been

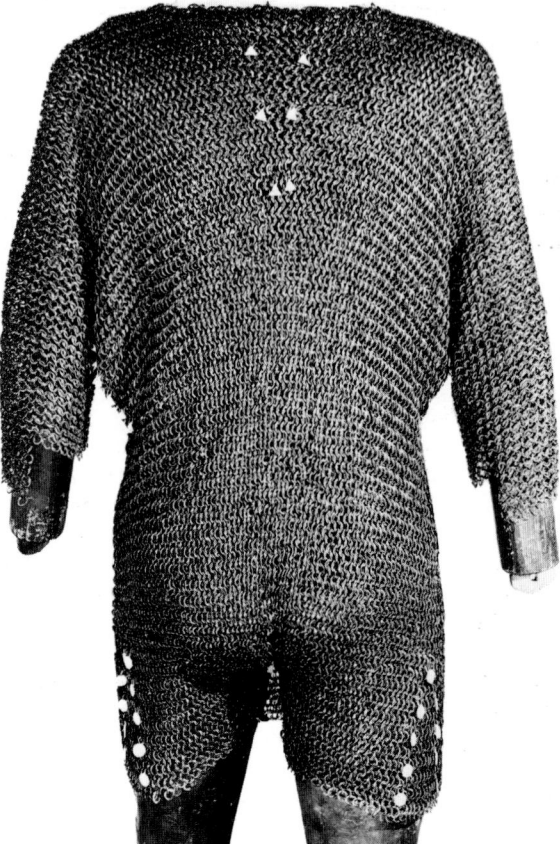

Above, left: A German engraving of the 16th century which shows the male and female costume of the period. The laced leather leggings of the man are of particular interest. **Left:** Armour formed a large part of equestrian military dress, often being worn over a shirt of chain mail, similar to the early example on the left. The suit of armour belonged to Henry VIII and can be seen in the Tower of London. **Below:** Chain mail stitched to leather jerkins was used by the Norman Knights of the Conquest. This particular example can be seen on the Bayeux tapestry.

Above: In this 15th-century picture of the hunt by Ucello the rough gartered trouser of previous years has given way to more elegant, tight-fitting nether garments made from wool or leather

great horsemen. Roman armour differed from that of the Greeks in its construction. The Greek cuirass comprised a back and a breast plate. Roman armour, however, was made of lames or strips of metal, which gave greater freedom of movement. A metal helmet, somewhat smaller than the Greek variety, was worn, with sandals or boots for the feet and legs. However, in the colder imperial provinces, Romans began to wear breeches. These, in their loose form with cross gartering, were to become the basis of European dress during the Dark Ages.

The Dark Ages themselves yield little material relating to the development of riding in Europe, but eastern art and literature are much more informative. They provide, amongst other things, fascinating information regarding the invention of the stirrup and its spread westwards. With saddles and stirrups in common use, it is safe to assume that the most comfortable form of male riding attire, even in hot countries, would have been some form of trousers and boots, the upper body being clothed in a garment suited to the climate.

The chief progression in armour at this time was the introduction of linked chain mail, a development of scale armour. With supple chain mail it was possible to make a single garment which gave protection to the body, neck, arms and thighs. Byzantine cavalrymen of around AD 500 are depicted wearing this type of shirt, together with breeches, boots and iron helmets.

Some 500 years later the Bayeux tapestry, depicting the Norman knights at the Battle of Hastings in 1066, shows that chain mail was still in favour. So, too, were conical helmets, not unlike those worn by Middle Eastern horsemen such as the Assyrians many centuries before. The great disadvantages of chain mail were its weight, which was supported mainly by the shoulders, and the constriction caused by creases forming when the arm was bent. Although it provided good protection against the weapons then in use, a heavy blow could drive it into the flesh, so it was necessary to wear thick, padded clothing under the mail to guard against this. Although it must have been extremely hot and uncomfortable to wear, mail was widely used until plate armour replaced it during the 15th and 16th centuries. At first, plate armour was used in conjunction with chain mail simply to give additional protection to knees, arms and shins, but its use gradually extended. By the middle of the 15th century—the golden age of armour—knights were covered in complete suits. These not only gave unyielding protection to the body but were so skilfully designed that they encouraged blows from an adversary's weapons to glance off, thus minimizing their effect. After this, chain mail was used only as a protection for the neck and to provide gussets at joints where the provision of plates was difficult.

Hunting and tournaments

As well as depicting cavalry, works of art of the period also provide a guide to the fashions adopted by horsemen and women when hunting or simply travelling from place to place. At the time of the Norman conquest male riding clothes, like everyday dress, consisted of a tunic worn over breeches. A woman either wore the normal long dress and sat sideways—alone, or pillion behind a man—or put on a divided skirt in which she could ride astride. Sitting astride was essential if she wished to ride at anything faster than a walk, since the true side-saddle, with a suitably positioned pommel over which the right leg could be hooked, was not invented until the early part of the 16th century. To sit sideways in a dress, a woman had to employ a man's saddle or a pad saddle, neither of which provided much security.

During the Middle Ages, the tournament became a popular pastime in many European countries, providing both a means of recreation and a good training for war. This provides an early example of the adaptation of general riding wear—at this time centring on military requirements—for a specific sporting purpose. Because the principal jousting weapon, the lance, was normally carried in the right hand and pointed across the horse's neck at the opponent's left side, specially designed tournament armour was devised. This was devised to give protection where it was most needed, being heavier and thicker on

CHAPTER TEN · RIDING DRESS

the left side than the right. It was also much more unwieldy than the armour used on the battlefield.

Flamboyance and fashion

From the time of the Crusades, the inhabitants of western Europe became aware of the silks and fine embroideries produced by the east and this soon had an impact on the riding clothes they wore. Although peasants and workmen continued to wear the simple, short tunic, great lords started to wear longer, richer clothes. Garments for both men and women began to be shaped to the body, with men generally wearing cloth or knitted woollen hose on the legs. Hoods gave way to hats, which at times became extremely large and elaborate, while the general increase in prosperity enjoyed by all classes of society was

Far left: Lady's driving habit of the late 18th century. **Left:** Military uniform of the late 17th century which has the high top boots of the period. **Below:** The 18th-century tapestry 'The March' from **The Art of War** shows clearly the type of boot which was in general use. The turned over tops could be pulled up for added protection in bad weather.

CLOTHES ANCIENT AND MODERN

Left: The well-dressed equestrienne at the turn of the century, when the modern side-saddle apron had yet to be introduced. **Right:** Two French fashion prints dated 1914 showing respectively a male and female swell.

reflected in all types of clothing. The courts of France and Burgundy in the 15th century, for instance, vied with each other for supremacy in this field. Their fashions spread to other European countries and, in due course, blended with the somewhat less flamboyant styles of the Italian Renaissance.

From the mid-17th century onwards men began to wear coats and waistcoats with breeches, the first step towards male clothing as we know it today. This started in France and soon spread across Europe. The great European riding masters of the 17th and 18th centuries rode in knee-length breeches, high boots, long-skirted coats and tricorn hats. All of these were pre-eminently practical, though they still incorporated a good deal of ornamentation as well.

Hard-riding squires

While Continental riders tended to specialize in elegant high school work, Englishmen were taking up the much more vigorous pastime of riding to hounds. Dispensing with unnecessary frills and decoration, these hard-riding sportsmen laid the foundations of what is today the accepted dress for universally popular equestrian sports.

Coats, breeches, boots and hats were devised as essentially practical items of equipment, the velvets, silks and satins of France and Spain being abandoned in favour of more serviceable woollens and leather. The tops of high boots were turned down below the knee to give greater freedom of movement to the leg when riding across country, a fashion which led to the hunting boot as it exists today, with its tan top. Decoration was mostly confined to cuffs, collars and buttons, distinctions which some hunts still employ. During the reign of George III, the tricorn hat finally gave way to the velvet cap which is now worn by riders, both male and female, the world over. By this time, too, most women had elected to ride side-saddle, dressed in long, flowing habits of great elegance, their long hair piled high on their heads and topped with elaborate hats.

The Englishman's other great sporting interest, which took fire and spread across the world with the development of the Thoroughbred, was racing. Here the essential requirements of lightweight clothing and colours easily identifiable from a distance have remained constant down the centuries; today's jockey's outfit of light leather boots, tight breeches and silks in the colours of the horse's owner have changed little since the earliest days of racing.

As far as the military was concerned, the introduction and development of firearms during the 16th and 17th centuries signalled the end of plate armour. While the armourers did not find it difficult to produce bullet-proof protection, the result became so heavy as to be quite impracticable. By the 17th century, only the metal cuirass and helmet were retained and by the 18th century all but the ornamental gorget worn by officers had disappeared. From then until the horse himself became obsolete, cavalrymen wore variations on the theme of breeches and boots, or trousers, with coats of varying lengths, plus helmets of differing degrees of elaboration,

CHAPTER TEN · RIDING DRESS

which served as a useful means of identification on the battlefield.

Clothing for cowboys

In North America a whole new genre of clothing was produced as a result of the rise of the cattle-ranching industry. Cowboys needed clothes which were hard-wearing but comfortable, cool in summer but warm in winter. They began by copying the clothes of the Mexican *vaquero*, but gradually adapted them to their own special requirements. From the leg-protecting leather flaps which formed part of the Mexican saddle, the cowboy devised chaps, which were usually made of cowhide or sheepskin and took the form of a pair of seatless leggings, worn over trousers for warmth, grip and protection.

The world-famous stetson hat was designed and introduced by John Batterson Stetson to provide a better fit than the high-crowned sombrero of the Mexicans. The stetson's wide brim protected the wearer from the summer sun, while in winter it could be tied down to cover the ears. It was useful for scooping up water for drinking. Then Levi Strauss, a New York tailor who travelled west to search for gold, invented the ideal cloth for cowboy trousers—denim. His 'Levi's', made of toughly twilled cotton, with flat non-twisting seams, a low waist, narrow hips and tapered legs to fit easily inside boots, were comfortable and practical.

In addition, a cowboy usually wore a woollen or flannel shirt with full sleeves to give maximum freedom of movement, and a sleeveless vest of stout cloth or buckskin. This was sometimes lined with sheepskin. Round his neck he wore a cotton bandana, which could be pressed into service when necessary as a bandage, a face mask or a filter for drinking water. Boots had to be extremely tough and, in addition to riding requirements, were fitted with high, forward-sloping heels which the cowboy could dig into the ground when holding on to a roped calf. Ornamentation tended to be restricted to hat bands and belts.

The clothes of today

The 20th century has seen significant changes in riding, notably the widespread abandonment of the side-saddle and the introduction of unisex clothes for men and women. The invention of man-made fibres have also had an effect on the design of riding clothes. Although in some countries horses are still used in their traditional rôle as working animals and their riders still wear traditional local dress—the herdsman of the Central Asian plains, for instance, wears a costume not unlike that of the nomads of 2,500 years ago—a great percentage of people who ride horses today do so not out of necessity but for pleasure, which includes competing in various sports. In this field the costume of breeches or jodhpurs, a style brought to the west from India, boots, shirt, tie or hunting tie, jacket and velvet covered cap, has become universally accepted for both sexes, while for less formal riding many people adopt more casual styles akin to those of the American cowboy. Unless a completely new use is invented for the horse it seems unlikely that these styles will undergo any radical changes in the near future.

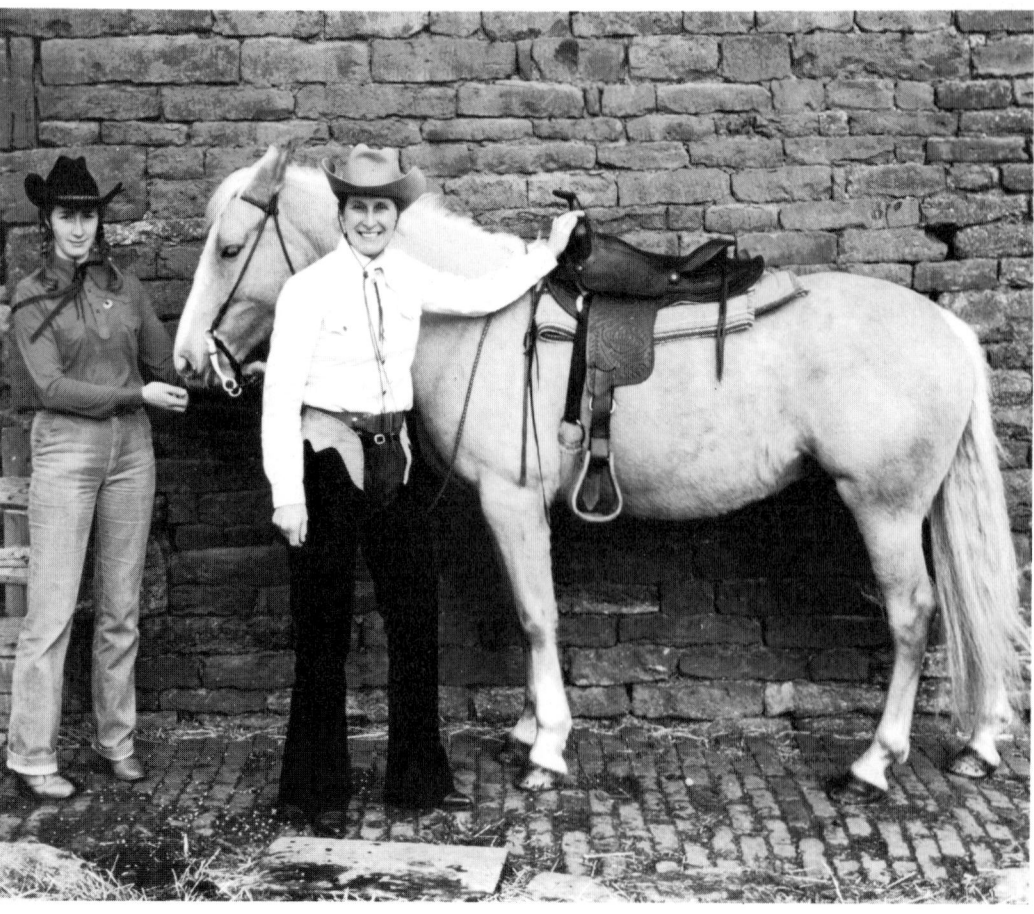

Right: Western dress is always practical and sometimes colourful as well. Both these riders wear stetsons which are sufficiently wide-brimmed to give shade from the sun and they also wear Western boots. The rider on the right is wearing a pair of tough leather chaps over her blue jeans.

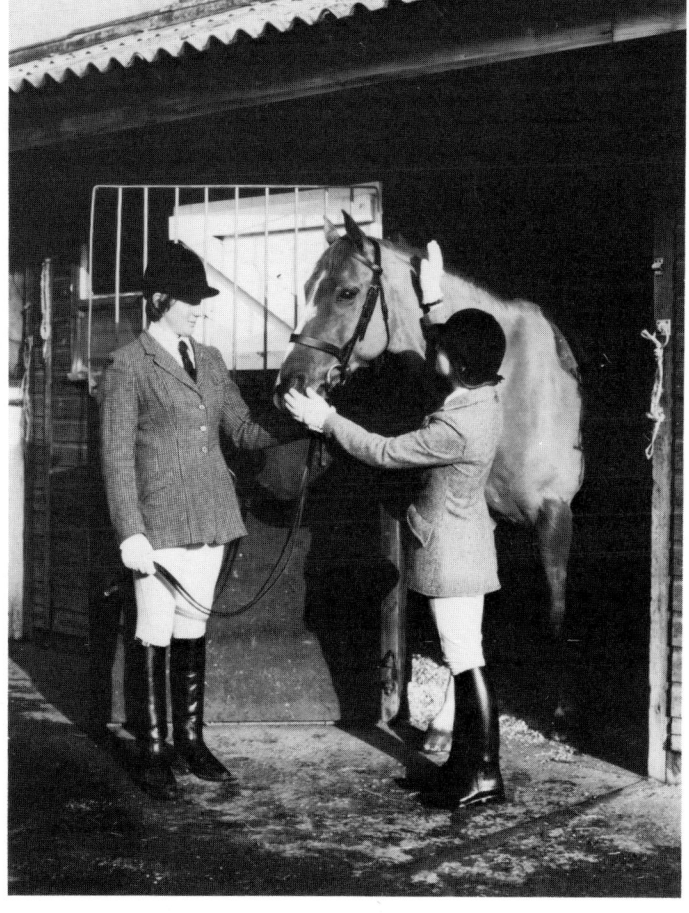

Top, left: Correct dress for advanced or even three-day event dressage is silk hat, hunting tie, black tail coat, white breeches and black boots. **Centre:** For cross-country, riders wear clothes copied from the steeplechase jockey; coloured jersey and crash helmet with a silk cover in whatever colours are favoured. **Right:** The polo player also needs a helmet for protection and frequently wears leather knee guards too. White breeches and brown boots are *de rigeur*.
Above: Formal hunting dress for a woman includes a black or navy coat and either a bowler hat or cap. Men who are members of the hunt may wear scarlet coats.
Right: Informal hacking dress is typified by the tweed jacket, neat collar and tie or polo-neck jumper.

Riding Dress · **Whips and Spurs**

In all probability, artificial aids have been used by riders ever since man first mounted a horse. Certainly it is known that there were accepted aids for training horses more than 2,000 years ago, since the Greek authority Xenophon described their application when teaching a horse to jump in his writings on horsemanship.

In their earliest form, whips would have been no more than switches cut from convenient bushes or trees—indeed one notable body of riders, the Spanish Riding School in Vienna, still employs this type of whip today. However, over the years man devised whips which were much longer-lasting, while whip-making itself became something of an art.

The structure of the whip

The main part of a conventional riding whip is the stock, which tapers from the hand-part to the lash end. Some whips are provided with a hand grip at the broad end and a plaited leather lash, or leather loop, known as a keeper, at the other, while others are left quite plain. Much depends on the use for which they are intended.

In former times, the centre, or stock, of a riding whip was made from whalebone, though in fact this was not bone at all, but rather a horny, elastic substance found in the upper jaws of certain whales. Carefully cut lengths of cane, known as splicings, were fixed round the whalebone with pitch. Then came the most skilful part of the whip-maker's art, which lay in the

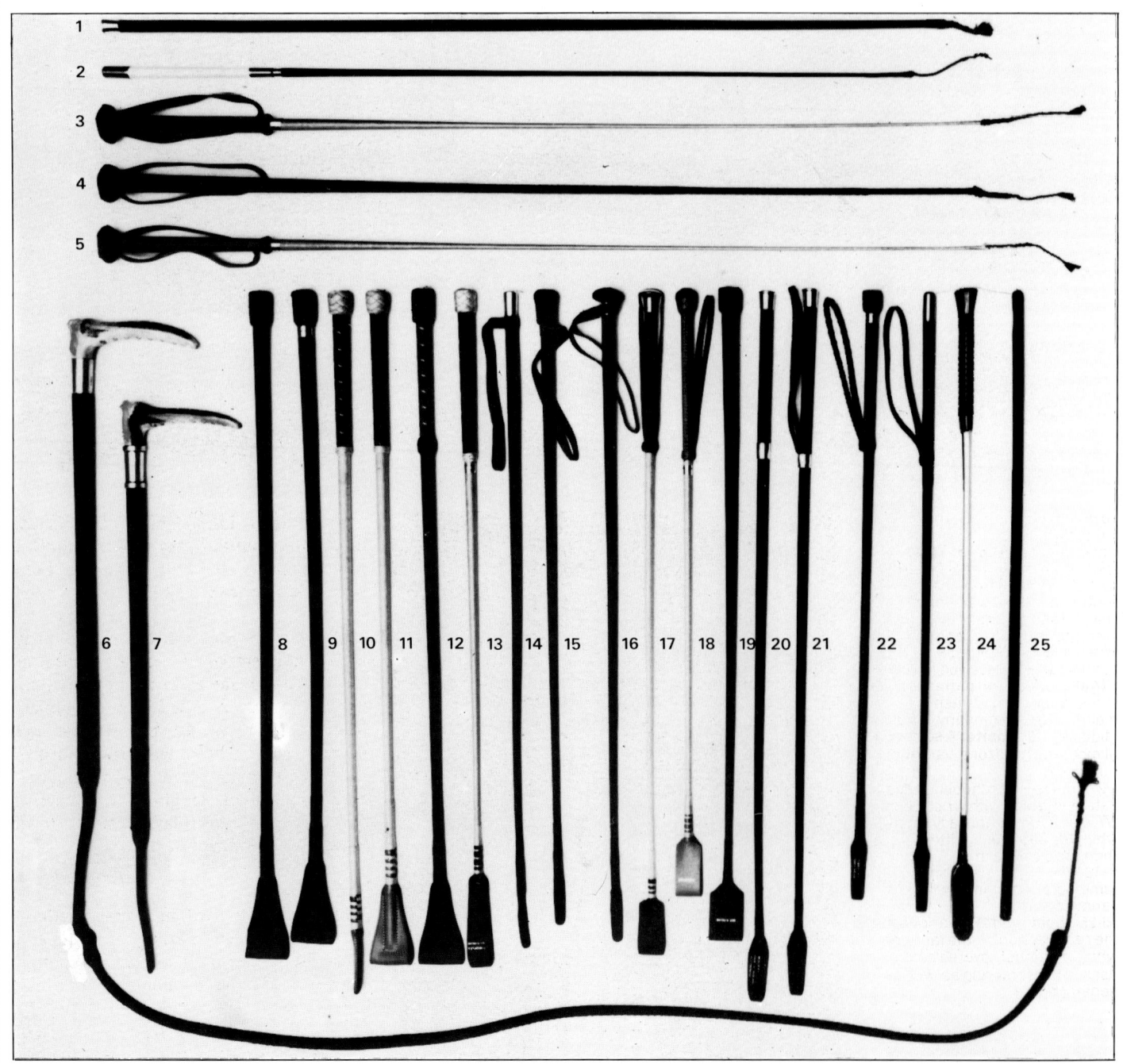

WHIPS AND SPURS

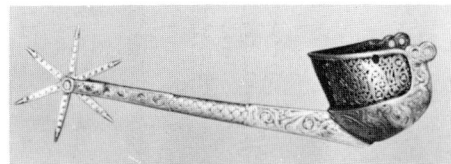

Top: A 16th-century German multi-rowelled spur of exquisite workmanship. **Above:** Three spurs from the Tower of London collection dating from the 15th-16th century. The spur was a mark of chivalry and originally the prerogative of those of gentle birth. When dubbed a knight, a gentleman also received his spurs.
Right: Spur and bit patterns filed in the foundry of a British manufacturing company in the Midlands. **Opposite:** A selection of modern whips for a variety of purposes:
1/2 Dressage or schooling whips
3-5 Polo whips with wrist loops
6/7 Gentleman's and lady's hunting whip, the latter being fitted with a thong and cord lash
8-13 Six race whips (or show jumping/cross country whips) of various patterns
14-25 Riding whips of various sorts, the cane version on the far right which is leather covered being used in the show ring as well as for general riding

planing down of this stock until it had just the right amount of play in it and until it bent equally well in all directions. Both these features are vital attributes of a good whip.

Fibreglass, which can be tapered fairly easily, now serves the same function as the old whalebone and cane combination. Steel is sometimes used in the manufacture of cheap whips, but it does not produce such a light, well-balanced product as does the more expensive fibreglass. The stock is given a protective covering either of plain leather or of braided rawhide, gut or thread.

Types of whip

Whips fall into two main types—those used by horsemen as an aid to riding and those used for specific jobs carried out on horseback. The latter include bull whips and stock whips, which are used by mounted herdsmen. Such whips consist of a short cane or wooden handle to which is

CHAPTER TEN · RIDING DRESS

attached a long plaited leather thong. Hunting whips are made in a similar fashion, having a plaited leather thong fitted with a silk or cord lash at one end and a horn handle at the other. The thong is used to control hounds, the handle for holding open gates.

A variety of riding whips has been developed for different purposes. Long schooling whips, which come in various lengths, can be used to activate the horse's hindlegs or to reinforce the action of the rider's leg without it being necessary for him to take his hand off the rein. Jumping and racing whips are a good deal shorter (under the rules of show jumping a whip may not be more than 2ft 6in long) and are used to encourage or correct a horse. There is also a wide range of canes, either plain or leather covered, which are generally used for showing purposes. In addition, the lungeing whip is used when training a horse by the dismounted trainer. Like driving whips, these need to be carefully balanced if they are to handle well; the best are normally of cane, steel being considered too heavy.

Spurs—design and use

The design of spurs has in a way come full circle since the aid was first devised. Early models consisted of a short metal goad strapped to the rider's boot, which is basically the same pattern as the one generally used in competitive equestrian sports today. Over the centuries, however, spurs underwent many modifications, at times becoming fearsome weapons. Generally speaking, the longer the rider's leg, the longer the spur must be if contact is to be made with the horse's side without undue movement of the rider's foot. For a long time horsemen rode with straight legs and this, coupled with the very restrictive leg armour used in combat and the rather common, cold-blooded type of horse much in evidence during the Middle Ages, led to the development of long-shanked spurs with enormous, sharp rowels.

Nowadays, spurs of this type are extremely limited in use. They can be seen on the heels of riders like the South American gauchos, who still use sharp rowels, and North American bronc riders, who favour blunted ones. They are also used on some ceremonial military occasions. The spurs in most common use are the short curve-necked pattern and the straight-necked pattern, which may either be blunt or fitted with a small rowel. The spikes of the latter are not unduly sharp and the longest neck does not, as a rule exceed about 1½in.

AMERICAN WHIPS AND SPURS

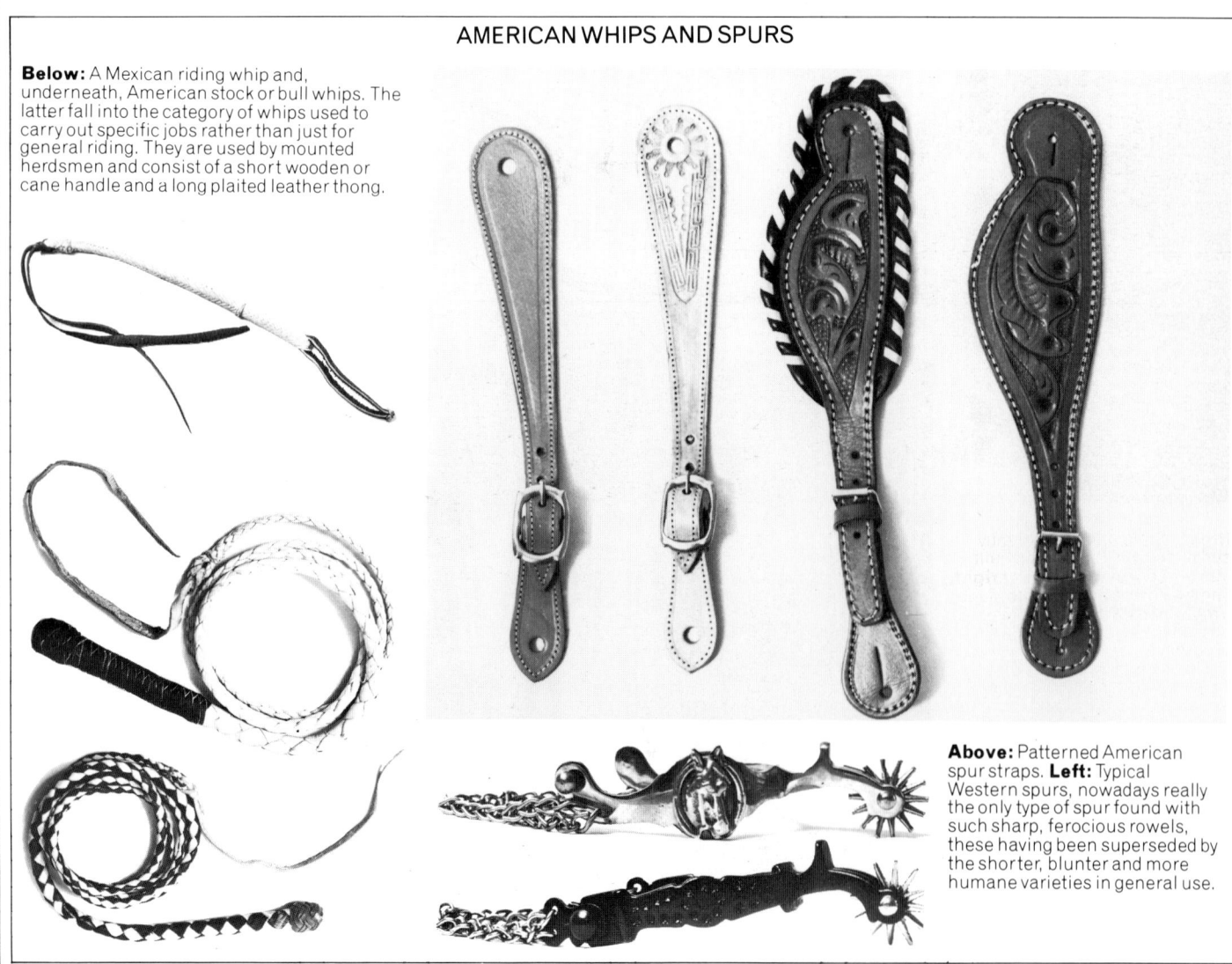

Below: A Mexican riding whip and, underneath, American stock or bull whips. The latter fall into the category of whips used to carry out specific jobs rather than just for general riding. They are used by mounted herdsmen and consist of a short wooden or cane handle and a long plaited leather thong.

Above: Patterned American spur straps. **Left:** Typical Western spurs, nowadays really the only type of spur found with such sharp, ferocious rowels, these having been superseded by the shorter, blunter and more humane varieties in general use.

USING WHIPS AND SPURS

Top, left to right: The hunting whip held in the conventional manner with the thong and lash hanging down; a dressage or schooling whip which is used behind the leg to support the action of the latter. It is of fairly rigid construction so that a single tap only need be given; a longer, more flexible schooling whip which can be used to activate the hindleg.
Left: A plain, leather-covered showing or riding cane.

Right: The spur fitted correctly and resting on a small stop built into the back of the boot. **Far right:** The spur being brought into play by a movement of the leg.

Index

A

Abbot-Davies Balancing Rein 190, *191*
    three positions *191*

B

Back chain 180
Backband 153
Balance of horse *see Point of balance*
Bandages 216, 219
    crêpe 216
    exercise 216, *217*
    leg *216*
    on showjumper *217*
    principal uses 216
    tail 216, *216*
    travelling *217*
    woollen stable 216, 219
Banner blanket 211
Barnum rein 194, *195*
Bearing reins *see Check reins*
Belly band 180
Benoist-Gironière, Yves:
    horse-breaking 194
Bitless bridles *135*, 145
    Blair's pattern *145*
    misuse of term 'hackamore' 141
    three types *144*
    use of 145
    William Stone Bitless Pelham 145, *145*
Bits, early development and use 17-18
    19th century 37
    Assyria 15, *17*
    Classical riding 33-4
    curb 18
    introduction of 10-11
    introduction of jointed mouthpiece 17
    Roman *21*
    'rough' (Greeks) 17
    snaffle 11, *16*, 19, 20, 26-7
    use by knights 26-7, *29*, 29, 31
    Western Asia 17
Bits and bitting systems 116-29
    Chifney 206, *207*
    double bridle (bradoon and curb) 123, 126
    fitting of 139
    for young horse being broken 192
    gag 129, *129*
    harness racing 167-8, *168*, 172, 173
    Latchford 116
    lorinery (manufacture) *118-21*
    manufacturers 117
    military (Army Universal Pelham) 230-1
    modern principles 116-17
    overcheck *172*, 173
    pair harness 161
    parts of horse's head affected *116*
    Pelham bridle 126, 129
    principal groupings 117
    Segundo's *New Method of Bitting Horses* 116, *117*
    selection of curb chains *127*
    single harness 154, *155*
    snaffle 117, 122-3, *124-5*
    tandem harness 157
    Western curb 143, *143*, 145
Blinkers on harness bridles:
    origins of use 13
    racers 173, *173*
    reasons for use 13-14
    working horses 178-9
Blinkers on racehorses 14
Bodkin method of plough harnessing 185
Boots and pads 218-19, 219-21
    brushing boots 218, 219, 220-1
    brushing ring *219*, 221
    coronet boots *220*
    cup fetlock boot *218*
    for harness racers 173, *173*
    good leather boots *218*
    heel boots 221
    hock boots *218*, *220*
    kicking boots 209, *209*
    knee caps 218, 219-20, *219*
    over-reach (bell) boots 221, *221*
    plastic travelling boots 219
    polo boots *220*, 221
    tendon boots *218*, 219, 221
Bosal 141, *143*
    two-rein *145*
Bradoon 123
Breaking a horse 193
    correct position of trainer *193*
Breaking aids 192-5
    Barnum rein 194, *195*
    basic equipment 192
    crupper 192
    first bit 192
    Galvayne's system 192-4, *195*
    long-reins 192, *194*
    lunge cavesson 192, *193*
    lunge rein 192
    lunge whip 192, *193*
    Rarey's *195*
    roller 192
Breast collar *see Single harness, etc*
Breastplate 81-2
    'Aintree' pattern, two types *81*
    for hunting 81
    for racing 82
    leather hunting *81*
    reasons for use 81
    Western *97*, 98
Breeching (cart harness) 180
Bridle, draught 178-9
    use of blinkers 178-9
Bridle, fitting of *138*, 139, *139*
Bridle, parts of *134*, *137*
Bridles, early development:
    Assyrian 14, *15*, 15
    Elamite *15*
    introduction of 10
    Persia 15-17
Bridles, manufacture of 53
Bridles, types and fittings 134-9
    bitless *135*, *144*, 145
    browbands *137*
    brush pricker *135*
    ceremonial 233
    double 123, 126
    gag 129, *129*, *135*
    hunting snaffle *135*
    hunting Weymouth *134*
    leather, buckles and reins *136*, *137*, *139*
    lightweight show *134*
    military (Pelham) *230*
    Pelham 126, 129, *135*
    rubber cheek guard *135*
    snaffle 117, 122-3
    stallion 208, *208*
    Weymouth *134*
Bridles for driving harness *see Single harness, etc; also Trotting equipment*

C

Californian saddle 96, *98*
    typical modern *102*
Caprilli, Federico 38-40
Cart harness 179-82
    back chain or ridger 180
    belly band 180
    breeching 180
    complete set on horse *179*
    crupper 179-80
    harnessing process in stages 180-1
    housen 179
    martingale 180
    meeter strap 179
    pad or saddle 179
    Shire ready to move *181*
    shutting in and out 180, *182*
    tugs 180
Cavesson:
    lunge 192, *193*
    plain 132, *132*
Ceremonial trappings 224-37
    American Indians *236*
    bridles and bitting 230-1
    cavalry furniture 231-3, *233*
    decoration of working horses *176-7*, 224
    mercenary pioneers 226-9
    military tradition 225-6
    pack saddle 229-30
    Pazyryk tomb finds 224-5, *225*, *226*
    Royal coaches, etc *234-5*
    Royal Mews collection saddles *227*, *228*, *230*, *231*, *232*, *237*
    US tradition 233, *236*
Chain harness *see Plough harness*
Chalon, Henry Bernard:
    George IV's Persian Horses 140, *140*
Chambon 189, *189*
    effect of 189
    parts of 189
Check reins 14, 171, *173*
Chifney bit 206, *207*
Children's saddles 76-7
    19th-century donkey two-seater *77*
    19th-century quilted *77*
    basket 76, *77*
    'Cobbar' felt *77*
    felt pad 76-7, *77*
    flexible leather pad *77*
Chin strap *173*
Cinches:
    centre-fire rigging 101
    cord *97*
    forward 96
    'in-skirt' rigging 101
    pleasure saddles 101
    rear or flank 96
    single- and double-rigging systems 96
    woven hair *97*
Classical riding, origins 33
    bits, etc 33-4
    breaking the horse 33
    saddle 34-5

Cleaning tack *200-1*
Clothes *see Riding dress*
Coach whip 164, *165*
Collar *see also Single harness, etc*
Collar, draught 178
    c. 880 AD *178*
    construction 178
    early 1900s, three examples *178*
    forewale and afterwale 178
    'improved' designs 178
    open-topped 178
Coronet boots *220*
Cowboy, clothes and saddlery *see Western dress, saddles*
Cross-country dress 247
Crupper (*see also Single harness, etc*):
    cart harness 179-80
    for young horse being broken 192
Curb bit 123, 126, 140
    16th-century German *140*
    Turkish design *141*
    Western 143, *143*, 145
Curb bit, early development 18
    use by knights 29, *29*, 31
    use in early Classical riding 33-4
Curb chains, selection of *127*

D

De Gogue 189-90
    points of restraint 190
    two positions 190, *190*
Distas bending tackle 191, *191*
Distas CP saddle 56
Double bridle 123, 126
    bradoon 123
    correct fitting *139*
    curb bit 123, 126
    diagram showing action *126*
    fixed-cheek Weymouth *127*
    length of cheek 126
    parts of *134*, *137*
    shape of curb mouthpiece 126
    slide-cheek Weymouth 126, *127*
Draw rein 188-9, *189*
    basic 188
    other forms 188-9
Dressage, correct dress 247
Dressage saddles:
    English-made 68, *69*
    German 69
    main features 67-9
    modern *68*
    Stubben 69
    tree 68
Driving harness (*see also Harness, Single harness, etc*) 148-85
    farm horses 176-85
    handling reins and whip 162-3, *162-3*
    present day 148-63
    trotting equipment 166-75
    whips 164-5
Duke of Newcastle 35, *35*, 188

E

Eclipse, picture by Stubbs *36-7*
European hackamore 145
    action of 145
    Blair's pattern *145*
    use of 145
    William Stone Bitless Pelham 145, *145*

F

Facsimile saddles 74, 75-6
Farm harness 176-85
   blinkers 178-9
   cart 179-82
   cart, complete set 179
   development of breast harness 176-7
   draught bridle 178-9
   first farm horses 176-8
   hames 178
   horses in tandem showing wheel and lead harness 185
   invention of the collar 177-8
   plough 182-5
   reins 179
   trace 185
   types 179-85
   working collar 178
Fiador 141
Foal slip 209, 209
Foxhunting, origins of 35-6

G

Gag bridle 129
   action, Balding 129
   Balding 129
   Duncan twisted 129
   eggbutt Cheltenham 129
   Salisbury 129
Gaited horse, attitude in movement 73
Gaited horse saddle 72, 73
   Walking Horse 72
Galvayne's system of horse-breaking 192-4, 195
Gaucho's saddle 21
General purpose saddle 65, 66-7
   British-made, good example 64-5
   cut-back head, three versions 67
   Jabez Cliff 66
   parts of 49
   Stubben Parzival 67
   'working hunter's' 65
Gibson, Colonel F E:
   Distas CP saddle 56
   Toptani saddle 41, 56
Gidden:
   Hermes pattern saddle 63
Girth sleeve, for soft horses 80-1
Girths:
   Atherstone 78-9, 78
   Balding 78, 78
   buckles 80, 80
   cord 79
   dressage (Lonsdale) 78
   Fitzwilliam (side-saddle) 79
   lampwick 78, 80
   leather 78-80
   length of 81
   nylon 79, 80
   racing 80
   Three-Fold 78, 79
   tubular web with rubber centre 79, 80
   variation of 'Humane' pattern 79
   webbing 79, 80
   woven horse-hair 78
Great Horse see Knights and the Great Horse

Grisone 33, 34
Grooming 202-3
   basic kit 202
   cactus cloth 203
   clipping 202
   grass-kept horse 202-3
   quartering 202
   rubber or plastic curry comb 203
   'setting fair' 202
   stabled horse 202, 203
   quartering 202
   strapping 202
   very muddy or sweaty horse 203
   wisp 203

H

Hackamore see Bitless bridles; European, Western, hackamore
Hacking dress, informal 247
Hance, Colonel Jack 56
Harness:
   cart 179-82
   farm 176-85
   four horse tandem 160
   handling reins and whip 162-3, 162-3
   historical accoutrements 148
   pair 158, 159, 161
   plough 182-5
   showing 148, 150
   single 148-9, 150-5
   tandem 154, 156-8
   team 161-2
   trace 185
   trotting equipment 166-75
   unicorn 161, 162
   variety of trace ends 158
   whips 164-5
Harness, early development 11-13
   Asiatic influence 13
   detail, Assyrian 14
   Egyptian 12-13
   Greek racing chariot 18-19
   Persian 12
   Roman improvements to yoke 12-13
   yoke system 11-12
Head pole 168, 169
Headstall, latigo 141, 143
Heel boots 221
Hermes pattern saddles:
   by Gidden 63
   by Jabez Cliff 63
Hermes show saddle 71
High School Movements, 18th-century prints 32
History and development 10-41
   Asiatic influence on harness 13
   blinkers and bearing reins 13-14
   British tradition 35-7
   Caprilli watershed 38-41
   carriage horse 37
   curb bit 18
   dominating the horse 33-5
   Duke of Newcastle 35, 35
   first equipment 10-11
   growth of saddlery 14-16
   influence of de la Guérinière 35
   influence of polo on saddle design 36
   invention of the stirrup 24-5
   jumping saddle 41
   Knights and the Great Horse 26-31, 33
   late 19th-century innovations 36-7

   origins of foxhunting and the hunting saddle 35-6
   Persia 16-17
   riding masters 33, 33
   riding styles, heavy and light cavalry 24-5
   Roman improvements to harness 12-13
   saddlery for American gaited horses 37-8
   saddles 18-24
   search for greater control 17-18
   shift in emphasis from east to west 25-6
   yokes and harness 11-12
Hobbles 171
   cross 171
   fit of 171
   fitting on horse 175
   half 171
   service 208-9, 209
Hock boots 218, 220
Holsters (cavalry) 232
Horsebox 204-5
   professional's 205
   trailer 205
   with side-ramp 204
Horseshoe, invention and early use 20
   early Greco/Roman 19
Housen 179
Housing 231-2
Hunting dress, woman's 247
Hunting saddle:
   conventional, deficiencies 63
   early examples 56
   origins of 36

I J

Inflatable saddle 76
Jabez Cliff saddles:
   general purpose 66
   Hermes pattern 63
   lightweight jumping 62
Jumping saddle:
   development of 41
   lightweight 62
   Jabez Cliff lightweight 62
   Pariani 57
   Pariani lightweight 61
   Stubben 'Danloux' pattern 60
   Toptani 56-62 (passim), 58, 59

K

Kimblewick bit 128, 129
Knee caps 218, 219-20, 219
Knights and the Great Horse 26-31, 33
   15th-cen. French tournament 31
   battle of San Romano (Uccello) 26-7
   body armour to counter long-bow 29
   chamfron 29
   curb bit 29, 29, 31
   German armour, late 15th cen. 29
   jousting saddle 31, 33
   knight in full armour 28
   knight's seat 29
   Luttrell Psalter illustration 30
   Norman (Bayeux tapestry) 26
   ring bit 29, 31
   St George killing dragon 26

   snaffle bits 26-7
   tournament and joust 31

L

Latchford, Benjamin 116
Latigo headstall 141, 143
Lines 182
Lip cord 173
Long-reins 192, 194
Loose box 198, 198, 199
Lorinery 118-21
   metals used 118, 119
Lunge cavesson 192
   correctly fitted 193
   with side rings 192, 193
Lunge rein 192
Lunge whip 192, 193

M

McClellan saddle 98, 100, 233, 236, 236
Mameluke (see also Ring bit) 24
Manger 198
Manufacture of bridles 53
Manufacture of saddles 44-53
   cleansing and liming of hides 44, 45, 45
   covering and padding 51-2, 52
   currying and finishing of leather 46, 46-7, 48
   cutting parts 52
   fitting panel 52, 53
   making trees 48, 50
   parts of a saddle 49
   possible defects in hides 44-5
   quality of leather 44
   scudding and rounding of hides 45, 45
   setting the seat 50-1, 52
   storing top quality leather 48
   tanning 45-6
   types of tree 48
   use of inferior materials 52-3
Martingale, false see Single harness, etc
Martingales 130-1
   bib 130-1, 131
   for polo pony 130
   Irish 131, 131
   Market Harborough or German rein 131, 131
   on cart harness 180
   pulley 131
   rein stops 131, 131
   running 130-1, 130
   standing or 'fast' 130, 130
Mecate 141, 143
Meeter strap 179
Military furniture 231-3, 233
   holsters 232
   housing 231-2
   officer's charger, c. 1860 232-3
   shabraque 231
   valise 233
Military saddles 226-37 (passim)
   American Indians 236
   Hungarian pioneers 226
   McClellan 233, 236, 236
   modern army officer's 229
   O'Dwyer and Nolan 227-8
   Polish, 17th century 232
   Royal Mews collection 227, 228, 230, 231, 232, 237
   Universal Pattern (Nolan) 229,
   Universal Purpose Pack 229-30

253

INDEX

Mountings, saddle 78-85
Mucking-out tools 199, *199*
Murphy blind 169, *169*

N

New Zealand rugs 211, *214*
Nolan 227, 230
Nolan saddle 229, *229*
Noseband, early development:
  Egypt 17
  Persia 16
Nosebands 132-3
  Australian Cheeker 133, *133*
  drop 132-3, *132*
  Flash 132-3, *132*
  Grackle, Figure 8 or cross-over 132, 133, *133*
  Kineton or Puckle 133, *133*
  plain cavesson 132, *132*
  raised show-type *132*
  sheepskin 133, *133*
Numnahs 86-7, *86-7*
  advantages and disadvantages 86-7
  felt 86
  foam plastic 86
  man-made fabrics 86
  seat cover 87, *87*
  sheepskin 86

O

O'Dwyer 227-8
Overcheck, Raymond *172*, 173
Overcheck bits 173
  jointed *172*, 173
  plain standard *172*
  Speedway *172*, 173
Overcheck or check rein 171, 173
Over-reach boots 221, *221*
Owen show saddle 70, 71-2
Owen side-saddles 112, *112*

P

Pair harness 158, *159*, 161
  attaching reins to bridle 158, 161
  bits 161
  differences from single 158
  fitting reins 158
  hames showing linking and false martingale *159*
  in position on horse *159*
  items on horses (engraving) *159*
  pad showing hame tug buckle *159*
  putting on collars, etc 158
  well turned out pair of bays *161*
Pariani saddles:
  early 'forward seat' 40, 56
  lightweight jumping *61*
  modern jumping *57*
Parker, Messrs George:
  Toptani saddle 41, 56
Pazyryk tomb finds 20, *22*, 34, 224-5, *225*, 226
Pelham bridle 126, 129
  advantage of 129
  arched mouth 126, 129
  in position *128*
  Kimblewick (Spanish Jumping) bit *128*, 129

mullen mouthpiece 129
original (Hartwell) mouthpiece 126
parts of 134, 137
rubber mullen mouth *128*
Scamperdale bit *128*
SM bit *128*
Pignatelli 33, 34
Plough harness 182-5
  Bodkin fashion 185
  detailed illustrations *182*
  drawing implement fitted with pole *185*
  harnessing variations 183, 185
  reins (lines) 183
  Shire in single harness *183*
  Shires in traditional English harness *185*
  two or more horses abreast 182-3
  unicorn method 183, 185
Point of balance of horse 62-3
  at increased pace 62
  in collected movements 63
  when jumping 62
Poll guard 213
Polo dress *247*
Polo equipment:
  boots (for horse) 220, *221*
  martingales 130
  saddles 75

R

Racing martingales 130-1
Racing saddles 104-5
  changing styles 105, *105*
  construction 104-5
  conventional tree *104*
  design and fitting 105
  exercise pad tree *104*
  flexible exercise pad *104*
  heavier pattern exercise *104*
  popular exercise, America *104*
  weight 104
  weight cloth *104*, 105
Rarey's breaking aids *195*
Raymond overcheck *172*, 173
Reins 136, 137, 139
  Barnum 194, *195*
  draw 188-9, *189*
  extra grip 137
  long- 192, 194
  nylon 137, 139
  plain 137
  side- 188
Reins for driving harness (*see also* Single harness, etc):
  how to handle 162-3, *162-3*
Reins for farm harness 179, 183
Ridger 180
Riding dress 240-51
  17th and 18th centuries 244-6
  advanced dressage *247*
  ancient Egyptians 240
  ancient Greeks 240-2, *241*
  ancient Romans 242-3
  ancient Siberian tribes 242
  Assyrians 240, *240*
  cowboys *246*
  cross-country *247*
  early 20th century *245*
  formal hunting, woman's *247*
  informal hacking *247*
  Middle Ages 243-4
  modern 246, *247*
  polo *247*
  Scythians 242
  whips and spurs 248-51

Riding halls, origins 33
Riding masters 33-5
Ring bit, early development:
  use by knights 29, *31*
  use by X Group 24
Rodeo saddles *see* Broncho busting saddles
Roller, breaking *192*
Rugs and travelling dress 210-15
  all-purpose rugs 211-12
  American sheets 214, *215*
  anti-sweat sheet 210, *211*
  banner blanket 211
  day and exercise rugs 212, *215*
  extra warm Australian rug *215*
  jute night rug 210
  Lancer turnout rug 211-12
  New Zealand rug 211, *214*
  nylon quilted rug 210-11, *214*
  rain sheets 212, *214-15*
  summer sheet 211, *212*
  Thermatextron rug 211, *215*
  traditional striped blanketing *211*
  travelling dress 212-13
  vintage American *212*
  winter stable rug 210
  Witney blanket 210

S

Saddle, early development 18-24
  16th-century Italian *34*
  Classical riding 34-5
  hunting 36
  influence of Caprilli 38-41
  jumping 41
  Sarmatian 21-2
  Sasanian 24
  Scythian 20-1
  Selle Royale 33, 34, 35
  Tang Dynasty, China *25*
  X Group *22*, 24
Saddle, manufacture of *see* Manufacture
Saddle, parts of 49
Saddle, to clean 200-1
Saddle, to fit 88-9, *88-9*
  clearance of withers and backbone 88
  fat horse 89
  importance of correct fit 88
  length of saddle 89
  rules 88-9
  sitting level on back 88
  tree 88
Saddle, twentieth century 56-89
  children's 76-7
  conventional, deficiencies in competition 63
  facsimile *74*, 75-6
  first prototypes 56
  fitness for purpose 56-69
  gaited horse 72
  gaucho's 21
  general purpose and dressage 64-5, 66-9
  German influence 69
  inflatable 76
  jumping (Toptani, etc) 56-62
  mountings 78-85
  numnahs, etc 86-7
  points of balance of horse 62-3
  polo *75*
  show 70-2
  some variations 70-7
  stockman's 72-4
  Toptani, disadvantages 63, 66
  trekking 74-5

Saddle cover, waterproof 87
Saddlecloths 86, 87
Saddles, specialist 92-113
  military 226-37 (*passim*)
  police work 229
  racing 104-5
  side-saddles 106-13
  Western 92-103
Saddles for driving harness *see* Single harness, etc; *also* Trotting equipment
Saddles for farm harness *see* Cart harness
Santini, Piero 40
Santini saddles 40, 56
Scamperdale bit *128*
Schooling aids 188-91
  Abbot-Davies Balancing Rein 190, 191
  Chambon 189, *189*
  controversial methods 190-1
  de Gogue 189-90, *190*
  Distas bending tackle 191, *191*
  draw rein 188-9, *189*
  side-rein 188, *188*
Segundo, Don Juan 116, *117*, 230
Selle Royale 33, 34, 35
Shabraque 231
Shadow rolls 169, *170*, 171
Show saddle 70-2
  Hermes ('English Saddle') 71
  modern straight-cut 71
  Owen 70, 71-2
  panel 70-1
  point strap 71
  stirrup bar 70
  tree 70, *70*
Show tack 204, 206-7
  Arabian horses 206, *207*
  brood mares 206
  leading from a bit 206-7
  stallions 206, *207*
  visitors from the Continent and USA 206, *206*
  yearling colts 206, *207*
Showing harness 148, *150*
  modern designs and materials 150
  most popular 148, 150
Side-rein 188, *188*
Side-saddle 106-13
  19th-century *106*
  changes dictated by fashion 108-9
  c. 1900 model *112*
  detail of doeskin and cut-back head *111*
  early designs 106
  fitting horse 112-13, *113*
  fitting rider 112
  great *marques* (balance) 109, 112
  heyday 109, 112
  improvements, 1800s 106, 108
  introduction of dipped seat 106, 108
  invention of balance strap 108, *109*
  invention of 'leaping head' (Pellier) 108
  lining *111*, 113
  nearside, parts of *110*
  nearside view *110*
  offside, parts of *110*
  offside view *111*
  Owen model, c. 1920 *112*
  Owen model, modern *112*
  pair of Queen Victoria's hacks *108*
  quick-release devices 109, *109*
  'safety' stirrups, 19th century 109, *109*

INDEX

underside of flap 111
Walsall model 112
Single harness 148-9, 150-5
  assembling and positioning saddle unit 152, 153
  attaching breeching strap 152
  backband 153
  bits 145, 155
  breast collar as alternative 151, 152
  bridle in place 155
  collar on first 150
  connecting traces 152
  crupper dock attachments 153, 153
  false martingale 153
  fitting crupper 153, 153
  full equipment in position 151
  importance of correct fit of bridle 154
  importance of correct fit of collar 150, 152
  importance of correct fit of saddle tree 152, 153
  positioning shaft tug 152
  putting on bridle 154
  putting on reins 153-4, 154
  safe 153
  stages in putting on collar 150, 150
  traces 152
  turnout to four-wheeled vehicle 148-9
Skull cap 213
Sling gear *see* Plough harness
Snaffle bit, early use of 11, 16, 19, 20
  by knights 26-7
Snaffle bridle 117, 122-3
  cheek snaffle with loose rings 123
  detail of flat ring 123
  eggbutt 123
  in action 122-3
  loose and fixed rings 117
  mouthpieces 117, 122
  parts of 134, 137
  range of bits 124-5
  straight-bar bit 123
  'strong' 122-3
  wire bits 122
Spanish Jumping bit 128, 129
Spanish Riding School saddle 34
Spurs 249, 250
  American 250
  how to use 251
  Roman 20
Stable (loose box) 198, 198, 199
Stable equipment 198-221
  at stud 208-9
  bandages and boots 216-21
  grooming 202-3
  horsebox 204-5
  manger 198
  mucking-out tools 199, 199
  ring for hay net 199
  rugs and travelling dress 210-15
  salt lick holder 199
  show tack 206-7
  tack cleaning 200-1
  tools and fittings 198-9
  water containers 198-9
Stallion bridle 208, 208
Stirrup, invention of 24-5
Stirrup irons 83, 84-5
  Australian Simplex 85
  knife-edge 84
  Kournakoff 84, 85
  Peacock 84-5, 84
  plain Prussian-side 84

racing 85, 85
  round eye side-saddle 85
Stirrup leathers 82, 82, 84
  cow and other hides 82
  'hook-up' or extending 82, 84
  racing 82
Stirrup tread 84
Stirrups and stirrup covers, Western 94, 97, 100
Stockman's saddle 72-4, 74
  features of 73-4
  shape 73
Stubben saddles:
  'Danloux' pattern jumping 60
  dressage 69
  Parzival general purpose 67
Stubbs, George:
  picture of Eclipse 36-7
Stückelberger, Christine:
  on Granat 40
Stud equipment 208-9
  kicking boots 209, 209
  neck cover for mare 209, 209
  stallion bridle 208, 208
  twitches and hobbles 208-9, 209

T

Tack cleaning 200-1
Tail guard 123, 213
Tandem harness 154, 156-8
  19th-century turnout 156
  bit 157
  bridle with Buxton bit 158
  hame terret 156
  leader in breast collar 156
  leader's saddle terret 156
  modern turnout 157
  wheeler's bridle 158
  wheeler's saddle terret 156
Team harness 161-2
Tendon boots 218, 219, 221
Toptani, Count Ilias 41,
Toptani jumping saddle 41, 56-62 (*passim*), 58, 59
  advantages of 59-60, 62
  and balance 62
  disadvantages 63, 66
  inset stirrup bar 58, 58
  panel 58, 59
  tree 58
Trace harness 185
Traces *see* Single harness, etc
Trailer 205
Training aids 188-95
  breaking 192-5
  schooling 188-91
Travelling dress 212-13
  fully equipped horse 210, 213
  poll guard 213
  skull cap 213
  tail bandage and guard 213, 213
Trees:
  'cow-mouth' Lane-Fox 73
  cut-back 51
  cut-back spring 50
  dressage 68
  fibreglass 48, 50
  heads 50
  manufacture of 48, 50, 50, 51
  Owen-type (show) 70
  points 50
  racing saddles and pads 104
  rigid 48, 50
  sizes and widths 50
  spring 48
  stirrup bars 48
  Western 92
Trekking saddles 74-5

Trotting equipment 166-75
  basic bit 168
  blinkers 173, 173
  boots 173, 173
  breast harness 167
  burr 168-9
  chin strap 173
  coping with pulling 171, 172, 173
  diagram showing items on horse 174
  driving bridle and bits 167-8, 168
  fitting hobbles 175
  Frisco June bit 168, 168
  harnessing a trotter 174
  head pole 168, 169
  hobbles 171
  keeping a straight course 168-9
  lip cord 173
  Murphy blind 169, 169
  overcheck bits 172, 173
  overcheck or check rein 171, 173
  pacer in harness 175
  Raymond overcheck 172, 173
  shadow rolls 169, 170, 171
  side-lining bit 168, 168
  slip-mouth side-lining bit 168, 168
  straight bar bit 168
Tugs 180
Twitch 208

U

Unicorn driving harness 161, 162
Unicorn method of plough harnessing 183, 185
Universal Pattern saddle 229, 229
Universal Purpose Pack Saddle 229-30

W

Western curb bit 143, 145
  in position 143
  selection of 143
Western dress 93, 246, 246
Western hackamore system 31, 34, 140-5
  adjustment and use of 141, 143
  bosal 141, 143
  bosal fitted to horse by headstall 141, 142
  fiador 141
  finished horse 141, 145
  from hackamore to bit 143, 145
  headstall 141, 143
  mecate 141, 143
  method of attaching *mecate* to heel knot of bosal 141, 142
  misuse of term 'hackamore' 141
  origins 140-1
  parts of a hackamore 143
  two-rein bosal 145
Western saddle 92-103
  addition of horn 94, 96
  breatplates 97, 98
  broncho busting 101, 102
  Californian 96, 98
  deep-seat cutting 103
  early Mexican-style 94
  enlarged skirts 94
  exercise, early 1900s 101
  exercise, modern 101
  fitting 96
  Grand Parade 100

Great Plains pattern 93
  improvements to Mexican-style 94
  introduction of fenders 94
  late 1800s pattern 93
  lightweight pleasure 98
  lightweight racing-type 99
  McClellan 98, 100
  Mexican blanket 97
  Mexican-style 92
  modern Californian-type 102
  modern changes 100-2
  parts of 92
  relatively lightweight 95
  side-saddle, early 1900s 93
  stirrups 94, 97
  strengthening cinches 96
  teenager's 98
  three-quarter size pleasure 98
  trees 92
Weymouth bridle and bits (*see also* Double bridle) 134
Whips, driving 164-5
  Coach ('bow-top') 164, 165
  Dealer's ('dropthong') 164-5, 165
  how to hold 162-3, 162-3, 164
  maintenance 165
  selection of (modern) 165
  selection of (Victorian) 164
  signalling to others 164
  specialist 165
  types 164-5
  woods used for stock 165
Whips, lunge 192, 193
Whips, riding 248-50
  American 250
  how to use 251
  selection of modern 248
  structure of 248-9
  types 249-50
Wither pads 86, 87
Witney blanket 210
Working hunter's saddle 65
WS Bitless Pelham 145, 145

X

Xenophon 11, 17, 18, 33, 240-1

Y

Yoke 10, 11
Yoke system, use on horses 11-13, 11

Picture Credits

Photographs and illustrations by or reproduced by permission of
Ashmolean Museum 243
Author 34
Beebee & Co 70l
British Library 26t, 30
British Museum 14, 17rt&rb, 19, 20r, 21r, 20lt, 240, 241
Cooper Bridgeman 12, 13, 18
Mike Davis 74t
Frank Dolman 113t & br
Mary Evans 15, 26b, 32, 35, 39, 77bl, 188, 191, 201b,242tl&br, 245
Michael Freeman 222
Giddens 165, 189c, 248
Kit Houghton 7, 40t, 41t&b
Hulton Picture Library 28, 29tl, 31 34t, 39, 83rb, 249t
Terry Keegan 224
Leslie Lane 235b, 247
Bob Langrish 40b, 70r, 177, 186, 189t, 190, 192, 193t, 194r, 205, 206, 207, 208, 209, 217t, 238
Janet Macdonald 112, 113bl

National Gallery 27
Photosources 22, 24, 25, 225, 226
QED 19, 49, 189bl&r, 199, 233
Walter Rawlings 236t
Peter Roberts 33, 198r
Ronald Sheridon 10, 11, 17l, 20l, 21l
Shire Horse Centre, Devon 181b, 183, 185t
Tate Gallery 39
Diane R. Tuke 48, 50rc&b, 53b
US Travel 40, 41
Victoria and Albert Museum 244
Harry Weber 176
The photographs on pages 29t&br&l, 242tr&bl, 249c are Crown Copyright
The photographs on pages 164l, 227, 228, 230, 231, 234 were taken at the Royal Mews, London and are reproduced by kind permission of Her Majesty the Queen
All other illustrations by Edwina Keene

G